'We value the work of the London School of Economics in the enlightening follow-through to "Phoenix Cites". What makes cities resilient and strong is critical to their future. Cities for a Small Continent offers a perspective on Leipzig and other European cities that sets them within a Europe–wide context.'

JAN RICHERT, *City of Leipzig official*

'It is inspirational to read about cities as the 'engines of new ideas' following their decline. These Phoenix Cities shows there is a road towards community integration and a greener future through a more creative, flexible and shared economy. Europe's former industrial cities have managed to reinvent and remake themselves.'

ALAZNE ZUGAZAGA, *City of Bilbao official, and Co-ordinator of German Marshall Fund in Bilbao*

'Anne Power's extraordinary capacity in observing, listening and learning from the field is here at its best: if you want to understand how European Cities are struggling to overcome the threats of the crisis, to face the challenges of innovation and to remain one of the best places to live worldwide.... this is the book!'

MASSIMO BRICOCOLI, *Politecnico de Milano*

'Anne Power has delivered a great gift to urban scholars and practitioners around the world. Her informed, thoughtful and passionate account of how cities can ride the tide of change is inspiring and practical.'

PROFESSOR RICKY BURDETT, *LSE Cities*

CITIES FOR A
SMALL CONTINENT

'Great cities like Belfast have been scarred by long periods of industrial decline and political upheaval. We are a small city in a small country, but part of a remarkable continent. This book will help those who care about cities, their citizens and our planet.'

JOHN MCGRILLEN, *Head of Northern Ireland Tourist Board.*
Formerly Belfast City Council official

'Anne Power's new book recounts the untold story of European industrial cities: a story of exploitation which led to a deep crisis. There is still hope for older European cities that have been exploring promising new paths out of trouble. Let us hope that she is right, for all our good.'

ANDREA BOCCO, *Politecnico di Torino and community entrepreneur*

'In "Cities for a Small Continent," Anne Power sets out a novel and compelling three- phase trajectory for Europe's older industrial cities – re-emerging time and again as the engines of Europe's economy. The continuing struggles of truly impoverished populations are balanced with truly solid foundations for future prosperity.'

LAVEA BRACHMAN, *Executive Director and a co-founder of the Greater Ohio Policy Centre, USA*

'Phoenix cities have learned! Having suffered and faced their fate, they have imagined new tools to shape cities of tomorrow in order to build a sustainable urban planet: through education, culture and mutual respect, they have placed human lives at the core of their vision.'

MICHEL THIOLLIÈRE, *Former Mayor of Saint-Etienne and former national senator*

CITIES FOR A
SMALL CONTINENT

International handbook
of city recovery

Anne Power

with Bruce Katz

Foreword by Richard Rogers

First published in Great Britain in 2016 by

Policy Press
University of Bristol
1-9 Old Park Hill
Bristol
BS2 8BB
UK
t: +44 (0)117 954 5940
pp-info@bristol.ac.uk
www.policypress.co.uk

North America office:
Policy Press
c/o The University of Chicago Press
1427 East 60th Street
Chicago, IL 60637, USA
t: +1 773 702 7700
f: +1 773-702-9756
sales@press.uchicago.edu
www.press.uchicago.edu

British Library Cataloguing in Publication Data
A catalogue record for this book is available from the British Library

Library of Congress Cataloging-in-Publication Data
A catalog record for this book has been requested

ISBN 978-1-4473-2753-0 paperback
ISBN 978-1-4473-2752-3 hardcover
ISBN 978-1-4473-2756-1 ePub
ISBN 978-1-4473-2757-8 Mobi

Cover design by Hayes Design
Front cover image: www.alamy.com
Printed and bound in Great Britain by CMP, Poole
Policy Press uses environmentally responsible print partners

Contents

List of figures, tables and boxes

Figures

Tables

Boxes

Abbreviations and acronyms

ANRU   *Agence Nationale de renovation urbane* (The National Agency for Urban Renewal)

EU   European Union

Eurozone   Fifteen countries that are within the European Union and share a common currency, the Euro

MEP   Member of the European Parliament

R&D   research and development

SCOT   *Le Schema de Coherence Territoriale* (SCOT). French planning requirement that all outer and inner communes or municipalities of a metropolitan area must collaborate to produce a coherent 10-year development and containment plan

SMEs   small and medium enterprises

ZUPs   *Zones à urbanisation prioritaire*. Large designated sites outside city boundaries that were used to build large, dense, publicly funded housing estates, known as 'Grands Ensembles'.

Acknowledgements

Many, many city experts have contributed to this book. Countless individuals have helped with our city visits, shared their experiences and shown us their projects. We cannot name them all, nor thank them enough. The following individuals have offered direct evidence or helped with preparing the text:

Juan Alayo, David Blunkett, Andrea Bocco, Diana Buckley, Ricky Burdett, Damien Chapuis, Andrea Colantonio, Cheryl Conner, Dorothée Delemer, Remi Dorval, Isobel Esberger, Mathieu Goetzke, Carolina Gutiérrez, Brian Hanna, Alex Jones, Eleri Jones, Bob Kerslake, Isabella Kohlhaas-Weber, Giovanni Magnano, Cécile Maisonneuve, Nathalie Martin-Sorvillo, Ana McDowall, Marie-Therese McGivern, John McGrillen, Clare McKeown, John Mothersole, Claire Patterson, Gianfranco Presutti, Jan Richert, Philipp Rode, Jessica Rowan, Tabitha Serle, Michel Thiolliére, Tony Travers, Oliver Weigel, William Julius Wilson, Christine Yip. I am immensely grateful to them all.

I owe special debt of thanks to colleagues who played a particularly important role in the development of *Cities for a small continent*: Bruce Katz began this study of former industrial cities with me in 2004 and we have worked together ever since. Jörg Plöger and Astrid Winkler were the main researchers for Phoenix cities, the predecessor for this book. Richard Rogers chaired the Urban Task Force, of which I was a member, and has shaped my thinking on the 'compact city'. Nicholas Stern helped me to recognise that the economic cost of investing in the new industrial revolution would pay back many times, both socially and environmentally. Howard Davies supported our City Reformers Workshops throughout the research process and has provided invaluable advice on how industrial cities like Manchester could, and would, recover.

Special thanks go to the researchers in the Centre for the Analysis of Social Exclusion; Eileen Alexander (Herden), Alice Belotti, Ben Grubb, Laura Lane and Bert Provan for contributing to and writing reports on the individual cities. Nicola Serle, research project co-ordinator for LSE Housing and Communities, has throughout played an invaluable role, in holding the research and all the implementation together. John Hills, director of the Centre for Analysis of Social Exclusion, supported the Weak Market Cities programme from 2006. This support was invaluable in writing this book. Richard Brown, Massimo Bricocoli and Anne-Marie Brady gave invaluable feedback and made helpful suggestions on the text. I owe them a great debt of thanks.

In the final stages, five people in particular pulled out all the stops; Emma Glassey in preparing, revising and checking the text, Bert Provan in preparing the many final charts and tables; Laura Lane and Alice Belotti in checking all content, endnotes and references; and Nicola Serle for pulling it all together.

I want to offer special thanks to Jenni Barkley, Belfast Harbour; David Blaszkiewicz and Karen Harris, Invest Detroit; Chiara Gionco and Mario Ferretti, Comune di Torino; Alazne Zugazaga and Esther Gonzalez Martinez, Bilbao International; Richard Bland, Sheffield City Council; Creative Sheffield; Lesley Holmes, Belfast City Council; EPASE. Guillaume Malochet of La Fabrique de la Cité came to us with the request to prepare this handbook, and has helped us throughout the process. I accept full responsibility for any mistakes, misunderstandings or shortcoming. Cities are in constant movement and I hope the pictures drawn here fairly reflect their evolution.

Copyright material

We gratefully acknowledge the permission granted to reproduce the copyright material in this book. All reasonable efforts have been made to identify the holders of copyright material and to obtain permission for their use. If we have unwittingly infringed any copyright, we apologise sincerely and would appreciate being corrected.

Figure and Table sources are listed in the book. Photographic sources are as follows.

Chapter 1 Bilbao
Photo 1.1: Mondragon Cooperative
Photo 1.2: Euskalduna Jauregia Bilbao
Photo 1.3: Bilbao Ria 2000
Photo 1.4: Bilbao Ria 2000
Photo 1.5: Mondragon Cooperative
Photo 1.6: LSE Researcher
Photo 1.7: Bilbao Ekintza
Photo 1.8: Bilbao Ekintza

Chapter 2 Belfast
Photo 2.1: Belfast City Council
Photo 2.2: Belfast City Council
Photo 2.3: Belfast City Council
Photo 2.4: Belfast City Council
Photo 2.5: Connswater Community Gateway
Photo 2.6: Belfast City Council
Photo 2.7: Belfast Harbour

Chapter 3 Sheffield
Photo 3.1: Creative Sheffield
Photo 3.2: Creative Sheffield
Photo 3.3: LSE Researcher
Photo 3.4: LSE Researcher
Photo 3.5: LSE Researcher
Photo 3.6: Creative Sheffield
Photo 3.7: Creative Sheffield
Photo 3.8: LSE Researcher
Photo 3.9: LSE Researcher
Photo 3.10: Creative Sheffield
Photo 3.11: Creative Sheffield

Chapter 4 Lille City Centre
Photo 4.1: LSE Researcher
Photo 4.2: City of Lille
Photo 4.3: LSE Researcher
Photo 4.4: City of Lille
Photo 4.5: LSE Researcher
Photo 4.6: LMCU

Chapter 5 Saint-Étienne
Photo 5.1: EPASE
Photo 5.2: LSE Researcher
Photo 5.3: LSE Researcher
Photo 5.4: EPASE
Photo 5.5: LSE Researcher
Photo 5.6: LSE Researcher
Photo 5.7: LSE Researcher

Chapter 6 Leipzig
Photo 6.1: Belfast City Council
Photo 6.2: LSE Researcher
Photo 6.3: LSE Researcher sourced from archival photography
Photo 6.4: LSE Researcher
Photo 6.5: LSE Researcher
Photo 6.6: LSE Researcher
Photo 6.7: LSE Researcher
Photo 6.8: LSE Researcher

Chapter 7 Torino
Photo 7.1: Archivio Fotografico Citta' di Torino
Photo 7.2: Archivio Fotografico Citta' di Torino
Photo 7.3: Archivio Fotografico Città di Torino
Photo 7.4: Archivio Storico Fiat
Photo 7.5: Archivio Fotografico Città di Torino
Photo 7.6: Arianna Forcella and Agnese Samà
Photo 7.7: Archivio Fotografico Città di Torino
Photo 7.8: Archivio Fotografico Politecnico di Torino
Photo 7.9: Archivio Fotografico Politecnico di Torino

Chapter 8 Detroit
Photo 8.1: Michelle and Chris Gerrard
Photo 8.2: Invest Detroit
Photo 8.3: Invest Detroit
Photo 8.4: Invest Detroit

Foreword

Richard Rogers

Cities have entranced me all my life. I love the life of cities, their surprises of form and activity, of buildings and people, of constant change.

I particularly love the best European cities for their density, their mixed use and their compact form. Barcelona, where I was architectural advisor during the Olympic period, is an amazing example. Yet it was deeply decayed after 40 years of dictatorship; its port was in steep decline; it had acres of scarred land; there were concentrations of extreme poverty in settlements on the periphery. But Barcelona had the life and mix of uses that many port cities exhibit; the very centre of the city was and still is crowded with immigrants from Africa mixed with traditional fishing communities. A succession of mayors with a powerful vision for the city helped it regain its former glory as the self-styled 'Capital of the Mediterranean'.

Barcelona's story exemplifies the strengths and challenges of Europe's industrial cities, former giants in the global economy, but left with vast dereliction, extraordinary levels of unemployment and devastating environmental damage. It is all too easy to spoil our cities. A combination of poor design, harsh social divisions, weakened economies, massive congestion, noise, dirt and total disregard for the environment has left many of them struggling to find a new future.

But Europe is a continent with an amazing urban history, resilient local leadership and citizenry, and imposing industrial architecture. Through a revival of local democracy and decentralisation, extraordinary energy was unleashed in Barcelona and through many small steps, a huge vision was delivered. This applies in different ways to the European cities this book is about.

Fifteen years ago, Anne Power and I wrote *Cities for a Small Country*, following our work together on the Urban Task Force. We argued that Britain, as an island, had no choice but to care for its cities, to run them differently, to stop sprawl and to concentrate on compact reuse. This required a very different approach to city reclamation, encompassing environmental protection, land use, buildings, design and social integration. Now *Cities for a Small Continent* takes up the baton for Europe's older industrial cities.

Across Europe, the cities that Anne Power calls Phoenix cities have shown a remarkable ability to re-emerge. Many were recovering in the early years of this century, but were hard hit by the financial crisis of 2007 and the recession that followed. It is amazing to me how far they have once again managed to reinvent themselves, developing mould-breaking solutions to the biggest social, economic and environmental challenges of our time. They offer powerful lessons for the 300-odd other European cities that have lost their major industries and are now searching for new futures. Europe needs its cities today more than ever.

This passionate, original and informative book tells how recovery and reinvention point to a new, more radical and more sustainable urban future.

Richard Rogers
October 2015

ONE

Lessons from cities in a crowded continent

We are the first generation that through its neglect could destroy the relationship between humans and the planet, and perhaps the last generation that can prevent dangerous climate change

Nicholas Stern, *Why Are We Waiting? The Logic, Urgency and Promise of Tackling Climate Change*

Box 1.1: Bilbao – a story

The ancient Basque city of Bilbao captures all the dense, compact, crowded variety of Europe's industrial cities. High blocks of flats, old in the centre, newer around the edges, are packed with residents jostling for space. Small shops fit tightly into street-level frontages. Cafes and bars spill out onto narrow pavements. Tourists mingle with local residents. Vascuence, the native tongue of the ancient Basque kingdom, is often heard. When you arrive at the station, you immediately sense the action. Suddenly the river comes into sight, and the wide pavement by the bridge is packed with noisy groups of protesters carrying banners and flags. It is June 2014 and the King of Spain has just abdicated. A new political force – 'Podemos', We Can – suddenly emerges.

In 2012, two years earlier, the same pavement by the river housed an impromptu encampment of young 'indignados' – the 'protesters' – who know they stand little chance of a job under Spain's harsh austerity programme. They demanded action against corrupt officials and a fairer, more open democracy. They became the springboard for this totally new political force in Europe, Podemos, capturing 25% of the regional Spanish vote in 2015.

Yet history and tradition remain strong in the city. Every August, the festival of Bilbao takes place on the same river bank. In August 1995, Bilbao was a gloomy, and occasionally violence-torn city, with few tourists, an idle port, silent steel furnaces. Crowds of locals packed the pavements in the dark evening, waiting for a ceremony that outsiders cannot fathom. An elaborately dressed, out-sized, crowned Virgin Mary hangs on wires over the black water as fireworks go off

1

all around. At the stroke of midnight, the robed statue bursts into flames, lights up the sky and river for seconds, then plunges into the deep. The ceremony still happens each year, challenging visitors and citizens to reconcile the past with the present, out of which a new future for Europe's cities is being carved.

Introduction: Europe's troubled and beloved cities

Europe is a small, crowded continent with compact crowded cities, often so close to each other that their boundaries almost touch each other. In between, there are also great green expanses, of forests, mountains and farms, increasingly populated by wind turbines and solar panels. Cities are connected by a dense network of long-established railways and new high speed trains as well as fast, modern roads, bridges and imposing motorway fly-overs. The economy of cities is like a large, thick tapestry, woven together with thousands of threads and multiple colours, each making the other stronger, working as a whole.

Europe's historic city centres look dense, busy, cared for, populated with cafes, small shops, monuments, churches, public squares and traffic. On the centre's edge, even in smaller, poorer cities, there are often concrete towers, gestures to modernity, banking and internationalisation. But there are also abandoned buildings and derelict spaces. It is easy to see the potential in Europe's battle-worn cities and their multi-tongued people, just as it is easy to see the broad sweep of world-shaping history. The paving stones and old buildings, the traffic and noise, the statues and war memorials tell a story of struggle, survival and resilience. People from all corners of the earth are crowded into them, banking on their future. But many city cores around the centre have become run down, underinvested, unloved, with too many jobless youth and too few enterprising job creators. All of Europe's cities were not long ago producers of goods. Today, most of those goods come from afar and too many hands, machines and spaces are idle.

This international handbook draws together ten years of ground-level research into the causes and consequences of Europe's biggest urban challenge – the loss of industry, jobs and productive capacity. The handbook explores the potential of former industrial cities to offer a new and more sustainable future for a crowded continent under severe environmental constraints and extreme, economic and social pressures. It focuses on cities that not only were the most productive and wealth creating in the not too distant past, but the most reliant on major industries and therefore the hardest hit by their demise. These cities have lived through many phases of growth and decline and they are experimenting in alternative futures. So they may show us new ways forward.

Why cities dominate in spite of loss of industry and jobs

Around 80% of Europe's over 500 million inhabitants live in around 500 large and thousands of smaller cities and towns.[1] Most of these cities are traditionally 'producer cities', where goods are made and services created to support production. Most still are in some measure producers, but large-scale heavy industries have often moved their investments and jobs to Asia, to cheaper labour markets, leaving behind underused assets and underemployed populations. They also left behind thousands of smaller functioning enterprises, and a huge public infrastructure on which far wider metropolitan areas depend – universities, hospitals, transport interchanges, housing, financial and legal services, cultural activity and much more.

With so much underused potential, cities are gaining rather than losing prominence as they continue to dominate the world's largest and densest economic union in Europe, now with 28 member countries and over three quarters urban. For in spite of Europe's economic troubles, its cities remain a major magnet for new opportunity, for living space, for social, cultural and economic activity. They also cause environmental damage far beyond their boundaries and a legacy of pollution and depletion that cries out for action. Yet these very problems offer potential solutions to our current dual crisis of financial unviability and finite environmental limits.

Europe's old industrial cities are famous today for their ugly, left-behind wastelands and underused buildings, their poverty, and their inability to catch up with their prosperous capitals or historic tourist centres. Yet they are rich in skills, ideas, connections and inventions. They are using their traditional engineering knowledge and expertise to rebuild entrepreneurial and problem solving skills. This could make them the cities of tomorrow, not yesterday.

Most things about them are undervalued: their railway lines, canals and rivers; their universities and small engineering companies; their vast and impressive town halls, civic institutions and 19th century factory buildings; their public libraries and swimming baths; their neglected neighbourhoods, underemployed young people and cast-off older industrial workers.

New breakthroughs may be around the corner. For as fast as old industries – coal, steel, textiles, shipbuilding – all but disappeared from the small continent, a massive new threat became an unforeseen opportunity for cities on the edge. Environmental damage and a warming climate caused through man-made activity, particularly the burning of fossil fuels like coal, affect Europe profoundly through our longer, more intense, industrial history, and our population density. Industrial cities paid a heavy price for the environmental damage they caused, losing not only their mainstay industries, but much of their wealth and status. They also destroyed their local environments and turned their social structures upside down. Yet below the radar over a 20-year recovery period starting in the late 1980s and 90s, they created a unique blend of invention, advanced engineering and manufacture, reclamation and social investment, giving them a head-start in tackling the largest global challenge of all times – planetary climate change.[2]

Producer cities across Europe have gone through booms, self-destruction, major industrial collapse, attempts to rebuild their fortunes, economic and environmental unravelling. The 21st century needs their high level engineering traditions and skills to remake the world of cities with their high consumption into a world of environmental care for the precious natural and man-made resources of an urbanised, crowded, city-dominated continent. This is the most challenging, yet most hopeful basis for a viable, carbon-light future.[3]

As scientific evidence of human-driven climate change becomes overwhelming, green innovations in which Europe is a leader are emerging in older, formerly declining industrial cities as a result of their engineering, technical and inventive traditions. The discovery in 2003 of graphene at Manchester University, a new 'miracle material', offering many energy saving possibilities, is one spectacular example.[4] Even cities with a long and deeply scarred industrial past have many surviving industrial workshops, innovative enterprises and start-ups, attractive vernacular architecture, historic parks and reclaimed wastelands. Dortmund in the Ruhr, Roubaix in Northern France, Stoke in the Potteries, Hull in North East England, and Burnley in Lancashire offer monumental examples of civic pride in the midst of decayed and abandoned industrial landscapes.

Yet these places formed the backbone of Europe's transformative industrial revolution. Former industrial giants and their ancillary cities, such as Manchester and the surrounding cotton towns, matter today to the health of capitals like London and Paris which also have their past industrial histories. But many cities are working to combat fierce decline. Cities like Lille, Saint-Étienne, Belfast, Torino, Leipzig, Bilbao and Sheffield are taking impressive strides towards recovering their position as wealth-creators. These are the cities whose stories we draw on.

This study picks up threads of change and signs of recovery, rediscovery and rebirth in cities across Europe, following our earlier study, *Phoenix cities*.[5] Thanks to strong public efforts at reinvestment across the continent since the late 1980s, the most acute decline was slowed and even reversed. However, just as these hard-hit cities showed signs of a fragile recovery, they were once more undermined by the international banking crisis of 2008. New resource limits emerged as this crisis threatened to swamp progress and the Eurozone entered a phase of deep instability, lasting until today. Former industrial cities like Sheffield were particularly hard hit by public spending cuts; while cities like Saint-Étienne were affected by the wider problems of the French economy and its own overhanging debt; and Torino found itself with an unfundable debt burden due to changes in national policy.

European cities under pressure

Cities in a small and crowded continent now face extreme challenges, taking different forms in different countries, shaped in part by different histories, cultures and economic paths. But five interconnected pressures influence the prospects of Europe's former industrial cities:

- The financial, banking and public funding crises across Europe are compounded in the Eurozone by the restrictions on a common currency, which affect all European Union countries.
- The great recession of 2008–14 and high unemployment, particularly youth unemployment, led to shockingly high levels of joblessness among under 25s, hitting over 50% in Spain, 30% in parts of France such as Saint-Étienne and over 40% in Italy.
- Insecurity of energy supply, price uncertainty and diminishing reserves of key resources, including land, raw materials, even food, are undermining people's confidence in the future.
- High levels of immigration from developing countries and Eastern Europe, particularly during a long, deep recession, create political and social tensions that cities must broker and manage.
- Unpredictable weather events, such as flooding, extreme heat and drought, all affecting cities, point to the biggest threat of all with the highest costs attached – climate change.[6]

These problems have created a political climate of great uncertainty where votes are harder to win, taxes harder to collect and jobs harder to find. Urban change in an already highly built-up, heavily exploited, urbanised environment does not 'start afresh', as America has so often done and as China is now attempting with its giant new 'eco-cities'.[7] How we rediscover, remake and reuse our urban pathways, worn deep into our cities and our landscape, will shape our urban future.

Europe's cities are forced to invent ways of coping with land pressures that offer a useful model to developing countries where cities are growing and spreading and to developed countries where cities are surrounded by vast, sprawling, car-born suburbs that have fatally weakened their cores and are highly energy intensive.[8]

European cities became the global hubs of modern industry in the 19th and 20th centuries – Sheffield's steel, Belfast's ships, Torino's cars, Lille's textiles. Today they again show clear signs of resilience and recovery; their 200-year-old industrial traditions, which were their life blood, have fuelled innovative ideas about recovery. The lessons of the past shape their path. Ten years of visits, close observation and on-site workshops about their survival and rebirth provide evidence for this handbook.

The rise, fall and rebirth of Europe's ex-industrial cities

Ground-level stories from seven struggling and reforming cities in six countries, representing seven distinct European regions, opened our eyes. Northern Ireland, with Belfast as its capital, part of the island of Ireland, is distinct from the rest of Britain, separated by the sea, with strong nationalist movements, and its own government; Leipzig in Eastern Germany was part of the former Communist Eastern bloc and bears many marks of that history; Saint-Étienne, a small and formerly almost exclusively industrial city in Southern France contrasts sharply with Lille, the dominant regional capital of north east France and one of Europe's most important international transport hubs; Bilbao is the industrial centre of the Basque country, a uniquely autonomous region of Spain, and a popular tourist centre; Torino, famous as the home and headquarters of Fiat, is also the historic capital of Italy;[9] Sheffield was the world's leading steel and knife producer. We could have chosen dozens, even hundreds, of similar cities, and much of our evidence draws on a wide urban canvas: Manchester, Glasgow, Newcastle, Liverpool in Britain; Essen, Dortmund, Bochum, Hamburg and Bremen in Germany; Barcelona and Sevilla in Spain; Milano, Genoa and Napoli in Italy; Larne and Londonderry in Northern Ireland; and many more.

We chose the particular seven cities because they represent seven geographically and culturally distinct European regions, but share four common characteristics:

- rapid growth in population, jobs and wealth creation during the first industrial revolution;
- significant loss of population, jobs and industrial prowess during their steep and rapid decline in the late 20th century;
- a private, public and civic alliance committed to reinvestment, recovery and reversal of decline in the 1990s and 2000s; and
- clear signs of resilience and recovery in spite of crisis.

Our grounded methods allow us to understand the lived experiences of citizens and city leaders alike, as they struggle to respond to wave after wave of change.

The long roots of Phoenix cities

The rise, fall and rebirth of great industrial cities in Europe calls up the image of the magical bird of ancient folklore, which in glorious plumage lives for hundreds of years until exhausted, it builds a giant funeral pyre, in which it self-immolates, but in which it has laid a giant egg. From the ashes rises a new Phoenix, to live again and endlessly recreate itself. Cities, like the Phoenix, arise and display powers of creation, energy, beauty, and wealth that are unrivalled, until they figuratively and sometimes literally burn themselves out and their prosperity turns to ashes, seemingly consuming their vitality. By a similar magic, cities are reborn, regrow in new forms that both mirror and transform the old. They find ways to reinvent themselves by reusing the form, legacy and talent of the old – as also happens in the film *The Full Monty*.

The Full Monty tells the tragic story of former steel workers in Sheffield, made redundant by mass closures of giant steel works. It captures the guts, determination and inventiveness of the 'stranded assets' of struggling cities, their people. The redundant workers feel 'stripped bare to the bone' and in a moment of genius, they turn their left-behind, discarded talents to good, earning money and restoring pride in revalued and newly discovered theatrical skills. This touchingly, hilariously true-to-life story captures the fate of Europe's former industrial cities. It seemed they had been stripped bare, like Sheffield's discarded steel workers, but they are reinventing themselves. The recession, banking failures, job losses and euro crisis, harsh and uncertain as they are, are together generating green shoots of new growth. We do not yet know if the green shoots are strong enough.

The story of the seven cities mirrors the story of Europe's rise, fall and hoped-for recovery. The seven cities all enjoyed a prominent pre-industrial history, giving them national and international status, which underlines their strategic importance in location, natural resources and political cross-connections. As these influences came together, they fed their manufacturing growth and accelerated their development when the industrial revolution got underway. For example Torino, at the gateway of the Italian Alps, was from Roman times a vital crossing point between Northern Europe and the Mediterranean. Lille had long been the strategic military and trade link between France, the Netherlands, Northern Germany and the Baltic. Belfast was a historic port close to the west of Scotland through which the British could settle on rich farm land in Ireland and reinforce their dominance. Sheffield held a royal prisoner in the castle. Leipzig was a critical trading centre between East and West. This history laid the ground for their future growth. Table 1.1 shows the historic origins of the seven cities.

The seven industrial cities went through an unprecedented population explosion in the 19th century, attracting migrant workers from poorer regions and more recently in the 20th century, from former far-flung European colonies and other regions around the globe. They were the pioneers in materials extraction, machine building, engineering and mass manufacture. They generated immense wealth not just for the cities themselves, but for whole countries, and the continent of Europe, by extracting valuable resources both from their surrounding land and from their colonies. For example Saint-Étienne developed its wealth and fame on the back of artisan crafts in metals and textiles dating from the pre-industrial era, eventually becoming the biggest centre of arms manufacture in France from which Napoleon commandeered vital military supplies for his foreign armies. It built France's first railway line and first bicycle.

The environments of the seven cities were rich in valuable resources like coal, iron, water, and their exploding populations quickly acquired skills which fuelled their growth. But both land and labour were overexploited during 200 years of intense growth. Table 1.2 shows the scale of early growth, where city populations sometimes doubled in a decade or two. Sheffield's population increased 7-fold in 150 years, Leipzig's 12-fold.

By the late 1970s Europe's industrial cities were losing populations, jobs and economic vitality. By the 1980s, their image was polluted, ingrained with soot, possibly obsolete, their workers deskilled and

Table 1.1: Historic origins

Leipzig	Medieval trading centre on major international routes across Europe Home of Johann Sebastian Bach Medieval university Rich coal deposits
Lille	Medieval regional centre on frontier of several countries – France, Belgium, Flanders – highly strategic location for international armies Inland port Rich coal deposits Early textile industry – linen
Saint-Étienne	Small pre-industrial craft based centre – became important for arms manufacture under Napoleon Rich coal and iron deposits Early lace making and iron goods Early development of mining technique
Torino	Medieval capital of powerful city state at foothill of Alps – critical crossing point between countries Confluence of major rivers Textiles, engineering, finance
Bilbao	Trading and fishing centre for ancient Basque kingdom Important port shipping Early extraction of iron Early engineering
Sheffield	Small pre-industrial settlement with famous medieval castle where Mary, Queen of Scots, was imprisoned Rich coal and iron deposits Early metal works
Belfast	Early settlement with strong links across the Irish sea to Scotland – became an important entry point for Scottish settlers in 16th and 17th centuries Major port shipping; textiles – linen; engineering
Comments	All the cities had some pre-industrial functions, often helping industrial development. All had a combination of mining, textiles, port activities, trading and engineering.

Source: City visits, 2006–15

underemployed. Large, factory-made housing estates, built for the mass of workers, became marginalised islands of poverty, underused, unpopular and increasingly home to poor migrants. Their economic raison d'être shrank as manufacturing giants sought out newer, cheaper, more profitable production centres. For example, Sheffield was the world famous inventor of Bessemer Steel, which allowed cheap mass production on an unimagined scale. Sheffield steel is still used for the advanced manufacture of engines, machinery, domestic and commercial goods, but in the 1980s, Sheffield lost most of its major steel companies and saw its economy shrink dramatically, even though some steel production continued. The threads of these old skills led to new inventions, such as fine precision cutting for advanced manufacture, and laser technology. But our cities still struggle to overcome their past and build their future.

Table 1.2: Population growth from the industrial revolution (1750–1980)

City	Date	Population number	Increase, 1750–1980
Leipzig	1750	35,000	
	1900	456,156	
	1950	620,000	+525,000
	1980	550,000	
Lille	1750	54,756	
	1900	210,696	
	1950	200,000	+165,44
	1980	170,000	
Saint-Étienne	1750	17,000	
	1900	146,000	
	1950	210,000	+183,000
	1980	200,000	
Torino	1750	58,128	
	1900	329,691	
	1950	740,000	+1,061,872
	1980	1,129,000	
Bilbao	1750	15,516	
	1900	93,250	
	1950	220,000	+414,484
	1980	430,000	
Sheffield	1750	60,095	
	1900	451,195	
	1950	570,000	+489,905
	1980	550,000	
Belfast	1750	8000	
	1900	349,000	
	1950	420,000	+292,000
	1980	300,000	

Sources: Plöger (2007a, 2007b); Winkler (2007a, 2007b); Power et al (2010)

Recovering cities need external support

The drama of de-industrialisation played out in city after city, until the local leadership was forced to abandon attempts to protect established but dying local industries and find new ways forward. In an attempt to fuel such recovery, national governments, with underpinning from the European Union, began to reinvest. European governments converged around the need to compensate for and make good the massive damage caused by industrial overexploitation. Every city we visited, along with hundreds of other cities like them across Europe, attracted major public investment to restore their environments, upgrade their infrastructure, reclaim landmark buildings, restore neighbourhoods and rebuild their skills.

Funds were levered in with public backing in the first phase of recovery, to restore city centres and inner areas, to reorient existing infrastructure, remodel city buildings and develop a new skills base. The most disadvantaged and most depleted regions, cities and neighbourhoods became conspicuous targets for European and national funding, particularly focused on regions hard hit by industrial decline. This helped equalise conditions and encouraged innovative projects. Private investors were gradually drawn back to join this public effort. The new shock waves of the 2008 international banking crisis, the bailouts, the austerity that followed, only made the value of reinvestment starker.

For example Bilbao, with its troubled, nationalist history, its terrorist attacks, the devastating loss of its giant steel furnaces and heavy engineering, attracted huge compensatory investment in the vast port areas and older inner neighbourhoods that were the legacy of its dying heavy industries and shipping. These public investments were not simply a disguise or cover-up for the inevitable shrinkage such cities were experiencing. They were both restoring liveable conditions and responding to local plans to create new out of old – an urban Phoenix. The external public support within countries was part of a much bigger, Europe-wide challenge. We set out to discover what real change this reinvestment has brought about, and what potential for new growth it now offers, given the loss of large-scale public funds since 2008 and the severe environmental constraints within which Europe lives.

Gathering concrete evidence of cities coping with change

A handbook for European cities cannot possibly capture every detail of the long struggle to reform, nor project accurately the rollercoaster trajectories of cities following the financial and employment crises of the past eight years. But cities surviving such turmoil can teach us a great deal about cycles of growth, decline and recovery, about how cities revive and renew themselves amid the ashes of the old.

This is a people story – how people created wealth, consumed and destroyed it; then laboriously built it up again; how communities were damaged by the very wealth creation these cities are famous for; and how city governments all over Europe attempted to integrate poorer areas into the mainstream. Will they now break through into what we think of as a new industrial revolution, following the first phase of extreme over-growth and exploitation; then the second of extreme decline and efforts at recovery? The third phase will point along a very different road to recovery, one that has few signposts and many unknowns – yet it is emerging in unlikely places as the ultimate Phoenix.

Cities for a small continent examines the actions that shape the course of cities for the future, and the global forces beyond their control that drive the changes. Did public reinvestment help cities bounce back? What actions helped most – skills or buildings, people or place? How did industrial cities come through the 2008 recession? Is a new economy emerging?

The value of this handbook is to demonstrate:
• what is being tried;
• what works;
• what the costs and benefits of different approaches are;
• what the pitfalls are and how they can be avoided;
• what the differences are between cities; and
• what common rationale and patterns of change emerge and what these patterns tell us.

The problems facing Europe's former industrial cities are so serious that economic, social and environmental conditions must be transformed. This long-term task involves building on and intensifying the partial recovery process that is producing many visible green shoots. Live examples which we document demonstrate action-learning in real places, showing what is possible, and inspiring further experiments. Hard-won experience generates confidence, which in turn attracts support. The ongoing upheavals of the last eight years make anything other than action-learning immediately out-of-date.

Cities do not work to prescribed recipes and procedures. They cannot simply be 'fixed', as their history, their geography, their flows of people and ideas make them bounded and fluid simultaneously. So this handbook is not a 'toolkit', but a guide to how cities are reshaping themselves. These cities have a history of learning by doing, of coupling research and innovation with producing things, of trialling ideas by turning them into practical experiments. There is no prescription, but many models, examples of what works and opportunities for places with leftover capacity – skills, people, buildings, transport, land and waterways. These cities are right now laboratories of change.

The unrealised potential of post-industrial cities has risen up the European agenda in part because of the financial crisis and the resource pressures on governments as European economies struggle to emerge from the worst recession since before the war. Former industrial cities point to a different kind of future, which is more than a cosmetic upgrading, a culturally or politically driven revival. The response of producer cities during years of upheaval and austerity creates a new and distinctive approach to city reform and recovery – truly transformative innovation. For although most of the big industries are now gone, there are literally thousands of surviving small and medium enterprises (SMEs) in each city, often the direct descendants of companies that operated as part of the powerful industrial supply chain, but now filling valuable engineering and production niches in the new economy. There is the potential for many new jobs through these SMEs.

A combination of reinvestment in infrastructure, backed at national and European levels, and the development of new specialisms, based on long-run expertise and skills, helps to shape a new economy within Europe's industrial cities. The 2008 crash reinforced this sense of direction as cities survived better than expected.

Learning from American suburban sprawl

Europe's cities are starkly different from their North American counterparts, which sprawl far outside their cores at extreme low densities. These 'ex-urbs' are linked and dissected by multi-lane freeways, only rarely by rail. Most American cities are more car-bound, less public transport-oriented and less pedestrian friendly than their European counterparts, simply because they are invariably too low-density to concentrate a critical mass in small spaces. They are overwhelmingly suburban in style. The lower urban density means that people walk the streets far less and public transport is less viable, making car dependence inevitably far greater. Small local shops are rarer and street life in most city centres, even in strongly populated, successful American cities, is usually sparser than in Europe.

Energy consumption in low-density US cities is far higher on average than in Europe.[10] Sprawl makes American cities more divided and more racially segregated than Europe's cities.[11] American cities also have far higher rates of violent crime and incarceration, about five times the European level, partly as a result of higher poverty levels and weaker public underpinning.[12]

The recovery efforts of European cities in the late 1990s and 2000s made these differences more visible, as recent American studies show.[13] Europe is locked into dense urban patterns, while America is locked into dispersed metropolitan patterns. In a land-constrained continent, and an energy-constrained world, European cities have no choice but to work to integrate diverse communities and harmonise social conditions. This reduces but by no means overcomes inequalities. Urban density accentuates the need for shared spaces and shared resources, while proximity underlines the potential for renewal.[14]

American cities have as dramatic and diverse a story to tell as European cities, but this history is less vaunted, partly because core cities have a shorter history.[15] Many legacy buildings and homes in older industrial cities in North America have been obliterated by careless modernisation or 'urban renewal', or simply by the scale of abandonment, usually for the outer suburbs. There is also a much weaker sense of world-shaping events in these sprawling agglomerations of wealth and poverty, because so much of American trade and development has been internal within a vast country, whereas European cities since Roman times have relied heavily on cross-border resource exploitation, colonisation, trade and exchange, forcing them to look outwards. War played a big part in this.

Yet across the United States, in old industrial cities, a similar recovery and rebirth is happening. Not only are US cities waking up to their potential, but green shoots of urban recovery under resource constraints are appearing in cities thought of as 'dead'. Detroit is an extreme example of this as we will show. Pittsburgh, Philadelphia, Louisville, Cleveland, Cincinnati, Baltimore, Detroit and many other cities illustrate the struggle in the US to reshape a monumental urban legacy that has become a vital resource for the future, far more than a liability. Many trans-Atlantic lessons reinforce the value of cities. Cities are making a come-back on both sides of the Atlantic.[16] This handbook pools these ideas.

Resource pressures and hopes of a new industrial revolution

European cities cannot sprawl or consume energy on the scale of North America. Therefore, a uniquely European model of city recovery is emerging that is based on high density, mixed use, recycling, conservation, custodial investment of semi-public, semi-private funds, an energy transformation and a pressing focus on social integration of diverse communities. Will this European model generate a more sustainable approach to the urban environment, a more solidaristic approach to city diversity, and a new dynamism that is capable of generating the new industrial revolution that Nicholas Stern forecasts is essential?[17] Finding and applying new, low-carbon ways of doing things that are more self-sustaining and more self-replenishing than in the past is the foundation of our shared future. The handbook proposes that a new industrial economy based on the assets of these cities offers a route to reducing the threat of climate change.

Nicholas Stern makes a powerful case for a radical restructuring of industrial economies. He stresses the imperative to reshape existing industrial methods, skills and infrastructure in favour of a 'new low-carbon industrial revolution'. He highlights evidence that this conversion process is under way. He argues that the risks involved in not doing it are unthinkably high; that the costs of doing it are affordable; and that escaping the gridlock or 'lock-in' of the dominant, existing infrastructure, production and consumption patterns is vital. Evidence from the seven cities suggests that they already far down this transformational road. These cities are already experimenting with the new industrial economy.

Our framework for understanding the way European cities have grown, declined and recovered is based on European studies dating from 1987.[18] Figure 1.1 sets out the three phases of a Phoenix city.

Figure 1.1: Framework for understanding Phoenix cities

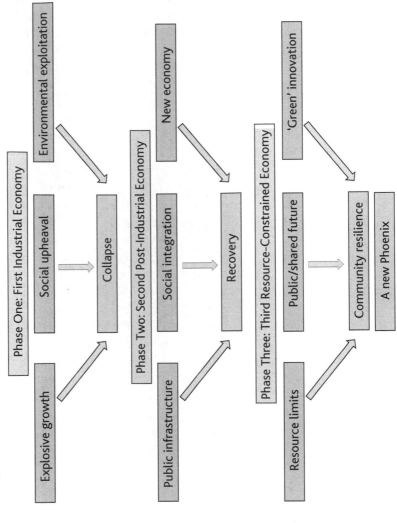

Outline of *Cities for a small continent*

The handbook is divided into nine chapters. Each chapter ends with a short 'Tale of a city' to illustrate the main arguments with a live snapshot of progress.

Chapter One, **Lessons from cities in a crowded continent**, has introduced the core idea that Europe is an old and crowded continent of dense, productive cities. They have survived the loss of major industries and adapted. Without these cities, Europe cannot survive. The handbook shows how former industrial cities are uncovering new breakthroughs to a different kind of future. This chapter has set out our framework for understanding Europe's industrial cities in three phases: growth and decline; recovery and new crises; and an alternative 'greener' future.

Chapter Two, **Divided and united Europe**, explains the bitter 20th century European experience of two World Wars which made industrial cities vital to survival. The legacy of the Second World War created a strong proactive social and public policy focus. This led to public investment in infrastructure, the building of welfare states and mass housing. The experience of deep, long-run conflict, followed by the Cold War, reinforced the value of economic cooperation, social cohesion and public underpinning. The idea that war should never happen again on European soil led directly to the creation of the European Common Market and the European Union. World wars, the Cold War, eventual collapse of the 'Iron Curtain' and the common market have strongly shaped, shaken and reinforced the role of Europe's many ex-industrial cities.

Chapter Three, **Grit and vision**, explains how Europe's post-war boom fuelled an unsustainable growth, over-scaling of industry and counter-movements of citizens that eventually contributed to industrial collapse in Europe's densely populated producer cities. As cities became mass production centres, bigness came to dominate the European way of life. Large-scale government action led to mass housing, motorways, mass goods and services. Full employment led to high immigration, while protest movements grew under the umbrella of state provision. Environmental limits became clear with the oil crisis and decline set in. Chapter Three explains Phase One of the framework for Europe's industrial cities – explosive growth and collapse.

Chapter Four, **Struggle and strive**, sets out how cities and governments responded to the challenge of industrial decline. The role of government, local, national and European, became even more important at this stage and strongly underpinned recovery. Citizens and private enterprise leaders became deeply involved in the rescue attempts. A big turnaround was underway driven by strong city leadership, government backing and the heavy involvement of citizens. Serious efforts were dedicated to restoring poorer neighbourhoods and integrating poorer, particularly minority, communities. By 2008, all the signs were that cities were improving. Chapter Four explores Phase Two of the framework – post-industrial recovery.

Chapter Five, **Threats and opportunities**, shows how the financial crisis of 2008 called an abrupt halt to the large-scale public reinvestment that was moving 'Phoenix cities' forward. However, earlier rescue attempts had laid the foundations for a different, 'resource-limited', energy-constrained, 'green' model of recovery, based on recycling existing infrastructure, buildings and skills. Troubled and struggling 'weak market' cities are practised at pulling through and now, while public and private resources shrink, cities learn to 'do more with less', coping on smaller budgets and operating at smaller scales. Chapter Five sets out Phase Three of industrial cities – resource constrained economy.

Chapter Six, **Over-scale and under-scale**, shows that cities learnt the hard way that over-large industry and over-reliance on the public sector no longer work. But earlier industrial skills and the over-arching role of government can be marshalled to create a new economy. The proliferation of SMEs becomes the multilayered backbone of a new economy when big businesses vanish. Cities slowly recognise the value of SMEs, often spawned by bigger institutions and enterprises (such as universities) and often inventing new goods and services. Manufacturing jobs continue to shrink, while new service and maker enterprises emerge. Advanced manufacture draws on the producer skills of the cities combined with their engineering prowess.

Chapter Seven, **The power of social innovation**, is about the social economy, social exclusion and inclusion. SMEs not only sustain production and services but also support a renewed social focus with many breakthrough social innovations in what is now called the 'Sharing Economy'. However, the skills gap remains a serious challenge for those most damaged by industrial losses – particularly among youth. The concentration of foreigners and ethnic minorities in the poorest neighbourhoods also challenges the European ideal of social cohesion.

Chapter Eight, **Shoots of growth in older industrial cities in the US**, is a voice from the States. Leading metropolitan scholars recount the story of urban turnaround in the most unlikely places, the cores of seriously damaged former industrial cities – the growth of innovation districts near the downtown areas, the recovery of some inner neighbourhoods, the reintroduction of public transport, and repopulation of the centre city. The American story powerfully reinforces the European one in spite of extreme levels of poverty and segregation. Our framework broadly applies to change and recovery in former industrial US cities.

Chapter Nine, **Finding new ways out of the woods**, debates the prospects for European cities. Struggling cities, with a heavy legacy of problems, are doing better than forecast and surviving draconian cuts in external public support. Resource use is shifting in favour of recycling, reinventing, renewing, remaking the economy in a new and almost unforeseen mould. New breakthroughs in advanced manufacture, which these cities are highly suited to develop, spawn thousands of subsidiary services and products even though they offer few jobs directly within their high-precision industries. A new economy, growing from smaller scale, more flexible, more innovative and bespoke production methods, using 3D printing, advanced engineering and computer technologies, is growing in European and American cities.[19] A lighter, leaner, more creative, more 'broken up', more experimental economy is beginning to grow in Phoenix cities. Chapter Nine illustrates how the three phases of our framework fit together and point to a greener future.

Conclusion

European cities industrialised earlier than elsewhere; they invented clumsy, heavy-handed industrial methods and were extravagant in their use of materials. They took the earliest steps along the path to factory production. Energy, natural resources and labour were cheap and plentiful until they became overexploited and unsustainable. Along the way, they devastated their environments in order to get ahead in production and stay ahead. Mass production became self-fuelling – the more we have, the more we want. European cities testify to the finite limits of both natural and human resources.[20] Nowhere illustrates the scale of over-reach and subsequent devastation more powerfully than the Ruhr in Northern Germany, with its preserved ghostlike giant relics of its industrial past, reminding us of the consequences of over exploitation.[21]

European cities have the strongest possible reason for treading a new path. They can become energy saving and resource efficient; they are attractive and valuable to the European economy, one of the biggest single markets in the world, in spite of its problems. Cities are the engines of new ideas after a period of decline. The seven cities are only at the beginning of this uncertain road and they form a small sample from a large pool of similar cities. However, wider studies bear out the evidence presented here and our case studies expose how and why city change actually happens. Cities are in constant flux but the changes we document may point to a more viable, more balanced, urban future in the world's smallest, most crowded, most city-loving, continent.

Box 1.2: Tale of a city – Bilbao

Bilbao exemplifies the dense, compact European city model that many other cities have come to admire and envy. At the heart of the País Vasco or Euskadi (Basque country), Bilbao is wedged between the Pyrenees and the Atlantic ocean, imbued with Basque laws and traditions, a sea-faring, outward-facing, entrepreneurial people. Bilbao flourished in pre-industrial times as an important fishing and trading port. It gained city status in medieval times, becoming wealthy through its early engineering, shipbuilding and valuable fishing trade. As early explorers of the New World, Basque fishermen and sailors frequently discovered new ideas – the early entrepreneurs of the Spanish renaissance.

Bilbao became the centre of Spain's relatively late industrial revolution, importing coal along the coast from Asturias and extracting iron and other minerals from its own rich deposits. Its industries flourished in the 20th century, and the Basque country became relatively prosperous. Under Franco's dictatorship, in spite of the defeat of Basque nationalism in the Spanish Civil War and strong political suppression of the Basque language and laws, Bilbao became Spain's industrial heart, with large-scale steel production, shipbuilding and heavy engineering.

In the immediate aftermath of the Second World War, a unique and world famous experiment in industrial producer cooperatives emerged in the valley of Mondragon, in the foothills above Bilbao, drawing on the cooperative and self-sufficient traditions of Basque peasant farmers, and the engineering traditions of Basque entrepreneurs and machine makers. Its early success and strong growth greatly strengthened the solidaristic traditions of Basque lore and influenced the development of cooperatives in Bilbao.

By the 1970s, when democracy returned to Spain and the País Vasco became a free autonomous region within the new Spanish constitution, Bilbao was far richer than other parts of Spain, host to large-scale immigration mainly from the impoverished south. It had become a highly successful manufacturing centre, and it flourished under the new democracy. But the massive oil shock of the 1970s set in train the collapse of Europe's mainstay industries, eventually hitting the País Vasco, and Bilbao particularly. Manufacturing jobs halved, youth unemployment soared, the city's population fell as many Southern Spanish migrants returned home. ETA, the illegal Basque terrorist organisation, fighting for independence, intensified its bombing campaigns in the city. The city was further devastated by floods in 1983, exposing the extreme decay of the old core city. The abandoned docklands and the closure of the huge steel works, the 'Altos Hornos', seemed like the kiss of death.

Photo 1.1: Mountainside view of Mondragon in the foothills of the Pyrenees outside Bilbao

When Spain joined the European Union in 1983, Bilbao and the País Vasco benefitted strongly from regional funds, social funds and the general opening up that followed. The autonomous Basque government, using its own tax-raising powers, together with the city of Bilbao, developed a plan to restore the core city following the flood, to reclaim the now derelict riverside port area, to upgrade and expand public transport, to build new bridges across the river that carved the city in two, and to generate new economic activity – high tech enterprises, advanced engineering and services. The most famous international architects were called in to design the metro, the bridges and Bilbao's now emblematic Guggenheim Museum designed by Frank Gehry. The Guggenheim receives around a million new visitors a year, the nearby international conference centre, Euskaldina, almost as many. These attractions are part of a far broader urban focus.

Almost entirely funded through the public purse, Spanish and European funds, these investments helped to catapult the city back to European centre stage. Its employment rate, its income per head, its public infrastructure moved far ahead of most other Spanish regions – though still lagging behind the European average. By now the threat of breakaway and violence had subsided and the nationalist party played a leading role in Bilbao's government.

Photo 1.2: Euskalduna Conference Centre

Since the crisis of 2008, Bilbao and the País Vasco have escaped the worst of the calamitous property crash of the rest of Spain. Two major Basque banks, the B.B.V.A. and the Mondragon-based Caja Laboral, have escaped the Spanish banking collapse, although both have been affected. Bilbao has a far lower level of unemployment than the rest of Spain, including youth unemployment. The city is virtually free of overhanging debt, having paid down its earlier borrowing and structured its investments so that the city pays its way and avoids high risk ventures.

Meanwhile, Iberdrola, the multi-national energy company, one of Spain's most successful companies, based in Bilbao, is now one of the biggest renewable energy providers in Europe and one of Europe's strongest renewable energy innovators – although Spain's economic crisis, severe austerity measures and cuts to renewable energy subsidies have made progress vastly more difficult.

In July 2011, the 140-odd industrial cooperatives in Mondragon together formed Spain's second largest industrial exporter; but by 2012, its biggest and longest running factory, Fagor, was forced to close due to the collapse in the domestic housing market. Fagor was Spain's major manufacturer of domestic white goods.

Photo 1.3: The new CEDEMI building façade-Barakaldo, a converted factory

Photo 1.4: The CEDEMI building interior-Barakaldo, now used as an enterprise and start-up incubator

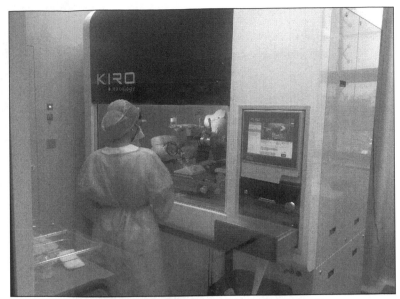

Photo 1.5: Kiro Oncology – hightech biomedical enterprise,
part of the Ondtagon co-op group

So Bilbao and its surrounding region did not escape wider Eurozone troubles. But the city's environmental enterprise park at Zamudio has grown in spite of the crisis. Ambitious new plans are on a slow burner but the city's imaginative social programmes encourage bright, young employment seekers towards microenterprises and cooperative creation.

The cooperative idea, which has a powerful hold in Bilbao, helps young people with a minimum of capital, a willingness to share profits and a bright idea to go out and create something while sharing the risk and the cost. The University of Mondragon now runs a full degree programme in Bilbao, 'Learning by Doing', based on the highly successful Finnish model. The four-year degree course takes groups of young people from a start point in developing a viable business to a fully-fledged enterprise over the four years – on a cooperative basis.

Bilbao has not escaped the general austerity, public spending cuts, reduced wages and chronic job scarcity for young people. Nor has it escaped the need for food kitchens and homeless shelters. But the city council retains a tight hold on its neighbourhood management, promotes the city's name and the city's products across Europe; it invests heavily in fast, efficient transport links, IT, conferences, business tourism and other export-oriented activities.

Bilbao's economy, housing market, youth opportunities are all affected by the wider, deeper crisis of the euro and the Spanish Doldrums – now showing signs of fading.[22] But it is surviving better than could have been predicted. A strong and unique Basque history and tradition, while ending ETA's violent campaign, no doubt play their part. We will see similar signs in other European cities. Bilbao has become a concentrated hub for design and showcasing, a laboratory and a shop front, a workshop for making and sharing ideas in one compact city space.

Photo 1.6: Azkuna Zentroa (Alhondiga): Converted 19th century wine store in central Bilbao – now a cultural and leisure centre with library, theatre, swimming pool, gym, community spaces. Each unique pillar is designed by an outstanding artist

Photo 1.7: Bilbao riverfront showing covered market and high rise housing in the background

Photo 1.8: Casco Viejo (The old town)

TWO

Divided and united Europe

A pioneer plant is one that can grow in harsh conditions and in poor soils, but is able to improve the area where it grows to make it suitable for other plants. Pioneer species are hardy species which are the first to colonise previously disrupted or damaged ecosystems. [1]

Box 2.1: Belfast – a story

Arriving into the port of Belfast by night ferry from Birkenhead reminds the visitor just how distant Belfast is from other British cities. It has a battle-torn history like no other.

John Hume, founder and leader of Northern Ireland's Social Democratic Labour Party, in 1998, won the Nobel Peace Prize for his tireless and often dangerous efforts to end the violence that almost tore Derry, his own city, Belfast, and his country apart for 30 years. The Republican fight for independence against the Unionist fight to remain part of Britain threatened to destroy Ireland, just as the Second World War had threatened to destroy Europe. Internal violence and deep sectarian divisions pushed Hume into a peace-brokering role amid the ugly 'Troubles'. A crowded community hall in North London in 2001 heard this quietly spoken Member of the European Parliament and member of Northern Ireland's own restored parliament at Stormont Castle explain how Europe became a key to peace in Ireland.

On his first visit to Strasbourg, home of the European Parliament, in the early 1990s, Hume stood with other MEPs from all over Europe, on the bridge over the river dividing France and Germany, two countries at war for over a hundred years. The immensity of the peace France and Germany had secured, burying centuries of bitter political and territorial divisions, made Hume realise a similar peace was possible in his small, divided country. Hideous wartime losses had led to a new, peaceful Europe. Northern Ireland must somehow fit into this European vision.

John Hume fought for and secretly helped negotiate several stages of the final Northern Irish Peace Agreement of 1998. 'He dared to look past centuries of

27

conflict' to 'a future where people of all religions can live together in peace and freedom'.[2] Chapter Two shows how wartime divisions shaped Europe's union and made peace in its war-torn cities.

Introduction: cities and the Phoenix

Europe's industrial cities developed within the wider European context of two world wars, the Great Depression, the Iron Curtain dividing post-war Europe, the rebuilding of Europe's devastated cities, the emergence of the European Union, post-war welfare states, post-colonial immigration, the rise of protest movements, and the Euro as a new European currency. This fast-moving journey has left deep traces within the seven industrial cities.

Phoenix cities only reflect the legend of the mythical bird of ancient Egypt if they are powerful and inventive enough to survive the struggle of past centuries and rebuild their fortunes from the ashes of that past. Acts of self-destruction do not always lead to the emergence of new growth. The legend of the Phoenix may not match the rise, fall and renewal of great industrial cities in Europe. This chapter sets out to show how connected Europe's industrial cities are with their past and yet how different and new they are today.

Not all cities recover from cycles of collapse and the ancient world is littered with the ruins of city civilisations that self-destructed through over-use of resources, over-aggressive domination of lands far beyond their boundaries, over-consumption of wealth in their growth period, and over-concentration of power. This pattern of social and economic collapse of urban civilisations is common to all continents.[3] But it is most conspicuous in the 'cradle of civilisation', the Mediterranean and Southern Europe – most spectacularly in ancient Greece and Rome.[4] It is easy not to learn the lessons of history.

The cities in this handbook grew to international significance nearly two millennia after Rome, gaining immense power and prestige through industrial development in the 19th and 20th centuries. Torino, our Italian case study, became important when Julius Caesar first built a fort there in 27BC to support his adventures over the Alps. It became for a short while the capital of a unified Italy in the 19th century and was weakened by the new capital of Italy moving after only two years to Florence and then to Rome. But its industrial growth, wealth creation and invention following this blow made it a powerhouse of urban progress in the late 19th and 20th centuries – a true Phoenix.[5]

Its position today, following its late industrial decline and recovery over the past few decades, bear these marks.

Industrial explosion and collapse

Fifteen hundred years after the fall of the Roman Empire and collapse of its cities, the industrial revolution changed the stakes and drove exponential urban population growth right across Europe, starting in England. Sheffield for example, the great early steel producer, doubled its population in the 50 years between 1800 and 1850, then quadrupled it in the following 50 years.[6] Our seven Phoenix cities were at the heart of this change of pace. Their founding strengths in natural resources, location and history gave them a head start in the race to make and grow.

Figure 2.1: Historic population development trends, 1350–2005

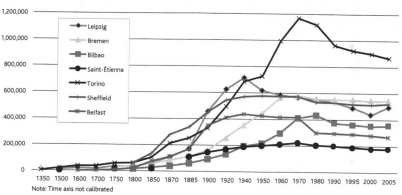

Note: Time axis not calibrated

Sources: Power et al (2010); Eurostat http://ec.europa.eu/eurostat/web/cities/data/database

The attempts to create wealth that had gone before paled into insignificance beside the new drive for invention, mass production and creative destruction. Unprecedented concentrations of energy and enterprise in the exploding industrial centres that grew up around earlier settlements shaped the first industrial revolution. Such growth – a long-run wealth and poverty bubble, as well as a population bubble – was eventually destined to burst but not for another 100 or more years.

The continuing urban industrial explosion, in the 20th century, sowed the seeds of its own destruction by using its natural resources over-intensively, taking no account of the costs in environmental damage, resource depletion and human exploitation. Just as earlier urban civilisations had done, it left behind a legacy of post-industrial damage and waste that the seven cities still display. Air, soil and water pollution reached extreme levels, while hectares of disused industrial land and abandoned infrastructure show the sheer scale and intensity of earlier production.

Industrial growth and decline affecting the seven cities – involving coal, iron, steel, shipbuilding, machine production, textiles, cars – reflect a Europe-wide pattern. Cities grew on the back of vast production systems, joined together by industrially built railways, laid

Table 2.1: Industrial growth and impact

Leipzig	Coal extraction Railway interchange International trade fairs Textiles
Lille	Coal and iron extraction Centre of linen and textile industry Also transport hub and logistics centre of international importance
Saint-Étienne	Coal and iron extraction Became major centre for arms manufacture Also built trains, bicycles and textiles Ribbon and lace making
Torino	Fiat cars, communications, typewriters Conversion to hydro-electricity from Alpine water sources Also built trains and lorries International logistical centre
Bilbao	Large scale steel production, with coal from Asturias carried along coast Became major port Used steel for shipbuilding and engineering of all kinds Machine production
Sheffield	Surrounding rich coal mining and iron ore extraction Invented Bessemer steel, stainless steel, silver plate Major engineering based universities
Belfast	Shipbuilding based around port Linen and textile industry Major engineering centre
Comments	All cities had strong engineering base All suffered social dislocation, extreme poverty among casual and immigrant workers Strong working class culture and neighbourhoods, educational gap Emergence of powerful unions Vulnerable to collapse under economic, social and environmental pressures Extremely damaging environmental impact of industry, extraction, growth, sprawl, and so on

Source: City visits, 2006–08

down during Europe's early industrial growth era over a century ago. In Britain, railways began their great expansion in the 1830s and by 1850 we had 5000 miles of track. This grew to 18,000 miles (25,000 km) by the end of the century. Most of those lines still exist today, thanks to which the industrial north of England, including Sheffield and Manchester, has the densest, if not fastest, railway network in Europe.[7] Railways transformed Europe's trading capacity and helped spread ideas as well as goods. A small continent became linked together in totally new ways, which today serve the goal of city recovery. Railways in Europe have made a strong come back and the seven cities are being re-shaped by that recovery.[8]

Across Europe, cities have long traded with each other, and learnt from each other in spite of language barriers, religious divisions, power struggles, high mountain ranges, such as the Alps and Pyrenees, and the channel distancing the British Isles by a narrow sea from the rest of the continent. Trade was a driving factor in industrial growth. Industrial cities originally flourished on a network of waterways, some man-made, many natural, that encouraged cheap, mass transit of heavy goods. Britain dug 3000 miles of canals linked to its main river systems and the sea to carry coal and industrial goods, early in the industrial revolution before railways were invented, only to see slow-moving canals overtaken by much faster and quicker to build railways a generation or two later. Europe did likewise. Many of Lille's canals were filled in and used for roads in the 1950s and 1960s. Now they are being uncovered again. Today, European waterways are aiding city recovery in unforeseen ways. They are also carrying more goods again, for example between Manchester and Liverpool in the industrial heartland of northern England, and around Lille.

Two World Wars changed Europe's fortunes

Modern Europe has a particular legacy of protecting and cherishing its cities because for over 2000 years, invaders, settlers, conquerors, kings, princes, barons, emperors, dictators fought each other across Europe's bitterly contested borders, often between small city states, in search of wealth and dominance. The wealth of resources that lay in Europe's early cities, their soils, rocks, rivers, mountains and coastlines made them the battleground for power. Endless European wars tell a tragic story of death, destruction, exploitation, colonisation, occupation and slavery. Torino, Lille, Belfast, Leipzig and Bilbao are all located in strategic positions where war has erupted and they have all seen their share of occupation, invasion, violence and domination. Twentieth century European wars were on a vastly different scale from their predecessors, and the seven cities as producers of machines, vehicles, textiles and armaments were the hubs of military-industrial production and conflict.

Wars in the end undermined Europe's domination as world leader in innovation, manufacture and wealth creation. The scars of two world wars in the 20th century, fought on European soil and between European powers, reminded populations of the dangers of over-ambitious growth and extreme exploitation, although they helped fuel the post-war industrial boom. War also shaped the response to the crisis of deindustrialisation, for it was still a living memory for most Europeans as acute decline grew in the 1970s and 1980s. Industrial collapse came as a shock, but their earlier resilience stood them in good stead. They reacted stoically and defensively, practised as they were in the art of survival and building anew.[9]

All seven cities in the handbook were involved directly or indirectly in the war of 1939–45, mainly through the production of armaments, vehicles and military supplies. War turned ship builders, steel workers, engineers, inventors, and textile, machine and tool makers of all kinds into vital players in an all-consuming war machine. Industrial cities thus became both strategically central to world war and vulnerable to attack. They were either heavily bombed or occupied or sometimes both. Bilbao was the partial exception as Spain was not a direct combatant, having experienced three years of bitter civil war directly before the Second World War broke out.

Following the overwhelming carnage and devastation of the Second World War, European countries pledged never again to fight each other. This had happened following the First World War and the Great Depression of the 1930s. This pledge, made on the border between Germany and France near Strasbourg, led directly to the creation of what eventually became the European Union. It also shaped industrial cities in a new productive fashion. They were both shaken in their foundations and set to grow again.

A lasting commitment to peace meant that the wartime boom in armaments, which had boosted innovation, skill and production methods in industrial cities like Sheffield, Belfast, Saint-Étienne and Torino was quickly converted to peacetime industries. Cities were crowded and the costs of war damage were clear, but governments stepped in to subsidise the conversion and regrowth of their traditional industries after the war, literally from the ashes of destruction. The post-war boom in production was based on mass production systems, operating on a vast new scale, using new methods that made goods cheaper and people richer. Many production innovations were introduced from the USA. European producer cities were set on a new path of explosive growth.

The Europe-wide experience of all-out war

Europe became almost totally state-controlled under wartime economies. Industrial cities, as military-industrial producers, became almost government-run. In countries occupied by Germany, such as France and Holland, industrial capacity in cities was diverted into Germany's war effort. Populations were often on the brink of starvation by the end of the war.[10] Even neutral countries, like Ireland, were affected and Belfast as part of the UK was a wartime arms manufacturer, warship builder, and target of enemy attack.

The impact of the Second World War on Central and Eastern Europe was if anything starker. Military occupation by Germany, intense fighting with Russia, chronic shortages of all necessities, floods of refugees, millions of deaths, huge Jewish round-ups, the persecution, forced labour and murder of other minorities such as Roma, made life unbearably harsh. Europe still shows those scars; the memories are often relived through multiple Remembrance Days; and the European Union is a beleaguered emblem of the attempt to overcome the barriers of history.

Europe's leaders had for centuries carved up European territory through cross-border marriage alliances which often preceded or provoked or followed wars. Cities shifted across borders between states or were the hubs for both conflict and sometimes unity. Lille, Torino and Leipzig as crossroad cities had sometimes belonged on one side or another of a moving border. Lille was besieged many times by invading armies. The moving boundaries across Europe were nowhere more contested than between Germany and France, and between Germany and its East European neighbours. Even today these borders are debated and occasionally contested. Some border cities straddle both. Other cities were the centre of armaments production, of which Saint-Étienne was maybe the most spectacular example, becoming rich and famous for supplying Napoleon's armies. Napoleon's military ambitions led to France's biggest national arms factory being built in the city, to produce precision guns up to the early 1980s. Sheffield, Belfast, Bremen and Torino were also large scale producers of valuable war supplies.

The industrial cities produced during the war, on a huge scale, by employing large numbers of women to compensate for the military draft of able-bodied men. The cities then became true war machines, leading to stream-lined and accelerated output, resulting from the imperatives of war, combining the engineering prowess of these cities and the sheer scale of need. Six of our producer cities became an integral part of the war machine – vulnerable to attack because of the indispensable function they fulfilled. Industrial cities played a huge part, but also paid a huge price.

The hardships of war were so extreme that doubling up in homes and shelters, recycling old clothes and equipment, making substitute food through industrial methods, rationing of almost everything, became accepted. Allotments, 'hand me downs' and 'any old iron'[10] were lifelines, not only for the poor, but for the masses affected by the war effort. War was above all a great equaliser. In Britain and throughout occupied Europe, sharing under duress became a way of life.

Normal life was severely disrupted at every level, not just because of extreme and bitter divisions that caused the war, but because of its long-run consequences. Loss of homes and vital infrastructure; loss of productive capacity; state domination of almost all aspects of daily life; chronic shortages; strongly equalising state-run systems; acute need and destitution for millions of refugees, orphans, broken families, returning soldiers and prisoners of war. People had no choice but to rebuild. Post-war reconstruction became an all-consuming task that shaped Europe's post-war generation of 1945–75.

A living bridge between wartime Europe and the industrial collapse of the 1970s and 1980s is the post-war generation of 1945–75, the baby-boomers. These 30 years witnessed extraordinary peacetime growth in manufacturing that shaped modern Europe – mass produced cars, telephones, televisions, air travel, supermarkets, welfare states, universal health care were all post-war experiences in Europe.

Legacy of war

War marked European cities deeply. Germany lost two thirds of its urban housing stock through bombing. Countless millions of its population were displaced and died, both through fighting and bombing, through concentration camps, mass executions and the Holocaust. Cities like Hamburg, Dresden, Cologne and Munich were all but destroyed. There were 12 million German refugees to absorb at the end of the war into Western Germany, following the new peace frontiers that were drawn across Europe. Eastern Germany became a separate communist state, profoundly reshaping cities like Leipzig and nearby Dresden, which was almost totally flattened by British bombing.

France, which had been occupied by Germany for most of the war, along with Holland, Belgium and Denmark, had an estimated deficit of 14 million homes in 1950, a political legacy of virtually continuous war with Germany for nearly a century and a weak and underdeveloped industrial base.[12] A strong communist party, strong trade unions, a radical worker–priest movement active in French factories, resistance fighters who had sacrificed all and wanted a united Europe. They all fed into unstable post-war governments. Lille was often host to these post-war movements, located strategically at a cross-border point with Belgium; while Saint-Étienne with its strong working class traditions, was dominated by the communist party for much of the post-war era.

Italy, a defeated ally of Germany, along with Greece, lost almost everything by 1945 as the Allies swept up from the south to defeat fascism. Italy was deeply impoverished by the war and its northern cities, particularly Torino, suffered severe bomb damage, having become involved in supplying military vehicles for Mussolini via the giant Fiat factory. Post-war Italy was dominated for 50 years from 1944–94 by the conservative Christian democrats, with the south dominated by organised crime, principally the Mafia. Greece meanwhile, having been severely war damaged, experienced a three year civil war soon after the Second World War, then a dictatorship. Its economic development has been unsteady ever since, and now threatens to destabilise Europe because of its unmanageable debt, its inability to collect taxes, and its banking crisis.[13]

Spain, having suffered a bitter civil war in 1936–39 during which most of its industry was destroyed and the German Nazis supported the fascist-leaning army leader, General Franco, helping him to become a military dictator in 1939 (lasting until 1976), did not join the Second World War. The country was dominated by a military regime allied with Germany. The dictatorship suppressed internal conflicts and held back Spain's post-war development. Bilbao suffered both heavy repression of Basque language and culture, and became Spain's industrial powerhouse after the war. Portugal fell under a dictatorship even earlier than Spain, in 1926 (lasting until 1974), made far worse by ugly colonial wars in Africa that sapped its scarce resources, making it Europe's poorest country for decades.

Britain, as a strongly defended island, remained unoccupied during both world wars but was directly under siege from Germany and heavily bombed between 1939 and 1944. The war effort led to total conscription and the militarisation of all British industries. Chronic food and material shortages, strict rationing, mass evacuation of families from cities, drafting all able-bodied women into factories and fields became a way of life in wartime Britain. Evacuees were billeted on families in safer, smaller places. Family and community life was disrupted. These sacrifices were accompanied by frequent night bombings and widespread damage to homes and industry in cities. Nearly a million homes were destroyed or damaged, only a fraction of the German toll, but causing extensive homelessness, and the rapid post-war boom in pre-fabricated housing, squatting, slum clearance and the ambitious construction of 10,000 mass housing estates – over 6 million homes. Sheffield, a major armaments and machine manufacturer, became a live example of all these trends, particularly steel production, bombing, slum clearance and concrete, mass produced housing estates.

Although the Second World War was truly worldwide, involving the USA, Russia, East Asia, North and East Africa, European colonies and the whole British Commonwealth, it was particularly a European war, both in its origin, its execution and its consequences. Understanding its significance for Britain and Northern Ireland, France, Germany, Eastern Europe, Spain and Italy helps us to understand the post-war evolution of our cities. For they were in many ways shaped in the post-war era by this wartime history, which in turn grew from the debris of the First World War. It is hard to make sense of European cities and their trajectories, except as part of a bitter, 20th century history of conflict, and desperate attempts at unity.

Repairing and rebuilding Europe's infrastructure: the US Marshall Plan

A path-breaking post-war gift was offered by the United States to address Europe's post-war economic ills, aimed primarily at rebuilding Europe's peacetime industries, but particularly helping to rebuild a flattened Germany, and integrate Europe. However, a larger share of the funds went to the Allies (France and Britain) compared with Germany. The Marshall Plan worked on the premise that a defeated and flattened Germany, without a viable economy, would not help unify Europe and heal wartime wounds.[14] All our industrial cities became involved in this process of reconstruction.

So harsh were social conditions and so acute the shortages of basic essentials after the war that rationing continued into the mid-1950s in Britain. Britain, densely populated and under siege for five years, was beset by chronic food shortages, while state involvement in basic services expanded rapidly. Housing, transport, education, health and industry all became largely state-run.

In contrast, Germany, defeated and almost flattened, was run until the late 1940s by a four-country allied peace occupation, with France, Britain, Russia and the USA. A new German federal constitution created a unique, devolved, federal form of government, with the aim of preventing a unified German state from ever becoming too powerful again.[15] This federal constitution has shaped Germany's post-war progress, particularly in relation to war, military intervention, the creation of the European Union and the Euro, and its attitude to austerity and bail-outs in Greece, Portugal, Spain and Ireland. Eastern Germany only joined the new federal Germany in 1990. The federal structure is still in place today, making the decentralised German model the envy of other more centralised countries, like Britain, France and Italy.

France had a series of weak governments and a strong communist-led, trade union movement. Eventually radical political reforms in the 1960s, led by France's wartime hero, de Gaulle, further strengthened the state. Italy was also highly centralised until the 1980s, also with some strong communist leanings, when Italy, like France, began a process of regional decentralisation.

Meanwhile, the Southern European dictatorships of Spain, Portugal and Greece held back post-war progress in their countries for more than a generation until the 1970s when the pull of post-war democracy and European integration became more powerful. The birth of democracy in Spain in 1978 led to strong regional autonomy, particularly for the Basque country and Bilbao. All of our industrial cities were caught up in these national policy shifts.

The Marshall Fund invested generously in new and restored infrastructure to get Europe working again, to create a new climate of collaboration and economic progress, and to bring European countries closer together. The European Union was at least in part built on the commitment exacted by the Marshall Fund that European countries would work together towards lasting peacetime progress, forged by stronger trade links and freer economies.[16] It was Europe's industrial cities that most stood to gain.

The American Marshall Plan for Europe required European economic cooperation and the vastly challenging tasks of rebuilding German and French industries on a cooperative basis, where they were often extracting coal and iron from adjacent mines on the basis of competition. The French and Germans, with the Benelux countries (Belgium, Netherlands, Luxembourg), set up the European Coal and Steel Community as a first step in this cooperation. In order to harness nuclear energy for peaceful purposes, they also set up Euratom, which the British, with their scientific nuclear capacity, collaborated in. Sheffield's Forgemasters, the oldest independent steel company, still has nuclear capacity today.

American Marshall Aid was conditional on greater cross-border collaboration within Europe, helped by the formation of the Organisation for Economic Co-operation and Development in 1961, thus underpinning the new Europe. When the United States came to Europe's rescue, Germany's engineering prowess, industrial strength and advanced machine production quickly began to recover. The wider public criticised the 'fairness' of helping Germany back on its feet. But European leaders, particularly France and Italy, were persuaded of the benefits of strengthening post-war Germany as an ally.[17] There was also a great need for Germany's industrial production skills to work in favour of all Europe – engines, machines, heavy equipment, domestic and industrial scale goods.

The Marshall Fund helped the rest of war damaged Europe too. Large scale American industrial investment in Britain turned Ford cars into a symbol of the new post-war economy. Giant American car factories were built, accelerating mass car ownership. The importation of American technical knowhow greatly extended mass production methods to many industrial fields, including industrial scale intensive agriculture, production of chemicals for food production and processing, and cheap mass consumer goods. American ideas, culture and influence were simultaneously embraced and resisted. They permeated nonetheless. Much less hampered than Europe by the hardships of war, the US had forged ahead in wealth creation, invention, and automation. It was far richer than Europe but needed a stronger Europe as ally in the Cold War against Russia and its East European satellites. It felt obliged to and could afford to support its European allies.

Advanced technologies, such as computing and automated conveyor belt production, encouraged a scramble for research and development funds. Competing countries tried to out-flank each other in precision instruments, technical efficiency and volume of goods. Scientific research, technological advances and new production methods were the byproducts of war, and favoured development in industrial cities.

The Iron Curtain and the Cold War

The separation of Eastern and Western Europe after the war in 1945 as a result of the Russian-backed emergence of communist governments across Eastern Europe was a particularly sad outcome for Western European leaders. Not only did it leave Germany divided into two separate states but it drew an 'Iron Curtain across Europe', with missiles, tanks and military bases drawn up on each side. Europe was yet again threatened by all-out war, placing one half of Europe apart from the other, and creating a 'Cold War', between East and West. A militarised communist front across Eastern Europe, cheek by jowl with the West, placed cities like Leipzig on the far side of a divide that was to last until 1989 and that constantly threatened the hard won, post-war peace. The USA was at one extreme, Russia at the other, while the whole of continental Europe was squeezed in the middle, half on one side of the Iron Curtain, half on the other.[18] In many cases families were divided, cities, towns and communities were divided, and Europe, over the long post-war decades, faced again the tensions and divisions that had beset its history.

Post-war European thinking in relation to industrial cities was driven by the desire for unity and the fear of further division. For war-battered Germany, the division of Europe after the war between East and West not only cut its country in two and displaced its capital, Berlin, to the East, deep inside the Iron Curtain. It created an illogical economic division, prohibiting trade, interrupting longstanding through trains, redrawing yet again Germany's Eastern borders, separating German families, creating millions of stranded ethnic German refugees on the far side of the Iron Curtain. The consequences for Europe as a whole were re-militarisation, the development in France and Britain of nuclear weapons, which Sheffield and Belfast, among other cities, were involved in, the deployment of American bases and missiles across Europe. Germany felt particularly vulnerable, with its long Eastern border, guarded by a heavy American nuclear protective shield. East Germany became the Soviet frontline in the Cold War, following Russia's loss of over 26 million lives and over half its industrial capacity.[19]

Americans were far more alarmed by the Cold War threat than Europeans. Communism itself became a much-feared system, partly because its core ideology of 'collective ownership' and state-run universal services was anathema to American ideas of freedom and enterprise creation. Yet it had a certain hold over European thinking, both West and East of the Iron Curtain.

In France, Italy and Spain, a different and new kind of communism was born, called Euro-communism. It embraced the idea of collective ownership of the means of production and collective provision of services either by the state, or by other communally-organised bodies such as cooperatives. It was an attempt by left wing thinkers to take the best of Western social movements and link them with the more sharing aspects of communist belief. Cities like Bologna in Italy were run for many years by democratically elected Euro-communists. In Torino, Bilbao and Lille, Euro-communists were widely represented.[20]

Euro-communists influenced the city government of Torino, where workers' protests over working conditions, acute housing shortages and inadequate welfare provision threatened the stability of the city and the fortunes of Fiat, the city's main industrial employer.[21] Similarly in Bilbao, workers' organisations, linked to the Catholic Church, were in clandestine alliance with Spain's progressive Euro-communists under Franco's dictatorship. In Sheffield, where radical miner's unions were based, the city's socialist council was strongly committed to state intervention, state control and state provision. The city backed the take-over by worker-owned mutuals of collapsing producer industries. Violent conflict erupted when the mines were threatened with closure in 1980–81.

Mines, railways and some of the largest steel works had been nationalised after the war and remained so until the 1970–1980s. A more reactionary form of Euro-communism held sway in Saint-Étienne where a communist elected mayor held power and vainly tried to save major industries through semi-public ownership, with French government backing.

Meanwhile, East Germany in 1961 built the Berlin Wall to stop East German citizens from fleeing to the West and to restrict West Germans visiting East German relatives. This catapulted Leipzig into centre stage, not only of the Cold War, but of the unravelling of East European communism. The Iron Curtain that divided Europe, harsh, rigid and oppressive as its public image was, allowed ideas and people to flow through it and influences worked in both directions, westwards and eastwards, as Leipzig's unique story shows. The rigid 'iron curtain' eventually collapsed under its own weight.

Box 2.2: Leipzig's Monday Demonstrations

In the mid-1980s, Leipzig became the centre of opposition to the repression of freedom, under the East German communist government. The Lutheran pastor of the Nikolaikirche, in the very centre of Leipzig, backed by other churches across the city, strongly advocated peaceful change, openness to ideas, freedom of speech and movement, an inclusive social system that was both egalitarian and tolerant. The Berlin Wall became a powerful symbol of oppression against all these principles.

The Pastor opened up his church to all comers, believers and nonbelievers, alternative groups as well as conventional communists, citizens who wanted to leave for the West, and those who wanted to stay to reform communism from within. Once a week, on Monday evenings, the Nikolaikirche held an open-door Peace Prayer service with the aim of bringing this disparate group of Christians and nonbelievers into a safe, supportive space where at least for that short hour, they would feel free and welcome. The Peace Prayers – Friedensgebet – encouraged participants to offer their own thoughts, doubts, questions, worries and direct experiences, as a form of active prayer.

Over several years, these prayer meetings built up into large gatherings of several hundred people. A particular problem, critical to East Germany's future, often came up – the conflict over whether East Germans should leave the country or stay and help to make the system work. The secret East German police, the Stasi, were aware of the pull of these prayer meetings, but recognised that they did not directly challenge the regime or the existing structure, only some of its methods, so the police remained as bystanders for a long time.

However, outside the prayer meetings, as the regime's hold on the economy and the population weakened, the police became more repressive. Arrests and imprisonments rose as overtly dissident groups became more vocal and protests over unjust treatment intensified. Outside the Nikolaikirche in the large square that opens onto the main street, protest demonstrations began to form on Mondays, after the prayer meetings, eventually spilling into the streets of Leipzig. As police action intensified, demonstrators posted the names of those arrested on the outside windows of the Church in the square, and vigil lights were lit to represent the peaceful transition the prayers called for.

As the demonstrations grew, so did police repression, until on 9 October 1989 70,000 people marched in the streets of Leipzig, calling for peaceful change. The German Democratic Republic's hold eventually crumbled, the Berlin Wall was breached and the communist government of East Germany gave up. An extraordinary combination of the Lutheran Nikolaikirche in the centre of Leipzig, the citizens of Leipzig, of all ages, beliefs and political persuasion, overflowed from peaceful prayer services in the church, onto the city streets, thereby effectively helping change the course of European history. Leipzig played a unique role in bringing down the Berlin Wall and the Iron Curtain.[22]

Europe's Common Market

The post-war generation recognised the vulnerability of national economies to wider forces. People had only survived the war through many forms of solidarity which belied the bitterness and violence of the war itself. Welding together common interests both within countries and across borders seemed essential to overcoming this fragility. Certainly the gradual emergence of the European Common Market in the 1950s, evolving into the European Community and then the European Union, followed from the need to spread a strongly social purpose across Europe's war-torn borders.

The post-war aim was to create more unity and collaboration between European nations, and more social support within them. Europe's generous post-war welfare states were largely the product of a wartime legacy which favoured shared responsibility, shared risk and rewards. Thus European states would rebuild solidarity from within and between each other.

The biggest challenge was the restructuring of European economies into a single European market. The early talk of European cross-border collaboration and trade was not just in response to the horror of war and the ambition to bury that history of European conflict forever. The urgency of cooperation was fomented by French anxiety to contain German ambitions and French ambitions to play a leadership role, following years of occupation. Germany, meanwhile, was anxious to wash away its nationalist, Nazi image and build a peaceful, cooperative international reputation – ideas that were strongly backed by survivors of European Resistance Movements, who had risked all to oppose nationalism and domination, and to end war in Europe forever. The very extremes of Europe's history, the vulnerability of its insecure and disputed borders, the precarious independence of many small states, made more extreme by language divisions and localised nationalism, made the goal of post-war European unity more important.

France wanted closer links with Germany, with which it shares a long and historically disputed border, to limit Germany's impressive recovery power by sharing in it. French Europeanist Jean Monet was a leading light in forming Europe's first shared economic–cum–legal structure, 'The European Coal and Steel Community', followed by Euratom. This evolved into the European Economic Community launched in 1957 – but excluding Britain, Scandinavia and most of Southern Europe, except Italy. Many industrial cities were part of this cross-border process, including cities like Sarrbruchen and Metz on the industrially rich but disputed German–French border. Jean Monet gave his name to the new university in Saint-Étienne, founded in the late 1980s to foster the city's outward-looking recovery strategy. By 1973, Britain, Denmark and Ireland joined the European Economic Community, with others to follow (see Table 2.2).

Trading freely across European borders in a small, closely inter-linked continent offered the prospect of economic growth, cheaper goods and the exchange of specialist knowhow in new, fast developing, and scientific fields. Cross-European research and development led to ambitious projects that pooled scarce resources and fostered new developments – in medical sciences, advanced engineering, computing, aviation, rail and logistics, inland waterways and intercontinental river networks, such as the Rhine.

European cooperation gave German, French and British cities the chance to rebuild their industries within a wider European framework of economic cooperation, leading to collaborative projects such as Airbus, based in Bremen, Toulouse and Bristol within the large trading area for European manufacture. Collaborative European research in advanced technologies, including nuclear, high speed rail, air transport, renewable energy, electric cars and hydrogen production, supported employment growth to increase prosperity and the development of new ideas. Deeply ingrained lessons in survival, conflict resolution and shared solutions helped shape post-war industrial recovery. Industrial cities were the heartlands of the new Europe, with their technical universities and colleges rapidly gaining status, and their workforces gaining access to new mass housing estates, free health care and increasingly higher education.

European economic progress helped end European post-war dictatorships in Greece, Spain and Portugal, and accelerated 'the fall of the Iron Curtain', and the reunification of Germany into the biggest and most powerful member state, still a somewhat feared outcome. Economic union also brought the whole of Eastern Europe into close union with Western Europe in the 1990s.

In 1957, six core founders of the European Economic Community signed the Treaty of Rome – Germany, France, Italy, Belgium, Netherlands and Luxembourg. Britain, insular in many of its attitudes and habits, but closely tied to Europe through history, trade, proximity, cultural links and the sacrifices of two world wars, wanted to join but its entry was vetoed by France's strong-minded President Charles de Gaulle in 1963 on the grounds that British customs and economy were too different – in spite of the core idea that Europe would be stronger together.[23]

A free trade area around Europe, with Britain, Scandinavia and Ireland, worked towards integration with the European Community and by 1971, these countries were admitted to Europe as we now know it. Spain, Greece and Portugal had to wait for the ending of dictatorships and for state democracy to emerge. And Eastern Europe had to wait for the Iron Curtain to come down and democratic governments to emerge in those countries.

Table 2.2 shows the evolution of the European Union from its founding six members, to its current 28, setting out the stages of post-war European integration.

Table 2.2: Evolution of the European Union

Organisation and date (and treaty)	Countries
1951 – Treaty of Paris **European Coal and Steel Community (ECSC)**	Belgium France West Germany Italy The Netherlands Luxembourg
1957 – Euratom Treaty **European Atomic Agency Committee (Euratom)**	As above
1958 – Treaty of Rome **European Economic Community (EEC)** **(Common Market)** **European Free Trade Area (EFTA) –** **created in 1960 by the 'Outer Seven':** Austria, Denmark, Norway, Portugal, Sweden, Switzerland, UK	1958: • France • West Germany • Italy • Belgium • The Netherlands • Luxembourg 1973: • Denmark • Ireland • UK 1981: • Greece 1986: • Spain • Portugal 1990: Former East Germany (GDR) on German reunification
1993 – Maastricht Treaty (11 Eastern European countries admitted) **European Union (EU)**	1993–94: Belgium; Denmark; France; Germany; Greece; Ireland; Italy; Luxembourg; Netherlands; Portugal; Spain; UK 1995–2004: Austria; Finland; Sweden 2004–06: Cyprus; Czech Republic; Estonia; Hungary; Latvia; Lithuania; Malta; Poland; Slovakia; Slovenia 2007–13: Bulgaria; Romania; Croatia

Source: EU, http://europa.eu/about-eu/eu-history/index_en.htm

The creation of a single currency was supposed to smooth the progress of European economic integration and the cross-border movement of goods, people and money. It was a logical progression from the common market and the European Union. However, the economic logic of creating a single currency for a single and unified trading area was weakened by the failure to establish sufficient political and financial integration to withstand the international banking crisis.[24] Table 2.3 shows the development of the Euro and its members.

Table 2.3: Evolution of the Eurozone

Key dates	Member countries	Total members
1999	Austria; Belgium; Finland; France; Germany; Ireland; Italy; Luxembourg; Netherlands; Portugal; Spain	11
2001	Greece	12
2007–09	Slovenia; Cyprus; Malta; Slovakia	16
2011–15	Estonia; Latvia; Lithuania	19

Source: EU, http://ec.europa.eu/economy_finance/euro/index_en.htm

For Europeans, different languages, different newspapers, foods, building styles, religions, forms of government, even dress are striking and challenging. Yet this super-diverse patchwork of peoples and places has somehow grown together since 1945 – now 70 years ago. From countries of 4 million people, like Ireland, to 80 million like a united Germany; from sub-tropical Canary Islands, to Arctic reaches of Sweden and Finland, the continent of Europe has to pull together or sink. Europe United is here to stay. The channel tunnel, permanently linking Britain to the continent by fast-rail in the 1990s, was a triumph of engineering, political collaboration and economic logic that reflected the European ideal. Britain is still part-island, part-European. It is outside the Euro and constantly questions its role in Europe. Yet, it is now quicker to reach Paris and Brussels from London than it is to reach Newcastle in the north of England. The idea of Britain leaving Europe seems highly unlikely.

Conclusion: progress is not plain sailing

In post-war Europe, trade unions and left wing ideas gained ground; wages and conditions improved beyond recognition; education spread; universities multiplied; and consumer goods proliferated. The transformation of Europe's industrial cities was extraordinary – from wartime arms and destruction, to post-war prosperity and growth. Yet there were tangible problems even while European economies were doing so well. The scale of production and growth created a sense of 'anomie' and powerlessness that undermined the very solidarity the European Union was born to create. A 'couldn't care less' attitude became the common charge from the wartime generation against the youth of the 1960s who had 'never had it so good'.

Meanwhile, post-war decolonisation and 'Third World' growth made competition for resources fiercer. In spite of comprehensive welfare states, some were left behind, particularly immigrant communities. Often length of residency and other citizen requirements precluded some immigrants from true equality within European Welfare States. Urban riots occurred occasionally, particularly in England and France where anti-colonial movements had most impact. Race relations were politically fraught, and a determination to avoid the American urban ghetto was balanced by a fear of losing votes and incurring high costs by fully integrating immigrant communities.

By the early 1960s an anti-government, anti-status quo mentality emerged in the post-war youthful generation. There were two kinds of radical urban movement – on the one hand, committed to the overthrow of the existing system, using violence if necessary; on the other hand, grass roots community groups arguing for more participatory, more local, more democratic, more egalitarian and more responsive forms of organisation within cities. Extremism was rare, but hugely damaging when it arose. One secret terrorist group, the Red Brigades, was active in the Fiat factories in Torino.[25] Re-emerging nationalist movements in Northern Ireland, the Basque country, some French and Italian regions, and within Belgium, also threatened the status quo and both Belfast and Bilbao were deeply affected by these movements.

As a counter-weight to the growing power of national governments, community groups rejected 'Big Brother', the state, and wanted the world to operate on a smaller, more local, more community-based scale, with the aim of integrating immigrant groups as part of the community where they worked, lived and added value. These popular community movements are discussed in later chapters.

Protest movements – against nuclear weapons and the Cold War in particular, but also against colonial wars and uprisings in Algeria, Eastern and Southern Africa, East Asia, and Latin American post-colonial dictatorships – rocked European governments. For a few heady months in 1968, students challenged the European status quo.

The American Civil Rights and anti-war movements had a powerful trans-Atlantic influence, and Europe was far from at peace with itself.

The loss of confidence in the post-war economic miracle and early signs of industrial decline ran hand in hand with political change and protest across Europe. Leipzig, far from being the exception among our cities, shared a common experience of unexpected change and upheaval with Torino, Lille, Bilbao and Belfast. European political leaders found it hard to accept that the post-war peace dividend might not last, and that all was not well in Europe's industrial economies.

Box 2.3: Tale of a city – Belfast

Belfast perfectly captures the problem of war and peace, industrial might and demise, the urgency of recovery and the evolution of a new sense of direction.

Every one of the seven cities over 1945–80 went through the monumental changes outlined in this chapter. Belfast reflects many elements of this rollercoaster ride.

Belfast's pre-industrial history helped shape its later functions. The British made Belfast a strong Protestant-dominated foothold in Catholic Ireland in the 17th century, by attracting Scottish Presbyterian settlers. It became famous for its butter, beef and textiles. Linen, a valuable natural product of Ireland, made it wealthy. In the industrial revolution, it became Britain's biggest shipbuilder. The Titanic, built in Belfast's Harland and Wolf dock at the turn of the 20th century, was the most spectacular example of its unrivalled prowess. The sinking of the Titanic on its maiden voyage, drowning most of its several thousand passengers, seemed to bring Belfast more fame than infamy. Yet it symbolised the absolute limits of industrial scale and might. The largest and most powerful passenger ship ever to set sail by that date was fatally holed by one of nature's fiercest defences, broken-off giant icebergs in a savage, untameable ocean.

Belfast was vital to Britain in the First World War and in the concurrent struggle to retain domination over Ireland, which was still formally part of the British Isles. When Ireland gained independence in 1923, Ulster (Northern Ireland), which was Protestant-dominated, unlike the new Republic of Ireland, opted to stay within the British Isles and was given its own parliament, Stormont in Belfast, as an exceptional privilege not granted to Scotland or Wales. The British thus retained the loyalty of the Protestant-dominated Northern Irish to the British crown, against the fierce opposition of Republicans (mainly Catholics) in most of the rest of Ireland, and a large section of Northern Ireland too. Belfast remained a major ship builder until the 1970s.

Belfast's industrial strength offered the dominant Protestant workforce well paid, skilled jobs, while their representatives dominated the Northern Ireland government. Public service jobs, as well as the police, were Protestant-dominated too. Catholic resentment simmered below the surface. As the shipyards and other industries closed in the 1960s and 1970s, so the skilled Protestant-based workforce lost its purchase on the economy. Violent troubles erupted between militant Republicans (mainly Catholic) and Unionists (mainly Protestants) which lasted for 30 years. The struggle for fair representation in elections and official organisations, and a fair distribution of jobs was only one part of a far longer, deep-rooted history of conflict.[26]

For nearly 30 years, the British Army was in occupation of Northern Ireland up to the late 1990s. Stormont, the Northern Ireland parliament, was suspended, and the IRA (Irish Republican Army) attacked civilian and military targets and ran an inextinguishable 'guerrilla' campaign to undo the established British-imposed system and 'occupation' of Ireland. Protestant paramilitary groups fought in defence of the Union with Britain while extremist politicians on both sides of the religious divide fuelled sectarian violence, causing thousands of civilian deaths. Reprisals, civil disturbances, increasingly segregated and guarded communities became common. Industry, jobs, housing, schooling, local government, planning, were all deeply affected. The population of Belfast declined steeply. Belfast became virtually a no-go city, with barricades, dividing walls between communities, army posts and militarised occupation. Internment, imprisonment without trial, became a standard method of containing violence. The Maze Prison, outside Belfast, housed interned violent combatants from extremist Republican and Unionist paramilitary organisations.

Belfast, the great former industrial city, became a shadow of its past, providing the most extreme example of a war-torn history playing out in the present. In all, 3600 died in the Troubles, many of them civilians.[27] The Troubles intensified Belfast's population and job losses. Belfast's economy was by the mid-1990s dominated by security and Westminster-appointed officials. The collapse of Belfast docks, textiles, manufacture and machine engineering was swift and drastic. Community divisions, mass unemployment, tight security, frequent civil violence, the introduction of internment (unusual in peacetime), barbed wire barriers between communities, road blocks, segregation and assassinations (including a near-miss bomb attack on Margaret Thatcher, then British Prime Minister) remarkably paved the way to a different kind of future. In the early 1990s the violent struggle seemed to both the IRA and the British government to be unwinnable and a covert peace process began while the conflict rumbled on. Secret talks lasted many years.

The British government attempted to improve housing conditions, to employ Catholics as well as Protestants in public positions and, under cover, to support the peace process. The peace agreement was finally signed in Stormont Castle in 1998, building in the release of hundreds of interned paramilitary prisoners from the Maze Prison. Since the Peace Agreement of 1998, there has been a reverse population flow into Northern Ireland and Belfast. Migrants from Eastern Europe and elsewhere were attracted to Belfast as it recovered, creating many new tensions, but greatly adding to the city's vitality and filling vital jobs.

In the 1990s while peace talks proceeded, the city centre of Belfast was restored as a pedestrianised, integrated 'Peace Zone' – an area of the city where people could mingle freely and walk without fear, regardless of background. The old port area of the River Lagan, Laganside, was converted into a cultural, commercial and sporting hub, with pleasure boats, open spaces and walkways – another neutral space. The most symbolic addition was the new Odyssey sports centre providing the first indoor ice rink in Ireland. The idea was that young people could learn a unifying and exciting new sport not associated with traditional divisions – as football is. The Water Front Hall provides international conference and concert facilities, which attract stars in music and song as well as politics and urban regeneration. The reclamation and development of shared spaces within divided communities was supported by a special European Peace Fund dedicated to Northern Ireland and particularly Belfast.

Northern Irish mediators, from both sides of the conflict, now go together to places like Iraq to show how reconciliation and post-conflict progress are possible. The urban riots in the famous but dying textile towns of Oldham, Rochdale, Blackburn, Burnley and Bradford in 2000 led to Northern Irish mediators stepping in to help communities of traditional Lancashire textile workers and South Asian immigrants cross seemingly impossible divides. This mirrored the help Nelson Mandela gave to Northern Irish leaders, following the end of apartheid in South Africa, a life-changing experience for Martin McGuinness, former IRA leader, and now Deputy First Minister in the Northern Ireland parliament.

Belfast has built a new future on the back of a dramatic past. In 2012, it celebrated the 100 years since the Titanic was launched on its only voyage. Maybe only with a history like Northern Ireland's can the launching of a giant disaster-marked wonder like the Titanic be a cause for celebration. Yet in many ways the failure of the Titanic to make it across the Atlantic symbolises everything that was eventually bound to fail in the vast industrial enterprises of Belfast and other European cities – too big, too clumsy and too inflexible, too resource intensive, and eventually self-destructive, like the Phoenix.

The Titanic Quarter is being rebuilt. The Harland and Wolf giant dry dock is in use. In 2007–08 it became home to the world's first commercial sea turbines – a huge feat of engineering that now delivers renewable energy far more reliably than their above ground counterpart, wind turbines. The lessons of the Titanic were not wasted and the old shipyards now house a new science park and manufacture wind turbines. They are currently gaining new port facilities to allow for the building of one of Britain's largest off-shore wind farms. Tapping the almost boundless wind and marine energy of the Atlantic coastline of Northern Ireland could transform Ireland from an almost 100% importer of fossil fuel energy to a net exporter of renewable energy. It needs a powerful upgrade of the connections to Britain to maximise this great economic and environmental opportunity. The Titanic Quarter now hosts Belfast's further education college, especially aiming to close the serious gap in basic skills among the large working class population of Belfast. Enterprise creation and handholding people into jobs are vital parts of the recovery process.

Many other parts of the city are also being restored; most neighbourhoods have ongoing renewal programmes; there is a new plan for the city centre involving Belfast's two main universities, Queen's and Ulster. They play a major part in the high level engineering required for new enterprises. They are also playing a vital part in the city centre expansion.

Photo 2.1: Titanic Belfast, opened in 2012, with the original Harland and Wolff Headquarters and Custom House in the background

Photo 2.2: Young people at the Girdwood Community Hub
in a low-income neighbourhood

Photo 2.3: Crumlin Road Gaol, now converted into a
museum and visitor attraction

Photo 2.4: The restored, lively Cathedral Quarter in Central Belfast

Photo 2.5: Sam Thompson Bridge, Victoria Park, Belfast. Part of the £35 million Connswater Community Greenway development

The joint parliamentary leadership by Unionists and Republicans is working again after a four year suspension from 2004 to 2008. It is a carefully crafted alliance that is forced always to work on a cross-party basis – unbelievably difficult at times. One of its greatest achievements – through unbelievably painful negotiations – is to give more powers to Belfast City Council, which until now has lacked control over planning, social services and many other local functions as a consequence of the 'Troubles'. This reform accompanies a major simplification of Northern Ireland government and greater powers to Stormont.

Photo 2.6: Victoria Square in central Belfast, opened in 2008

But the recession of 2008–14 hit jobs hard and caused a 50% fall in house prices as well as the loss of inward investment. Belfast was protected for a few years from the worst of the austerity measures imposed in mainland Britain because of security fears, but it is now paying the price. Northern Ireland is part of the island of Ireland and shares a long border with the Republic. It has been deeply affected by the banking and Euro crisis in the South, and lost considerable investment as a result.

Belfast's troubles are far from over, but the city is full of positive signs. Tourism is a big growth industry, and Belfast has gained rather than lost in appeal due to its turbulent history. Cross-border links with Dublin are strong and growing. The new port of Belfast is expanding in capacity and activity. Renewable energy potential is pushing Northern Ireland out in front in the European race for renewables. Belfast's remarkable resilience in the face of deep divisions encapsulates the most central elements of the European story so far.

Photo 2.7: Belfast's expanding port showing development to facilitate giant off-shore wind turbine

THREE

Grit and vision

The earth, our home, is beginning to look more and more like an immense pile of filth... We need only take a frank look at the facts to see that our common home is falling into serious disrepair. Hope would have us recognise there is always a way out, that we can always redirect our steps, that we can always do something to solve our own problems.
Pope Francis, Laudato Si' [1]

Box 3.1: Sheffield – a story

A visitor arriving at Sheffield by train stands inside the lovingly restored, sand stone Victorian station, with its ten ornate wide arches spanning the frontage. Outside, a new square has been carved out of a former carpark and turning point, cut off from the busy dual carriageway through the city centre by a modern high steel wall sculpture-cum-barrier. The functional sculpture acts as a noise shield against the roar of traffic. It is also a gentle waterfall as a film of sparkling water flows down the shiny, undulating steel surface, linking the new space to the city's steel making past. This popular new square hosts special events, exhibitions and public gatherings, displacing cars with people.

Above the station, straddling the steep hillside, loom the gleaming high rise concrete blocks of the Park Hill estate, a listed monument to the brave 1960s vision of replacing old slums with new hope, now being refitted and reoccupied by old and new residents. Between the station and the estate sits the Olympic-size swimming pool, built in the heady 1980s when Sheffield bravely resisted the Thatcher government's cuts to its budget and hosted the World Student Games. These different monuments unite Sheffield's past and future.

Sheffield's vision is best captured in the giant metallic sculpture inside the Winter Garden made entirely of Sheffield cutlery. Sheffield's fame had already spread by the 1740s as the world's leading knife maker when it invented crucible steel and silver plating. Today, cutlery is replaced by blade making and other ultra-modern manufacture. Its engineering prowess, its super-strong steel, its blades, fuel a new economy. Advanced manufacturing is a race Sheffield wants to win against huge odds, following the boom and bust of the post-war years.

Photo 3.1: Ponds Forge, Olympic size pool, built for the World Student Games in 1991, Sheffield

Photo 3.2: Winter Gardens, Sheffield, housing trees, plants and the giant cutlery sculpture

Introduction: the grit of European cities

Europe's industrial cities survived two world wars, with the 'Great Depression' in between, within a single generation. Cities bounced back to full employment and the long post-war expansion in the 1950s and 1960s, only to see them fade in the 1970s and 1980s following the international oil crisis of 1974. They then battled to recover, only to be hit again by the international financial crisis. Their grit and vision grew from this unpredictable trajectory. This chapter explores the extraordinary era of urban–industrial expansion, confidence and creativity between 1945 and 1975, leading to calamitous decline.

Europe's post-war recovery was about much more than a united Europe at peace with itself; or the division of Europe between East and West that led to the Cold War; or rebuilding bombed cities and reconverting war economies to peacetime purposes. It was about creating prosperity where previously there was poverty; spreading the gains of production across the mass of citizens where previously only the elite had cars or telephones; moving into large scale operations in order to meet the social and economic aspirations of post-war Europeans.

The ambition to raise the conditions of the masses, to spread the goods of industrial scale production as widely as possible and to provide the social underpinning for everyone that was part of the post-war consensus led to an unprecedented growth in scale – scale of production, scale of government, scale of intervention, and scale of consumption. Post-war society was changed out of all recognition by these shifts – most maybe by scale.

The seven cities grew rapidly post-war. High American investment in European industrial recovery helped large scale production systems expand. The sheer volume of mass produced goods led to falling prices, high consumption and higher wages as all available workers were drawn into the industrial boom. 'Smoke stack' cities were the powerhouses of the new economy at the very heart of mass production and cheap goods for universal consumption. This new prosperity brought with it higher wages and many conflicts over conditions.

The capacity and potential of industrial cities seemed boundless. The driving idea that machinery, materials and human invention could combine to improve the lot of the masses underpinned post-war optimism in a uniquely European way.

Government underpinning

Wartime controls over all goods, services and people during the six years of war created the infrastructure for governments to tax and spend in order to rebuild industry, and develop welfare states to fulfil wartime pledges to reward the masses, meet post-war aspirations and make good the damage of war. Governments became key orchestrators of industry, housing, infrastructure, transport and social underpinning. The new post-war Europe would have at its heart the idea that all citizens should be part of and benefit from a broad system of solidarity – often called Social Europe.[2]

The idea that governments should expect and demand contributions from all citizens in the form of taxes to fund collective infrastructure and services became widely accepted across Europe, partly to counter the threat of Communism with its universal 'free' provision of public services, partly to make up for the deficiencies of the market and private provision.

Governments were voted in on their promises of spending on:

- health – more hospitals and doctors;
- education – new school buildings, more trained teachers, more years of schooling, new universities;
- transport – motorways, ring roads, petrol subsidies, special company car concessions, upgraded trains; and
- industry – special incentives to locate and expand in poorer, already struggling old industrial areas, special support for backbone industries already under threat, particularly coal and steel, ports and shipping
- housing – subsidised government-driven construction of mass housing estates

A transformational shift was the financial underpinning by governments of household incomes for all citizens in regular work, although in most European countries recent immigrants did not qualify and nor do informal workers. In health and education, no one was excluded. In poorer Southern European countries, provision was sparser and less was offered free but underpinning became the norm. Spain and Italy had much bigger rural populations at the end of the war and much larger informal economies with small family businesses. They collected less taxes and their universal services and investment in infrastructure were less comprehensive as a result. Those in the informal sector – small traders, solo maintenance workers, café and bar owners, peasant farmers – benefitted less from cash transfers, but did gain access to health, transport and education.

The long-run impact of European welfare states has been to create a sense of security and weak incentives to move in search of work when jobs dry up. There is far less movement in Europe in search of better jobs than in the US.[3] Cities that lose a major part of their industry usually retain a large residual population of underemployed and deskilled former workers. Europe today has high levels of unemployment – except for Germany, which has underpinned jobs during the recession. Even with this help, many former East German cities struggle with high unemployment, and Leipzig has above the German average.

The role of the state in growing the public sector limits private initiative and shields firms from risk. Its great benefit is that it blunts harsh market decisions and creates a stronger sense of shared responsibility. It can create better conditions for research as the sense of security it confers creates confidence to do things.

Sheffield, Belfast, Lille, Saint-Étienne and Bilbao illustrate how governments took control of large sections of the economy. This favoured larger industrial structures, fostering a false sense of security. When the industrial crisis came, the response was inadequate, as large scale industries disappeared and large scale public structures were too inflexible to respond. As the public sector shrank under waves of austerity programmes, so the cities have struggled to reinvent themselves in a more private sector-oriented fashion. Interestingly, the surviving small and medium enterprises that were often offshoots or even sub-contractors of big companies adapted better, but grew too slowly to make good the losses.[4]

Torino is an unusual case. There the Agnelli family, private entrepreneurs who built Fiat up to the hugely successful post-war car producer, tied themselves closely into both the city and regional governments of Torino and Piemonte, and to the central government in Rome. This gave it privileged access in seeking funding and tax advantages. In exchange, it became a major funder of many aspects of Torino's welfare and social provision – including worker housing. In this way, Torino's 'welfare state' was more a mix of public–private benevolence than public or private welfare.

Leipzig is also exceptional, with a Communist government that ran almost everything, from industry to schools – real cradle-to-grave provision. Giant mass housing estates like Grunau, on the outskirts of Leipzig, comprehensive full employment, universal, free, all-day child care, state ownership of all industry, were Leipzig's reality. Bilbao, until the late 1970s, was tightly controlled, funded, and managed from the authoritarian centre. Following the transition to democracy, the public authorities running the city and region have retained tight control over investment, spending and conditions, with a strong public service ethos.

The sheer scale, uniform rules and protectionism of the public sector eventually gave way to more market-oriented reforms, spearheaded by sharp privatisation moves in the UK. This happened early in Britain partly because the country was more statist and more centralist than most of the rest of Europe;[5] partly because large state owned industries – coal, steel, shipping and railways – were virtually bankrupt by the mid-1970s, partly because the public debt on housebuilding became unpayable following the oil price hike of the 1970s, high inflation and high interest rates. Other countries followed with more gradual shifts to a mixed economy. However, the idea of state underpinning and universal provision remained deeply embedded, including in Britain.[6] Without welfare states, inequalities would be far greater, and social cohesion far more at risk.[7] European governments today are sacrificing aspects of the universalist ideal that had become embedded. It remains unclear whether universal welfare underpinning will survive under the pressures of European integration, continuing international migration, global competition, and austerity.

Mass production revolution

Mass communication was part of the war effort. The BBC became a wartime lifeline across Europe.[8] In the 1950s, television became a miracle messenger. It was as magic. By the 1960s, television was close to universal and blamed for dominating or even destroying family life. So much now depends on instant visual communication of news, weather, entertainment, consumer advertisements, children's education, politics, popular culture that it is hard to imagine life without this instant access. All kinds of communication technology – almost universal phone lines, mobile phones, clumsy post-war mainframe computers, universal, portable micro-computer pads, camera phones – have transformed the production systems of industry, the management systems of government and private enterprise, the day-to-day lives of citizens. Information technology is also opening up opportunities in advanced manufacture, music, entertainment, social organisation. The pre-war world where few people had telephones, cars, home computers, mobile phones or televisions is hard to imagine.

Mass production systems were swiftly applied to the car industry, very much an elite luxury until the post-war era. Torino, with its Fiat factories and links to the Detroit giants of Ford, Chrysler and General Motors grew unbelievably rapidly in the 1950s and 1960s. Fiat is often credited with driving forward Italy's 'economic miracle' from a broken, impoverished peasant-based economy to a wealthy modern industrial country. The rapid spread in car ownership fuelled two other post-war booms: road building and house building beyond city limits – in other words, sprawl. It led to a shift away from rail travel, significant growth in dependence on oil, a great expansion in lorries, vans and other petrol-powered vehicles, an energy transformation that would undermine the industries it was fuelling by unleashing runaway climate change.[9]

Other more mundane, but influential, technology-based revolutions were in food and clothing. Supermarkets became all-pervasive, replacing small corner shops. Farming was transformed into a mass production industrial system, leading to giant processing, packaging, distribution and logistics systems. The advent of pre-cooked meals, the choice of 20,000 products under one roof, the reliance on self-service have all transformed the way we buy, prepare and serve food. Remarkably, purchase costs fell.

Much the same happened with clothing, which before the war was generally locally produced on a small scale. The advent of cheap, high tech, synthetic materials, block cutting with advanced machinery, such as that which Sheffield still specialises in today, and automatic sewing machines with 20 or 30 stitching functions, as originally invented in Saint-Étienne, transformed home-based enterprises into mass production, eventually landing us with a glut of 'stuff'.

The biggest and most expensive post-war shift was towards 'mass production' of homes as well as goods, using factory methods to produce extremely large and imposing estates of usually high rise towers, to house the mass of workers at a subsidised rate. The seven industrial cities and towns within their orbit generally built very large estates on the cities' edge, often emptying out inner areas and reducing urban vitality. The idea of 'mass' remained popular until the late 1970s.[10]

Many other high tech developments shaped post-war Europe. The aeroplane is an obvious example, increasing mobility and cheap access. The development of regional airports in major cities like Manchester, Milano and Lyon fuelled ambitions for airports in cities like Sheffield, Torino and Bilbao, wanting and needing easy international links. Bilbao broke through into urban tourism and international conferences, acquiring a prestigious new terminal for its airport designed by Santiago Calatrava. One of the early fields of European technical cooperation was aircraft development.

Clothing, food, TVs, computers, air travel, cars all became cheaper and more readily available to the 'common man' – though not the 'bottom man'. The combination of high tech, mass production destroyed a lot of small scale, local, informal provision, making it harder for poor people to be part of the new economy, doing away with many low-skilled jobs. The steep rises in many forms of production post-1950 are known as the Great Acceleration. Human activity has accelerated so fast that its impact on the environment has quickly become visible.[11] The post-war explosion of activity soon pushed climate change and resource threats to the fore. Figure 3.1 shows this.

Figure 3.1a: The Great Acceleration: Socioeconomic trends

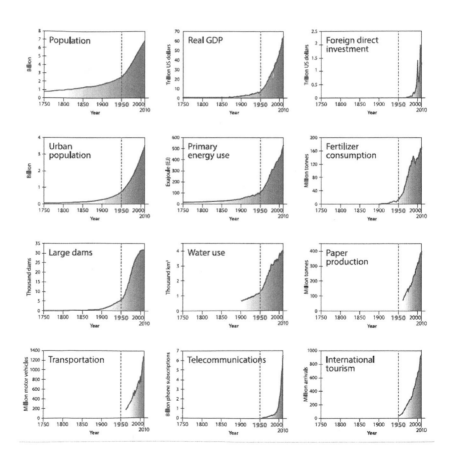

Figure 3.1b: The Great Acceleration: Earth system trends

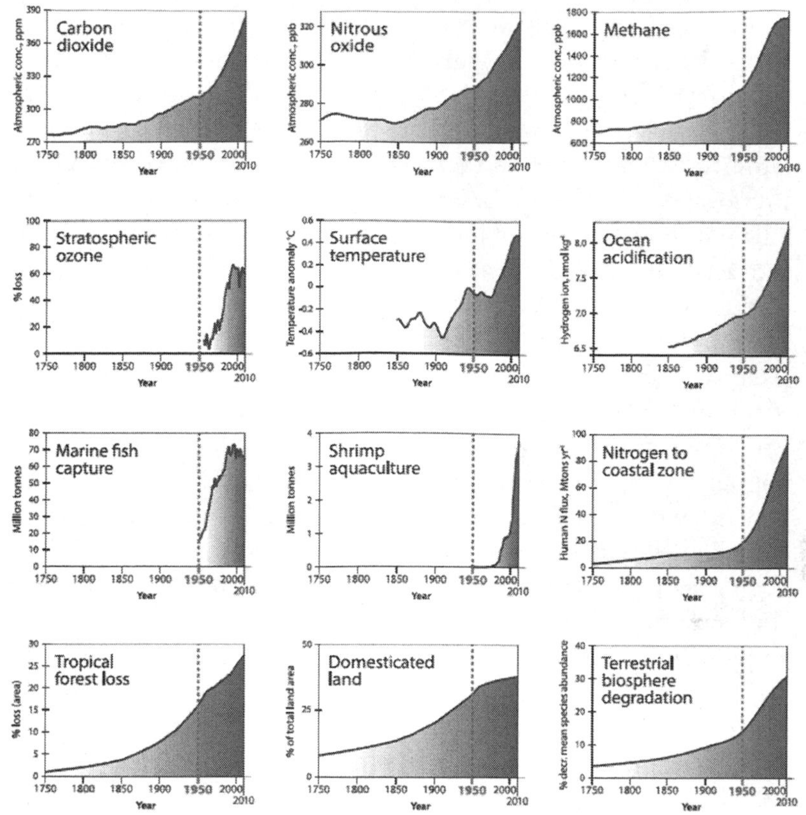

Sources: The Trajectory of the Anthropocene: The Great Acceleration (2015) - (1) HYDE database; Klein Goldewijk et al. (2010). (2) Maddison (1995, 2001); M Shane, Research Service, United States Department of Agriculture (USDA); Shane (2014). (3) IMF (2013); UNCTAD (2013). (4) HYDE database (2013); Klein Goldewijk et al. (2010). (5) A Grubler, International Institute for Applied Systems Analysis (IIASA); Grubler et al. (2012). (6) Olivier Rousseau, IFA; IFA database. (7) ICOLD database register search. Purchased 2011. (8) M Flörke, Centre for Environmental Systems Research, University of Kassel; Flörke et al. (2013); aus der Beek et al. (2010); Alcamo et al. (2003). (9) Based on FAO (Fisheries and Aquaculture Department online) online statistical database FAOSTAT. (10) International Road Federation (2011). (11) Canning (1998); United Nations Statistics Division (UNSD) (2014). (12) Data for 1950–1994 are from UNWTO (United Nations World Tourism Organization) (2006) and data for 1995–2004 are from UNWTO (2011), data for 2005–2010 are from UNWTO (2014).

Job growth, full employment and migration

Mass production systems gradually cut the jobs per unit of output but over the 1950s and 1960s expanded the overall number of jobs due to the expansion in services and sheer volume of production, linked directly to the post-war growth in industrial cities. Rapid economic growth fuelled rapid job creation. From fears of unemployment among returning, demobilised armies and refugees, all over Europe, the new fear became a shortage of workers and the search for cheap labour.

Major enterprises, both state and private, recruited workers from abroad. Germany favoured 'guest workers' from Turkey; France recruited North Africans, particularly Algerians, but also sub-Saharan Africans from its former colonies; Britain went to the Caribbean,

Mauritius, India and other colonies; Belgium went to Congo; Holland to Indonesia and Suriname. All northern European countries also hosted large numbers of migrants from poorer Southern European countries. The Irish continued to flow into Britain until the 1980s, when a reverse migration began. So did Sicilians and Southern Italians into Torino and other northern cities, while Andalusians flowed to Bilbao and other industrialising cities in Spain, like Madrid. The inflow of migrants helped industry but unsettled many communities and racial prejudices deepened as the flow of migrants grew. Immigrant communities became concentrated in the poorest areas of the cities.

Meanwhile, rising expectations among the established workforce eventually undermined the wartime values of sharing, sacrifice and equality of treatment. Skilled workers gained power in negotiating with bosses as they became more valuable and harder to recruit. This not only led to growing industrial strife in Britain, France, Spain and Italy, shown in Sheffield, Saint-Étienne, Bilbao and Torino; it also created an elite of workers, highly paid, specialised, ambitious, who became removed from the lower-level and more casual workforce. An increasing exodus of better off workers from core cities to the growing suburbs fuelled this problem. Full employment could not last and the import of cheap migrant labour having filled the short-term gaps eventually undermined the ideals of a skilled workforce and full employment of the 1960s. When the major industries declined, those jobs shrank massively, the hardcore industrial workforce found itself stranded and had huge difficulty adapting. More recent migrants were even harder hit.

Planning: Big Government in action

European cities were short of space, industries were expanding, housing needed to be built, and other services such as schools and hospitals needed to expand, so planning became a vital tool in managing growth. Industry and economic activity took precedence – but housing and transport, energy, water and waste were vital for industry. So were education and health, policing and maintenance.

New industrial zones were designated, often with low taxes, and lax environmental and quality controls over design. Industry tended to sprawl wastefully around the edges of built-up areas, polluting as it went. The expansion of the Ruhr, the Lower Don Valley in Sheffield and the Port of Belfast illustrate this.

Housing was a much more complicated planning issue. Better off, older populations dreamt of a peaceful home outside the city with a garden. Inner suburbs had already exploded in the early 20th century. Now in the 1950s and 1960s, governments were ready to help those who could afford to move out, build and buy. All countries saw a big expansion in suburban owner occupation, although the expansion was more moderated in Germany. Owner occupation was particularly strong in Spain and Italy, where it was virtually impossible to acquire a flat, except by buying. Bilbao became ringed by high rise, dense, subsidised, owner-occupied flats.

The sheer scale of housing shortages after the war was mind-boggling, and workers needed to be housed. Governments developed mass housing programmes, most often on the periphery of existing cities, building in the region of 20 million concrete, factory-produced homes across Europe. The seven cities all gained mass housing estates, and also gained a large immigrant workforce (apart from Belfast), creating more housing demand. Mass housing estates and high rise block building helped over 20 years to ease the immediate housing shortages. Housing conditions improved immeasurably and by the mid-1970s there was broad parity between housing need and housing supply in most of our cities.[12]

At the same time, planning systems did in the end constrain outward growth and refocus on city density. Hence the agreed plans in Saint-Étienne and Lille to stop sprawl building;[13] and a similar ban in Northern Ireland on the construction of single family homes scattered in the rural outskirts of Belfast.[14] Sheffield is constrained by its green belt, as are all British cities.

Maybe the biggest planned transformation of industrial cities came with the construction of urban motorways. By the late 1970s and 1980s, most European cities were linked by motorways or auto-routes. Fast roads were built not only for cars but also for lorries as goods were increasingly transported by road, rather than rail. It was cheaper, more flexible and door-to-door. It especially suited the booming consumer, retail and supermarket economy. In fact, the indirect costs were huge, not only in environmental damage, pollution, road building and repair, but also in development impact. Trees and topsoil, biodiversity and agriculture, hedgerows, rivers, streams, and other water sources were all affected and damaged. The environmental footprint of cities grew extremely fast in this period.[15]

Sheffield, Lille and Saint-Étienne have 'improved' and speeded up inner dual carriageways that damage and dissect the city. All European cities became heavily congested as a result of road and car expansion, and a transport planning system that did not plan for the end game – where to park and what to do if better roads generated more cars, which they did. It became difficult to stop lorries thundering through cities. Cities became less attractive to residents and fuelled further exodus. Tables 3.1 and 3.2 show changes in transport in Britain since the war, both the huge rise in overall volume and the tripling in road travel compared to a doubling in rail. However, rail travel is now growing as road travel declines. A similar pattern prevails in Europe.[16]

Table 3.1: Total passenger kilometres in Britain (billions)

Year	All road	Rail
1955	200	38
1965	312	35
1975	401	36
1985	504	36
1995	669	37
2005	719	52
2013	688	72

Source: Department for Transport (2014)

Table 3.2: Total annual goods moved in UK by method of transport (billion tonne kilometres)

Year	Road	Rail	Water	Pipeline	All modes of transport
1955	38	35	20	-	93
1965	69	25	25	1	120
1975	92	21	28	6	147
1985	103	15	58	11	187
1995	150	13	53	11	227
2005	163	22	61	11	257
2010	151	19	42	10	222

Source: Department for Transport (2014)

Mass housing and urban motorways transformed the shape and image of industrial cities, leaving a costly legacy today that is hard to change. Once cities had become car-born, their goods became increasingly lorry-born, and Europe's industrial cities became far dirtier, noisier, more polluted than they had ever been. When the oil crisis happened in 1974 and oil prices shot up, Europe's car and lorry transport suddenly became liabilities instead of assets.

Today European cities and governments have retained planning controls, albeit within the language of 'markets'. As they are increasingly land-strapped and space constrained, they have focused their powers on urban density, traffic reduction, and pedestrian and cycle-friendly spaces (see Chapter Five).

Alienation and radical social movements

As the 1960s advanced, alienation became common parlance, both within huge, monolithic factory systems and within state bureaucracies, especially among working class populations in industrial cities.[17] While most permanent workers relied on some form of social security, subsidised housing and unemployment benefit if they lost their jobs, the sense of purpose evaporated when industries became so big, so mechanised and so multi-layered. Experiments in alternative, more varied, more worker-controlled methods of production, including the famous Volvo experiment in Sweden and the Mondragon co-operative outside Bilbao, showed positive results and have in fact influenced new working structures, but too late for the embedded factory system.[18]

Meanwhile, large scale city planning generated a strong growth in small scale community activism and grassroots movements – fighting for more local control of decisions, more community based services, more local jobs, more access to housing for minorities and other excluded groups, more action to defend public services as they came under threat. Eventually when the seven cities faced steep industrial decline, community activists would find their ideas brought into new focus as they responded to large scale unemployment and cutbacks. They forced governments to give credence to popular grassroots protests – for example over the demolition of poor, decayed, crowded housing that would leave some inhabitants homeless; over the need for play spaces and nurseries; over harsh policing of young people, particularly minority youth; over discrimination against black people and other minorities in workplaces; over unfair housing access. Governments became acutely aware of the underlying threat of disorder in poorer communities if they were left to fester where industries were no longer flourishing.

Mass housing estates provided new, more spacious and better quality homes for traditional workers, but they disrupted community networks and undermined the community viability of older areas. Inner areas continued to decay and became neglected leaving space for incoming minority migrants who were generally excluded from subsidised mass housing. The density of European cities, the poor conditions in older, inner neighbourhoods and the divisions between social groups all interacted, as people of different backgrounds and incomes were forced into relatively close proximity. City governments in the 1960s and 1970s increasingly worried about and responded to community conditions. As conditions became more conflict prone, new forms of urban participation emerged. Grassroots organisation and community provision within poor neighbourhoods worked in favour of city recovery and social cohesion. Table 3.3 illustrates the decline of inner areas.

Social movements brought together young activists – often students who moved into poorer, older, cheaper areas as university access expanded – with traditional residents, some elderly and longstanding, some new migrants. Local organisations and services such as churches, schools and small shops also got involved as they had a stake in the future of urban neighbourhoods. This alliance of seemingly different yet actually shared interests contributed significantly to saving and restoring value to declining inner city areas across Europe. San Salvario in Torino, the Casco Viejo in Bilbao, Burngreave in Sheffield, Tarantaize in Saint-Étienne all exemplify today the outcome of a long-run post-war struggle for the protection of inner city communities.

Photo 3.3: Ashram café, a locally organised community-owned enterprise centre in Burngreave, a multi-racial area of Sheffield

Table 3.3: Declining inner areas, 1970s–2000s

Leipzig	Inner East Leipzig dominated by 19th century housing blocks, workshops and small factories Extreme decay under communist rule as established residents moved to new estates Attracted East European immigrants post-reunification due to old cheap housing Socialstadt and other housing programmes helped improve it
Lille	Lille Sud – dominated by early post-war social housing – poorest area of city Unemployment became severe in 1970s with economic decline – increasingly isolated from wider city progress City then determined to upgrade the neighbourhood in mid-2000s
Saint-Étienne	Inner city areas – Tarantaize and Cret de Roc became extremely rundown, neglected and poor - filled with new migrants in crowded conditions French government launches Grands Projets de Ville, major investment programme in poor urban areas – both inner areas targeted and upgraded
Torino	Inner Torino became rundown as many richer inhabitants move out, leaving spacious apartments to be filled by immigrants and other poorly housed residents San Salvario became one of the most crowded neighbourhoods in the seven cities Neighbourhood upgrading and community organising takes off in the 2000s
Bilbao	Inner Bilbao decayed seriously from the 1960s, becoming more overcrowded with immigrants from Southern Spain and North Africa Serious floods in the 1980s caused severe damage and exposed appalling conditions – major upgrading of property with protection for residents and shops from late 1980s
Sheffield	Inner Sheffield was blighted by long-run, far-reaching slum clearance programme – many areas cleared and rebuilt such as Park Hill, Hyde Park, Kelvin Other areas like Burngreave partly survived but became very rundown with very high immigrant concentrations – after 1998, Burngreave received New Deal for Communities funding Many examples of upgrading and community development
Belfast	Inner Belfast, with densely built, small, terraced houses, interspersed with post-war estates, became deeply implicated in the Troubles in Northern Ireland from the 1970s Many communities divided by sectarian violence and physical barriers – but significant investment in housing and community facilities Peace Agreement in 1998 led to significant community regeneration
Comments	All the cities have poor inner areas All have reinvestment programmes – both in buildings and community provision Are without exception still poor but upgraded and potentially attractive

Source: City visits, 2006–15

Industrial cities consumed by growth

The development and growth of the European idea led to the growing recognition of environmental limits. Industrials cities were at a particular disadvantage. Not only were they seriously damaged by more than a century of heavy industry, mining, air and soil pollution, the extraction and burning of coal, deforestation for extensive building, loss of agricultural land for suburban housing and industrial expansion, poisoned river systems and so on. Now with intensive, post-war and mass production systems, the volume of waste and byproducts rose exponentially, causing massive scars on the land around cities through giant landfill sites, toxic effluents poisoning rivers and polluting land with dangerous waste. Thousands of highly polluting, intensely wasteful landfill sites grew all over the continent. Belfast's giant North Foreshore landfill site gives off dangerous methane gas on the edge of the city, illustrating reckless treatment of waste and land, a problem the city is now attempting to rectify and convert into a renewable energy source.

The faster, more 'mass' the production systems became, the greater the volume of waste offcuts, damaged goods, byproducts, overproduced lines, obsolete goods. One growing industrial practice was 'built in obsolescence', so it became more profitable for companies to produce goods that would last only a year or two and be replaced, by ensuring that older spare parts were not available. Suddenly, everything could be replaced with new – from buildings to materials, goods to gadgets – more cheaply than they could be recycled or repaired. Material inputs were cheap and available and were still expected to be available at low cost for the foreseeable future. Therefore, they were used without regard for the outputs of waste, a product that was not counted or costed until waste itself became unmanageable, and materials started to run short.[19] Landfill sites became so vast and so polluting of themselves that eventually they had to be controlled. The European Union came to the rescue. Across Europe, landfill taxes were introduced.

From the oil crisis onwards in the mid-1970s, energy became vastly more expensive with knock-on effects on the cost of manufacture, including building materials and other energy-intensive products. Suddenly the value of everything changed. Environmental limits loomed, and Europe's industrial cities paid a double price. First, their industries were undermined by the previously uncounted cost of waste and environmental damage in their production system. Second, when their big, heavy industries failed, they were left with the pollution, contamination, damage of centuries of exploitation. This had long-term consequences for the cities.

Environmental limits

Serious environmental problems were emerging from the industrial systems of producer cities. News began to hit the headlines that pollution from Germany's industrial heartland was causing acid rain many hundreds of miles south in the Black Forest causing trees to die. Industrial effluents into major rivers were killing off all life in river systems, such as the Rhine, while polluting beyond remediation the water systems of downstream cities. Welsh coal mines were no longer productive, and slag heaps from their spoils became dangerous. Mining accidents, such as the Aberfan disaster in the 1950s, signalled the over-reaching power of industry: 116 primary school children, almost an entire young generation in the isolated Welsh village, were killed when a slag heap of coal residue slid down the mountain side of the Welsh coal mining valley and buried the village school with all the children inside.[20] All Welsh mines closed by the early 1980s, while a few of Sheffield's surrounding coal fields survived until recently.[21]

Energy shortages followed the oil crisis in the 1970s causing deep economic recession, accompanied by high unemployment, particularly in industrial areas. Hot on the heels of Europe's post-war full employment and high immigration, it came as a terrible shock to the industrial and urban system. The stark realisation dawned that endless supplies from the earth might run out. The cost of manufacture grew as energy supply shortages drove up energy costs, leading to shorter working weeks, electricity blackouts, a crash in demand for cars and other consumer goods.

The first signs of an oversupply of publically subsidised housing emerged around the same time giving a wake-up call to cities and governments that demand was finite and population growth was no longer a 'given'. Nor was big planning perfect. France's publicly subsidised 1000 giant concrete, high rise, peripheral estates ('ZUPs'[22]), with 5000–8000 units each, were entering a period of acute difficulty with riots breaking out at Les Minguettes on the outskirts of Lyon, not too far from Saint-Étienne in 1981.

Birth rates were falling across Europe and older people were living longer, so the population structure was changing too. Europe was changing in ways that were worrying and cities were no longer prospering as they had. Figure 3.2 shows the population of the seven cities levelling off from the 1970s as jobs declined.

Figure 3.2: Population slowdown and decline after 1970

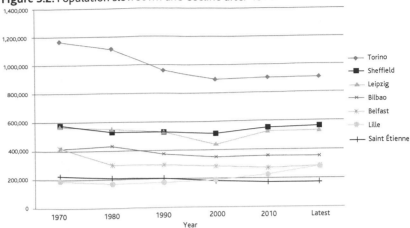

Source: Power et al 2010; Lane and Power, 2016a and 2016b; Provan and Power, 2016a and 2016b; Herden and Power, 2016; Power 2016a and 2016b

The decline of big industry

New economic challenges confronted European cities. For example, coal, the mainstay of most of the industrial cities, was already a declining industry as oil, gas and electricity gradually eroded the power of coal in post-war Europe. Shipbuilding, textiles, machine production gradually saw a similar transformation with increased mechanisation and reduced labour inputs. Textiles shifted almost entirely to South Asia and this had a dramatic effect on Lille, Saint-Étienne and Leipzig, as well as the Lancashire cotton towns around Manchester, and the Yorkshire wool towns around Bradford and Leeds.

There was a gradual convergence across Europe of the pattern of growth, immigration, automation, job shrinkage and decline of mainstay heavy industries, leading to eventual collapse. By the late 1980s, dockyards in Belfast, Bilbao, and Bremen were closing. Coal and steel all but vanished from Sheffield, Lille, Saint-Étienne and Bilbao. Change was most visible in the 'titanic' industries, the giants of production that had become too unwieldy to adapt, and in the extractive industries like coal and steel, where it became uneconomic to go on extracting at ever higher cost. Big industry went from the life blood of our industrial cities to the fugitive. The idea of 'small is beautiful' appeared suddenly captivating.[23]

It was a bitter pill, only one generation after the severe wartime hardships, that Europe's beleaguered industrial cities, which had been at the frontier of the industrial economy, and post-war recovery, faced an acute crisis of confidence. Government funding to support faltering industrial giants in the seven cities did not work for long, while the growing reliance on cheap labour from abroad also proved controversial, generating local costs and local conflict as public resources for housing and schooling came under pressure and jobs started to disappear. The writing was on the wall for Europe's wealth-creating cities.

Manufacturing job losses

Unemployment rose to a frightening level in the mid-1970s in the seven cities and remained high in the 1980s and 1990s, driven by the steady decline in the manufacturing industry and the closure of large factories. In France, Germany, Italy, Spain and the United Kingdom, state-supported industries, such as coal, steel and other major industries such as shipping, railways, aeroplanes, arms manufacture and car production, continued to dominate city economies, even as they began to fail. None of our cities had all of these industries, but all had some. State actions helped to keep declining industries going for some time after the rot began to show.

The biggest challenges and changes were heavily concentrated in Europe's manufacturing heartlands: the north of England and Northern Ireland; northern France and its south eastern coal belts around Saint-Étienne; Piemonte in northern Italy, including Torino; the industrial Basque country around Bilbao; eastern Germany, including Leipzig where heavy industry was propped up by the Communist regime until 1989. These regions where our seven cities are located all experienced sharp industrial job losses, strong suburban growth and regional population shifts. However, although manufacturing plummeted over 20–30 years, sometimes by as much as 70% or even more reaching almost 90% in the case of Leipzig, populations dropped far less, leaving large cities intact, albeit thinned out. The figures tell a stark and startling story.

Decline sets in

By 1970, the population of major industrial cities started to decrease. Some declined earlier, for example Leipzig. Population exodus became more pervasive as job losses grew. The shock to city leaders was so severe that at first they reacted defensively. The hope was that strong action would protect the traditional industrial base, where jobs were disappearing at an alarming rate. But there was a mutually reinforcing process of decline underway. Industrial jobs went because costs of

Table 3.4: Manufacturing losses

City	Number of jobs lost	Loss of manufacture (%)
Leipzig	1989–96: 87,000	86.5 (city)
Lille	1968–2006: 38,000	73.2 (city)
Saint-Étienne	1977–2001: 29,000	41.1 (metropolitan area)
Torino	1971–2005: 171,000	34.7 (province)
Bilbao	1970–2001: 56,000	45 (metropolitan area)
Sheffield	1971–2004: 86,000	73.7 (city)
Belfast	1973–2001: 51,000	76.4 (city)

Sources: Germany: Stat. Landesamt Sachsen; City of Leipzig; Stat. Landesamt Bremen; BAW Research Institute. UK: ONS; Nomis (2007); Sheffield City Council; NISRA: DFPNI. Spain: Eustat. Italy: ISTAT. France: INSEE; Assedic

materials and manpower had risen too steeply while environmental limits constrained expansion. Demand shrank as economies were hit by recession, and oversized systems proved too inflexible to adapt easily to new conditions. Production methods and products were also changing faster than big industries and their workforces and infrastructure could adapt.

Outer suburbs expanded in the 1970s, 1980s and 1990s as conditions within industrial cities declined. Europe seemed to be following the example of the United States' 'rust belt' – the large band of older industrial cities covering the north eastern and mid-western states as far as the Mississippi. As large old industries declined and eventually closed, their industrial infrastructure literally 'rusted' while their outer suburbs grew. The signs were alarmingly similar in Europe. One big difference was that in the US there were plenty of other regions to the south and west that had space, resources and growth potential. In Europe, space was at a far higher premium. For this reason, many European city dwellers stayed within the city. Table 3.5 shows the population loss of cities, between 1970 and 2000, with the steepest loss in Belfast.

There had been early signs of the limits of industrialisation. 'Smog' – the combination of dense coal smoke particles and common winter fog that envelops much of Britain, northern France and Germany – had particularly damaging health impacts in industrial cities like Manchester and Sheffield, the Ruhr and north eastern France. Manchester's 'smog' was known as a 'pea souper' as you could not see anything. Every home was heated by coal fires; trains ran on coal-powered steam; every building was blackened with soot. Britain, in the late 1950s,

Table 3.5: Population loss, 1970–2000

City	Total population, 1970	Total population, 2000	Actual loss	% of population lost
Leipzig	566,630	437,101	129,529	22
Lille	190,546	184,657	5,889	3
Saint-Étienne	223,223	180,210	43,013	19
Torino	1,167,968	899,292	268,676	23
Bilbao	410,490	349,972	60,518	15
Sheffield	572,000	513,234	58,766	10
Belfast	416,679	280,054	136,625	32

Source: Power et al 2010

banned domestic coal burning in urban areas to reduce chronic air pollution and to allow cities to function normally. The effect on coal mining was as strong as it was on air quality. Chinese cities are now facing similar problems, with a promise to scramble out of coal and an actual decline in use already. The entire industrial system was hitting up against hazardous environmental limits that added to costs and restricted further growth. Europe's industrial economy was near exhaustion because industry itself was extracting too high a price in health, social wellbeing and even the prospects of survival.[24]

Many factors came together to push a crisis of confidence among Europe's producer cities. Decolonisation and the oil crisis coincided with intensifying international competition for control over resources. The oil crisis was only one symptom of this with countries, previously thought of as 'backward', flexing their muscles and discovering both their own strengths and a way to make Europeans and Americans pay what producer countries saw as a reasonable price for their dependence on raw materials extracted from other parts of the world.

Meanwhile, more advanced Asian economies were industrialising fast to compete with European and American goods. Cheap, mass produced US goods that brought the US great prosperity after the war as they were imported into Europe were quickly displaced by even cheaper mass produced Japanese goods. The combination of the oil crisis, the loss of control over resources of cheap, raw materials, the competition from Japan, and the 'copy-cat' production of cheap consumer goods in the Far East made governments realise that the post-war growth and public spending bonanza was over. Europe no longer commanded global supplies through colonies, energy had become a crunch issue, and cheaper producers overseas were out-competing them in world markets.

Wartime memories were fading and the strong solidarity it bred in the wartime war generation did not infect the younger post-war generation into the 1970s and 1980s in the same way as it had in the 1950s with the birth of a 'new Europe'.

Limits to growth and de-industrialisation

The oil crisis underlined a dramatic change – resources are finite; the planet does not belong to Europeans; and industrial production has to pay for the full cost of its activity.[25] Our extravagant post-war boom was bound to end and the price has been paid by the industrial cities which were at its centre. However, people around the world are increasingly affected by climate change which is the long-term consequence of the industrial explosion in Europe and North America. Cities everywhere are particularly badly affected because of their vulnerability to climate-related disasters.[26]

For the first time, the argument around the limits to growth hit the headlines. The projections of imminent catastrophe in the 1970s were exaggerated and proved wrong, but a new consensus emerged that it was impossible to go on as before. European city leaders faced a real clash between local unions fighting for their jobs, industrial leaders seeking cheaper production methods in order to survive and national governments fiercely cutting spending under the pressure of international oil prices and runaway inflation. There seemed no way to protect core industries. Costs rose dramatically while revenues fell due to the oil crisis. In the case of Britain, the overspending by the state on national industries, steel, railways, roads, coal and infrastructure – but particularly on mass housing and motorways – caused a debt crisis that brought in the International Monetary Fund. This economic disaster paved the way for 'Thatcherism', an attempt to adopt the extreme 'free market' model of the US. Table 3.6 shows how the industrial crisis played out in the cities.

European decision makers in the private and public sectors realised that importing products from abroad was cheaper than struggling to retain increasingly unviable local industries. It became more profitable to trade in high tech skills, IT, medical and educational services than in heavy goods that could be made at lower cost elsewhere. Banking and financial services grew in some bigger regional cities, such as Torino. The market economy which dominates Europe's social democracies dictated that we allow poorer countries to step in and develop a new phase of dirty industries, which were no longer competitive in Europe. In this way we transferred our environmental problems and industrial dead-end out of Europe.

Table 3.6: How severe was the industrial crisis?

Leipzig	Up to 1989, industry protected under Communist East Germany 90% loss of industrial employment at reunification Still Germany's most unequal city
Lille	Went from being dominant regional capital with rich industries, to decayed infrastructure, fragile, impoverished, out-of-work population Port activity declines Very depressed by 1980s/early 1990s
Saint-Étienne	City economy almost entirely reliant on mining/manufacturing collapsed State all but withdrew, forcing change France's biggest factories for shells Saint-Étienne seen as Communist basket case
Torino	Slow decline of car and vehicle production at Fiat Big conflict with unions over wages and conditions Major loss of production jobs Urban terrorism Steep decline of factory housing areas
Bilbao	Major steel works and shipbuilding close; port declines Major political conflict in part driven by industrial decline and loss of former prestige industries Nationalist violence and urban terrorism Devastating impact on city infrastructure and image
Sheffield	Almost complete loss of volume factory jobs – *The Full Monty* was true Many major steel works closed Mining in region declined Most prestigious steel producer in the world 'shamed' by losses City seen as ultimate 'smoke stack'
Belfast	Early loss of industry, jobs and population Complete collapse of shipbuilding, textiles and related manufacture Generated massive conflict between divided communities – 30 years 'civil war' and army occupation Highest unemployment in UK
Comments	Hard to conceive of worse outcome, after 150 years of sweat and toil Huge economic progress reflected massive local struggle and huge losses Cities have struggled with jobs, skills, labour relations all through their history The bigger the companies the more vulnerable the industry became to disruption Large factory systems bred hierarchies and rigidity that eventually locked them in and made them less adaptable Deindustrialisation crisis lasted around 20 years

Source: City visits, 2006–15

Thus flagship industry after flagship industry disappeared from within Europe's borders: shipbuilding from Belfast, Glasgow, Newcastle, Bremen, Bilbao, Genoa; coal from South Yorkshire, South Wales, south east and northern France, eastern Germany and the Ruhr; armaments from Saint-Étienne, bicycles from Nottingham. Some surviving threads of older, previously dominant industries survived in Belfast, Sheffield, Torino, Bilbao, Saint-Étienne and Lille. One of the story lines for the future is the revival of a new generation of manufacture in the same cities, invariably descended in some way from the older industries that were fading. We return to this later.

One of the biggest costs facing declining industrial cities was their oversized infrastructure. Sheffield, Leipzig and Bremen built too many large, publicly-funded housing estates in the 1970s for their declining populations and have since demolished significant numbers. Dortmund in the 1960s built an underground rail system for a city twice its size on the assumption that Dortmund, in the heart of the Ruhr, would double – whereas it shrank. Leipzig built a railway station for the busiest rail interchange in Europe – but from 1940, its population shrank and by the 1980s, the city was a shadow of its former scale. Saint-Étienne's giant arms factories, built to support extensive French military activity, became too big and too grand as France's imperial status declined. Shipping itself was a vast enterprise in the heyday of industrial production in Belfast, Bilbao, Newcastle, Glasgow and Bremen, only to collapse as economies shifted, leaving huge, unused docks, such as the Titanic dock in Belfast. Car production, the backbone of Torino's growth, moved most of its factories to cheaper places closer to its markets, as costs rose and industrial strife in the city disrupted production. This left behind large empty factories and disused housing. Fiat nonetheless survived in Torino as its small, economical, energy-efficient cars became popular following the oil crisis.

An acute process of industrial and urban decline affected Communist-run Eastern Europe in parallel ways, in spite of large differences in economic and political structures. Overscaled industry, overexploitation of the environment, overuniform mass production, overcentralised decisions, and many other factors were, in the end, to make the communist system unviable, a process greatly accelerated by citizen protests. In strange and uncomfortable ways, their industrial and political collapse reflects similar problems of scale, environmental damage and overuse of resources, only in a far more acute forms.

Figure 3.3 sets out how Phase One of our framework for European cities played out. It shows the disastrous consequences of overexploitation and overconsumption that were hallmarks of our great industrial era.

Figure 3.3: Phase One of the framework

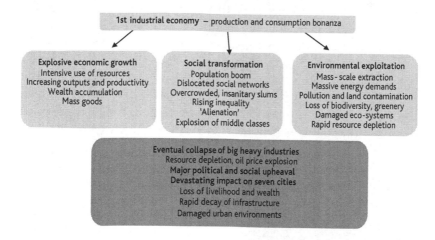

Industrial cities did not lose their maker traditions. All modern European cities have some local centres of industrial activity, including materials for building activity, transport, heating, water, wiring, plumbing, pipes, energy, food and waste. Physical structures, material usage, processing, and logistics on which every modern city relies, require significant making and doing enterprises. Nonetheless, as the 20th century waned, so did our reliance on locally produced goods, including the machinery and equipment with which modern cities run, although the need for them in all modern cities provides the basis for a new industrial revolution.

Urban regrowth in Europe

The trend towards outer urban metropolitan growth around European cities, which began in the early 20th century, with the expansion of suburban railways, greatly accelerated in the post-war years under the planning regimes that prioritised new housing for the growing workforce. Older industrial cities with their 'smoke stack' image had developed affluent inner suburbs in the late 19th century to house their factory owners, but usually to the west of the cities, so the prevailing trade winds across the Atlantic would carry the smoke away from their residences. Sheffield sustains this sharp pattern of west (prosperous) and east (poor) to this day, as does Manchester – and London. So do Saint-Étienne and Leipzig.

The density and proximity of European suburbs compares sharply with US suburbs. Bilbao and Torino epitomise the high density suburban form, but even lower density cities like Lille, Belfast, Leipzig and Sheffield are far denser than their US counterparts. European suburbs generally have a much tighter geography than their American equivalents, and are invariably connected by public transport, even though this is sparser than in dense inner cities. The shortage of urban land and space has led to continuing support for urban public transport systems including suburban areas. Urban motorways which became the fashion in the 1960s in imitation of the super-fast, super modern American highway model quickly stalled for lack of space and money. Nonetheless, Sheffield's centre is still divided by a heavily congested dual carriageway. Saint-Étienne says it needs a second dual carriageway to Lyon to ease congestion!

Suburban growth creates many problems – congestion, decline of city services, environmental problems, city decline, social inequality, traffic and environmental damage. Cities like Newcastle, Liverpool, Belfast, Manchester, Sheffield, Lille, Saint-Étienne, Torino, Bremen and Leipzig all struggle with the problem of outward growth and inner shrinkage. European national and city governments have progressively attempted to rein in metropolitan growth, with ever tighter planning controls and city-regional plans to curtail the urban–suburban competition for population. All seven cities are implementing plans to regrow their city centre populations and draw families back into cities. Table 3.7 shows this.

In Europe, cities can only spread out so far before hitting a natural boundary, with the protected Peak District National Park in Sheffield; or the next city boundary in Lille; or into protected land, in Saint-Étienne; or mountains in Bilbao or Torino. Both urban and suburban land are highly valued in Europe because of their scarcity, proximity to centre cities and well-developed infrastructure, particularly public transport links. Density is inevitable in Europe's closely connected cities.

By the 1980s, when industrial cities were losing populations heavily, national and regional governments intervened to halt sprawl and focus on core cities. National and local budgets were expanded to be dedicated to city recovery, rather than diverted to further suburban growth. Using land more carefully was simply making virtue out of necessity, as sprawl could not continue as a solution, and pro-urban European policies favoured density, compact, mixed uses, urban conservation, urban energy and transport systems.

Table 3.7: Inner city densification and repopulation

Leipzig	Built new terrace family housing in inner west Leipzig to attract young families Pioneered Houseguard system to encourage young people to live in the city and keep derelict blocks going Incentive for conversion of old flats in inner city into modern, attractive dwellings Allow old buildings to be converted into alternative uses
Lille	Modernising and letting flats over shop fronts in city centre Building eco-neighbourhoods with family housing in centre Responding to residents' calls for more security and higher protective railings around resident's squares Building new attractive private housing in Lille Sud Upgrading homes in preserved neighbourhoods of La Grande Deule
Saint-Étienne	Building new homes in city centre to attract younger households into the city Upgrading poorest inner neighbourhoods to hold onto residents and attract newcomers Infilling on bare sites in old neighbourhoods to densify population 'Selling' the city as cheap and attractive to nearby Lyon
Torino	Upgrading central areas such as San Salvario Converting disused buildings into housing Attracting students into central areas Offering grants for residents to make homes more energy efficient
Bilbao	Building dense, new mixed hosing within inner city area, Miribilla, and around coach station Upgrading old homes (mostly flats above shops) in city centre Conscious attempt to attract middle class into expensive replacement homes, following demolition of old, decayed stock
Sheffield	City centre flats built by private developers Inner city terraced housing in Burngreave upgraded and attracting middle class incomes Park Hill flats restored and reoccupied by mixed income groups Many student areas and residences in city
Belfast	Renovation and new housing in inner neighbourhood helps sustain population New incoming migrants help repopulate private housing Efforts at limiting outer and rural housing building around city New city centre plan brings both big universities into city centre, attracting thousands of students
Comments	Serious efforts to limit sprawl building beyond city boundaries in wider metropolitan area All cities aim to attract more middle class, working population Upgrading of old inner city homes becomes an attractive offer New purpose built centre city flats also attractive

Source: Site visits by author up to 2014

Steady flows of public subsidy and investment helped retain the viability of essential infrastructure – including extensions of urban transport networks, re-use of ex-industrial land, waterfronts, canals, civic buildings, public squares, parks, former industrial warehouses. Even smaller 'shrinking' cities in declining regions of northern England, the Ruhr, the eastern Länder (states) of a united Germany, or former mining and industrial towns and cities of northern France around Lille, fought back.[27] The idea of 'shrinkage' generated resistance and counter-investments.[28] Most cities in fact managed to reverse their shrinkage although this still has not happened in some Eastern European cities, like Chemnitz in eastern Germany.[29] Across European cities and governments, a 'rescue approach' to declining industrial cities, strongly supported by governments, battled to combat decline. Chapter Four will explore this reaction.

Conclusion: Europe's density

A large share of Europe's land, people, culture, wealth and infrastructure is concentrated in older urban areas, for Europe is an old and urban continent. Our cities are where most of us live, and we expect proximity, local shops, buses, neighbours, parks and social spaces. We have no choice but to make cities work, as they are home to 80% of Europe's citizens, who work in them and depend on them for their survival.

One consequence of Europe's pro-city, pro-density stance is that conservation, environmental protection and energy saving become both more important and easier: buildings can be reused more readily so the incentive to restore them is higher; transport infrastructure is easier to retain, modernise and extend; it is also easier to curb traffic; urban parks, playgrounds, public spaces become more essential and more valued at higher densities. Sharing space, facilities, and services reduces energy requirements. The makings of a more sustainable economy are laid by these imperatives.[30]

Urban growth and regrowth is part of a global trend towards city living, with over half the world's population now living in urban areas.[31] Europeans cannot abandon their cities, consume their land and overuse finite resources such as energy, when their economies are so hard pressed and their resources so constrained. There is simply not room to do so without incurring massive social and environmental costs that would in turn undermine our economic prospects. In practice, the drivers of change in Europe are strongly pointed towards a new economic, social and environmental model that confronts the real resource limits we face, the deep social divisions created by our history and earlier growth, and that offers creative economic and environmental solutions to our current troubles.

In spite of extremely high unemployment, immigration pressures, economic fragility and deep austerity cuts, producer cities retain their viability and fare far better than was forecast. They house millions of people, most of whom are self-supporting and in work. They invent, make, build, restore. They have been forced to innovate in ways that will shape our common urban future. The story of their recovery from industrial decline comes next.

Box 3.2: Tale of a city – Sheffield

The city of Sheffield epitomises the story of extreme growth, extreme decline, environmental damage and the discovery of a new industrial revolution.

Sheffield has passed through many ups and downs of intense growth and severe collapse. It is a classic industrial city and epitomises the vast wealth-creating power, energy and inventiveness of England's first industrial revolution. It is also one of the starkest examples of the harsh impact of industrial over-growth and decline. It stands out sharply as a city bent on recovery, and shows how remarkably adaptable and inventive cities can be when faced with major cuts in public funding and deep recession. It is a clear example of extreme rise, extreme fall and long haul towards a new economy.

Sheffield's population grew from 50,000 in 1800 to 600,000 in 1950. Its iron and steel industries ransacked the desolate moorlands that surround it for coal and iron ore. Its early engineers and entrepreneurs invented the strongest, most usable forms of steel, silver plating, knives and blades of all kinds, turning it into the Cutlery Capital of the world. 'Made in Sheffield' and 'Sheffield Steel' became the ultimate badge of quality.

Steel and blades have many uses, and both proved invaluable in 20th century warfare. Sheffield steel became indispensable in wartime Britain (both 1914–18 and 1939–45), making it also a bombing target. Sheffield became a rich city to be envied and emulated in the post-war generation with a booming economy and virtually full employment.

Photo 3.4: Halcar Street, Sheffield. Some old industrial landscape survives

This version of history does not allow for the human misery reflected in the rapid population growth, the atrocious conditions in mines and steel furnaces, the low wages, long hours and poor housing conditions of the mass of industrial workers. Poor housing and overcrowding were constantly made worse by inflows of new workers, poor sanitation, lack of basic amenities and, in the Second World War, extensive bomb damage.

Sheffield has traditionally been a progressive city and after the war civic leaders resolved to put right the housing deficit, with an effective blank cheque from central government to clear the rubble of war, demolish the late 19th century terraced slums and build the 'New Jerusalem'.

As with steel, so with housing. The most avant-garde architecture, the most advanced high rise concrete building techniques, the enthusiastic embrace of Le Corbusier's 'Streets in the Sky' and Mies van de Rohe's 'worker housing' led to a series of imposing concrete and steel 'implants' – oversized blocks of flats, climbing the hilly urban landscape, riding rough-shod over communities, with little long-term thought of how to fund the management or maintenance of such expensive monoliths. Whole communities were displaced as estates such as Park Hill and Hyde Park were built where Victorian brick-built terraces once stood.

A similar process was under way with industry. Larger and larger steel companies, most eventually nationalised by central government in the post-war era, led to a clumsy, expensive, unadaptable business model. Industrial workers and miners meanwhile organised themselves into powerful unions, fighting for better wages and conditions, shorter hours, more privileges. The weapon of strikes became insidious. Bosses in effect seemed powerless in spite of their 'ownership of the means of production', and workers gained status and recognition, without a collaborative method of production and decision making developing. Heavy industry was organised on a very large scale, was centralist, top heavy and confrontational, in part because of the dominant role of government following the war; it compared sharply with Germany's more consensual, more decentralised management structures and methods.

By the 1970s, it was too late to save Sheffield's industries. Coal was already waning and the long painful national coal strikes of the early 1980s were headquartered in Sheffield where violent clashes with the police took place. Coal, a nationalised industry, brought the country almost to its knees. Lights went out, literally, and workers were put on a three-day week because of coal shortages. The National Union of Mine Workers, with its headquarters in Sheffield, witnessed the closure of mine after mine until nationally almost every mine was gone by the late 1980s – a few mines did survive in South Yorkshire. The voice of the miners was eventually drowned out, even though the mining union fought a hard and bitter fight to prevent this outcome.

Photo 3.5: Park Hill estate, now being converted by Urban Splash into ultra-modern apartments for existing and new residents. Glass fronted lifts are imported from Mondragon where they are made

Steel gradually went the way of coal, though many of the smaller ancillary enterprises and the high class advanced engineering which had grown out of the steel industry remained strong along with some advanced forms of steel production. Sheffield lost half its manufacturing jobs in the 20 years to 1995, all its large blast furnaces and most coal mines. It became a depopulating, job-short, ex-industrial relic of its former self. Except that it did not.

The city council in the early 1980s fought strongly to support local industry and defend the conditions of local workers. It introduced a costly and inadequately funded bus subsidy and built an expensive new tram line; it hosted the World Student Games, and expensively converted the publicly owned Hyde Park flats, now demolished, into athletes' accommodation. It initially rejected a government-imposed, public–private development corporation that would be outside its control but would have brought in government money to fund conversion of its now defunct, giant industrial areas in the Lower Don Valley. It encouraged worker takeovers of failing industries which led to a sadly failed mutual buyout by the workers. The government limited local spending by introducing rate-capping, thereby making the city highly indebted. The standoff between Sheffield's famous leader, David Blunkett, and Margaret Thatcher has gone down in Sheffield's history.

Sheffield's spirited defence failed to reverse decline, although it did ingrain a tough and enterprising response to trouble. After battling against closure, privatisation and job losses, Sheffield switched to a different modus operandi with a new chief executive in the mid-1990s forged partnerships with local companies, communities, neighbouring councils, central government, the European Union, and its own outstanding universities. Sheffield became a leading light in the core cities group, a loose association of England's eight major industrial cities. The core cities were England's former industrial giants, decimated by job and population loss. Sheffield's problems were so severe that the city region was granted Objective One status by the European Union, recognising its extreme post-industrial condition and the urgency of reinvestment. European money flowed in partnership with central government support and the region backed the city too, recognising that only if Sheffield recovered as the core city would ancillary towns like Rotherham, Barnsley and Doncaster thrive too.

In the late 1990s, Sheffield turned a corner – buildings restored, public spaces created and enhanced, neighbourhoods upgraded, social enterprises fostered, new enterprises encouraged, inward investment made attractive. The city became an 'entrepreneurial hub' and its technically-oriented universities became the incubators for new branches of advanced engineering, digital enterprise, start-ups, and advanced research, partnering with big-name companies like Siemens, Rolls

Royce, Boeing, Tata Steel, among others, attracted by its Advanced Manufacturing Park, established in 2004.

The city sustained its strong focus on community cohesion and the integration of poor neighbourhoods. It supported pro-active neighbourhood renewal and community enterprise all across Sheffield's poor neighbourhoods. The commitment was to equalise conditions in a hugely unequal city, but without a firm economic base and sense of direction this would prove an elusive goal.

The clean-up of the industrial waste lands, left by fleeing, polluting industries, was a prerequisite. Government and the EU helped – in a sort of payback for Sheffield's giant contribution to the nation's and Europe's progress. A major site for advanced manufacturing was developed on acres for formerly industrial land on the outskirts of Sheffield, towards Rotherham. Progress seemed firmly under way until the crash of 2008.

Before the financial crisis, Sheffield's official unemployment rate had fallen to below the national average, even though economic inactivity remained extremely high. The city's population was growing again. By 2010 it was clear that Sheffield, heavily dependent on government funding, much of its population de-skilled from manufacturing losses, would be harder hit than almost any other city. Prospects looked grim, and Sheffield City Council forecast a severe funding crisis with many job losses.

Sheffield, the leading city in a large city region, drew up a 'City Deal' with central government, and with the surrounding metropolitan authorities, that gave it new 'combined authority' status as a city region allowing it, as the combined authority of South Yorkshire, to take control of major infrastructure, investment, transport decisions, economic development. Sheffield was only one of four cities to receive this new status by 2015 – along with Liverpool, Leeds and Manchester. The city developed a major skills and apprenticeship programme, business support for the expansion of SMEs, enterprise zone status, and a new technical college to fast-track young people into engineering and industrial technical skills development to match employers' needs. Under the City Deal, Sheffield receives special business support for SMEs and the opportunity to take on bright graduate trainees with technical skills under an innovative graduate recruitment programme called RISE. The Advanced Manufacturing Park took off quickly, in partnership with the University of Sheffield, and has over 700 jobs on site. It is now expanding to a second site.

Photo 3.6: RISE: a graduate employment initiative across the Sheffield City Region providing internships within local SME businesses

Photo 3.7: The expanding Advanced Manufacturing Park, Sheffield

SMEs form the backbone of Sheffield's private sector, employing around 85% of all private sector workers. Many are new micro-enterprises with under ten employees. Many are working in avant-garde fields and inventing breakthrough technologies related to digital, wind, hydrogen, electric vehicles and water-saving, among others . Many of the new industries are low-carbon, such as wind and hydrogen. Therein lies the future of the new makers. Sheffield has recently been awarded special government funding to create a Maker Hub in the city centre, in a disused large retail store.

Photo 3.8: The Peace Gardens are an award winning public space located next to the Town Hall in Sheffield City Centre.

Photo 3.9: Sheaf Square is a public space immediately outside the railway station providing visitors with an attractive entrance to Sheffield city centre

Photo 3.10: The Tour de France went through Sheffield in 2014
causing a great upsurge in enthusiasm for cycling. Sheffield now has an ambitious
cycling strategy and a cluster of outdoor pursuits and activities linked to the Peak
District National Park

Photo 3.11: Peak District National Park, on Sheffield's Western
boundary, supporting Sheffield's new economic strategy, promoting outdoor activites,
cycling and tourism

Sheffield's population and jobs have continued on their recovery trajectory in spite of the recession. Advanced Manufacturing is expanding and although the number of specific high tech jobs is limited, the ancillary services are highly job-intensive if relatively low value – many of the SMEs have proved to be Sheffield's economic lifeline. In fact, South Yorkshire, where Sheffield is the core city, has the fastest regrowth in manufacturing of all regions of the country.[32]

Sheffield is still a very divided and unequal city, poor in the east, rich in the west. It has a serious skills gap among the former industrial population and is still heavily reliant on public sector jobs, nearly a third of the total. But it shows many signs of resilience. It is poorer by far than London, but also possibly more sustainable. As a symbol of Sheffield's grit and vision, its "ruinously expensive" tram line of the 'red' 1980s has increased its passenger usage and mileage so much that it now pays its way. Sheffield, with its advanced manufacture, its great engineering universities, its social commitments, and its renewed focus on cycling and outdoor sports, may pave the way to the new industrial revolution.

FOUR

Struggle and strive

All living things must take from nature in order to survive based on renewal and regeneration. But it does mean the end of the extractivist mind-set, of taking without caretaking

Naomi Klein, *This Changes Everything*

Box 4.1: Lille – a story

Eurostar, connecting London, Paris and Bruxelles by train through the Channel Tunnel, makes a hasty stop at Euralille, the super-modern station surrounded by futuristic office blocks representing the new Lille. The outsized new square visitors have to cross to reach the city centre looks underpeopled and underused. Yet on foot it is only a few minutes to the heart of medieval Lille, lovingly restored and heavily zig-zagged with red city bicycles. In the great medieval central square, cafes spill out onto the pavements. On one corner sits a Paul's bakery, a popular, specialist French bread chain that has spread all over France and southern England, from its early beginnings as a family enterprise in Lille. A strong Catholic tradition in Lille of investing in family businesses in the city generates jobs and wealth for the city, always industrious and struggling, somewhat of an ugly sister in urban France.

Lille wears its past well. A small, charming hotel near the centre is converted out of an ancient monastic refuge for destitute people. Its original cells now make quaint bedrooms. Its preserved chapel reminds guests of a dedicated past.

Euratechnologie, based in the giant converted textile mill on the edge of the river and canal that create a protective island around the old city, is another emblem of ancient and modern Lille. There are at least four oversized brick built textile mills on the site, monuments to the huge industry of specialist linen production that Lille was famous for. Lille's linen was coarse, unrefined and especially useful for many commercial, agricultural and industrial purposes. Today, Euratechnologie is at the cutting edge of the digital revolution with over 200 companies, many international, based there. It also houses many start-ups.

Photo 4.1: *Original Pauls Bakery, founded in Lille*

Photo 4.2: *Euratechnologie Atrium showing converted interior of an old textile mill with huge factory floor spaces*

The historic neighbourhood around the mills is unique – terraced Flemish weavers' houses, a reminder of Lille's divided history, part Flanders, part France, sometimes occupied by Spain, Austria or Germany. Eurostar's super-speed, super-modern trains, built with significant cross-Channel public investment, today depart from Lille in opposite directions – to London in England, Bruxelles in Belgium, or to Paris in France, and on by train across Europe, putting Lille firmly back on the European map, and unifying a small continent.

Introduction: public framework for action

A 'public investment' approach to cities has long roots in Europe, originating in Greek and Roman times; it was popular among the landed aristocracy and churches in pre-industrial days.[1] Major industrialists in the 19th century saw the urgency of creating decent conditions for their workers, increasing workers' productivity through better health, ensuring social order and long-term profitability. At the peak of the Industrial Revolution, the 'social agenda' acquired political power, captured most vividly in the French novels of Victor Hugo and his English counterpart, Charles Dickens. In England local government emerged in the 19th century as broker, arbiter and provider of urban sanitary conditions.[2] A similar consensus emerged in France and Germany.[3] Housing conditions became a key driver of reform, transforming health, a family's ability to work and wider conditions. Therefore government intervention became stronger, controls tighter, taxes and subsidies for action on housing provision stronger.[4]

The imperative to control urban conditions expanded under the impact of two world wars as we have seen. The high involvement of government in the life and survival of citizens became the entrenched norm which the oil crisis of 1974 and its de-industrialising, impoverishing aftermath only served to intensify. Survival against the odds was proved possible but only with the strong, unifying government structures that underpinned the struggle. Struggle led to striving, but only with wider support. A fundamental reason why Europe's industrial strongholds, in spite of severe decline and job losses, managed to fight back and lay a path to recovery lies in the role played by city governments, backed by regional, national and European Union programmes.

The overarching role of government

The development and expansion of the European Union strengthened the sense of an overarching public responsibility, as European investment funds are strongly directed towards regions in difficulty, under the European Regional Development Fund (ERDF). The problems of de-industrialisation afflicting our seven cities attracted significant investment from the EU on the condition that it was matched by national governments and as long as it targeted physical renewal, new economic opportunities, skills development and social inclusion.

Europe simply cannot allow 'market failure' in cities on a scale that is happening in many American 'rust belt' cities.[5] 'Welfare states' and collectivist ideas are far more embedded in European cities than in 'frontier' American society. Federal and state government intervention and support does not happen on anything like the same scale in the US for very distinctive reasons, such as the original federal structure of the founding constitution, giving states power and control over *all* local provision. The US is continental in scale, more comparable to Europe as a whole than to a single European country like the UK or Germany. Smaller European countries are roughly the equivalent of populous American states. American state governments give far higher priority to their wider state-level populations than to their impoverished core cities for electoral reasons. Thus American cities have struggled with declining populations and a declining tax base to fund interventions; and they have survived by their wits, paying a high social price and taking longer to round a corner to recovery than European cities.[6] Chapter Eight on US cities explores the contrasting trajectories in greater depth.

Governments developed in the growth eras when industrial power houses needed taming in their excesses, to establish public control over basic conditions, but also in their decline when it became clear how much of Europe's wealth derived from them, how much damage the process of growth had caused, and how large their now much poorer populations still were. They could not be simply 'left to rot'. Governments that had supported their major industries now supported their deindustrialised shells.

Governments intervene in cities

In the last quarter of the 20th century, urban social divisions and ethnic tensions, unemployment and de-skilling, disused buildings and underutilised infrastructure, pollution and environmental damage, population and job losses created such pressures in industrial cities that they could not be ignored. Remedial measures were driven by national interests, national priorities and the scale of need.

In Britain, in the early 1980s, in a perversely centralist act, every major industry was denationalised and privatised, both as a consequence of decline and an acceleration of the engine of decline. This privatisation drove core cities rapidly downhill. Sheffield was at the centre of this whirlwind change. The 'short, sharp shock' of privatisation, led by Britain's confrontational prime minister, Margaret Thatcher, if anything reinforced the powerful role of the state, and galvanised a new sense of purpose in core cities.[7]

In Germany the Federal government intervened strongly over a long period to curb environmental damage. Federally regulated controls over pollution, energy use and waste laid the ground for Germany's sustained industrial strength today, as it directly supported the growth in green technologies, energy efficiency and renewable energy production, all job-intensive industries.[8] Rapid progress in adoption of renewable energy, the 'Energie Wende', gave the German government the confidence to reject the nuclear option in 2012 and go all out for a renewable energy conversion. Leipzig certainly benefited from this policy direction with major growth in solar, wind and electric cars.

European urban programmes

In city after city, action by European national governments, backed by the European Union, began to tackle the problem of urban industrial decline, of which our cities were principal beneficiaries. Cities with a strong forward vision and clever plans to revalue their cities won out in the Europe-wide competition for resources.[9] Both Leipzig and Torino were particularly strong in this. Box 4.2 sets out some of the actions.

Box 4.2: European urban programmes

UK
- 1981: Urban Development Corporations in London, Sheffield, Manchester, Liverpool, Birmingham, Newcastle, Bristol and Belfast. They took over control of city centre ports, canals, derelict former industrial land – with full planning powers, generous public funding to 'lever in' the private sector, development driven; for example, Lower Don Valley, Sheffield; Laganside, Belfast.
- 1998: Urban Task Force – to pinpoint the problems and propose solutions for Britain's core cities, including Sheffield, Manchester, Newcastle, Liverpool, Birmingham

Northern Ireland
- 1999: Peace Fund in Northern Ireland – European Union
- Targets divided areas of the city
- Builds community cohesion through shared spaces and shared activity
- Belfast benefits greatly from this programme

France
- 1982: Ensemble Refaire la Ville – 'together remake the city'; following severe urban riots
- 1987: Delegation Inter-ministériale a la Ville – Inter-ministerial Commission for Cities

- 2005: Grands Projets de Ville – both Lille and Saint Etienne are targets for these programmes

Germany
- 1980s: urban renovation and estate renewal programmes
- 1999: Sozialestadt, a Federal programme, targeting troubled neighbourhoods
- 1991: 'Stadt Umbau Ost' – investment fund for demolition of surplus housing and renovation of decayed stock targeting East German cities first Leipzig receives major investment via multiple Federal German and European funds

Italy
- 1995: Decision making and budgets devolved to cities and regions allowing elected mayors for the first time. Torino developed transformative urban policies under this change

Spain
- The Basque country, Spain's semi-autonomous northern region, under the new Spanish constitution of the late 1970s, raised local taxes with provincial and city governments.
- Regional and city autonomy is strong throughout Spain.
- Bilbao prioritised regeneration and major infrastructure investments

Source: City visits and government reports

At the turn of the Millennium, older European cities as far apart as Thessaloniki in northern Greece and Cork in the west of Ireland, Chemnitz in Eastern Germany, and Naples in southern Italy were crying out for renewal. Our seven cities lay in between the more extreme cases of decline and cities that were on the up, like Nantes in France, Hamburg in Germany and Barcelona in Spain. The seven cities and many others have one feature in common: a strong focus on regeneration and renewal, backed by governments and by the European Union. A newly emerging local, national and international consensus proved willing to put weight behind the renewal effort. The fact that Europe is made up of small, densely populated countries, with many small, crowded together cities, reinforced the need for renewal and helped overcome barriers to progress.

The European Union supports city equalisation

The European Union, recognising its limited powers and the principle of subsidiarity, sought to enhance learning between cities rather than attempting to impose solutions. So participation became a strong and recurring theme. In 2004, the European Union established an

Urban Audit covering initially 350 cities across Europe to map more accurately what was happening to Europe's cities and to measure progress. This audit collected evidence on over 150 indicators and ranked urban progress depending on the economic strength, skills, social conditions, governance and a host of other measures in each city. The findings show the continuing strength, resilience and significance of European cities; but also their uneven performance, skills gaps, lack of competitiveness, and in some cases decline. Interestingly, the Urban Audit, a trans-European attempt to gather essential information from cities on their progress, unleashed an intense sense of competition between cities on how they ranked in the progress from failing and shrinking to prospering and growing.[10]

The European Commission funded many peer-to-peer urban networks across Europe in an attempt to galvanise action to reverse the spiral of decline, promote positive change and inspire innovative action. Former industrial cities were keen to engage in these networks in order to learn, and also to promote their new ideas and projects. Belfast, Bilbao, Saint-Étienne and Torino were strong participants. They became a seedbed of change, persuading city leaders that multiple actions on many fronts, rather than the magic bullet of showcase projects, were the answer. Among the cities in our study, a similar network has emerged and there is an almost infectious spread of ideas and mutual reinforcement of experimental approaches to problem-solving. These exchanges allowed cities like Saint-Étienne to learn from Barcelona, Torino to learn from Munich, Bilbao to learn from Lille.

Regional development funds from the European Union were focused on highly underdeveloped regions, like Southern Italy and Southern Spain, and on 'overdeveloped' regions, where the industrial restructuring of the 1970s, 80s and 90s provoked a serious economic and physical crisis of decline. This required 'structural' funds, alongside social investment to restore the cities' viability. All the cities received generous European Union backing, via their national governments, for both physical works, industrial restructuring, skills development, social investment and urban interchange of ideas. National welfare states drove the goal of integrating poor communities, also backed in most cities by European funding. In spite of these efforts, European regional inequality remained, as more prosperous regions pulled ahead further and faster than declining regions.

The ERDF, set up specially to rebuild prosperity in Europe's most depressed regions, poured significant support into hard-pressed regions around our cities, such as South Yorkshire (Sheffield), Merseyside (Liverpool), Nord-Pas de Calais (Lille), the Basque country (Bilbao) and

Piemonte (Torino), to help reshape their infrastructure and build new skills in favour of knowledge-based, high tech industries, green technical innovation, more attractive urban environments, neighbourhood restoration and inclusion.[11] The cities, their surrounding regions and national governments had to match major European funding to help declining cities and regions recover.

The Basque country account of European funding is staggering in its scale and reach.[12] Almost without exception, support from governments and the European Union has allowed former industrial cities to reverse the extremes of decline.[13] It is unlikely that local survival strategies alone would have worked, as Sheffield's initial rejection of government diktat shows. The same is true of Saint-Étienne. We conclude that government intervention and investment in cities, at regional, national and European level, has greatly enhanced the potential for urban recovery and regrown the capacity of cities that seemed smashed by the loss of industry.

Some argue that 'shrinking cities' are inevitable given the flight of manufacturing, the outward sprawl of suburbs and the predicted long-term decline of Europe's urban population.[14] However, although some smaller cities and towns in industrial regions are still declining, it is not true for most cities.[15] Over time, Europe's ex-industrial cities have progressed, even in the harsh recession post-2008, and grown rather than shrunk, thanks in large part to the investments in renewal that governments made, often matched by the European Union. It is this that has levered back the private sector, as Michael Heseltine, Thatcher's powerful cities minister, predicted. Leipzig owes its recovery to help from the Federal government and the EU, without which it would have faced immense barriers to progress.[16] However, the reality today is that Leipzig is growing, not shrinking, and is on a strong recovery trajectory (see Chapter Six).

Eastern Europe intensifies problems of urban decline

The Europe-wide focus of ERDF programmes quickly spread to East European countries and cities, once they set out to join the European Union following the collapse of the Iron Curtain in 1989. Eleven have joined the Union, extending Europe's reach to the borders of Russia, increasing its markets and scope for learning.

Eastern Europe is in many ways very different from Western Europe, not least in its languages, history and urban industrial legacy. Yet so much history, culture, trade and development is also shared and always has been that the expansion eastwards of Europe resonates strongly and has its foundations in our history, geography and economies. It brings great opportunities as well as risks. Eastern Europe is generally far poorer than Western Europe and its industries, under Communism, did untold environmental harm.

Eastern European cities were seriously damaged by Communist rule between 1949 and 1989. Their inner core was allowed to decay and was stripped of working populations who were moved to giant outer estates. The mass housing drive in Eastern European cities was vastly more ambitious, larger scale and more monolithic than we saw in Western Europe, over-scaled as that was. Their private enterprises were generally taken over by the state and their working populations were drafted into state-run industries. Leipzig epitomises this experience – state-run development of large scale industries; seeming disregard for the environmental consequences of polluting, extractive industries; giant mass housing on the urban periphery – Grunau in Leipzig initially contained 30,000 units. The inner city lost population and old housing decayed or, as in Romania, Hungary and elsewhere, was used to house the Roma community.[17] Trade was restricted to state-produced goods based on an almost total rationing system.

We are still in the middle of the process of integration across European boundaries. The complexities of the transition defy any simple or universal ways forward – difficult-to-master foreign languages; inherited contrasts in assets and liabilities; new political and economic structures that still tangle with the Communist past. The journey of urban recovery has become less predictable and more precarious. However, there is more that unites than divides the now 28 countries of the European Union and its several hundred cities.

The European Union expanded to incorporate Eastern Europe, partly for historic and geographic reasons, partly to recompense for the war and its aftermath when Eastern Europe suffered hugely, partly to gain access to a very large market with development potential. Eastern Europe is bound to Western Europe by a geographical and political logic. Eastern Europeans are Europeans and therefore these much poorer countries, including Eastern Germany, have drawn large amounts of European funding eastwards, particularly to their distressed cities and declining industrial regions.

One major impact of European integration and widening is the strong, almost one-way flow of Eastern European migrants to Western cities, causing serious tensions in some of our cities. For example, a large encampment of Roma families, settled on scrap land near the dual carriageway in Lille Sud, its poorest neighbourhood, was evicted from the site when the city began the upgrading programme. There was a major increase in attacks on Eastern European migrant workers in Belfast since 2008. There have been tensions between Eastern European immigrants and more traditional residents in poorer neighbourhoods in Torino, Bilbao and Leipzig. The road forward to European integration is rocky, but it is built on our rocky history – wars, colonisation, over-scaled industrialisation, rapid deindustrialisation, huge underused infrastructure, state-backed social support systems, peacetime cooperation, cross-border pacts, and now the European Union.

Eastern Europe, with which we share long borders, history and generally common values, is a regional cousin to whom we are bound by proximity and affinity. Its declining cities have become our problem, but they deserve further, detailed study.

Post-industrial 'blues'

The seven cities have struggled in the 1990s and 2000s with a recovery agenda that might or might not work and in any case would take decades plus a scale of resources that the cities certainly do not have. In spite of this, a striking characteristic of the cities is the commitment and inspiration of city staff and citizens to put their weight behind recovery efforts. Urban experts from the US said of Sheffield in 2006, 'We need entrepreneurial, committed city staff like this'.[18] Cities wanted government support, but often fought against the restrictive conditions imposed by central government. City leaders, imbued with a culture of public responsibility and an urgent need to modernise public infrastructure, began to invent new ways forward. For example, they created arms-length bodies, part-public, part-private, that were detached from local and central government, yet operated within its broad framework, to drive forward complex regeneration and land reclamation projects. Partnerships became a byword for recovery (see Table 4.1).

The most pressing goal was to save jobs and prevent social breakdown; so much of the early action in the recovery mode of the 1980s and early 1990s was reactive, protective and in the end not enough to stave off the inevitable decline. Demoralising and expensive as this was for city governments, their interventions slowed and diluted the most extreme impacts of manufacturing closures and the harsh realities of mass unemployment. Many would regard this as 'throwing good money after bad', but it bought time, helping cities to build their recovery on a firmer base than would otherwise have been possible. Often with government subsidies, major manufacturing industries kept going for longer than expected. Small and medium enterprises (SMEs)

Table 4.1: Partnerships to foster recovery

Leipzig	Links between city, major companies and Federal Government to attract major investors, BMW, Porsche, Amazon, DHL – including help with recruitment Links with housing companies to take action on empty homes, such as Hauswachter (house guardians) Citizen organisations, including Stadtforum, to guide city policy
Lille	Partnership with universities on major health, ICT, textiles and renewable energy development Partnership with metropolitan communes and region to develop 'Third Industrial Revolution' Partnership with business in Euralille (International Eurostar hub) and Euratechnologie (ICT hub)
Saint-Étienne	Design partnerships to attract enterprises and support SMEs Collaboration with surrounding communes and with Lyons to strengthen Saint-Étienne Partnership with national agencies to manage state investment in city, such as ANRU, EPASE, EPURA
Torino	Strong partnership with Politecnico di Torino to develop new skills, enterprises, incubators and attract R&D City partnerships with charities, civic and citizen associations, church and voluntary organisations to provide services city cannot provide and to secure external funding
Bilbao	City-backed organisations to invest in regeneration, major development projects, international links and promotion, including Bilbao Ria, Bilbao Ekintza Sponsored enterprise hubs and start-up centres Partnerships with cooperative organisations, such as University of Mondragon, and with charities, including Caritas Links with civic organisations, for example Bilbao Metropoli
Sheffield	Umbrella bodies, led by city council, to work in partnership with business, universities, government, surrounding local authorities Civic partnerships with community trusts and associations to deliver community services City sponsored business parks, apprenticeship schemes, training City contracts for management of public facilities and spaces
Belfast	Partnership with multiple community organisations, political and religious representatives to deliver all locally based projects including housing, community facilities and many services Regeneration partnerships to plan and oversee investment in local areas Partnership with universities to develop and deliver city centre renewal Partnership with NI Government, Westminster, EU to sustain investment, progress in devolution
Comments	City councils work in multi-layered partnerships from communities to central government and EU All have partnerships with Metropolitan areas All have strong links with universities and local businesses

Source: Author's visits, 2006-2014

helped in this; as bigger industries disappeared, they often left behind specialist sub-companies, sometimes independent parts of the bigger supply chain. SMEs are important in Torino, Saint-Étienne, Bilbao and Sheffield. They provided a base for city recovery and the growth of new jobs, as we will see below.

European governments were searching for new solutions, as they saw a Europe-wide pattern of industrial change, rather than total collapse, taking hold. Older industries were being replaced by lighter, smaller, more technologically-based industries, but new industries — such as mobile phones — were growing in other less damaged cities away from the industrial heartlands of Europe. The core industrial cities were at risk of being left high and dry.

A new sense of direction

Big, new, high visibility investments were no longer affordable. Urban motorways were left incomplete in Newcastle and Glasgow, for example. Planned housing estates were not built or were left unfinished. Governments now worried as much about pollution, troubled housing estates, minority concentrations, congestion, as they did about industrial troubles. The world had changed around and within these cities and they would either become obsolete or they had to change too. The pace was different in different cities; the direct impetus behind change varied; leadership came from different sources. But a radical shift in direction got under way in all seven cities, fomented by big changes across industrial regions all over Europe. It took about 20 years for this change process to emerge clearly, but by the late 1990s, all the cities and their surrounding industrial regions had adopted a new kind of leadership focused on restoration of centre cities, reuse of existing assets and infrastructure; the development of new skills and enterprise.

Urban leaders shaped events differently in different cities, as Box 4.3 shows.

Box 4.3: Urban leaders in the cities

In Lille and Torino, two large regional capitals, powerful mayors broke the mould. In Lille, the mayor in the 1980s was a former prime minister, Pierre Mauroy, part of the French political establishment, and a fighter for the city of Lille. He persuaded the British and French governments to reroute Eurostar through the city centre, transforming the public transport infrastructure and international fast rail connections across Europe – the transport of the future for the small continent.

Torino's first directly elected mayor emerged from the university sector, with no traditional political baggage, but with a strong commitment to participation and open government. He promoted an inclusive, participative, visionary approach to city recovery, linking citizens, bank foundations, industry, universities and government.

Leipzig, Bilbao and Belfast were shaped by cataclysmic political events that overwhelmed the past and forced a new settlement – Leipzig, through its role in the collapse of East German Communism; Bilbao, because of powerful Basque nationalist movements and violent opposition to the Spanish state; Belfast, through the sectarian troubles that led to 30 years of violent conflict in the city and province.

In Saint-Étienne, a conservative national senator, with strong roots in Saint-Étienne, became mayor and broke the mould of the old style, Communist-run city government and developed a radical, pro-business, pro-investment new strategy.

In Sheffield, a skilled, new public-spirited and open-minded chief executive was able to rise above the long-run labour battles and bring together divided interests around a new agenda for reform and change – developing partnerships, working with universities, restoring the city centre and run-down neighbourhoods.

Mayors and civic leaders, having recognised the need, were driven to pull out all the stops. They were voted in by their desperate electorate on the promise of change. So change they did, often in many small as well as some big ways. Table 4.2 sets out the main actions each city took to change the ways things looked, felt and functioned.

Table 4.2: Road to recovery

City		Signs of recovery	
		Jobs	Population
Leipzig	Strong mayor with local roots led recovery before becoming a national politician Replanning, redensifying, reclaiming, restoring Attracts major new industry, such as BMW, through special subsidies	+	+
Lille	Major national politicians become powerful mayors of Lille Successful battle to win international fast rail links Strong university base helps to build new enterprises Strong cluster development Government investment in Grands Projets – inner and outer areas	+	+
Saint-Étienne	New conservative mayor as old regime falters Restoration of many city spaces based on Barcelona model Renovation/reuse of huge former factories Grands Projets de Ville in inner and outer areas Developing links to wider region and Lyon New enterprise clusters	-	-
Torino	Big clean up and conversion of central rail artery Successful bid to host winter Olympics New consultative mayor spreads involvement New civic alliances Crucial role of Bank Fondatione San Paolo Fiat factories converted – Lingotto/Mirafiore	+	+
Bilbao	Strong Basque leadership and nationalist government Urban tourism – business related Diversification of economy Development of cooperative enterprises Strong neighbourhood renewal Clean up of port area and river	+	+
Sheffield	Strong new partnerships on every front Successfully taps EU funds – gains Objective 1 status Strong neighbourhood commitment Central city restoration and flagships Advanced manufacture develops	+	+
Belfast	After the ceasefire (before Peace Agreement, 1998), decision to restore city centre as neutral zone for multipurpose, cross-sectarian activities Reclamation of River Lagan Reuse of collapsed dock area Community partnerships	+	+

Note: Saint-Étienne began to recover population after 2010.

Source: City visits, 2006–15

Former industrial cities, overexploited, overdeveloped and environmentally abused, contained valuable but damaged resources, as Box 4.4 shows.

Box 4.4: Damaged and undervalued city resources

- Heavily contaminated land
- Oversized factories, furnaces, shipyards, docks
- Imposing civic buildings housing local government and with potential for cultural events
- Out-dated, inefficient but valuable public transport infrastructure, both rail and bus
- Underused ports, canals and river systems with potential for new uses including transport
- Underinvested and under maintained housing stock, polarised between rich and poor
- Anchor institutions, such as hospitals, universities, specialist schools of engineering and design
- Public space, parks, squares, streets, courtyards, play areas
- Cultural institutions, such as orchestras, choirs, theatres, churches, civic societies.

Reclamation and restoration

Public and social institutions serve the wider community far beyond the city boundaries and attract a much wider population. Their assets were put at risk by decline; and their value far beyond the urban boundary explains why struggling cities became a national as well as local responsibility. Their huge potential makes them irreplaceable.

Land reclamation and environmental clean-up were long-term and expensive necessities if the damaged assets of declining cities were to be revalued and reused. Truly vast wastelands existed in the very heart of all the cities and only public intervention made their swift reuse possible. Decontaminating former industrial land could generate a critical mass of new activity.

Restoring buildings was slow, costly and sometimes too daunting. Some buildings were simply dismantled or sometime left to decay beyond repair. One of the biggest challenges was finding new uses for giant industrial legacies, such as the Fiat Lingotto factory in Torino, the Spinnerai textile mills in Leipzig, the Grande Deule textile neighbourhood in Lille, the Harland and Wolff docks in Belfast, or the Park Hill estate in Sheffield. But ideas emerged, as the potential of the buildings and sites became clearer – enterprise clusters, creative industries, conference and exhibition centres, University extensions, new industries, tourist attractions, concert venues, even housing and hotels, restaurants and museums.

Civic buildings, constructed at the zenith of industrial achievement as a symbol of 'the New Jerusalem', required a different kind of care. Majestic town halls reflected the status and power industrial cities enjoyed in the industrial era. They matched the cities' former glory better than current functionality. Belfast, Leipzig, Lille and Sheffield all have historic town halls, built to mirror the grandeurs of national parliaments coupled with the ornate decoration of churches and palaces. Their restoration displayed a new civic pride and underlined the real importance of city governments as they sought to reaffirm their staying power and dominant role in the transition to recovery. The upgrading inspired action around other important public buildings and spaces such as central libraries, concert halls, theatres, public squares and streets.

By removing the worst eye-sores and by enhancing the most respected and attractive buildings in the heart of the cities, a new image was growing of cities that were moving forward, as places to visit and uncover new experiences. 'Urban industrial tourism' or 'city breaks' came from these beginnings. Belfast, Bilbao, Torino and Leipzig became major visitor attractions, creating many new enterprises and jobs.

Traffic calming

One of the biggest challenges facing cities in the post-industrial era was the urgent need to tame traffic, which had grown to have a strangle hold on city centres over the post-war boom period. City centres, originally the civic heart of dynamic city regions, were increasingly taken over by cars, delivery vans, lorries – often a deluge of through traffic simply dissecting the city in many places as a quick through-route. Cities were after all the original crossroads of traders long before cars were invented.

Ubiquitous parking, with the accompanying noise and pollution, not only damaged people, shops and trade, but also affected people's health and the urban environment. Making city centres people-friendly, accessible on foot, by bus or bike, traffic-tamed, sociable spaces became an inspired priority for city governments.

Traffic taming requires public transport reinvestment and public support for a different kind of city, less car bound and more foot-bound. But public transport into the city centre needs to be fast and efficient, in order to displace cars, restrict parking and create more public space. Unless buses and trams are frequent enough to justify dedicated road space, car owners will outvote the city traffic engineers. It took these cities a long time to tackle traffic. But when they did, civic spaces were restored and people returned to the centres.

In city after city, grand central squares were no longer traffic roundabouts or parking lots, as cars were excluded or confined to limited road space. The Peace Gardens outside Sheffield's Town Hall, the Porto Palazzo in the centre of Torino, adjacent to its civic buildings, and the Grande Place in the old city centre of Lille, all demonstrate a similar trend away from car domination and towards people priority. Sheffield's Peace Gardens is extremely popular because its low level water fountains make it a 'beach' for local children.

Central public squares now act as magnets for many new cultural activities and for the flowering of street cafes and street activities that make cities so attractive and special. Main shopping streets running from the central squares now dedicate significant space to pedestrians and shoppers. Browsers have returned to city centres and entrepreneurs of all kinds needing meeting places now commonly use cafes. Belfast city centre stands out after decades of blockades, bombs and boarded-up buildings. A similar recovery transformed Bilbao where nationalist violence took away the city's street life for years. Torino, Leipzig and Lille have all seen a dramatic rebirth in their city centres. Table 4.3 shows the changes in public space and traffic.

The change of image and activity in city centres brought two immediate benefits: it attracted new investors and enticed in new residents so the populations living in city centres began to grow; and it created many new service jobs and encouraged tourists. City centre shopping became fashionable again and out-of-town shopping centres lost ground. In several countries, notably the UK, Spain and Germany, cities proactively use their local planning powers to promote city centre shopping. Bilbao has a key target of sustaining the hundreds of small shops in the old city centre. Leipzig and Sheffield had both severely damaged their city centres by supporting the rapid growth of out-of-town shopping as a way of generating jobs in the late 1980s and 1990s. Both cities are now attempting to reverse the trend of out-of-town shopping.

Table 4.3: Public spaces and public realm

Leipzig	Renewal of main central area including station Main thoroughfare linking Nikolaikirche, town halls, university, Thomas Kirche and central square pedestrianised Canals greened with planting – cycle and walkways throughout city Demolition sites turned into temporary parks Damaged industrial and mining brownfields turned into Lakeland parks
Lille	Gare St Sauveur in city centre converted into public square, market place, events venue Medieval city centre square made traffic free with strong promotion of city bike hire Canal and river sides cleaned up and made accessible Euralille plaza makes hub for large events Bois Habité and other eco-neighbourhoods made green with planting
Saint-Étienne	Many small central public spaces created with planting – also central verges planted along streets Street and squares in centre pedestrianised – some cycle ways being formed Old coal mining area turned into museum and public park Area around station upgraded with new train link to centre
Torino	Central square pedestrianised, along with several main shopping streets River banks cleaned up and opened to public access – with parks Popular city bike scheme 'Spina Centrale' – redevelopment of former railway tracks to place them underground, covered by a new public space with shops, cafes Many small squares close to traffic and trees planted Upgrading of local environment in Mirafiore neighbourhood
Bilbao	New parks along river banks from centre toward Guggenheim Old city 'Casco Viejo' pedestrianised and dense with small businesses Covered public space created at base of the vast Alhondiga building, a converted wine store Green route – for cycling and walking – right around edge of city New public square created in Barakaldo
Sheffield	Creation of new square in front of main station Development of large Peace Gardens in front of Town Hall Winter Garden built in centre to create indoor greenhouse-like, tree-planted public square Impressive, award winning city farm with animals, park and activities New cycle routes being created through city Parks in outer neighbourhoods on hilly slopes of city
Belfast	Creation of pedestrianised streets and squares in city centre Conversion of banks of River Lagan into public open space Upgrading of banks of canal/river into Connswater Community Greenway, cycle and pedestrian way Conversion of giant landfill site on edge of city as large ecopark Many 'peace' areas created throughout inner city
Comments	Impressive focus on city centre restoration Creation of squares, pedestrian streets, parks, walking and cycling in all cities Neighbourhood open spaces also created Canal and river sides upgrading very popular

Source: City visits, 2006–15

110

Public transport

Public transport investment is a high priority, and highly significant in its scale, cost and impact. City by city, modernisation was tailored to the particular situation, and sometimes mistakes were made. Sheffield's tram is a celebrated case of near bankruptcy which eventually made good. Bilbao, Torino and Leipzig expanded and extended their underground systems; modernised their central stations; negotiated faster train connections to nearby main cities; built or upgraded train lines linking city centres to nearby suburbs; created dedicated bus lanes to speed up journey times. The improved transport connections have been vital to the development of new enterprises, the ability to attract new investments, the expansion of the universities, access to cultural events and a new kind of urban tourism. The density of public transport services has grown in all the cities, adding value to the cities, in economic and environmental terms – attracting investment and cutting pollution.[19] In general, cities feel much more welcoming places as a result, strongly linked to traffic calming measures.

International transport links are also extremely important. Airports are contentious developments in cities due to noise, pollution and high environmental impact. They are at least three times as energy intensive as fast trains, when considering within Europe flights, and they greatly add to CO_2 emissions.[20] Nonetheless, they are favoured by cities like Bilbao and Belfast that otherwise would be hard to access, cut off as they are by mountains and sea. Much stronger airport links have developed in Leipzig, Bilbao and Belfast that have encouraged a growth in both tourism and new business.

There is growing competition with airlines from fast train links on international and within-country lines. Fast train links have helped Torino, Lille, Belfast and Leipzig. Belfast is now much closer to Dublin, as is Leipzig to Berlin, Torino to Milano, Lille to Brussels, Paris and London. Torino's drive towards internationalisation has been strengthened by links to France, particularly to Lyon and Paris. The Eurostar link between London, Lille and Brussels, Amsterdam, German cities, Paris and the south of France, has helped Lille recover. So has Leipzig's fast train to Berlin, and on to west, north and Eastern Europe. Its 24 hour airport at Leipzig-Halle has had a different kind of impact, attracting the modern logistics of DHL and Amazon. Sheffield is fighting for the new proposed fast train line linking the south and north of England to include an extension via Sheffield, greatly accelerating its slow train links to Leeds and Manchester, its nearby big cities. Currently it takes almost as long to make the 40 mile journey across the Pennines to Manchester as it does to get down to London. Saint-Étienne now has much improved train links to Lyon and is part of the national TGV fast rail network.

A startlingly low impact, but transformational, transport investment in Lille, Leipzig, Torino and to a lesser extent in the other cities has

Table 4.4: Public transport links, upgrading and expansion

Leipzig	The city has expanded and upgraded its tram and bus system. It is building an underground metro system. A new fast rail link with Berlin has greatly reduced travel time. The upgraded 24-hour airport at Leipzig-Halle now handles the second largest amount of cargo of any German city.
Lille	The city's public transport system works very efficiently. Winning the argument for Eurostar to be routed through the city centre has captured a great market for trans-European rail passenger and freight travel. Journey times from London to many French destinations are now shorter than air, allowing for airport access.
Saint-Étienne	Saint-Étienne upgraded its railway station and built a new tram line into the city centre. It has a fast rail link to Lyon and is linked to the TGV network.
Torino	Torino built a new urban metro system. There are controversial plans to build a high speed rail link to Lyon, thus shortening journey times from Milano to Paris via Torino by 3 hours. It now has a fast rail line to Milano, almost halving the journey time.
Bilbao	Bilbao has upgraded and expanded its metro system, its suburban trams and its buses, including long distance buses to the French frontier. The high speed rail link between San Sebastian, Bilbao and Vitoria is half built. The costs are highly contentious, and parts of the new link will remain at conventional speed. Bilbao airport has been expanded and upgraded and now handles many times the volume of traffic.
Sheffield	Sheffield built a new tram line in the 1980s which the city was forced to fund itself. Bus fares were frozen. Both these measures harmed the city's finances but lay the ground for a modern, efficient public transport system. The tram line has been extended since 2000. Sheffield's train links to London have speeded up. There are discussions about accelerated train links across the north, linking Manchester, Leeds and Sheffield.
Belfast	Belfast has a relatively weak public transport system and is heavily reliant on car transport. But its bus services are now much more reliable with the addition of dedicated bus lanes, some faster and more frequent bus routes and services, and the planned introduction of Rapid Bus Transit on dedicated road space. The train link to Dublin has been upgraded and speeded up. The airport capacity has been greatly expanded, so has the sea port and access by boat to Scotland and England.
Comments	All cities have fast rail links to other cities. All have a strong city-wide and suburban public transport system. Five of the seven have public bike hire schemes. Four of the seven have major airports.

Source: City visits, 2006–15

been the restoration of cycling as a cheap, quick, non-polluting, healthy way of getting around most cities for most people. In Lille and Torino, city cycle hire schemes have generated ubiquitous red and yellow cycle wheels – free of noise and pollution. Hilly cities like Sheffield, Bilbao and Saint-Étienne, are clearly much harder work, except for the young and fit. But even there, 'green routes' are being created. Following the high profile start of the Tour de France in Yorkshire in the summer of 2014, which passed through the centre of Sheffield with a fanfare, Sheffield has launched a super ambitious cycle programme that will transform the hilly city into a cycle-friendly hub with ready access to the Peak District National Park.[21] The regrowth of cycling goes hand in glove with traffic taming, bus lanes, pedestrianisation and the conversion of public spaces for people. Polluter cities are becoming greener.

New enterprise and the regrowth of industry

People had to find the cities attractive and usable for new purposes. The physical upgrading and reinvestment in city assets were a prerequisite for attracting new business and generating new enterprises. New ideas and activity grew on the back of city reinvestment, attracted by the assets, amenities, and space. City leaders worked closely with universities, private companies, central government and external backers, including the European Union, to devise plans to realise the ambition of regrowth, often derived directly from the city's historic strengths in manufacture and engineering. City universities were grounded in many fields of applied engineering and these research institutions helped develop the skill base for new industrial ideas:

- laser technology and fine steel cutting processes in Sheffield, derived from the traditional knife industry;
- design and optics in Saint-Étienne based on the long-run skills in precision lenses and arms manufacture;
- turbine technology (for marine and wind energy generation) in Belfast, based on powerful turbines for shipping;
- hydrogen and electric technology for advanced automotive industries in Torino;
- digital technologies and advanced textiles in Lille;
- advanced engineering in Bilbao; and
- international trade fairs and alternative energy in Leipzig

These are just some examples of the advanced industrial and technological fields that the cities specialise in. In practice each city developed several new strands of research and development at once.

City governments were not usually the instigators of the applied work that was needed to shift economies so radically. Rather they fostered, pulled together and underpinned partnerships between private investors, universities, research centres and local business. The cities by providing a collaborative framework and core city services, helped attract research funding which in turn generated private interest. The new fields of enterprise in post-industrial cities are still at the early stages of development after a decade or two of growth, and they have not come near to operating on the scale of the old industries. But they hold the promise of future breakthroughs, in transport, renewable energy, biotechnology, energy saving, advanced high performance materials, health technologies, machines of all kinds. Although new industrial enterprises do not create jobs on anything like the scale needed, they do create many spin-off jobs in small supporting services.

Surprisingly for many city leaders, a few large industries have been replaced by many SMEs which continue to function and develop, while new ones start up literally in their thousands. In fact, in the period of recovery, most of the economic activity in the private sector was based in SMEs. This was partly because, under-recognised in the industrial era in the shadow of big industry, SMEs had filled much of the supply chain, engineering, components manufacture and service back-up needs of big industry. Their skill base and productive capacity remained in demand even after big industries had moved to cheaper places. Their low overheads and more informal methods were both cheaper and more flexible. In the early 2000s, when European economies were growing again, ex-industrial cities like Saint-Étienne and Sheffield were worried about the sheer scale and density of small enterprises,[22] compared with the loss of big name companies. Yet gradually they came to realise that small and medium businesses were in fact the lifeblood of new growth.

The hidden strengths and added value of SMEs encouraged the universities to develop incubators and start-up spaces for their bright young engineers, inventors and entrepreneurs. Supported start-up work spaces, in old converted factories, such as Euratechnologie in Lille based in a giant converted textile mill, is one example. But there are other more modest examples, for example in a former engineering and machine production factory in Bilbao, Cedemi. The cities are desperate to hold onto enterprising young graduates and this is one way to do it.

The sharing of ideas and business support that these incubators foster is hugely helpful to the development of new businesses.

The Politecnico di Torino has gained a world reputation for both training the best engineers and for generating new enterprise. Sheffield's Advanced Manufacturing Research Centre within the university is now firmly linked to the city's Advanced Manufacturing Park which is attracting big industrial names like Siemens, Boeing and Rolls Royce, but also many far smaller, newer companies. These cities have remarkable strengths in advanced technical research and are not going to fade away in an era where new technologies are vital to tackling energy shortages, energy saving, climate change, modern communication and production methods.

The development of new enterprises happened within the context of continuing overall manufacturing decline. All in all, job recovery and regrowth in most cities was impressively strong as the new enterprises and industries generated a plethora of back-up and ancillary services. This ran hand-in-hand with population recovery. Figure 4.1 shows significant job regrowth overall in all cities up to 2008, in spite of steep and continuing decline in manufacturing. Four expanded jobs further, after 2008.

Figure 4.1: Job regrowth in recovery

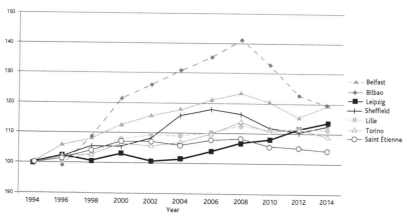

Source: LSE Metromonitor, 2014

Poverty and skills mismatches

Cities face a daunting, possibly unending, task of picking up the human pieces from the workings of the economy. Unemployment, particularly youth unemployment, withdrawal from the labour market, deskilling, have all taken a heavy toll in former manufacturing cities. Poverty goes hand-in-hand with joblessness in the poorer areas of the cities. Whole neighbourhoods, particularly the outer estates built for the industrial workforce, became 'islands of inactivity' in the 1980s, although there were always residents who found new work, and a dwindling minority who held onto existing industrial jobs. The new jobs in services required new skills, the use of more advanced technology and softer skills in communication and customer relations. Part-time jobs became more common. New employers often complained they could not find workers with the right qualifications, skill and knowhow in the city and sometimes brought higher skilled staff with them. This happened in Leipzig with BMW.

The skills mismatch imposed a heavy economic cost on the cities, in spite of the value of new investors. Universities could help at higher levels but at the middle and lower levels, special adaptation and basic skills programmes were needed. In Sheffield, the City Council worked with schools, colleges, neighbourhood organisations and private companies to recruit and train poorly equipped young people for the new openings. Coming from a manual tradition where skilled, semi-skilled and unskilled factory jobs had always been readily available and pay was relatively good, the new jobs often looked unattractively insecure, flimsy and unsuitable for male industrial workers. Female workers took many of the part-time service jobs that became available.

Persuading young people with low confidence and a poor school record to return to desk-based learning has proved a hard sell that is still ongoing, and there are still many skills barriers, particularly concentrated in the lowest income neighbourhoods among the more traditional working class. Belfast City Council is worried about the divisions this skills gap is reinforcing. Job access initiatives, run by the cities, help to bridge the gap between low skilled, poorly qualified young people and the new, more service-based jobs coming up.

Meanwhile, many minority communities, with poor language skills, face even higher barriers, unless special measures are adopted to bridge that gap. This often happens through special neighbourhood support projects like the Arbeitsladen (Job Shop) in East Leipzig. Lan Ekintza in Bilbao ran a similar job links programme (see Box 4.5). The GEMS NI employment programme in Belfast, running for over 10 years now, targets the most deprived areas and the most vulnerable, hard-to-employ people. It works by 'handholding' workless people through every stage of accessing jobs. The JobNet programme in Sheffield worked on similar lines until it lost its funding. These special employment projects are immensely important bridge builders, but they are a drop in the ocean of disadvantage that faces struggling neighbourhoods. Nonetheless, the efforts to bridge the skills gap face-to-face are critical in reducing the sharp extremes that would otherwise prevail. The hard-core human waste of deindustrialisation is still taking a heavy toll on communities in the cities. A more recent focus, in Torino, Sheffield and Bilbao particularly, is on increasing the work-related technical skills of young people to overcome a mismatch of skills; and the loss of traditional links between communities and employers. The following box gives examples of the different kinds of training linked to jobs.

Box 4.5: Job-linked training

Sheffield
- The University Technical College (UTC): giving 16-18 year olds technical skills for new jobs in industry
- Job Match: linking unemployed people in low income areas to job opportunities
- RISE: apprenticeships for graduates in SMEs

Torino
- Special engineering courses at Politecnico di Torino for advanced technical training
- Incubators attached to the Politecnico to help young graduates
- Porta Palazzo Apolio Centre: helping illegal immigrant informal workers into the formal economy

Bilbao
- Incubator for start-up businesses in Barakaldo
- The 'Learning by Doing' university degree: a four-year programme linking study with business development

Saint-Étienne
- Design courses and mentoring: helping small design companies and start-ups use design to succeed
- City-based 'Maison d'emploi' (employment centre)

Leipzig
- Passivhaus Retrofit training school: to train builders in Passivhaus methods for retrofitting homes, schools, and so on
- City employment agency to help new employers recruit locally

Belfast
- Further education: a major effort to push up the basic skills levels of young people from disadvantaged backgrounds
- GEMS NI project: offering training and support to low skilled people far from the jobs market

Neighbourhood upgrading

Several common neighbourhood measures have arrested decline, stabilised populations, and attracted incomers:

- Upgrading the older housing stock
- Developing neighbourhood management
- Opening and supporting community centres
- Encouraging social enterprises and local voluntary initiatives
- Working in partnership with independent civic organisations, such as ZEST community centre in Sheffield, social caretaking in Torino, Templemore Community Project in Belfast, Neighbourhood Association Children's Centre in Saint Etienne.

Even in the 2000s when the cities were doing much better and their economies were growing, they were struggling with intense concentrations of poverty and were taking action to try and reduce them. Nowhere in the seven cities was the decision taken to 'let whole neighbourhoods go' in order to focus on the parts of the city that showed more promise. On the contrary, the poorest areas attracted most support. This reinvestment effort has paid off in preventing the extremes of American ghetto poverty, which actually intensified over the 2000s.[23] Whole areas of Bilbao, Torino, Leipzig, Lille, Saint Etienne, Sheffield and Belfast were tackled in a fundamental attempt to draw them out of a vicious circle of decline. All the areas targeted this way were diverse areas with residents from many different places. So the cities embrace the ambition of social inclusion, alongside their aim to upgrade the neighbourhoods.

The potential for gentrification is obvious and in several cities – Bilbao, Torino, Leipzig, Sheffield, Lille – this threat looms. Residents were acutely aware they might be displaced and put up a strong case for benefitting from the upgrading. In practice, the desirability of attracting some new residents while retaining existing residents meant that efforts were made to do both. There was some dispersal, invariably voluntary, some 'low level' gentrification, and considerable continuity. The poorer the neighbourhood, the more important it became to retain and attract working residents who would support local enterprise and bring in resources. Table 4.5 gives examples of neighbourhood upgrading.

Table 4.5: Neighbourhood upgrading

Leipzig	Selective demolition of derelict blocks Restoration of pre-First World War residential blocks Creation of small temporary green spaces awaiting redevelopment Investment in energy efficient upgrading of outer estates
Lille	Comprehensive improvements to poorer social housing areas, involving selective demolition, environmental improvements, new social facilities
Saint-Étienne	Major refurbishment of two poorest, most rundown inner neighbourhoods Major investment in biggest, most problematic outer estates
Torino	Special 'Projetto speciale perifeire' organised by city, supported by EU, targeting help at poorest neighbourhoods – significant resident involvement Upgrading of disused factory housing
Bilbao	Big reinvestment in oldest city centre neighbourhoods following severe floods in 1980s – some demolition of worst blocks Dense new building around periphery as population expands
Sheffield	Demolition of several large, poorly managed council-owned estates Slow upgrading of others – one area completely rebuilt Neighbourhood renewal in many older, inner city terraced areas
Belfast	Terraced streets of inner city renewed or replaced Estates of public housing renovated Significant investment, both in upgrading and new facilities Residents play very significant role
Comments	Support for social and community enterprises Resident participation became increasingly important All cities targeted public housing estates and the poorest, most rundown inner areas

Source: City visits, 2006–15

Greening European cities

Sheffield is on the edge of the Peak District National Park. Many of the former extensive coal mines are now leaking toxic fluid from flooded mines into the protected environment. This illustrates long-run environmental consequences which are difficult to put right. The environment of ex-industrial cities became one of their most urgent liabilities. Industrial soot blackened the cities and crowded out greenery. The burning of gas and oil, constant outpourings of chemical waste and dumping of toxic materials burnt the ground and left cities with high levels of dangerous pollution. Since the offending companies had invariably gone, there was no way to enforce the logical 'polluter pays' policy. Governments therefore had to step in at extremely high cost. This task is still not complete after 20 years.

As the cities rebuilt their image, they gave increasing priority to creating green spaces, planting trees, restoring clogged-up and cemented-in river systems, cleaning up canals, giving city land over to gardens. Former industrial cities became much more attractive, particularly to families and the elderly through these measures, making their cities literally greener. If cities are to reduce the impact of climate change, then green infrastructure – literally trees, grass, gardens, parks, allotments, waterways – are vital, according to the Intergovernmental Panel on Climate Change's 2014 report.[24] It is impossible to detail all the careful steps in environmental reclamation and greening that were taken but a few stand out as striking examples.

Box 4.6: Greening the city

Leipzig was a major centre for open-cast coal mining during the post-war Communist era. The scorched earth approach of this form of extraction left not only unplantable, unusable hectares of bare poisoned land but also leached toxic minerals running off over the already damaged soils. This vast, scarred area was reclaimed, cleaned up and replanted, cleverly creating large lakes to fill the moon-scape craters of the open-cast mines, surrounded by parkland, woods, cycle ways and forests.

Throughout Leipzig there are small allotments and communal gardens along reclaimed canals that citizens can cultivate.

Leipzig also turned many small sites within the city, left bare by demolition, into temporary green spaces. This both reduced the blight and involved residents in community rebuilding.

In **Belfast**, the vast landfill site at North Foreshore, now capped, is being turned into both a methane energy source to save the lethal gas from escaping; and an environmental park reaching out to the estuary and the Irish Sea.

Another magic Belfast area is the Connswater Greenway, made famous by its native superstar, Van Morrison. It was formerly a clogged and filthy industrial effluent channel, and is now a green, wild, natural waterway running right through the middle of the city joining different communities together. It is used for cycling, walking, canoeing, school nature quests and peace building.

Sheffield supported several 'greening' initiatives, including Healey City Farm, which recently won awards for its enterprise, environmental care and contribution to nature education. A new park was also created near the Manor Community Trust where the city encourages wild areas.

The city of Sheffield also supported the creation of a community forest; it has many allotments.

Sheffield has recently launched a new enterprise cluster based on outdoor activities, cycling and hiking, using the city's proximity to the Peak District National Park.

Torino has reclaimed and restored parkland along the River Po.

Torino also plays host to Terra Madre, an offshoot of the Slow Food movement that supports small-scale organic agriculture.

Lille has created a whole green neighbourhood, called the 'Bois Habité' (the lived-in wood), right in the heart of the city, which has running waterways of clear, cleaned waste water, full of reeds and water plants, willows and other trees and bushes. It also has many cycle ways.

Lille has a large central park, full of mature trees around the citadel.

Lille has built links to organic farming in and near the city, providing organic vegetables for schools

Saint-Étienne adopted the Barcelona model of creating small public squares and gardens throughout the city, and planting them. Green verges are planted along all city roads, often with ornamental, multi-coloured cabbages.

Bilbao has created several new parks in the city, cleaned up its rivers and created a 'green way' round the whole city where it is possible to cycle and walk the whole outer circle of the city.

All the cities have created pedestrian areas within the city centre. Six of the seven cities have cycle schemes and cycle development plans within the city.

Green areas are only part of a much bigger shift towards green technology, green innovation and new environmental enterprise which we come to in Chapter Six. What mattered in the recovery phase was that the clean-up of the city and its surroundings created an acute awareness of environmental limits and vulnerabilities. It led city officials to discover the value to city recovery, of creating and protecting green spaces, and greening the existing dense industrial cores so that they acquired a new viability.

In the course of the clean-up, the environmental potential of previously heavily polluted waterways, warehouses, factory buildings was rediscovered. As places were cleaned up, so new parks, walkways and cycle routes were created; new homes and workplaces were developed; and new enterprises emerged. The economic benefits of greener cities was immense. The warehouses became start-up workshop spaces, in Bilbao, Leipzig, Lille and Torino, making the environmental gains double as economic development. The reinvestment in cities was environmentally beneficial in ways that had not been foreseen by revaluing earlier investments that otherwise could have become redundant. Old warehouses and industrial and port buildings gained value as they were saved and reused (see Table 4.6). The very rescue of these seemingly useless buildings generated ideas about how to do things differently.

Landmark projects – symbols of recovery

Post-industrial cities were determined to create a new image in order to attract new activity – no longer the dirty, polluting producers of the past, but part of the 'knowledge economy', 'service economy' and 'new communications'. The different strands of reclamation, renewal and new enterprise this chapter has outlined all point to a new kind of city. But cities wanted to showcase their progress visibly. Throughout the seven cities, there was a serious attempt to create a new image and presence through major international events, requiring local venues. The Winter Olympics in Torino in 1996 are a perfect example of the city itself becoming a physical showpiece. It was catapulted onto the world stage. Leipzig's unsuccessful bid to host the 2012 Olympic Games was driven by similar reasoning. The city however gained a serious image boost as host to several games for the football World Cup in 2006. Several other cities aimed to create international tourist attractions. The most eye-catching example is perhaps the Guggenheim in Bilbao, built on reclaimed port land, on the banks of the previously highly polluted river Nervión. In its first year it attracted 1 million visitors and has held up with similar numbers ever since. There is now a large international conference centre next to it, also drawing in nearly 1 million users, visitors and conference guests a year.

Table 4.6: Examples of reuse of old and industrial buildings

Leipzig	Conversion of large textile mill with 20 factory buildings into an avant garde, alternative, artistic enterprise and residential community – Spinnerai Conversion of old workshops and shop fronts into new alternative enterprises Conversion of central station into covered shopping mall
Lille	Conversion of large group of disused textile mills into new international technology centre and new business space – Euratechnologie Conversion of old railway station into a conference, meeting and events venue, plus restaurant and outdoor space for further activity
Saint-Étienne	Conversion of abandoned pit head, mining buildings and mine into a museum to recreate industrial history Restoration and conversion of Imperial Arms Factory into new Design Centre and incubator space for design businesses
Torino	Conversion of old railway sheds into exhibition space which house the 150th Anniversary of Italy's unification Conversion of Fiat's giant and historic Lingotto factory into a large exhibition and events space; also as university training and research space for the Politecnico di Torino Large, disused factory turned into supermarket for Slow Food products
Bilbao	Conversion of vast wine warehouse in city centre into multi-use public and leisure venue Conversion of 19th century machine engineering factory into incubator, start-up and SME work space Use of old industrial warehouse in the port area to develop Bilbao's home-bred Maker Movement
Sheffield	Conversion of Park Hill mass housing estate into a mixed income, high quality, council-built flat complex Conversion of old vestry building in Burngreave into community learning centre Conversion of abandoned cooperative store in city centre into a government-backed Fab Lab
Belfast	Conversion of old Custom buildings in Belfast dock into exhibition, event and visitors centre Conversion of old bank in Cathedral quarter into five star hotel Upgrading and preservation of Crumlin Road Gaol into museum and visitor attraction Conversion of Titanic dock area into a science park

Source: City visits, 2006–15

Box 4.7: Landmark changes in image

Belfast, a city with a long history of conflict and community divisions, focused on unifying showcases. The sinking of the Titanic was hardly Belfast's finest hour, since the liner had been built in the Harland and Wolf dock and set sail from Belfast. Yet built in Belfast's port area, leaving a highly visible heritage of buildings, docks and machinery, the city managed to turn the Titanic's international fame to its advantage. The 'Titanic Quarter' has restored buildings, created striking new buildings, restored docks and renewed industry. Although the return of industry is on a much smaller scale than previously, nonetheless in Belfast it is set to grow rapidly thanks to the development of offshore wind and the major port expansion that goes with it.

With great foresight in 2004, the City of **Sheffield** and the University of Sheffield established its Advanced Manufacturing Park, which is becoming the world centre for blade technology and other forms of advanced manufacture. This new focus has put the city well and truly on the international map.

Lille has used its success in winning the Eurostar link to turn the city centre into an international business and cultural hub – Euralille. Lille became the cultural capital of Europe. Transport has played a major role in the city's transformation.

Saint-Étienne has developed several conspicuous projects. The most impressive is undoubtedly the Design Cluster, reusing the famous 19th century factory buildings that were forced to close in the heart of the city, thereby linking its past industry with its future. Saint-Étienne has become the 'City of Design' which French railways now advertise in London as an international tourist attraction! A most unexpected outcome.

Leipzig rebuilt its historic international trade fair, dating from medieval times and made famous in Communist times. As a result, Leipzig hosts many international fairs and conferences – of books, industry, art, design, the environment.

Bilbao became suddenly internationally renowned for the Guggenheim, but its cooperative industrial tradition also put it on the map.

The strong presence of landmark activities, events and show pieces highlights the transformations this chapter is about: environment; new enterprise; culture; tourism; international events; new skills; new transport hubs; economic regrowth.

The full payback from the high investment involved in these different examples is not clear. Most of the cash to deliver the projects came from public resources, local and national as well as the European Union and sometimes private sponsors. On the whole, the bold moves forced the cities to galvanise their plans, deliver to a timescale, and market their attractive but undervalued assets. Therefore, the indirect benefits of image-boosting landmark events and places are generally significant. Local residents take great pride in the changes provoked by these landmarks – mostly because the city governments have to galvanise their citizens behind them if they are to work. Landmark projects are arguably the 'gilt on the gingerbread', but it is hard to argue against the benefits they have brought to these cities in underpinning and reinforcing the more 'bread and butter' transformations. A lot hinged on the landmarks offering some long-term purpose and functionality, which our evidence suggests they are doing.

Did recovery take root?

There are constant worries in the cities about how firm the recovery is, given the high level of public support they have received. This is particularly true in the cases of Belfast and Leipzig, because of their particular histories and extraordinary funding in response to historic transitions. Leipzig still receives significant subsidies from the German Federal government to help with the equalisation of Eastern and Western Germany. Leipzig's signs of growth are extremely robust and the hope is that by 2019, when special subsidies end, the city's recovery will have taken root. Belfast also received 'protective' funding – 25% more than the UK average.[25] This funding is now restricted by the UK government's welfare reforms which impact the province's high dependence on welfare. At the same time, Belfast is holding up, some would say against the odds and belying expectations.

Given the long period of industrial growth and prosperity – 100–150 years in most cases – and the decades of decline, starting in the 1970s, or even earlier in some cases, the period of post-industrial recovery looks relatively short – little more than 15–20 years. In spite of this, certain trends are clear and encouraging. Following several decades of fairly steep population decline, that process was arrested and reversed in six of the seven cities over the recovery period. Only Saint-Étienne continued to lose population, albeit much more slowly than before; Belfast, by the end of the recovery period, began to gain population again. Lille even managed to recover population almost to the peak it had reached before decline set in. All the other cities rounded the population corner – one of our key measures of recovery. Figure 4.2 shows how population gradually began to recover.

Figure 4.2: Population change in cities 1995-2014

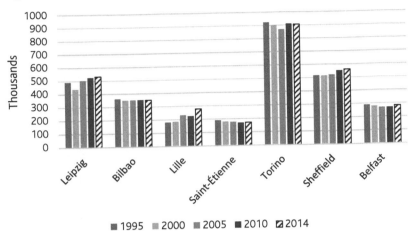

Source: Power et al 2010; Lane and Power, 2016a and 2016b; Provan and Power, 2016a and 2016b; Herden and Power, 2016; Power 2016a and 2016b

Jobs in manufacture continued their long-term decline, although they did not disappear, and cities like Torino still had about 35% of total jobs in industry. Other cities like Bilbao and Leipzig retained a smaller manufacturing base.[26] Jobs in services grew fast and other ancillary jobs in administration, health and social care, construction, retail, finance, real estate, professional services continued to expand. Overall, cities gained jobs but due to the skills mismatch, some new jobs went to incomers rather than locals, attracting new population – a vital sign of city recovery. But unemployment often remained stubbornly higher than regional or national averages, particularly in poorer areas of the cities – a sign of the fragility of some elements of recovery. However, unemployment moved close to the national average, and Bilbao, Torino and Sheffield moved ahead.[27]

Government financial support for enterprise, skills and the physical regeneration of buildings and land made it far easier to attract new firms, sometimes quite major ones. However, since the firms needed confidence to invest in the city and bring their enterprises there, the ground had to be prepared within cities themselves, in the shape of restored physical spaces, adequate housing and other services, support in job recruitment and training. This combined with the multi-faceted effort of cities and governments, backed by European funding represents Phase Two of our framework. Figure 4.3 shows Phase Two of city recovery.

Figure 4.3: Phase Two of the framework

Conclusion
==========

The different strands of action within cities combined to change their image – Bilbao, Torino and Belfast are major tourist and conference destinations; Sheffield is extremely popular with students, scientists and specialist producers, from many parts of the world; Saint-Étienne attracts many thousands of design-oriented visitors to its Design Biennale; Lille combines its pivotal function as an international transport hub for much of Europe, with its historic, medieval city, now also becoming a major tourist attraction; Leipzig has become the new hub for alternative, creative and artistic enterprise, pulling in young creators, innovators and alternative groups from all over Europe, as well as leading Europe in electric cars and solar energy.

These changes are far from ephemeral, for cities thrive on interchange, ideas and links to the wider world. Recovery has put cities that seemed set to decline on the European map as places to go, learn from and live in. Huge challenges remain unresolved – concentrations of poverty, joblessness, and ethnic tensions are the most serious of these. But cities are not balking at these challenges or burying them. In fact a hallmark of cities struggling to recover for the longer term, in a context of severe economic problems, is the imperative to target, include and offer new opportunities to those who would otherwise be left behind by industrial collapse.

It is the combination of new enterprise within a strong civic framework that marks out recovering cities.

Box 4.8: Tale of a city – Lille

Lille is perhaps the archetypal rise-and-fall European city. In so many ways it prospered and yet suffered unspeakable damage in both world wars, recovered and then hit the economic buffers when coal and textiles, two of its mainstay industries, collapsed in the 1970s and 1980s. France's northernmost major city and capital of the Nord-Pas du Calais region, Lille has a special place in European history. The city spreads over into Belgium; it is within easy reach of the Netherlands, Germany and now England, thanks to the Channel Tunnel. Its history is dotted by changes of ruler, country and status. Originally part of Flanders, it was ruled by the Spanish, then taken over by France. Under France's last ruling monarch in the 17th century, a great star-shaped defence citadel was built to protect the city from attack and conquest. It is surrounded on two sides by rivers and early on a canal was built linking them to improve defences and increase navigation. The city withstood several long sieges, including by the Austrians, Dutch and English. The citadel is today a centrepiece of the city, surrounded by protected, tree-covered park land, replanted after the Austrians stripped it during a long siege but were defeated in 1801.

Lille expanded as it industrialised in the 19th century, with a rich textile industry, surrounded by coal mines and plentiful iron. The canal and river system helped this growth, offering cheap, large scale transport. Proximity to Belgium's coal mines helped fuel the boom. The population grew fast from around 10,000 in 1800 to around 200,000 in 1960. The metropolitan area, including 85 communes, is many times bigger.

In the First World War, Lille was a prime military target, given its strategic location, and was occupied by the Germans amid strong resistance, large scale destruction and deaths. In the Second World War, the same happened again, and the German occupiers destroyed the war memorial to the French victims of German occupation in the First World War – still a bitter memory revived in the rebuilding of the memorial.

By 1940, Lille was France's third city, housed its third most important university, and was its second largest industrial producer. But by the 1960s, decline set in, most rapidly in textiles, but also in agricultural products from the surrounding region, and coal mining. In all by the early 1980s, nearly 300,000 jobs had been lost in Lille Metropole. The city acquired a grey, down-at-heel, empty feel, although it retained its key role as a crossing point with major logistics businesses flourishing, including the pioneering catalogue company, Redoute, first established in the city in 1930.

Before industrial decline had really taken hold, Lille attracted funding from major government house building programmes, and developed a whole new dormitory city, Villeneuve d'Ascq. This, along with other satellite cities like Roubaix and Tourcoing, made city governance potentially complicated. The French government devolved powers to the city, allowing it to form Lille Metropole, joining the 85 surrounding communes into a cooperative governance structure with each commune retaining certain autonomy but collaborating on more strategic issues such as transport. This structure continues to function today.

The city of Lille was the dominant partner in the Metropole. This became clear when Pierre Mauroy, a former French prime minister, became mayor in the 1980s. He fought and won the battle for the Eurostar high-speed train route joining London, Paris and Bruxelles to go through the centre of Lille, reinforcing its hub status and opening up new economic opportunities within the city. The plan was to develop large public spaces, major office developments and eventually residential accommodation to draw new life into the city centre. Alongside this ambitious Euralille plan, the beautiful but sadly neglected medieval city centre was restored and upgraded. A big step in rebuilding the city's image was the much sought-after status of European capital of culture, which Lille won in 2004. This turned the city into a new kind of hub, fostering popular and community-oriented events as well as big stage shows. The city's population began to grow again, a sure sign of recovery. Unusually for a former industrial city, the current population outstrips its industrial era peak, reaching 230,000 in 2011.

Many new SMEs emerged and grew under the strong 'cluster' strategy encouraged and supported by the city and Lille Metropole. Euralille today provides a strong office development cluster, and Lille became France's second most successful city at attracting and building new office developments. Euratecnologie, located in a huge former textile mill complex near Lille's old docks, has become an international IT cluster, ranging from the small micro-start-ups to major international names like Nike and Price Waterhouse. Eurasanté is another major cluster, building on Lille's outstanding medical and biotechnology research within its universities. A fourth important strand or cluster influencing the city's policies significantly is the environmental focus. Building retrofit, new-build eco-urban villages, renewable energy and new green start-up companies stand alongside strong community level plans to 'green' the city.

These economic clusters played to Lille's strengths and aided recovery. Nonetheless the city has struggled with higher than the French average unemployment and is still a 'poor city' by French standards. When the international banking crisis erupted in 2008, Lille was hard hit. Industrial jobs had continued to go but between 2008 and 2012, there was a 15% fall in employment. Interestingly, this was less than the French average of 22% because of growth in ICT and optical technologies. Unemployment rose to 11% while the surrounding Metropole hit 15% – worse than the French 10%.[28]

Lille is used to crises and responded to this new challenge with vigour. Recognising the global significance of the crisis, it ranked itself next to New York and Tokyo on a single measure: the concentration of population within a 300 kilometre radius of the city centre. On the other hand, 29% of the city's population depends on benefits, higher than any other French city. It also underperforms on tourism and in housing, and is a relatively low density city, with still too many bare, former industrial sites and buildings. There remains a lot of ground to cover.

A new economic recovery strategy following the Eurozone crisis majors on five main themes: health, ICT, environment, enterprise and housing. The city provides business support, international links, physical upgrading, IT development, social inclusion and support for key industries such as advanced textiles, electronic commerce. Amazon located its French and European distribution headquarters in the city. Progress was rapid in environmental innovations, linked to Lille University's research strength in low-carbon energy.

One potentially significant recent step is the adoption by the region, including Lille, of policies supporting the Third Industrial Revolution. The idea is to completely de-carbonise the whole region of Nord-Pas de Calais through a systematic shift to major energy saving and domestic and community level renewable energy generation – linked through multiple connections to the electricity grid – an 'energy internet'.[29] Lille Metropole and the region have enough wind and other renewable energy potential to achieve this. The plan to turn the whole region carbon neutral is ambitious indeed, but it offers the potential to create many new jobs, as has happened in Germany with its long-term plan to cut CO_2 emissions by up to 80%.

Meanwhile at a more modest level, Lille fosters environmental care through its open-door advice service to households, its eco-village developments where energy and water saving are linked with waste reduction, recycling, tree planting, bio-diversity, cycle and pedestrian priority, public transport, and so on. The new eco-village within Euralille, Bois Habité, incorporates all these elements. It also mixes social and private housing and includes some passive house (Passivhaus) experiments. The 'village' is walking distance from the city centre.

Photo 4.3: Le Bois Habité – a new-build green neighbourhood
adjacent to Euralille

Jobs and enterprises have regrown since 2008 and Lille's strong artisan and SME sector has continued to flourish – mainly around the cluster growth and new advanced manufacture, design, textiles and ICT. The whole region is now pushing for industrial regrowth and there are ambitious plans to reclaim 1000 hectares of brownfield unused sites within the city. This fits with the conscious policy to re-densify the city and counter the sprawl tendency of the past.

Nonetheless, Lille remains a deeply unequal city in spite of the social policies pushed by its progressive mayor, Martine Aubry. Five neighbourhoods with far higher than average poverty, joblessness and low skills are part of the national

131

neighbourhoods renewal programme (ANRU) and receive significant state funding. The core aim is to increase the social mix of these neighbourhoods, make them open and attractive to people in work, and turn their schools into lively cultural music centres.

One remarkable initiative is to introduce the teaching of musical instruments and performance to all school children in Lille Sud, Lille's largest and poorest area. These schools are also linked to the city's environmental agenda and 50% of all school food comes from organic sources. A new and popular theatre has been built in the area as a way of attracting people from all over the city and opening up the area. A similar 'opening up' and 'linking in' is symbolised by the rescue and restoration of the Gare Saint Saveur in the very centre of Lille, next to the Town Hall – turning it into a public space, used for popular events, markets, festivals, outdoor family gatherings, and large indoor spaces for conferences, meetings, a restaurant and events. These social, cultural hubs enliven the city, bring people together and attract tourists. The medieval central square meanwhile is criss-crossed with city cyclists on city hire bikes, another popular innovation. Regrowth within the city is visible and inspiring.

Photo 4.4: Family events at the restored Gare Saint-Sauveur, in the centre of Lille

Photo 4.5: Allotments in Lille Sud – a large social housing area

Photo 4.6: Euratechnologie – converted textile mills, now an international digital industry hub

FIVE

Threats and opportunities

Anyone who believes in indefinite growth in anything physical on a physically finite planet is either mad or an economist.

David Attenborough, quoted in *New Statesman*, 21 December 2015

Box 5.1: Saint-Étienne – a story

Determined efforts to put Saint-Étienne back on Europe's map are working. Even the London underground carries giant tourist advertisements for Saint-Étienne and its new design centre. With an early start, you can arrive at Saint-Étienne's main station by train all the way from London. You then climb onto the new tram that will carry you into the city centre.

The young press assistant in the Mayor's Office explains why she moved to Saint-Étienne from nearby prosperous Lyon: "The housing is cheaper, more accessible and more people-friendly." The regeneration officer working in the old, dilapidated inner city neighbourhoods, a born-and-bred returning Stéphanois spends his working hours going door-to-door to uncover people's real needs and encourage residents to stay and enjoy the improvements underway. "We learnt our lessons from the 1960s – wholesale demolition and brutal estate building. We tore up communities. Now we want to hold onto them."[1]

Out on Saint-Étienne's largest estate, young residents of North African origin are angry. They work in the city-funded youth centre, have ambitions and want to get on, but still feel excluded. They do not 'buy' the official French rhetoric that they are equal. There is still a severe lack of jobs for most young people they work and live with. Tensions are everywhere. An old, disused coal-mining shaft within the city is being turned into a mining museum. On its edge is a travellers' encampment, due to be moved away as the site is restored.

European cities increasingly face such conflicts over city space as now many Roma communities belong within the European Union. Many migrants are crossing the Mediterranean and heading north. No-one is quite sure how Europe will cope.

Introduction: troubling recession

In 2007 when the international banking crisis first broke, Europe's former industrial cities were in recovery mode. Now the most troubling European recession since the 1930s has hampered recovery and posed many new threats. When the Big Crash happened, our cities were hard hit. Yet industrial cities bounced back from two world wars, and the chronic 'Great Depression' of the 1930s. There is reason to hope they will bounce back again. This chapter looks at how they fared in the longest, deepest recession since before the war.

The seven struggling producer cities were heavily dependent still on external public support for their progress. Former industrial cities had contributed so massively to the growth in their countries' wealth that they were owed compensation for the major environmental and social damage caused by that very growth – an otherwise over-heavy burden they were left to carry. This suggests that their recovery was propped up, and if the underpinning was removed, they would collapse. So we examine what happened when the major international financial crisis hit Europe in 2008 and public funding shrank drastically, an ongoing situation.

Consequences of international crisis

The impact of the crisis on the cities was harsh, and as yet the longer-term consequences are unclear. Table 5.1 summarises the main ways in which the seven cities have been affected by the international crisis.

Some European governments kept their support in place in the hope that flows of cash injected into the economy would facilitate a recovery and contribute to the end of the banking crisis. It certainly offset the most extreme consequences of the crash, although on all standard measures, the impact was still severe – job losses, programme spending cuts, a stalling on new investment projects, and gradually a cutback on all kinds of public spending. Between 2008 and 2010, European cities went from mild optimism about a swift recovery to serious gloom. Large infrastructure projects were put on hold and private investment shrank. The figures in Tables 5.2 and 5.3 show the immediate impact of the crisis on jobs and unemployment. Two cities, Leipzig and Lille,

Table 5.1: How the financial crisis of 2008 hit weak market cities

City		Examples of programmes affected
Leipzig	Block on major urban development plans Poorer areas lose out as Leipzig becomes most unequal city in Germany East Leipzig project funding shrinks Benefits from strong manufacturing developments Solar, electric cars, Amazon, logistics Logistics holds up; car production shrinks in volume Alternative/artistic scene continues to grow	Centre city plans left incomplete Neighbourhood restorations also incomplete Leipzig protected by special reunification funds but still loses
Lille	Up to May 2011, little sign of reduced flows of public funds Ambitious plans still being promoted New clusters being developed But unemployment high – city still poor	Big slowdown in Euralille Affected by poor economic performance in France
Saint-Étienne	Debt crisis because avant garde reformist mayor signed up to risky loans Grands projets still carrying on Anti-sprawl plan also working – SCOT Design village attracting support SME sector very strong	Local spending curtailed by debt repayments
Torino	High youth unemployment – over 25% Big cutback to regional funds Job losses within city Fast growing role of Politecnico Continuing growth in tourism	Ending of neighbourhoods programme Council funding cut by loss of local taxes
Bilbao	Loss of resources for new regeneration schemes, such as Zorro Zaure Construction of earlier schemes stalled Pay cuts in many organisations, Bilbao Ria, Council Still some new initiatives, including business tourism Mondragon co-ops managed crisis - but lost key factory	6% pay cuts in publicly funded agencies Amalgamations to save money Several regeneration schemes stalled
Sheffield	Struggling with big public funding cuts and big job losses in council Advanced manufacture holding up and innovating Universities play major role in advanced manufacturing New stress on economic development	End of New Deal for Communities Cuts in Energy Saving Programme Big city job losses
Belfast	Budgets kept more or less intact in spite of wider UK cuts Private investment shrinks Tourism holds up due to deep crisis in Ireland but continuing visits to North Retail jobs affected Big investment in renewable energy because stuck without energy source	Slow progress on major investments, such as transport Problems over welfare reform Big slowdown in house building
Comments	Overall, cities held up and many local programmes continued at reduced levels in spite of external pressures Resilient because of past experience of struggle against overwhelming odds Emergence of advanced manufacture as hopeful route helps them	

Source: City visits, 2006–15

saw an increase in jobs due to public underpinning, and Leipzig saw an actual decline in unemployment. Five cities experienced some losses. Bilbao was extreme, losing 20% of its jobs.

In four metropolitan areas, Leipzig, Lille, Sheffield and Saint-Étienne, jobs increased. Unemployment levels increased among the least skilled in all cities except Leipzig (protected by special government measures) and the same applied to metropolitan areas. The rate of unemployment was pushed up by population growth in response to jobs, helping the cities sustain growth, but intensifying competition for jobs. Unemployment was lower than the national average in two cases, Bilbao and Lille, and the same in two others, Leipzig and Saint-Étienne.

The Re-economy

Between the 1980s and 2000s, European governments stepped in to rescue declining cities because millions of citizens live within and immediately around them. There are two powerful reasons why

Table 5.2: Change in total jobs following recession and Eurozone, % change

City	City level			Metropolitan area		
	Year	Total jobs	Increase/ decrease	Year	Total jobs	Increase/ decrease
Leipzig	2008	281,000	11,511 +4.1%	2008	392,000	10,180 +2.6%
	2012	292,511		2012	402,180	
Lille	2009	509,000	2,239 +0.44%	2008	503,000	6,040 +1.2%
	2011	511,239		2012	509,040	
Saint-Étienne	2009	159,000	-2,069 -1.3%	2008	223,000	4,019 +1.8%
	2011	156,931		2012	227,019	
Torino	2008	367,000	-995 -0.26%	2008	754,000	13,570 -1.8%
	2009	366,005		2012	740,430	
Bilbao	2008	181,000	-36,611 -20.2%	2008	459,000	55,547 -12.1%
	2012	144,389		2012	403,453	
Sheffield	2008	246,000	-3,200 -1.3%	2008	456,000	1,368 +0.3%
	2012	242,800		2012	457,368	
Belfast	2010	199,000	-4,385 -2.2%	2008	294,000	No change
	2012	194,615		2012	294,000	

Note: Overall jobs increased in four of the seven cities.

Source: Eurostat, http://appsso.eurostat.ec.europa.eu/nui/show.do; OECD, http://stats.oecd.org/Index. aspx?DataSetCode=CITIES#; NISRA, Quarterly Employment Survey.

Table 5.3: Unemployment, 2000s

City	Year	Unemployment rate	Increase/decrease %
Leipzig	2008	15.7%	
	2010	13.6%	-2.1%
Lille	2009	14.6%	
	2011	15.7%	+1.1%
Saint-Étienne	2009	13.3%	
	2011	14.9%	+1.6%
Torino*	2008	5.6%	
	2012	9.8%	+4.2%
Bilbao	2006	8.6%	
	2011	16.5%	+8.5%
Sheffield	2008	6.7%	
	2011	10%	+3.3%
Belfast	2008	2.9%	
	2011	6.6%	+3.7%

Note: In all cities except Leipzig, unemployment levels increased significantly. The same was true of the metropolitan areas. * Figures for Torino are for the Metropolitan area.

Source: Eurostat, http://appsso.eurostat.ec.europa.eu/nui/show.do; OECD. http://stats.oecd.org/Index.aspx?DataSetCode=CITIES#; NISRA, Quarterly Employment Survey.

European governments support city recovery. First, the large urban populations of a small and crowded continent like Europe cannot realistically abandon their cities. There are too many of them, they are too close together and there is simply not enough capacity in faster growing areas to absorb such an outflow, in spite of suggestions that this makes economic sense.[2] Within cities, communities are anchored by tradition, culture and local ownership. Some residents do emigrate, many now move around Europe far more freely than before, but the vast majority stay in cities that have the potential for recovery.

Second, as we showed in Chapter Four, city recovery was based on solid potential for regrowth – forgotten assets, underused capacity, specialist skills, a history of innovation, valuable infrastructure, impressive universities, hospitals, cultural and civic institutions, with the makings of a knowledge economy embedded within them.

The recovery methods adopted by struggling cities were distinctive, far removed from the rapid growth, high speed, high tech, financial services model of more recently successful and global cities, with all their associated glamour, spin-offs, property booms, high pay, fast track allure and suspected 'bubbles'. The distinction lies in the focus of former industrial cities on **Re**newal, **Re**clamation, **Re**cycling, **Re**building, **Re**discovery – the **Re**-economy – a new model with lower inputs, lower outputs, less waste and more sustainable **Re**growth. The most important innovation was possibly the **Re**discovery of science-based knowledge and engineering prowess, the **Re**valuing of irreplaceable infrastructures, and the **Re**making of places. The cities began to reorient their thinking and economic strategies towards a new industrial revolution.

As the financial crisis unfolded, harsh economic realities hit home. Though these cities were recovering, the process was far from complete and their growth had not gathered the momentum of more successful places. Financial centres like London and New York caused their unravelling but also allowed them to bounce back more quickly. They, like their banks, were 'too big to fail'. Ironically, weaker cities had less far to fall, so they fared less badly than feared and they were only indirectly caught up in international banking disasters, although Bilbao did lose the headquarters of its home-grown but now international BBVA (Banco Bilbao Vizcaya Argentaria) bank.

So while the ex-industrial cities could not escape the crisis and its aftermath, they adjusted to it more quickly than at first seemed likely. However, government cuts hit these cities extremely hard, far harder in practice than capital cities which governments were inescapably tied into – like Paris, London, Madrid, Rome or Berlin. European governments did not withdraw from their commitment to helping weak market cities. They rather drew in their horns and became more cautious in what they supported, more focused on economic than physical **Re**investment.

There is another explanation for the recovery reflex of the cities, backed by our own research: these cities are so used to struggling and surviving, so ready for problems and so practised at problem solving, that they simply carried on, found new ways and generally coped. The results show how the cities have continued to develop up to today.

The Euro: a dream or hard currency?

The Euro in 2000 effectively became the single currency of 11 European countries, expanding to 19 over the following 15 years, without a fully-fledged central bank, without a fully integrated governing body, without including all European countries, without the European Union having taken on the political mantle of being responsible for the new currency. So while Euro leaders, notably

Germany, set stringent tests for entry to the Euro, they allowed Italy, Spain, Portugal, Greece and Ireland to join without any certainty that they would be able to follow or apply the rules that had successfully governed the Deutschmark. Even France and Germany breached these rules during the crisis. The brand new trans-European currency under tough new rules that proved hard to enforce faced serious trouble when the banking crisis hit Europe.[3]

The new currency opened the door to new borrowing and lending across a very wide area giving poorer countries in southern and peripheral Europe the chance to borrow on an almost unprecedented scale during the boom years of the new millennium. In effect they accessed cheap loans through the Euro, a form of 'subprime mortgage' to boost their economies, cheap and attractive at the outset but becoming toxic when the crisis hit. This was somewhat akin to the US house-lending bonanza that triggered the financial crash in the United States, where cities like Detroit were devastated by cheap loans to poorer households to buy houses they could not really afford and that were destined to sink to even lower values.

The Euro offered easy credit to poorer countries within Europe, for a debt that was then too big to repay, in a market that was risky to both lenders and borrowers if things went wrong. In Spain and Ireland, this fuelled a housing boom that was destined to crash, causing awful pain and often homelessness to households and causing banks to collapse, including the main bank of Ireland and many government-backed savings banks in Spain. Being part of the Euro created a short-term sense of prosperity, but when trouble struck, the currency could not be devalued in the countries over-burdened by debt, and exports to the rest of Europe therefore became less competitive. Their economies suffered acutely. New house building in a major bubble in Spain and Ireland suddenly ran out of credit as housing loans could not be repaid. The housing market crash that followed made some house purchases worthless. House values in Northern Ireland fell by 50%. Cutbacks in jobs and closures of companies became inevitable. Meanwhile, whole countries became engulfed in the collapse of important banks when debts could not be repaid.

In Spain, the government and local authority-sponsored savings banks – the Cajas – were in many cases on the verge of bankruptcy, forced to merge and unable to lend. The Mondragon bank, the Caja Laboral, had to merge with another Basque cooperatively owned Caja to save the latter from bankruptcy. Over 1 million Spanish homes were repossessed and families not only evicted but saddled with an unpayable debt. Bilbao was not as badly affected as other parts of Spain but its housing market was shaken and construction plans halted.

In Italy the Berlusconi government, in a frantic attempt to stay in power, cancelled local property taxes that allowed local government to borrow and spend, leaving cities like Torino without an obvious means to pay down the huge debt it had built up in implementing its bold recovery strategy.

All the countries in our study became caught up in the triple blow of the banking crisis, the deep recession and the Eurozone crisis in different ways. The European Union has lurched from one crisis to another for five years and the currency problems around the Euro are still unresolved. The cities that had lost their major industries 30 years before now faced the loss of, or at least serious reduction in, public underpinning at both national and European level, as well as losing private finance for enterprise. Resources of all kinds were suddenly in short supply, and city governments had no choice but to find new ways forward for themselves.

This unforeseen pressure came on the back of deeper structural problems in the European economy that had long shown signs of slowdown. This sluggishness, for long the target of US critiques of Europe's 'old' economy, was disguised by the strong growth and prosperity of the 2000s. But the symptoms were clear: slow growth; high unemployment, particularly youth unemployment; long-term unemployment; weak competitiveness in international markets; continuing loss of manufacture; low investment in research and development; low levels of market innovation; high taxes constraining market freedoms and profits; and rising costs of pensions and health in an ageing continent. These major structural problems were played out in the seven cities. Table 5.4 shows how the crisis hit the seven cities and how the crisis played out over the following 2–3 years.

Inescapable European-wide problems

The European Community greatly expanded inter-European trade. Britain benefited strongly and eventually around 80% of its economy was tied in to the European Union, including 44% of its international exports, even though the UK was not formally part of the early years of Europe's development. The same applies to Scandinavia, Spain and Ireland. European economies have become tightly bound together. Even so it remained far from the US model of federal states, bound by a common currency, common language, borderless trade and a unifying federal government, federal laws, federal taxation and federal bank.[4]

Table 5.4: Immediate impacts of Eurozone crisis and new austerity

Leipzig+	Major national company based in Leipzig closes – Quelle BMW shrinks workforce but keeps going and moves into electric cars Major rebuild plans slow down, some are deferred East Leipzig renovation struggles with negative pressures Independent and alternative initiatives grow Special German government funds continue, helping Leipzig retain jobs – special subsidies to support underemployed workforce and jobs for youth
Lille*	City funds keep flowing – mainly from central government Some enterprising ideas working well, for example Euratechnologie Big political differences between local (socialist) and national (CU) levels, 2012 Big poverty problems in social housing and outer areas Growing hostility to Roma migrants
Saint-Étienne*	Funds severely reduced for other developments Youth unemployment very high City continues to lose population
Torino*	Massive debt problem in city and country Major restrictions on replacing public jobs – only 1 in 5 can be filled Neighbourhood reinvestment programmes ended Big housing affordability crisis – social initiatives to help Several smaller programmes rescue derelict housing blocks Bank foundations play a big role Very high youth unemployment Hostility to Roma is compounded by unemployment
Bilbao*	Very low city debt compared with other parts of Spain Big cost reductions; 'voluntary' salary cuts across the board Many land/development plans on hold – private sector withdraws from land deals New industries hold up with difficulty Very high youth unemployment Bank (BBVA) moves HQ
Sheffield*	Most programme funding goes Sustainable energy saving programme is in disarray due to funding uncertainties Continuing job losses in heavy manufacturing (steel and related industries) Advanced manufacturing still progresses but not many jobs City management retains strong sense of direction SMEs hold up and multiply, but do not expand in scale Budget more protected than rest of UK but cuts still coming
Belfast*	House price collapse, halt in building Loss of private investment, particularly from Ireland EU Peace Fund continues Some big projects still go ahead more slowly, such as Titanic quarter, North Foreshore Attacks on Roma and other immigrants Emigration returns, and many recent immigrants leave
Comments	Cities suffered immediate funding and debt problems Unemployment rose, youth joblessness very serious City populations steady and some growth due to students and return to city Governments react by both protecting programmes and cutting Looming Euro crisis as Spanish and Irish housing markets crash and banking crisis overtakes them

Source: City visits, 2006-15
Note: *Youth unemployment is a big problem. +Liepzig has relatively low youth unemployment compared to the other cities due to special Federal German employment support measures.

The creation of the Euro, a common currency to solidify the free trade arrangements of the Union, and strengthen the political bonds to direct it, reflected the idealistic vision of a united federal Europe that was able to play its part as a real powerhouse in the world, as well as economic arguments in the single currency's favour. It was a euphoric moment for its leaders. But not all countries were included – the UK opted out of the Euro following its painful experience of having to withdraw from the European Exchange Rate Mechanism in the 1990s to stabilise its currency. 'Black Wednesday', as the critical withdrawal date became known, was seen in the UK as a precursor of trouble for countries that needed to raise or lower the value of their currency to cope with fluctuating economic conditions. The UK, with its advanced financial services, did not want to risk a second currency 'lock-in'. Europe was 'not ready' and nor was the UK. The other countries in our study took the plunge and the UK, as usual, appeared insular, narrow and conservative.

Problems were almost bound to arise in the European Union's poorer member states on the periphery, such as Spain, Portugal, Greece and Ireland.[6] Yet they would be prevented from adapting to the crisis by being in the Euro. They were the countries benefiting most from having joined the Union – rapid growth, large exports of cheaply produced goods, tourism and European regional investment funds to equalise conditions. They hoped that signing up to the Euro would bring them even more prosperity and more ready funds to invest in further growth. Initially, it did just that, on the assumption that the growth potential was endless and the resources to fund it were all but bottomless. The momentum behind the Euro was unstoppable and the arguments in its favour around a European super-economy, if not super-state, seemed convincing in the face of global competition from fast-rising powers like China, India, Brazil and the constant foil of US growth and prosperity.

Once most European currencies had joined the Euro, the 'outsiders' had no choice but to trade partly in Euros and adjust their banking systems, finances and economic policies to that reality. They thus became entangled in its ups and downs. The situation in Northern Ireland illustrates this. As part of the UK, Belfast and Northern Ireland were initially protected from the Eurozone crisis. But much of the investment, tourism, commerce and trade which helped Belfast's recovery following the Peace Agreement of 1998 came from south of the border in the Republic of Ireland. Ireland was one of the countries worst hit by the Euro crisis. Its leading national bank was forced to accept a humiliating bail-out; its booming housing market collapsed;

its public sector was hacked back; its welfare system massively shrunk. The impact on Northern Ireland by 2011 was a withdrawal of Irish investment, and an acute shrinkage in the construction and housing boom that was underway.

On the other hand, Belfast and Northern Ireland were heavily protected by the Westminster government from the cuts in the UK, and additional funds ensured that Northern Ireland did not experience the severe upheavals of other parts of the UK. There was too big a risk of trouble. Sheffield, on the other hand, was unshielded, in contrast to Belfast, and hard hit by the UK coalition government's harsh austerity measures.

Austerity and its aftermath

The financial crisis of 2008 forced the UK government to take over several major banks and bail out others. This is still sending shockwaves through the economy. The cuts in public spending in the UK were partly driven by the massive rise in public debt in the immediate aftermath of the financial crash of 2007–08, first to fund the bail-out of the banks and second to increase public spending to keep the economy and jobs going in the face of private shrinkage. This double funding could not last and by 2010 a new coalition government drove through an austerity budget, nowhere near as harsh as southern Europe's or Ireland's, but for cities like Sheffield tough beyond their deepest fears.

The British government bail-out of leading banks shares many similarities with the Eurozone bail-out of Ireland, Portugal and Greece. The Spanish government, with deeply indebted regions, unfundable government commitments, a collapse in the housing market and the near bankruptcy of many publicly owned Cajas, or savings banks, managed avoid a humiliating Eurozone bail-out, but only with the most severe austerity and cutbacks, a de facto underpinning of its banking system, a bail-out in all but name, and the same shocking level of unemployment as Greece – over 50% among young people.[7] Figure 5.1 shows the steep rises in youth joblessness in all cities except Leipzig following the 2008 crisis.

Former industrial cities, far more dependent on public underpinning than their more prosperous non-industrial counterpart cities, were particularly badly affected. By 2010, Sheffield was uncertain whether any but the statutorily mandated services provided by the city would survive. Economic development, enterprise, regeneration, large scale investment plans, energy saving, public services like libraries, social

Figure 5.1: Youth unemployment (%) in metropolitan and provincial areas, 2000–13

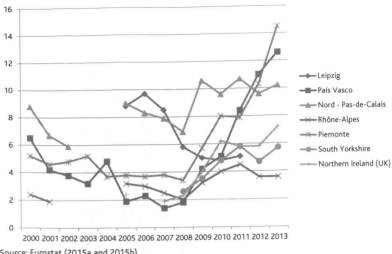

Source: Eurostat (2015a and 2015b)

programmes, support for voluntary and community organisations, were all shrunk, put on hold, cancelled, or collapsed into one another. European austerity compares sharply with the US Federal stimulus budget under Obama (the American Stimulus and Recovery Act, 2009) which unleashed massive government five-year spending programmes to help refloat the economy. The more rapid economic recovery in the US compares with the continuing crisis of 'austerity versus growth' in Europe. Paul Krugman, the Nobel prize-winning economist, put his finger on it several times, arguing that Europe is stifling its own recovery, punishing instead of coaxing the heavily indebted countries into collecting taxes, decimating rather than restraining the public sector while encouraging the private sector.[8]

Spain and Ireland applied deep cuts under the vigilant eye of the International Monetary Fund, the European Central Bank and the European Union. Italy and France were supposed to reform their labour markets and their pensions, and 'free up' their economies from over-restrictive state controls and over-heavy taxes. But both were slow to move. Germany was in a far stronger economic position due to its industrially-oriented and export-driven economy, its high savings and low borrowing. In large part it de facto funded the bail-outs and shaped (if not dictated) the terms of austerity to other European countries. This put a big charge on the German government and many forms of milder austerity were introduced there – such as cutbacks in unemployment payments, the introduction of low paid, short-term job contracts, and reduced job protection.[9] Some major investment programmes in our seven cities were cut back or delayed – for example, new transport, large site developments, new public buildings.[10]

Bilbao and Torino both show how austerity plays out in practice. In both cities, large scale physical regeneration projects have either been scrapped or deferred; some of the most innovative city-led organisations such as Bilbao Ria, responsible for land reclamation and the Guggenheim, and 'Progetto speciale periferie', responsible in Torino for the special neighbourhood projects in poorer former industrial areas, were either massively curtailed or reabsorbed.

In Bilbao, city employees agreed a 6% pay cut across the board and only voluntary redundancies. The city manager reduced the city's debt to zero with tight management of resources, so that spending stayed within budget, while neighbourhood, park and street services were carefully maintained. The result was rising satisfaction, impressive neighbourhood conditions and zero debt, but almost no room for manoeuvre. In this way, the city retained control of its local conditions – a truly impressive achievement. A similar process in Sheffield led to the amalgamation and reincorporation in the city of several arm's length partnership bodies, specially developed in the recovery period. Social investment programmes have disappeared. Interestingly new strands of social innovation have appeared in their place – far patchier, smaller scale, more ad hoc and unpredictable, but nonetheless imaginative, possibly pointing to the future for cities across Europe in a new era of resource constraints and slow growth.

Work and skills

The weakness in recovery lay partly in strong reliance on public sector support and relatively weak private sectors. But the skills change needed for the new economy to grow highlights further weakness. Conversion from industrial and manual to service and knowledge-based jobs has only been partial and very large numbers of people could not find jobs for this reason, particularly young people without experience. The reluctance of enterprises to take on additional workers or risk expanding even when they were surviving relatively well made this worse, due to shortage of credit and fears of further trouble. This problem was compounded in several countries, particularly France, by strict labour laws that deter jobs creation. Only now is France proposing significant measures to open up the job market – Lille has seen a sharp rise in self-employment as a result of the changes.

The fear of taking on workers was one of the issues the German government tackled, first with its labour market reforms, which allowed semi-casual, low paid jobs to be created, which in turn were easier to terminate. Second, it provided generous funds for employers to help firms to keep workers on their books even when there was not enough work. Third, it supported apprenticeships and training jobs for young people to ensure high access to work and low youth unemployment. These reforms kept German unemployment low in the crisis, and Leipzig stands out among the seven cities as staving off the worst of youth unemployment. Italy, Spain and the UK all adopted more flexible employment and offered some public underpinning to keep the lowest paid and most precariously employed in work. Other measures eased the crisis of jobs:

- Self-employment, introduced in France to make it easier for 'solo enterprises' to be created, led to a huge boom in self-employment.
- Working tax credits and part-time jobs in the UK led to a rapid increase in extremely low paid but government supported jobs.
- Employer job subsidies, funded by the government in Italy, helped to protect existing jobs.
- Shorter hours and pay cuts across all levels of the public sector in Bilbao helped to keep budgets manageable and protected jobs.

These measures helped to keep jobs in place, but it still was not enough, and the worry is that recovery, slow and feeble as it is, is not creating enough new jobs to take up the slack. Also, many new jobs are short-term, part-time and low paid. This remains a huge challenge, but growth signs are turning positive.[11] Table 5.5 summarises what happened in each city over the vexed question of jobs. Figure 5.2 shows which employment sectors did better or worse in each city.

Table 5.5: Job and skill trends through decline, recovery and new crisis

Leipzig	Sudden collapse of DDR meant 90% of all manufacturing jobs disappeared in 1989–90 Big success in winning companies back: BMW, Porsche, Amazon, DHL Many service jobs created City agency to link new jobs to existing workers Reskilling of population Many jobs held up by government subsidies Special job support centres opened to help local residents access available jobs Also special help to companies to recruit local workers
Lille	Slow decline from mid-1960s New clusters following industrial collapse – high tech, bio-medical, advanced textile design, logistics Focus on new and green technologies – Third Industrial Revolution Higher than average unemployment but held up quite well during crisis Many new enterprises and big growth in self-employment
Saint-Étienne	Most solidly manufacturing city, along with Sheffield Recovery road is steep and very difficult Success with design – linked to industry Attracted HQ of big French supermarket chain, Casino, bringing many new jobs Hard to attract/hold higher skill – high unemployment rose in crisis Large number of SMEs offering a majority of jobs
Torino	Auto-decline carefully managed – some elements retained to create new transport industries Also advanced communications, engineering, design, sustain jobs Continuing growth in tourism and events Renewable energy and green innovation are important Social cooperatives are very significant Very high youth unemployment
Bilbao	Manufacturing hard hit but bigger share of manufacturing jobs retained than other cities – helped by Mondragon cooperatives Spin-offs in Bilbao such as 'learning by doing' university degree programme Many jobs in 'business tourism', conferences High unemployment (16%) but far lower than Spanish average
Sheffield	Major job losses and stranded populations Strong economic recovery and advance manufacturing growing quite fast but with few jobs – ancillary services are job intensive, more openings there Poverty and inequality are still serious SMEs employ the largest share of workers Only slightly above average unemployment
Belfast	Long decline and regrowth frozen by Troubles Urban tourism still growing – millions of visitors, helping investment and jobs Gateway for Ireland so increasing logistics role Strong US links attract inward investment Major development of renewables Retail creates jobs because of volume of shopper/visitors from Republic Big gap between high and low skill workers creates employment gap Collapse in house prices undermines construction jobs Jobs in hospitality often takes by East European migrants Some protected jobs in local government and security shrink

Source: City visits and interviews, 2006–15

Figure 5.2: Job trends, 1994–2014: main sector gains and losses for each city

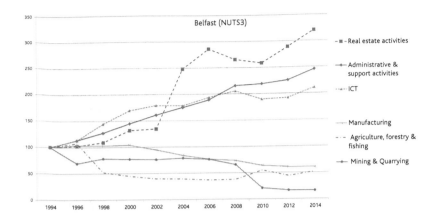

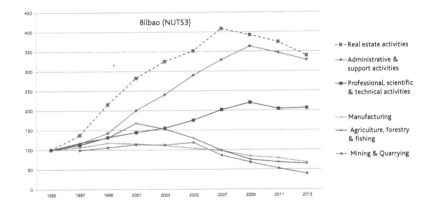

Threats and opportunities

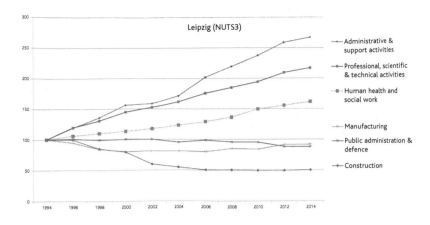

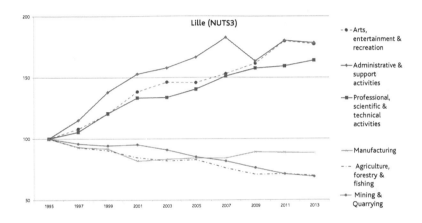

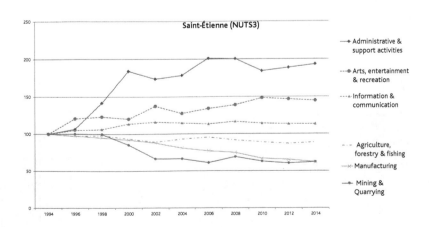

Cities for a small continent

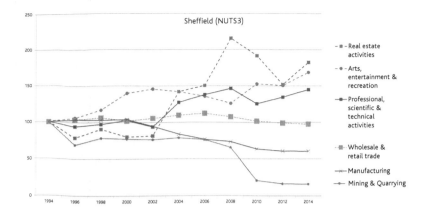

Sheffield (NUTS3)

- ■ - Real estate activities
- ● - Arts, entertainment & recreation
—■— Professional, scientific & technical activities
- ▦ - Wholesale & retail trade
—✕— Manufacturing
—●— Mining & Quarrying

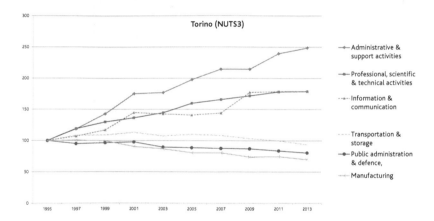

Torino (NUTS3)

—▲— Administrative & support activities
—●— Professional, scientific & technical activities
--▲-- Information & communication
----- Transportation & storage
—●— Public administration & defence,
——— Manufacturing

Source: LSE Cities European Metromonitor Website

Third phase of development in Europe's industrial cities

By 2010, European weak market cities were coming to terms with the new era. There was little hope of a quick and easy return to rapid growth. There was a realisation that public sector cushioning was significantly reduced – levels of pay and pay rises; pensions and retirement age – while job insecurity, redundancies and shrinkage increased. Voluntary and community organisations, particularly those helping the poorest and hardest hit areas, were struggling to survive with shrunken public support and more impoverished local communities. They also faced rising demand for their services while new demands were emerging – particularly for food banks, homelessness shelters, debt relief and advice. Some local programmes and organisations did in fact disappear, but new emergency provision appeared in their place, particularly around emergency food supplies and eating centres; emergency housing provision and hostels, often based on sharing; special initiatives to support minorities and combat racial tensions; and advice centres to help people with financial, legal and claimant problems.

Special measures were tried out within the cities to help people get by; they too signalled a new sense of direction, a new phase for cities – doing more with less; inventing more, depending less; finding new solutions to old problems. Cities quickly discovered that many of the measures they had experimented with in Phase 2 – reclaiming land and buildings, recreating public spaces, repopulating under-occupied cities – had laid a solid foundation for a new phase when such investment would no longer be made but the infrastructure of old industrial cities was in vastly better shape and ready for reuse – ready to act as a shock absorber and spring board for renewed action.

Our seven cities, which gained then lost so much in the first phase of industrial boom and bust, then recovered slowly but surely, with a great deal of public support in the second phase, now face a totally new phase of austerity, mainly falling under four headings: public, private, physical and environmental. We examine each in turn.

Public austerity and its wider significance

Public austerity programmes reflect the real resource constraints we face. Many think they are here to stay. They appear extremely harsh because they are hitting places and people very unevenly, but they are not just a flash-in-the-pan response of the moment. They reflect a deep-set problem within European democracies that voters and taxpayers support public services but vote against paying the necessary taxes to fund them. Raising taxes in one European country immediately leads to talk of seeking refuge somewhere else – both the French super-tax of 75% on the very rich; or the United Kingdom's temporary tax of 50% on higher incomes had this effect. The opposite effect is produced by any tax concessions such as the Irish reduction in corporation tax to entice foreign firms into Ireland. The movement created by these new taxes and tax breaks is somewhat destabilising within the European Union without there being counter-measures that might work to integrate tax and spending systems.

In response to economic difficulties, cutting taxes has become a political game of high stakes when the reality is that European governments and cities need to raise more money, and need to harmonise their funding policies, rather than diverge to undermine each other. The pooling of resources and support that taxes bring and that the European Union was in part set up to achieve has been melting away under pressure of the crisis, to be replaced by the harshest measures being imposed on the poorest communities. In practice the austerity measures, triggered by the double financial and Eurozone crises, reduced tax revenues so drastically through unemployment and falling wages that the economies of cities and countries shrank even faster than was already happening.

Governments had less to spend, could support fewer jobs, and therefore provided less resources that could flow through the economy. It was a vicious circle. The hope that the private sector would step in and fill the breach was belied by the reality of 'leverage' in recovering cities – private investment followed public funds in all our cities, as we showed in Chapter Four. As public funds dried up, so the private sector lost confidence. Public and private finance was also severely limited by the need to 'recapitalise' banks – to save rather than to spend.

The fall in public funding for cities was real and harsh, as Box 5.2 explains. The resulting cutback in funds for cities sent shockwaves through local economies:

Box 5.2: How the financial crisis played out

- Slowdown in flows of funds from governments and from the European Union
- Reduction in tax income due to the recession and wider austerity measures
- Some tax cuts to encourage investment
- High resistance to paying more taxes from voters, due to greater insecurity, falling real incomes and higher costs

- Political fear of raising taxes, even where they could be justified because of public mistrust of government
- Need to keep public debt under control at a time when repaying it could cripple capacity to spend – as played out in Spain, Portugal, Greece and Ireland
- Cities themselves being saddled with high debts resulting from the high level of borrowing for major infrastructure investment during the recovery period

---

It is easy to see how the drying-up of public funds damages struggling cities. It is hard to see how the resource constraints of Phase Three would help Europe along the road to recovery.

Private retrenchment

Private sector firms were seriously hit by the crisis. Often firms were over-extended and taking big risks before the crisis – particularly in the building industry, leading to major financial losses once the crisis happened. In other industries such as car manufacture, over-production became a major barrier to survival. Car production not only fell, car sales plummeted, jobs were lost and factories shrank or closed.

Construction fared particularly badly in all cities and there were many job losses. Even where housing was not deeply affected – for example, Leipzig – the rate at which new houses or flats were being built slowed, and the value of existing property was dampened. Big physical investment projects also slowed right down or stopped completely, causing further loss of construction jobs. On the other hand, repair, upgrading and retrofit work continued in most cities and this kept many smaller building firms going.

A major consequence of the banking crisis was the loss of credit resources, which limited the ability of firms to keep going; this undermined motivation. Bigger firms were struggling with cash flow; small and medium enterprises (SMEs), which were gaining prominence, had limited capacity to invest or expand or take on new ventures.

These three examples – construction, cars and finance – ran right through the economies of our industrial cities. In producer cities, many SMEs supplied the construction and auto industries with parts, materials, services. Once the financial industry was in trouble, it became extremely hard to borrow, particularly for SMEs. This made investment, growth and recovery extremely difficult and very slow. Our cities today are still struggling with the lending and investment barriers that began with the crisis.

In practice shrinkage in the public and private sectors went together, leading to the long, deep recession of 2008–14. Overall private sector problems were driven by factors linked to public sector cutbacks – high indebtedness, shrinking resources, high costs, over-staffing and underperformance. In many private companies this quickly results in bankruptcy; in the public sector it provokes cuts and austerity budgets.

Some major companies were propped up by governments. Having struggled to survive, Fiat in Torino managed to make alliances with the troubled American giants, Chrysler and General Motors. Fiat finally moved its headquarters out of its Torino birthplace in 2014. BMW in Leipzig also survived – thanks in part to generous German government subsidies. But it too has reduced its workforce and production lines. On the other hand, BMW has recently launched its revolutionary 100% electric car there – with some hope that this may open up a new direction for manufacturing in the city, a revolution in car transport, a much cleaner, safer environment, and thus BMW remains a crucial player in Leipzig's economic future. Fiat is also involved in developing 'clean' engines – for trains and buses, as well as cars, and hydrogen as a renewable fuel. Resource constraints and tougher European environmental regulations are helping this transition.

Physical constraints

Europe is many times more populated and more built up today than it was when the industrial revolution took off. There is far less physical space surrounding the cities than there was, partly because populations have spread out to improve housing conditions. Pressures on land and restrictions on sprawl have helped these cities stay fairly compact and not lose populations during the recession. Small businesses have continued to open up in these cities because their physical infrastructure is good, density and proximity help, public transport connections are helpful, and space is cheaper than in major cities.

An ageing population and historically low birth rates are projected to lead to a Europe-wide decline in population, but inward migration and the natural increase that comes with the higher birth rates of younger migrants are still pushing up the population totals in most countries. These factors come strongly into play in our seven cities. Torino, Belfast, Sheffield and Lille have all experienced a major growth in foreign minority ethnic populations, due to rapid in-migration before and following the crisis. Bilbao has received migrant settlers under a dispersal policy by the Spanish government from the southern regions of Spain. Leipzig has received migrants from Eastern Europe.

Environmental limits

We have shown how industrial cities had got close to their environmental limits. In effect their economic viability was undermined by resource constraints. Environmental pressures became even more serious over the crisis period due to mounting evidence of climate change impacts and costs particularly in Europe.[12] The most crucial factor forcing European cities to shrink their environmental impact is the absolute finite limit on the natural resources on which cities depend. This applies to land above all, but also air, water, energy, all of which support their multiple functions. It particularly applies to fossil fuels; to energy intensive building materials such as concrete, steel, glass and bricks; to copper pipes and many other essential material resources.[13] Physical and environmental resource limits force cities to move into the third phase of our framework, the resource-constrained economy. The banking crisis proved to be an extreme version of what was an inevitable shrinkage of resources that was happening anyway. However, it is the financial crisis that triggered the public and private resources available to our cities to shrink. It was this that triggered such serious job losses and retrenchment.

Meaning of a resource-constrained new phase

The four strands of austerity – public, private, physical, environmental – created a whole new phase in city development, a post-industrial, post-recovery, resource-constrained economy with only one option: to find new ways to manage. Phase One involved exuberant growth, over-use of resources, high social and environmental costs, and an eventual crash. Phase Two describes post-industrial recovery, based on a different, more cautious revaluing of cities following the serious damage and losses caused by Phase One. Phase Three is the phase that European cities reached during the harsh austerity period of 2008 to 2014 when they had to cope with resource limits. Figure 5.3 sets out the main characteristics of Phase Three.

Figure 5.3: Phase Three of the Framework

Source: Power, 2013

The third phase of the industrial revolution is by no means uniform across Europe. The resource-constrained economy is strongly influenced in Europe by many pressures, as shown by Box 5.3.

Box 5.3: Pressures on resources in ex-industrial cities

- Unstable energy supply problems that European countries face
- Europe-wide drive for renewable energy
- Deep, inescapable and pervasive legacy of manufacturing and its decline
- Desire to reignite the industrial production engine
- Advanced scientific knowledge-base in European research institutions
- Innovation focus of cluster growth
- Continuing rise in flows of migrants
- Severe limits on space within cities
- Ongoing pressures of traffic
- Slow-moving but influential democratic decision making of a continental union of 28 countries with many layers of governance

---

This new third phase harks back to our early post-war visions of a Europe that is united and cooperative, working against the odds to create peaceful, cross-border collaboration. Only this way can a resource-constrained economy work. Our working model is our early post-war recovery era, when austerity was the order of the day, and where burying our differences allowed us to create the world's largest and densest trading area.

During Phase Three, the hope has emerged that scientifically driven solutions could help to close the widening gap between resource limits and current needs. There is a parallel notion that **Re**cycling in every sense could combine with **Re**newable energy to create a new type of economy. Nicholas Stern describes this economy as more socially benign as well as more custodial of our planet, more inventive in new technologies, and more integrative within cities.[14] Energy saving in building goes hand in hand with restoring buildings, and with the potential for relying on renewable energy. It is not yet clear how Phase Three will pan out.

The new European economy

The seven cities are hard hit by five dominant aspects of the post-2008 crisis:

- further loss of industry and construction jobs;
- withdrawal of financial support, both public and private;
- the unstable Euro currency;
- deep recession; and
- climate change itself.

The major driver behind these problems lies in the reality of depleted resources of all kinds. It is this resource depletion that makes Phase Three inevitable. As European economies began to recover, the pace of regrowth proved extremely slow, and regrowth itself has taken a new and somewhat hesitant shape. The following five changes are the most salient.

1. Real wages fell in both public and private sectors, particularly at the lower end of the scale, and particularly for young people. The only exception is at the very top of the scale, most significantly in the financial sector.
2. Revenues fell along with wages as more people are in subsidised jobs and more people unemployed.
3. The cost of some social services, considered essential, is rising, such as health, disability provision and elderly care.
4. The need for higher skill levels and new skills is pushing up training costs and making new jobs inaccessible to less skilled workers.
5. The reality of climate change and the environmental impact of human activity is hitting home hard in Europe and is visible in many ways.

Table 5.6 sets out the changes and pressures.

Table 5.6: Strands of change and pressure

Regrowth in Phase 2 Recovery in the job market; most new jobs in services Upgraded civic centres; reuse of buildings; public spaces; improved transport links New support mechanisms, social enterprises and neighbourhood services bridge poverty divide Cities practically transformed by the environmental clean up Citizens far more widely involved
Changes in approach A new kind of leadership with focus on city-region and economy Continuing physical and infrastructure upgrading Economic development and diversification Social and community investment and neighbourhood renewal Environmental reclamation and upgrading
Impact of crisis Loss of industry and other jobs Withdrawal of public and private investment Unstable currency conditions in Europe Deep recession Climate change
New shape of recovery Real wages have been falling in both public and private sectors Revenues have fallen along with wages The cost of some social services is rising The need for higher skill levels and new skills is pushing up training costs The reality of climate change and the environmental impact of human activity is hitting Europe
Climate uncertainties Loss of tree cover and water conservation problems Melting and shrinkage of Alpine permafrost Rising sea levels, loss of top-soil, bio-diversity depletion and extinctions Rising temperatures Threats to European cities from flooding, storms, heat islands and droughts

Source: Author's city visits, 2006-2004; IPCC, 2014

The Intergovernmental Panel on Climate Change in 2012 and 2014 produced reports on the specific threats to European economies of climate change relating particularly to European geography, level of development and population density.[15] Climate scientists have issued severe warnings about many impacts of Europe's climate uncertainties on cities:

- drought, overheating and water scarcity;
- heavy and unpredictable rain leading to severe flooding;
- desertification and loss of tree cover around the Mediterranean causing more intense heat and water conservation problems;
- melting and shrinkage of Alpine permafrost and glaciers causing landslides, avalanches and faster run-off, feeding Europe's rivers and affecting both flooding and water supplies; and
- many more general and barely visible threats to Europe's viability such as rising sea levels; loss of top soil, biodiversity depletion and extinctions; loss of tree cover; all coupled with increased concrete, tarmac and buildings.

Underlying the severe weather warnings lies the reality that Europe's reliance on fossil fuels is dented, causing a continuing rise in CO_2 emissions, in spite of rapid growth in renewable energy production. The impact of CO_2 emissions on climate change is cumulative over time, as is the impact of development and growth, both causing serious environmental damage right across the continent. All kinds of economic activity including new building affects ever more extensive areas and has major knock-on effects on soils, water systems, tree cover, biodiversity, farming, flooding and resource use, as well as energy use. The volume of embodied carbon going into Europe's infrastructure alone is terrifyingly large. The development impact on land, water, materials, energy is huge.

These high-impact factors, when coupled with the rapid rise of fast developing economies, and their demand for resources, determine the new shape of the European economy. Interestingly, ex-industrial cities, exemplified by our seven case studies, are strongly placed to develop in a new, environmentally 'light' direction, suggesting a way forward under now heavily limited resources, widely recognised environmental pressures, climate change imperatives, and the need to survive. These pressures on struggling cities can be reduced by reusing the assets and gains that accrued over their original growth period and the second phase of recovery. Their assets and gains also fall under five main headings:

- A new kind of leadership and approach.
- Physical and infrastructure reinvestment.
- Economic change and diversification.
- Social and community investment and neighbourhood renewal.
- Environment reclamation and upgrading.

The gains from the five strands of remedial investment had in all cases spurred some regrowth showing in population and job recovery or at least slowed population decline.

- A recovery in the job market, with most new jobs in services, led to new enterprises and new growth in the clusters of economic activity that city governments encouraged
- Cities had invested in upgraded civic centres, the imaginative reuse of buildings and public spaces and improved transport links. These investments helped the cities continue to attract people and activity even in a period of serious decline.
- Social inequalities and skills mismatches in the job market remained, but new support mechanisms, social enterprises and neighbourhood services were in place to help bridge the great poverty divide that threatened social cohesion.
- The environment of the cities was practically transformed by the environmental clean-up – rivers and canals, parks and squares, industrial sites and left-over relics of the industrial age. The heavy pollution and contamination were on their way out. This created many opportunities for new economic activity, which cities like Sheffield, Torino and Belfast expanded into *during* the crisis.
- Citizens had become far more widely involved and new leaders generally recognised that citizens were their life-support in the recovery battle. They also knew that only by working with all sectors of the community in an innovative and entrepreneurial way could their economies recover.

Table 5.7 summarises some of the assets that the cities had acquired over their long growth period and their recovery following acute decline.

Building on these assets, the cities developed their new economy. The city stories show that the current economic position of struggling cities is substantially different from earlier. They no longer have the wealth creation capacity of Phase One nor the public underpinning of Phase Two; but they have the knowhow and experience, the infrastructure and motivation to respond to new challenges; and they do understand the Re-economy and its potential to create a new kind of low or tamed growth form of prosperity.

Table 5.7: Assets that can help in a new economy

Leipzig	International trade links to East are rebuilt through Trade Fairs New high speed rail link to Berlin BMW launched production of electric cars City centre attracts significant tourists, but periphery declines Outer edge looks ugly and neglected Large outer estates have been 'thinned out' and upgraded Universities are very important Big poverty divides Green spaces, cycle routes, land reclamation have high impact Big retrofit programme Solar manufacture still big Some regeneration continuing; but big spending of past 20 years is over
Lille	Major international rail hub – many cross border links Major logistics centre, including road and canal/river as well as rail New technology hub in disused, restored textile mill Big universities and major bio-medical research High sustained public spending, but tailing off over the next two years Significant tourism Strong drive of city leadership for social and economics reinvestment continues – large scale funded projects still continuing Densification of city generates commerce, culture, tourism

Saint-Étienne	Slowly recovering from huge city debt built up over decades
	Casino (national supermarket chain) HQ moved to Saint-Étienne, bringing
	   many jobs
	Plan in place to restrict suburban growth – some success in attracting
	   residents back into city
	Links with Lyon progressing and positive
	'Design village' based in huge old factory and Biennale successful, also
	   optics cluster
	Improving public transport – new train line, TGV connection
	Now major debt under control; regeneration efforts holding up
	SCOT plan to control sprawl and concentrate growth is functioning under
	   Metropolitan control

Torino	New advanced transport manufacture alliances to develop new hydrogen
	   buses, trains, electric cars
	City centre is extremely prosperous and attractive
	Slow Food movement expanding and generating international associates
	Strong energy saving focus – retrofit old buildings, centralised combined
	   heat and power system for most of city
	Innovative social enterprises
	Multiple sharing and cooperative initiatives
	Major events focus and tourism
	Major debt crisis in city council; leads to job cuts
	Some agencies closed down, including neighbourhood programmes
	Strong anti-immigration sentiments
	Fiat struggling to reinvent itself – smaller, more research oriented.

Bilbao	Strong investment in city infrastructure Multiple SMEs, cooperatives and social enterprises Sustained manufacturing, engineering, high tech sector Land reclamation in port and river, also old neighbourhoods Strong growth in tourism (Guggenheim) Mondragon industrial cooperatives are a beacon Autonomous tax revenue from Basque government helps; also high tech engineering Strong entrepreneurial culture; outward looking focus Business tourism is big and growing
Sheffield	Major loss of public investment and special funds Business tourism is big and growing Strong developments in advanced manufacture Universities with engineering focus doing well Some prospect of energy-related nuclear revival – linked to University research Energy saving and retrofit lost funding – but renewable energy research growing Engine making, machine cutting and advanced steel all still important
Belfast	City still highly segregated – slows economic progress Major focus on Titanic centenary – huge publicity – restoration of old customs building New visitor exhibition/events centre and Further Education College opened Major new Science Park and renewable production R&D link to universities Politics difficult but progressing Benefits from Southern Ireland visitors and shoppers Attempts at improving public transport Tourism holding up though affected by crisis in the Republic of Ireland Some new manufacture, including London buses Some infrastructure: North Foreshore landfill site becomes methane producer; looking at light rail for Belfast, copying Dublin Jobs drive still strong; but big skills divide
Comments	Major budget and spending constraints on all cities Public investment pays off everywhere Big refocus on advanced manufacture and high tech industries – everywhere Italy, Spain hard hit by Euro crisis – affects France too Youth unemployment huge problem – 20% plus – particularly Torino, Bilbao, Saint-Étienne Cutting carbon use dominant in all cities especially Germany – many avant garde models, particularly Leipzig, Lille, Torino

Source: City visits, 2006–15

The Re-economy and the benefits of density

The **Re**-economy is based on the idea that resources that have already been used, or created for other purposes, can be used again. People who once seemed redundant and 'on the scrap heap' are a valuable new source of manpower for the low level maintenance and custodial jobs cities now need. The engineering and technical skills that looked obsolete in these cities when their big industries went can become the new applied skills of innovative enterprises. The spare capacity in housing and neighbourhoods, industrial and commercial areas can be taken up and *re*used as populations continue to expand. Trams, trains, metros and buses, underused and rundown 20 years ago, have been *re*instated and upgraded and are now an urban lifeline in Europe's cities. Public spaces, neighbourhood services and essential public functions are retained, albeit at a lower level than before, so the main framework of jobs stays in place.

With much diminished government support, reinvestment has been slowed, but the idea is not lost, for example better rail links. However they are being challenged or revised, on grounds of cost and environmental impact. The high speed train links from Torino to Lyon, from Bilbao to Madrid and from Birmingham to Manchester, Leeds and potentially Sheffield, are increasingly questioned on environmental and cost grounds. Their long-term viability is in question. Instead, upgraded, faster rail links between these cities are almost guaranteed and in fact already developing. Train travel in Europe speeds up all the time, often with incremental improvements, and it has around one third of the environmental impact of internal European flights.[16] The European rail networks are pivotal to our cities and support the new economy of cities in Phase Three.

Basically the cities moved from a 'make-do-and-mend' phase, which was one of the hallmarks of their Phase Two recovery, into a Phase Three characterised by 'how to achieve more with less'. They are well placed to do this as they are no strangers to adversity, shortage and setbacks. They are also well versed in the need to innovate. Through war and peace, economic ups and downs, they have learnt the value of **Re**making, **Re**-doing, **Re**forming and **Re**-instating. It is a very different idea of older industrial cities than the notion of 'shrinkage', which seems anathema among all levels of city actors that we met.[17] Increasing urban density has become a key to sustaining cities with many benefits, as Box 5.4 shows.

Box 5.4: Benefits of density

- Saving energy
- Bringing diverse communities closer together and increasing social integration
- Raising revenue for city investment and recovery action
- Maximising the value of public space and city facilities
- Increasing street life and vitality
- Creating innovation through the density of ideas and exchanges
- Appealing strongly to young people and therefore offering prospects of holding them in the city
- Encouraging anchor institutions like universities and hospitals to stay and invest
- Reinforcing the value of public transport, cycling schemes, pedestrian streets, and so on
- Plugging holes and gaps in the urban fabric that were not filled in Phase Two
- Reusing existing infrastructure

Conclusions

Even during the industrial revolution, when conditions were grim beyond our imaginings, industrial and public leaders, citizens and communities invented new solutions on a routine basis to improve the workings of booming industries, overcrowded cities and highly vulnerable communities.[18] In the era of collapse in the 1970s and 80s, conditions and prospects again looked their grimmest and most hopeless. Yet out of that collapse at the end of Phase One, the whole of Phase Two, the recovery era emerged. In Phase Three, yet a further process in the evolution of cities is unfolding, offering the prospects of a more benign, more planet and people-friendly growth, as Nicholas Stern expects.[19]

Many questions remain unanswered. But the reality of resource constraints, the concerns over climate change and the commitment to cutting reliance on fossil fuels underpin a new industrial economy.[20] We know that the Eurozone crisis is far from over. The recent Greek and Spanish elections demonstrate the readiness of large populations to opt for radical change, to reject traditional parties and programmes, to escape the austerity that has decimated their public services, destroyed their safety net and left large numbers all but destitute, with over half their young people out of work. The rise of the Scottish nationalists, on a crest of youthful optimism about a different kind of future, almost matches the mood in southern Europe.[21] The forecasts suggest that public sector austerity is here to stay, but it will take different forms as the politics of youthful rebellion take shape.

Regrowth in the context of austerity is proving difficult. But there are positive signs. The crucial driver of change in our cities is both the reality of resource constraints and the fact that cities have resources that can be reused. Cities are the places that illustrate best the fundamental causes and drivers of climate change – man-made climate change through *over*-extraction, *over*-burning and *over*-reliance on fossil fuels leading to *over*-pollution of the atmosphere, *over*-use and contamination of land and water. Now we are in a different phase.[22]

Inventive, industrial cities can lead Phase Three, a resource light economy, not only by undoing the damage, reusing what has already been made, but also by actually making things again. This is what they have always been good at. This time around, it will require new ways, using new, non-polluting forms of energy. If they can do this without extra resources by *re*using currently underused space and capacity, *re*-employing underused populations, then the third phase may evolve from the ashes of the first phase and the ground laid by the second.

Box 5.5: Tale of a city – Saint-Étienne

Saint-Étienne's story illustrates most clearly the three phases of industrial cities. Its future progress still hangs in the balance so it is a very powerful illustration of the uncertainties that lie ahead for struggling cities. The international financial crisis, a recession and the Eurozone all took their toll on the city.

Saint-Étienne is a city of contradictions, poor, working class, small, lacking 'residential appeal', with a long declining population. Yet it has a conspicuous role in French history as a central arms producer for the French Revolution, for Napoleon's foreign excursions and in the First and Second World Wars. It is also potentially a very attractive city, with dense, quaint, narrow, winding, hilly streets, old squares, ancient buildings and enterprising, resilient Stéphanois, the natives of Saint-Étienne. The city is within sight of hills, a national park and the Loire Valley.

Saint-Étienne has a long maker history dating from the 14th century when coal was first discovered and pre-industrial iron foundries produced knives and firearms. A thriving textile industry turned ribbon and lace-making into local specialities. Saint-Étienne was famous early on for its arms production and in 1764 the landmark Imperial Arms Factory was founded in the city. Saint-Étienne's critical role in the French Revolution of 1789 was magnified many times when Napoleon became emperor. The city's population grew quickly in the 19th and early 20th centuries, from 15,000 in 1800 to 230,000 in 1970.

Photo 5.1: *Aerial view of Saint Étienne with Mont Pilat National Park in the background*

Powerful local craft-based producers dominated Saint-Étienne's development until large scale investors and entrepreneurs, drawn to Saint-Étienne by its rich resources, mining and engineering skills, brought a new dynamic industrial class to the city, focusing on large scale industry. This unleashed long-run political tensions in the city between smaller scale, more traditional, artisan-based business forces and more adventurous progressive opportunistic investors. Saint-Étienne's dominant production was in armaments but many other path-breaking inventions were born in the city, including France's first steam engine carrying coal.

Saint-Étienne's inventors, designers and producers forged ahead to make the first bicycles, sewing machines, modern arms, specialist optic lenses and many other modern goods, mass produced in the giant factories of Manufrance and the Imperial Arms Factory. The First World War greatly expanded Saint-Étienne's national role as a major arms producer. In 1944, American bombs fell heavily on Saint-Étienne, destroying its military bases following the German occupation.

Social and housing conditions in the strongly working class city were shocking and overcrowding was so serious that two large outer estates were funded by the French government after the war to relieve the housing pressure. This coincided with the large influx of post-war immigrants, mainly from North Africa, to work in the foundries, factories and workshops of Saint-Étienne. In the early 1980s, the estates became crowded with immigrant families while the indigenous population began to move out to the suburbs. Outward sprawl was an early and continuing problem for the crowded city. Mass estates then became part of the problem rather than the solution.

Saint-Étienne's mines began to close in the late 1950s, eventually costing 25,000 jobs. After the 1970s oil crisis and recession, another 25,000 jobs went from industry. Textiles, steel and other industrial jobs decreased and Manufrance, the huge mass producer of goods, began its long decline. So important was it and Saint-Étienne to the country's economy that a large bail-out to the declining factory was agreed in the late 1970s. There were several further bail-outs.

Meanwhile the outward flow of population and small enterprises continued and by 2000 the population had fallen by 25% to below 170,000, a serious blow to Saint-Étienne's leaders. The political leadership was on the defensive with a Communist mayor and council fighting to protect industrial jobs, with more loans to the giant Manufrance, backed by the government. The rear-guard stance of defending the industrial workforce against inevitable change led to more debt for the city without turning the city's fortunes around. Eventually the near bankrupt Manufrance closed in 1989, a symbolic death knell to the old industrial world.

Saint-Étienne's unstoppable downward spiral led to a new conservative mayor being elected in 1993, on a platform of creating new economic openings, improving the image of the city and making an anti-sprawl deal with the surrounding, and often competing, communes. Mayor Thiollière, a committed Stéphanois, wanted to make the city into an attractive residential and commercial magnet. Over his long period of office to 2008, he steered the city towards recovery based on this new image. A new tram line linking the main station to the city centre; a new concert stadium, Zenith, designed by Norman Foster; new and restored housing within the city; and firm new agreements on containing sprawl with the metropolitan communes, of which there were 34, all shaped the recovery. The core aim was to combat the loss of population, recognise the city as the core of the metropolitan area, and attract population and jobs back into the city. The approach was partly successful as the rate of population decline slowed significantly. However, Saint-Étienne is still battling to rebuild its image. Since 2010 its population has begun to grow again and its new economy is gathering pace, in spite of continuing losses in manufacturing.

Photo 5.2: *Montreynaud open air market*

Photo 5.3: Restored street in central Saint Étienne

Photo 5.4: Street Café in central Saint Étienne

Photo 5.5: Graduate School of Art and Design

Photo 5.6: Restored manufacturing buildings hosting the City of Design

The recovery plan set out to tackle the vast tracts of former industrial land and buildings and the rundown urban environment. The French government, anxious to back Saint-Étienne's recovery plan, sponsored and largely funded two state-led agencies to head up the reclamation of ex-industrial sites and turn them into economic assets. These agencies were responsible for decontamination, new infrastructure, reuse of the city's damaged assets and new growth points within the city. Four major neighbourhood renewal projects, funded by government, tackled the entrenched problems of decay, crowding, poverty and joblessness that beset the city. Two severely rundown inner neighbourhoods and the two giant outer estates were targeted with a ten-year investment programme.

The city went through a transformational process of upgrading and image change from the late 1990s to 2008. The city designed multiple cluster strategies to increase economic opportunities. One radical new departure was to create 'the City of Design', turning Saint-Étienne into an international hub for design companies with new ideas, linked to industrial and other uses. With great foresight and flare the city decided to base the design cluster in the shell of the historic Imperial Arms Factory – with capacity for many small new enterprises, a design school, business support, design advice, exhibitions and events. This move placed Saint-Étienne on the map again with a highly successful Design Bienniale that attracted thousands of international visitors. Saint-Étienne also features in many international design exhibitions and events. It sponsors design engineers to help local companies adopt more environmentally friendly, less energy intensive, less wasteful methods.

Other clusters include an optics cluster, based on a nearby site, building on Saint-Étienne's tradition in specialist lenses, leading to the invention in the city of the revolutionary zoom lens camera. Several other clusters include food, health, ICT and eco-design. The environmental focus makes several important connections: reclaiming derelict sites, restoring old industrial buildings, combating sprawl, greening the urban environment, protecting natural assets around the city, creating green corridors and cycle routes in the city, promoting renewable energy and eco-design, innovating in environmentally friendly de-contamination methods.

One big shift in economic thinking has been in favour of SMEs, where two thirds of Saint-Étienne's workforce are employed. Small and medium companies always were a big part of the city's industrial fabric, suppliers of specialist components and services, while being makers in their own right. SME's survived the earlier industrial crisis while major companies failed. The growth in new clusters over the past 15 years generated many new SMEs which receive business support. Many start-ups have arisen in the new technology and design fields. There were over 40,000 SMEs in Saint-Étienne in 2014.

Saint-Étienne gained its first official university in the 1980s, named after the great pro-European founding father Jean Monnet. Specialist schools in mining, engineering, industrial design and art have promoted and spread new ideas and practice for a reshaped economy. Its 'Écoles Supérieures' have become hubs of advanced learning. Student life helps enliven the city.

In spite of such far-reaching ideas, programmes and progress, the city has struggled with continuing high unemployment, higher than the regional or national average; poorer educational attainment and lower skills than average; and extreme concentrations of poverty and worklessness, most conspicuously in the four neighbourhood areas receiving national renewal funding. The upgrading of the two inner neighbourhoods is helping existing residents to stay in vastly better conditions as well as in-filling the many bare and derelict sites. But some of the conditions waiting to be tackled are shockingly overcrowded, tumble-down and occasionally lacking the most basic amenities, such as indoor toilets. The outer estates suffer from extremely high worklessness and are the target of many special employment training initiatives, often embedded in local social enterprises.

Photo 5.7: Crêt de Roc where the Grands Projets de Ville is investing in major renovation of old buildings

Saint-Étienne is still a struggling city, with strong competition from Lyon, its far bigger and more powerful neighbour, but also from its surrounding suburbs. The city has now finally managed to agree a metropolitan plan that builds in strong environmental protection, agreed anti-sprawl measures, and policies to re-densify the city and enhance its core functions, which in turn will make the city more attractive and more functional, offering amenities to the more spacious and generally more affluent suburbs. Saint-Étienne, partly as a result of these progressive plans and efforts, is now much more closely allied with nearby Lyon, at last burying old rivalries, and cooperating on a wider metropolitan basis, linking Saint-Étienne firmly into European markets.

In 2008 the international financial crisis hit Saint-Étienne just when the signs of recovery were most positive and the city, helped by state regeneration agencies, was on the cusp of a breakthrough into recovery. The impact was extreme. Unemployment shot up. Youth unemployment rose to three times the high French average rate – a terrible price to pay. Firms closed or shed workers, and the city's large overhanging debt from historic bail-outs and from costly borrowing for ambitious investments under Thiollière became an unfundable burden.

A new socialist mayor was elected in that year, determined to pay down the debt and continue on a reforming track. But from 2008 onwards, progress was lacklustre, hampered by the additional burden of France's wider economic troubles. In the new local elections in 2014, the socialists lost control and the city continued to struggle to recover with a new conservative mayor.

However, the city's focus on design, linked to environmental resources, has made the city into a progressive and imaginative green innovator, affecting the way industrial components are designed, the way buildings and industrial sites are reused, the way the city reclaims contaminated land, uses public space, fosters public transport, and upgrades homes. Saint-Étienne today has many assets – new enterprises, strong specialist skills, successful new clusters, with around 1000 small new companies forming each year. The city struggles to create a critical mass of enterprise, employment and population that will put it firmly on the road to recovery, but its recovery path is pointing in a positive direction.

SIX

Over-scale and under-scale

Cities will not be smaller, simpler or more specialised than cities of today. Rather, they will be more intricate, comprehensive, diversified and larger than today's and will have even more complicated jumbles of old and new than ours do

Jane Jacobs, *The Economy of Cities*

Box 6.1: Leipzig – a story

Leipzig's central station reminds a visitor of a cathedral. Its huge, arched, glass roof covers scores of railway lines departing all over Europe, particularly eastwards. Its gleaming shopping arcades, built into the now oversized structure, are teaming with shoppers. Outside the station, the cobbled square, criss-crossed with trams, looks to the narrow main street where new jostles with old.

There are two showstoppers: first, the open square outside the Nikolaikirche where demonstrators braved the mounted police in the late 1980s and, through daily peaceful protests and weekly prayer meetings in the church, accelerated the cataclysmic collapse of East German Communism in 1989. Leipzig's peaceful stand helped reshape a whole continent.

The other showstopper is a scruffy shop window further down the street where Leipzig's citizens still hand in for sale relics from the Communist past – old state regulated clothing, standard issue metal cups and plates, lamps and torches for when the electricity failed, school books, army boots – anything that curiosity-seekers value as reminders of 40 years under strict East German Communism.

On the edge of the city is another showstopper, the ultra-modern BMW car plant, designed by Zaha Hadid, the famous architect of London's glorious Olympic pool. If you could ever call a car factory glorious, this would be it. The huge glass front, under the sweeping roof, reveals the automated conveyor belt with shiny cars rolling along it, high above ground. Visitors gaze upwards as a motor drama rolls by. It is home now to the most advanced breakthrough in electric cars – with zero carbon emissions and potentially fuelled on 100% renewable energy.

Young people crowd to the city, and bemoan the loss of free space as others follow in hot pursuit of opportunity. Leipzig has truly gone from bust to boom, against all predictions.

Introduction

European cities are deeply affected by the turmoil of decline, recovery, then the still-rumbling financial crisis of 2008 which has cost them jobs, cut public resources and dented their recent recovery. The economy of cities, having been shaped by mass industrialisation and private institutions, became much more broken up, fragmented and backed by local, central and European governments. It is unclear in the new period of austerity how they will survive. Former industrial cities have been up and down a steep and slippery slope more than once – growth, decline, recovery, shock, crisis are written into their stories. How they are facing the challenge of renewing, recovering, reshaping their prospects, under current constraints will shape where they are heading; and will show whether remaking old places with modern and traditional skills can work.

The curse of over-scaling

The industrial revolution got its name from its transformative character – every aspect of production grew out of all scale to previous experience, from extracting coal and iron, to firing furnaces and driving machines, to attracting human labour, building factories, warehouses, town halls, banks, schools, universities, hospitals, mass estates. In the 19th and 20th centuries, private enterprises and public services grew to a scale that was eventually unmanageable and destined to break up, as Jane Jacobs argues in *The Economy of Cities*.[1] This over-scaling turned bigness itself into a hallmark of modernity, leading to the overuse of energy and materials, over-large, unmanageable structures, unrecyclable waste – too much heat, too much power, too much throughput, too much thrown away, and no plan for turning redundant materials or wasted energy back into the cycle of production.

The depletion of a finite natural environment was not factored into the industrial city model we have described as Phase One, the first industrial revolution (see Chapter Three). This damaging economic model is driving climate change, since we still live on the overuse of finite resources. Unless we change the model, we are stuck.[2] Figure 6.1

represents the unsustainable economy that continually extracts resources and dumps waste, including carbon emissions, back into the finite environment. This pattern of intense energy use causes immeasurable, hard to reverse damage, as our cities testify.[3]

Figure 6.1: Unsustainable economy

Sustained by burning fossil fuels
– Oil, gas, coal
– High environmental impact

Production

Pollution/waste

Extraction

Waste

Resource inputs

Consumption

Wealth creation

Inequality/exclusion

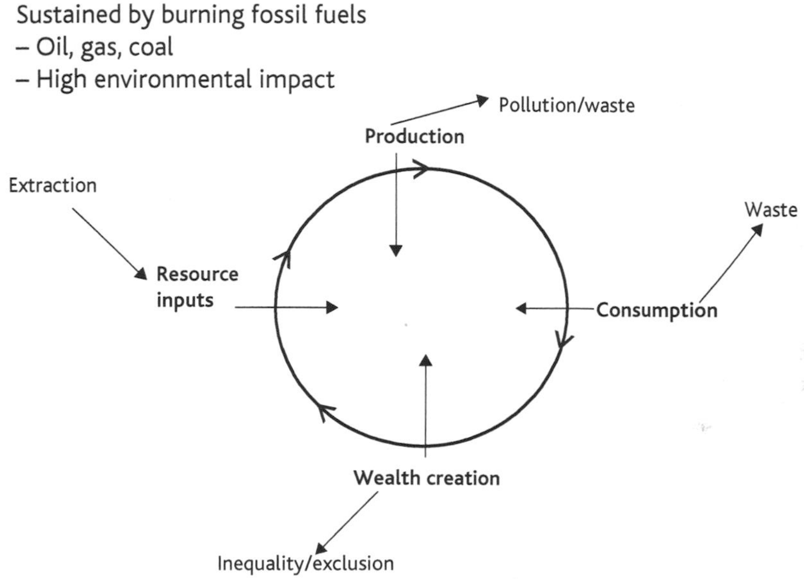

A new synergy – public and private

The first industrial revolution was almost entirely privately initiated and driven, but business urged the creation of the public sector to regulate the essential conditions of survival.[4] In the second recovery and rebuilding phase, following the collapse of Phase One, recovery was strongly public-sector-led but developed important partnerships with the private sector. In Phase Two, European cities developed a new synergy between private and public activity that aimed at restoring and rebuilding. The two have become increasingly interdependent. A pattern of pro-active public intervention became common across Europe. Over-scaling in the public sector had led to steeply rising costs, clumsy, bureaucratic structures, and loss of motivation.[5] But during the recovery period to 2008, programmes, partnerships and new strategies were developed locally within cities which became more fine-tuned, more variable and more broken up; governments became enablers.[6] In this period of recovery and rebuilding, the private sector did not stand alone, partly because Europe's war-torn 20th century history created such a strong public framework, partly because the creation of the European Union added a further layer of decision making, regulation, and pan-European rules. Local governments in Europe grew more powerful as cities declined because there was a large vacuum left by declining economic activity and the large public infrastructure could fill some of the gaps left by the disappearance of major industries. City governments, knowing how dependent they were for funds and jobs on private enterprise, set out to create new partnerships in an interdependent relationship. While the public sector depends on private enterprise for funds, jobs and investment, private enterprise depends on local government for the infrastructure and services the public sector provides.

Public intervention in Europe's former industrial cities, backed by central governments and the European Union, has played a strongly equalising role between less economically troubled cities and struggling cities. Public investment has proved a magnet for new private interest, always hungry for opportunity. Arguably, without public backing, many of the new growth industries we are now seeing would not have arisen.[7] It is public reinvestment between the 1980s and 2008 that has revalued the 'stranded assets' of industrial cities and created new opportunities for enterprise. In fact, the recovery from industrial collapse outstripped expectations. Not only did the cities offer attractive environments, large, old buildings and houses, rivers and canals, public amenities and easily accessible, protected countryside – in others words 'residential appeal' – they also offered scope to grow businesses and capacity to attract new enterprises. The seven cities gained several big name companies each as inward investors. This boosted civic pride, morale and confidence. It also generated ancillary activity – even more small companies.

An extreme example of the need for public investment is Liverpool, a city that lost nearly half its population through a combination of a splurge of publicly funded outer building in the 1960s and 1970s, the collapse of the gigantic docks, the loss of its major associated industries, sugar and food processing, decline in most forms of manufacturing, and a recklessly overgrown public sector, determined to clear existing property and rebuild. This desperate basis for recovery led to Liverpool becoming a perfect illustration of the 'shrinking cities' theory – the idea that old, industrial cities enter an inevitable period of decline which needs to be managed – often referred to as 'managed decline'.[8] And yet as Phase Three begins, Liverpool shows signs of recovery, through public investment attracting private enterprise.

Box 6.2: Liverpool's dramatic public–private turnaround

Liverpool is an extreme example of industrial collapse, illustrating how public investment levered in private resources. In 1981, in the very depths of recession with large scale industrial closures followed by the early, brutal Thatcher cuts, serious riots broke out in the city and the council was taken over by extremist militants.[9] Thatcher appointed one of her toughest henchmen, Michael Heseltine, as Minister for Merseyside. He took private sector leaders, bankers, developers, industrialists, commercial bosses in a large luxury bus around the decayed but still majestic city centre and the riot-torn inner areas of Liverpool. He showed them the disused historic buildings, empty docks, abandoned sites, Georgian sea captains' homes, presenting 'mouth-watering' opportunities for almost free.

The city's population had fallen from 857,000 before the Second World War to 442,000 in 2001. The business answer was then uniform: 'We left this because it was broken. Without public sector investment, we cannot put it together again and make it work'.[10] Liverpool matched the US story of abandonment. In the words of a local urban expert, 'Liverpool is still on a life-support machine, not yet fit for intensive care'.[11]

Liverpool is 'off the stretcher' at last. After years of public investment, European Objective 1 funding, and multiple recovery initiatives, Liverpool, still one of Europe's poorest cities, is growing again.[12] Much of this rebound has happened since the 2008 crisis. Two of Liverpool's growing industries are creative arts and culture. It became the European capital of culture in 2008. It also became one of the first cities in England to gain an elected mayor. It has a strong and growing film industry because of its legacy of listed historic buildings. There is the prospect of rich sources of tidal energy in the Mersey; the city attracted major investment from Grosvenor, one of the biggest property companies in the UK, owned by the Duke of Westminster, turning the city centre into a powerful magnet. The basic, public infrastructure is working, the population is growing and recovery seems possible.[13]

Breakaway structures

In the recovery period, public bodies had the resources to invest, thanks to government backing, pooled revenues and a pro-recovery orientation between business, civic institutions, local government, public–private agencies and citizens. Partnerships across the full spectrum of city life became an obvious way to strengthen weak market cities – a role that eluded strictly private sector leaders. This partnership approach encourages citizen involvement, social enterprises and is entrepreneurial in itself. It helps cities escape an over-scaled and now fast vanishing past.

Even the giant mass housing estates reflect this. The estates still house large numbers of lower income residents, but now in a more broken up form. Many of the estates have combined selective demolition of some surplus blocks, upgrading of remaining blocks, creation of community enterprises, injection of private housing in the gaps left by demolition and high quality conversion of the blocks themselves. The conversion of ground floor spaces into small private shops and businesses has added a new dynamic mix and new job opportunities to residents. Park Hill flats in the centre of Sheffield, Monreynoud in Saint-Étienne, and Grunau in Leipzig have become much less monolithic, separate and uniform; more diverse and attractive.

This symbiotic relationship between public and private sectors is reflected in Boeing setting up its research headquarters in Sheffield, BMW building its new factory in Leipzig, Casino, the French supermarket chain, moving its head office and many back-up services to Saint-Étienne. None of these 'lighthouse' companies create a fraction of the jobs that have been lost, but their success depends on many of the smaller companies that now proliferate. New industry indirectly creates many new jobs. According to studies in Europe and the US, around five ancillary jobs can result from the specialist jobs we are describing.[14] This broadly matches the experience of Sheffield, Lille, Saint-Étienne and Torino. Public backing plays a crucial role in all these developments. Many private enterprises – engineering, construction, law, finance, materials, supply chains, trade – flourished over the recovery period under the shield of public sponsored partnerships, receiving publicly funded contracts, carried out by private contractors. Public underpinning offered many investment opportunities as cities rebuilt. This brought private firms in where otherwise they would have stayed away, for example, Nationwide moving to Sheffield and Halifax (now part of Lloyds) moving to Belfast, or Grosvenor investing heavily in Liverpool. Figure 6.2 shows the rapid growth in jobs in all seven cities over the whole period to 2014, in spite of significant continuing loss of manufacturing jobs, and a decline in some sectors and cities following 2008.

Figure 6.2: Changes in employment sectors, 1994–2014

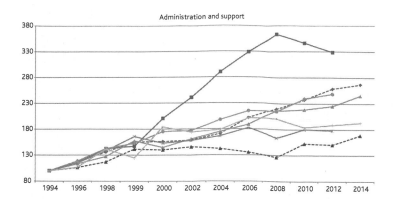

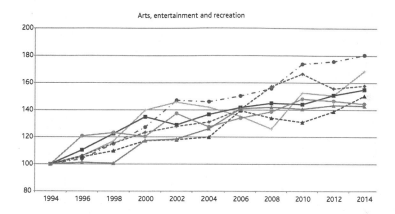

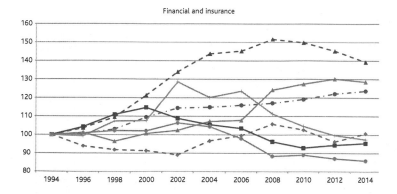

Cities for a small continent

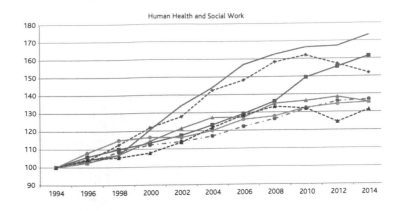

Human Health and Social Work

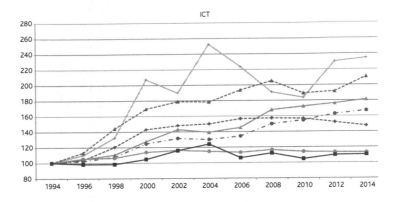

ICT

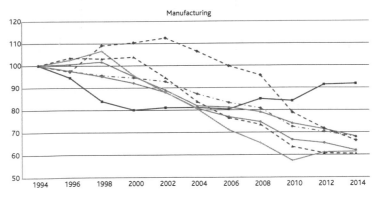

Manufacturing

Over-scale and under-scale

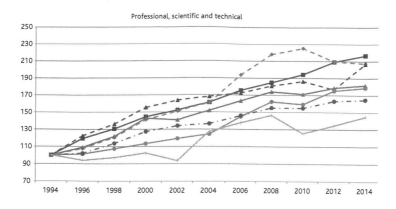

Professional, scientific and technical

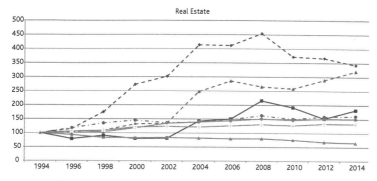

Real Estate

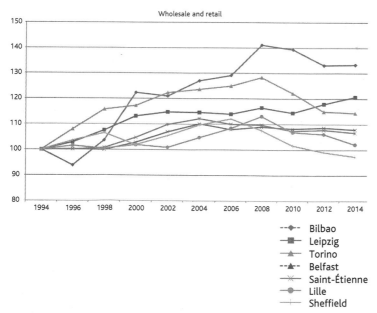

Wholesale and retail

- --◆-- Bilbao
- --■-- Leipzig
- --▲-- Torino
- --▲-- Belfast
- --✕-- Saint-Étienne
- --●-- Lille
- --+-- Sheffield

Source: LSE Cities Global Metro Monitor
http://labs.lsecities.net/eumm/m metromonitor#3/43.58/3.74

Phase Three is starkly different

Chapter Five showed how the carefully woven tapestry of recovery was put under intense pressure by the international banking crisis of 2008. European cities that were heavily indebted suddenly faced insolvency. This restrained further borrowing and affected enterprises in the cities, particularly smaller businesses where risks are greater. It particularly affected the public financial underpinning on which city recovery was built. The funding tap was turned off – or so it seemed at first. Far wider pressures within the European Union and beyond hit national and local economies.

As public investment fell steeply, so did spin-off activity in the private sector, also struggling with over-indebtedness, credit limits, demand shrinkage, reduced profits and therefore job losses. Unemployment rates, which had fallen to near or below national levels during the recovery, now doubled again, to far above. The loss of public funds and structures, a disarrayed and threatened private sector, a realisation that resource limits were real made Phase Three of our model, the resource-constrained economy, inevitable[15] In this new phase, our cities lost some public–private partnerships that had spurred their recovery. The entrepreneurial approaches that had worked through them were threatened by lack of resources, loss of capacity and talent as job cuts took their toll. Some of the brightest sparks left local government and the hard-hit cities for good.

Reuse of infrastructure and rebirth of industry

While prospects were looking gloomy, the cities' industrial identity re-emerged as an unexpected plus. In practice it had far from disappeared, albeit it had shrunk massively as industrial buildings became industrial incubators, like the old disused machine-making factory in the working class suburb of Bilbao, Barakaldo, turned micro-business centre.[16] Small new engineering and technical start-ups were offered not just space but also advice, business knowhow and ideas-pooling. It is impressive to visit the stark, oversized emblems of industrial history converted to new activity hubs. The Jahrhunderthalle (Hundred Year Hall in Bochum), in the Ruhr, is one of the most original. Its preservation reminds us that "we were poisoning our planet", in the words of a local planner.[17]

Box 6.3: Jahrhunderthalle in the Ruhr

In the heart of the industrial Ruhr stands a massive factory, with giant machinery and gas pipes big enough for a man to walk through running overhead into the factory on huge pylons, and massive, ugly, metallic structures, supported by giant iron girders. Rusting machinery is stacked inside, built on a scale that is almost unimaginable. The factory no longer pumps toxic gases and effluents into the surrounding land and water systems, but its rusting carcass remains a relic of a time of immense wealth creation and destruction. The workers are gone, the machines are silent and in its place, the unending 'factory floor' has become a venue for concerts and major events. People now pour into this industrial relic-cum-monument, drawn by the bar, reception, staff, facilities, music, dwarfed as they are by the iron girders, gas pipes and over-sized disused machines.

These reminders of the 'producer city' signify more than at first appears. In 2000 the city of Sheffield planned a science park, to link the strengths of its technical and engineering-based universities with private companies keen to develop advanced manufacturing, a clear development from the specialist skills of heavy industry. The city council was the broker.

Advanced manufacture requires high-level engineering and design skills, advanced materials that are super-light and incredibly strong, advanced technology of every kind, with other quality features that far outpace traditional materials or methods. Advanced manufacture requires extreme precision in the design process, production, assembly and highly skilled workers. Most modern equipment, technology, construction, consumer goods, and even 'non-material' sectors like banking rely on it. Advanced manufacture is used in computer technology, advanced lighting, heating and cooling systems, and virtually all sectors of the modern economy, particularly health and digital technologies, but also in almost every other branch of manufacture from lift-making and glass, to textiles, coffee pots and outdoor equipment, spare body parts and dental fixtures, food processing and logistics.[18] For these reasons, Sheffield's Advanced Manufacturing Park is a world leader today.

European cities win back industry

Manufacturing is now growing again in many parts of formerly industrial Europe. The transport and logistics costs, uncertainties and quality control problems of importing goods from afar are beginning to offset the value of cheap labour in countries like China and India. The environmental damage that over-scaled industry is now causing in the fast developing countries carries huge risks of precipitating climate change beyond danger.[19] Yet much of the demand for their cheap production comes from European cities, and Europe is called to account for this indirect pollution it causes.

The costs to China in environmental damage, pollution, labour difficulties, housing, infrastructure and shipping all push up the real costs of previously dirt-cheap production, making some European goods more competitive. Although other, lower-value Asian economies like Bangladesh, the Philippines and Vietnam are filling some of the gaps, similar limitations are emerging there. Space limits and environmental costs are mounting in these countries too, just as they did here, but more rapidly, and China already has many declining former industrial cities.

Strengthening Europe's industrial base starts from the demands for precision engineering; the high value attached to advanced manufacture, design and production methods; the greater ease of communication within the single common market; shorter turnaround; and above all the value of proximity. Thus several former industrial regions of the UK, including the West Midlands, Wales, the North East, Northern Ireland, Glasgow and South Yorkshire, where Sheffield is regional centre, have seen a significant regrowth in manufacturing jobs since 2011.[20] Sheffield and South Yorkshire have seen the strongest manufacturing growth in the UK, but other industrial areas are showing green shoots too, as Box 6.4 illustrates.

Box 6.4: Green shoots in industrial areas

Stoke on Trent

The 'Potteries' comprise a string of towns with Stoke on Trent as the main city where Royal Dalton, Wedgewood, Denbyware and other world famous makers of china and pottery operate. Royal Dalton won back the contract to make specially designed bowls and mugs for Disneyland Paris from a Chinese firm, because Disney found that Stoke-made pottery lasted ten times longer without chipping or cracking, compared with China's product. Quality, strength, design, production, communication were all sufficiently strong to make this shift back work. There are now other examples of the Potteries, almost dead 20 years ago, restoking their kilns and firing pots again.[21]

Bradford

Industrial rebirth is often happening on a small and highly specialist scale. Recent efforts to revive the production of worsted wool, a textile process specific to Bradford and West Yorkshire shows this. Worsted wool uses specialised local skills, looms and fine woollen thread; but they had all but disappeared. Because of the strength, lightness, durability and warmth of the cloth, it is in demand and is being revived on a small scale, using the disappearing skills of the surviving loom operators and restored machines in the struggling city of Bradford.[22] It may prosper and expand, as handwoven Harris Tweed is now doing in the Outer Hebrides. Bolton, a Lancashire textile town in Greater Manchester, is also producing textiles again among its Asian population.

South Wales

A local industry in a former mining area has been developed by Rockwool, a Danish insulation company and large international producer of external and internal cladding for buildings. Based in a South Wales coal mining valley near Newport, the Rockwool factory 'spins' local rock into fine threads or wool, giving the insulation its name. The company trains local unemployed youth in applying the insulation material to old and new buildings and runs special retrofit courses. Rockwool is used as energy saving cladding in the retrofitting of concrete high rise estates.[23]

The circular economy

One important and very different area of manufacturing return is the growth in reprocessing and conversion of used assets, often building on earlier industry. Ship-breaking seems a deadly activity when the rust-encased hulks are towed into former shipbuilding docks like giant, dark shadows reminding cities like Belfast and Newcastle of their former glories. However, the wealth of steel, copper and other precious materials within that hulk are both valuable themselves and vital for the new 'circular economy'. This is a simple idea that extracts new value out of waste, as an alternative to dumping it expensively in the environment. There are many examples:

- new building techniques that create close to zero waste from a standard of one third of materials thrown away;
- methane capture from landfill for energy use in which form it is far less environmentally damaging;
- capturing energy from brakes on vehicles and turning it into electricity, as happens with hybrid buses and cars;

- using waste to convert it into electricity and heat, such as feeding over half the city of Torino with power and heat and heating most of Sheffield's city centre.

Figure 6.3: Sustainable economy

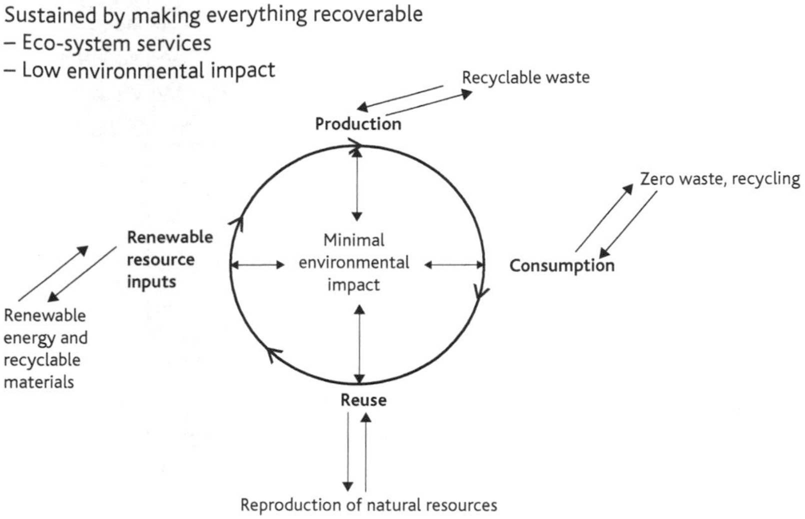

Sustained by making everything recoverable
– Eco-system services
– Low environmental impact

Although some of these methods are far from perfect, they are far less damaging than what they replace.[24] Figure 6.3 shows the way a zero waste, 100% renewable economy works.

Using the technology, infrastructure and sometimes machinery that was developed to make engines – for cars, buses, trains, ships – it has become possible to develop turbines for energy generation from wind and sea. Sheffield, Belfast and Torino are three cities where this is happening. Bremen University hosts the European wind energy research centre. In the case of Sheffield, it is the historic specialist skill in blade making, precision engineering and high grade steel that attracted Siemens to invest in a wind research centre in the city's university. Powerful, ultra-strong blades are vital to wind energy.

Adapting gasification methods, used in coal, it is now possible to create biogas from many forms of organic waste. Methane, a seriously dangerous and intense greenhouse gas that arises from rotting waste, many times worse than CO_2, escapes in large quantities from landfill sites. Belfast is now developing a new renewable energy source from its largest and now sealed North Foreshore landfill site to produce burnable methane, in which form its most harmful environmental effects are neutralised. For Northern Ireland, with very few ready sources of energy, the methane 'renewables' industry is a huge bonus.[25]

New technology and the shift to green growth

The environmental challenges of ex-industrial cities brought 'green growth' to the fore, helped by the economic and social drive to create new jobs, find new markets and do more with less. Five concrete areas of expansion in the 'green economy' are: energy generation and energy saving; water conservation; more environmentally friendly ways to re-activate brownfield sites; building conservation and new construction methods; and infrastructure to support a low carbon, low impact economy.

In response to the need to save water and prevent expensive, energy intensive leakage and waste, a small engineering and design company in Sheffield has devised new technology and instruments to measure, locate and avert water leakages, saving potentially thousands of tonnes of carbon a year. Unknown to most of us, and largely out of sight, water collection, purifying and pumping uses considerable carbon-based energy in the process. What is worse, up to 40% of this purified, energy intensive water leaks away from faulty pipes.[26] Even more is wasted simply by running a tap in an uncontrolled way.

Bilbao has developed a highly successful business park at Zamudio on the edge of the city, concentrating heavily on environmental enterprises. It is now crowded with successful green enterprises. Torino set up a similar environmental business park. It is now just breaking even, though it is yet to galvanise a critical mass of new green enterprises, which Zamudio is doing. Many forms of advanced manufacture are in practice light on materials and energy because there are powerful drivers in that direction.[27]

In the energy conservation field, new inventions are too numerous to list. For example, more efficient and more environmentally friendly battery storage would not only save energy loss and the leakage of highly toxic substances used in batteries but, as important, would help to crack the problem of intermittent renewable energy – there is too much energy when the sun shines or the wind blows; too little when it is still or cloudy. The European Union has sponsored research on improved battery storage to overcome the waste and pollution problems of current batteries. An engineering company in Sheffield has broken through in the design of batteries for electric cars which will reduce the cost, increase storage, reduce leakage and help make electric vehicles more accessible and reliable.[28] Giant-scale flasks to store the heat captured by concentrated solar reflectors, as an alternative to batteries, are still being developed.

There have been several breakthroughs. The discovery of graphene at Manchester University offers the possibility of a more lasting breakthrough. There is now an impressive National Graphene Institute at the university and researchers there have recently shown how graphene, often called the miracle material, can greatly increase the capacity to recover heat losses, and therefore energy losses, over a wide range of energy intensive industrial processes, as well as medical and building processes. Graphene, a super-fine, super-strong material of nano-dimensions so fine that it is described as a 2D material, offers myriad possibilities in new technology, renewable energy and other advanced manufacturing fields. Discovered by Nobel prize-winning Russian scientists, who came to the University of Manchester for research, graphene is one of these rare breakthroughs that results from multiple experiments. The British government and European Union are now investing in specialist graphene research to help turn graphene into an energy saving, wonder of multiple applications.[29] Most of these more advanced energy saving technologies are in their infancy, but they offer real promise.[30]

New ideas are constantly being tested on a small scale, with potential to magnify them many times into mass production. Sheffield's Proving Factory is an industrial resource base for testing prototype ideas, machines, inventions and specialist small scale production to the point where they can be manufactured at a larger scale with lower costs. The Proving Factory is essential to the new advanced breakthroughs manufacturing needs to become commercially competitive, since small scale innovators and inventors of new technologies do not have the resources to prove their value at scale. Until they are produced at scale, the unit cost will remain high. So the Proving Factory is a largely public investment in enterprise development used, for example, for testing energy saving vehicles.

Brownfield reclamation often involves releasing toxic waste, impregnated in the soil and the water systems, unless it is purified in an environmentally friendly way, as opposed to simply sealing sites over or digging out contaminated soils and materials and dumping them elsewhere as commonly happens. Saint-Étienne is pioneering work on environmentally friendly clean-up of polluted land with a cluster of small enterprises. It is possible to reuse almost everything on an abandoned site if enough care is taken. This includes soil, industrial buildings and materials, pipes, foundations, left-behind machinery, access roads, associated housing and other services.

It is also possible to at least halve future energy use, for example in heating or materials treatment, using known and tested techniques. If renewable energy is used, alongside energy saving measures, then it is possible to reduce energy use by at least 30% by 2020 – a goal the European Union has proposed.[31] More energy efficient, resource-limited, waste-reducing activity requires higher labour inputs. But the cost of labour is falling relative to the value of land and other material resources, which are becoming scarcer over time. From 2008, the value equation begins to tip in favour of labour intensification. Labour is a resource which industrial cities currently have in surplus. The rapid growth in services as ancillaries to the new industries in these cities take up some of that surplus, in back-up jobs in recycling and environmental care.

Back-up jobs do not show up strongly in gross value added, but they do show up in longer-term sustainability, a different and generally unmeasured increase in value. The process of reclamation has great value in cities with land and existing infrastructure. People relocate to Saint-Étienne from nearby Lyon, as it is cheaper and there is more space for the same money. This in turn generates services in Saint-Étienne. The same is true of Sheffield, from London and Leeds; or Lille from Paris and even London! In spite of some regrowth in jobs, economic inactivity and youth unemployment remain big challenges. The 'green', energy saving economy has not yet gone nearly far enough.[32]

Applying old skills to new

Universities have driven the research, development and new skills that fuel regrowth in our cities. Advanced research requires large funding, involving both government and private sector. Large companies often commission university research, using their large institutional infrastructure, research tradition and declared independence of commercial or political bias, to test ideas. Many industrial city universities – Sheffield, Belfast, Torino, Lille and Bilbao – grew as a form of support to industrial growth. General Motors sponsors auto and train engine research in Torino. In Bilbao, an extraordinary alliance has been forged between the University of Mondragon, the founding centre of the large industrial cooperative cluster outside Bilbao, the city of Bilbao and local enterprises, to develop a four-year 'Learning by Doing' degree course, in which students spend four undergraduate years learning how to set up a cooperative enterprise as a going concern. The degree course uses avant-garde study methods, borrowed from Finland. The key measurable output of their four years' study and practice is establishing a new, cooperatively owned and run business as a going concern.[33]

Advanced manufacturing is highly specialist, requiring extremely well-qualified people, in order to deliver goods that are extremely costly to produce and require a very different set of skills from traditional metal bashing. The existing workforces of our cities are often underqualified and the adaptation needed does not come readily. The Politecnico di Torino has laid on new courses to meet the demand for specialist skills; it has also developed highly successful 'incubators' and generated hundreds of new enterprises and jobs via its renowned research institutes and enterprise clusters, using advanced manufacturing techniques.

Sheffield is trialling an important innovation – a technical university college, offering post-16 courses for young people interested in developing more hands-on technical skills in STEM subjects (science, technology, engineering, maths) in order to work in the advanced industries. So far it is attracting strong take-up – as are Torino's engineering courses. Saint-Étienne, Leipzig, Lille, Bilbao, Torino and Sheffield all run specialist design engineering courses that fuel the new economy.

Box 6.5: Torino's green design skills in action

An example of how this helps is Pininfarina in Torino, a small but world renowned highly successful design company using new design technology to pioneer an electric car-share system called Auto-Lib, trialled successfully in several Italian cities, exported to Paris in 2014 and planned for London. The design involves not just the electric car, with the built-in robustness that a large, public car-share system requires, but the technical simplicity, docking and charging stations, payment systems, repair and distribution networks that will make it work. It is high tech design, plus highly energy and space efficient, lower cost than car-owning, non-polluting within the city, and potentially 100% fuelled by renewable energy. The Pininfarina car-share, car-hire scheme hits every button – renewable energy (potential); very low emissions and no pollution; light weight; reducing traffic and congestion; reducing materials input; increasing sharing; saving resources.

It is not always clear how 'green' displaces 'grime'. However ex-industrial cities have learnt to their cost that the filth and waste of old industry is a killer – literally and figuratively. Green innovation is almost daily finding ways to change the equation. Progress in advanced manufacturing is pointing towards energy- and materials-light processes. There is a long way to go, but in Europe many factors are pushing in the same direction, and inventions on both sides of the Atlantic are pouring out of the Maker tradition. Making things free of pollution and other environmental damage opens up new opportunities for yet more invention and more making. There is a massive body of interest and skill bound up in ex-industrial cities that links their big anchor institutions, their historic big industries and their new small enterprises, as the following example shows.

Box 6.6: Norwegian fjords need Glasgow engineers

One extraordinary example of these connections comes from Glasgow, Scotland's severely declined industrial capital. The links between Norwegian fjord settlements and Glasgow are tenuous – on the one hand, an almost pristine and icy environment only polluted by the extravagant use of cheap, locally produced oil; on the other, Britain's former industrial giant and now its poorest city, with vast, obsolete dock areas, majestic city buildings and powerful design engineering traditions and institutions. A small unknown Glaswegian engineering firm called Star Renewable has won a breakthrough contract to design and build a water source heat pump to extract heat from the freezing waters of a fjord, 40 miles from Oslo, enough to produce electricity and heat to power up to 100,000 homes and businesses in surrounding towns and villages – an unexpected triumph for an old industrial city, embittered by its loss of status and prowess, yet also buzzing with excitement at a new, more environmentally friendly dawn in the left-behind city. As the engineer from Glasgow said, "if you can do it here, you can do it anywhere". [34]

Craze for clusters

The loss of scale in industry – and now possibly in finance too – has generated considerable enthusiasm for clusters of enterprises, working in close proximity, in particular fields or specialisms. Local and national governments play a strong role in encouraging clusters, but in the end, they are highly dependent on private initiative to take up the opportunity. Instead of a giant company containing multiple specialist units, under one often unwieldy umbrella, many related enterprises are encouraged to form a cluster, often backed by a core service centre. There are many clusters in the seven cities, and each city has a strategy for developing clusters, some more ambitious than

Table 6.1: Economic clusters in the seven cities

Leipzig	Healthcare and biotechnology Logistics Media and creative arts Automotive supply chain – includes electric vehicles Energy and environment International fairs Rail transport
Lille	Advanced textiles/logistics/plastics Environment and green technologies (decarbonisation) ICT and advanced technologies Design engineering/new low carbon materials/health
Saint-Étienne	Design and engineering Advanced materials and manufacture ICT High performance textiles Medical technologies Optics Transport and logistics Digital and nano-electronics Ecological and green industries
Torino	Wireless, telecommunications, ICT Design engineering Environmental and green technologies Advanced scientific research and enterprise Creative and digital enterprise Aerospace Transport technology and engineering – electric and hydrogen Tourism and events Renewable energy
Bilbao	Biotechnology Construction Energy, including marine, wind renewables Environmental industries Maritime engineering Automobile Aerospace
Sheffield	Advanced manufacture and advanced materials Renewable energy Aerospace Digital and ICT Health and health technologies Sports and outdoors-related industries Technology and engineering
Belfast	Renewable energy and environment Tourism, hospitality Scientific, technical, engineering and ICT Health Construction Arts
Comments	Not all cities use the term 'cluster' All cities have groupings of specialist industries that play to their strengths and use traditional skills of related enterprises All cities foster networks, incubators, industry-linked research, SMEs Leading industries often form their own networks or 'clusters', grouping together and sharing facilities, experience All the cities have clusters of advanced engineering, designs

Source: City Visits, 2006-2015 and City Reports (2016)

others – Lille aims for nine; Leipzig, seven; Saint-Étienne, nine. The Advanced Manufacturing Park in Sheffield acts as a de-facto cluster of many smaller enterprises as does the Science Park in Belfast.

The dense concentration of skills, ideas and complementary enterprises, within minutes' reach of each other, creates a different kind of economy of scale from the less and less common giant factory, with its problems of routinisation, remoteness from control and highly segmented production systems. The economies of scale in clusters derive from the inter-relatedness of enterprises, and the common services they need and can share. It derives from the theory that work autonomy, working in small, specialist teams, generates a level of innovation and motivation that is highly creative. But it requires fluid, easy and frequent interaction at close proximity to work. In Europe, the idea of clusters became embedded in recovering cities at the point where reinvestment and reclamation was far enough advanced to make the cities attractive again to business. In all seven cities, clusters have grown since the mid-2000s. Table 6.1 shows the main cluster developments in the seven cities.

Box 6.7: Clusters work – Saint-Étienne

To illustrate how clusters emerge from industrial traditions, Saint-Étienne's optics cluster (2006) arose from Napoleon using Saint-Étienne's then super-advanced iron ore and coal industries to commission armaments for his expansive military adventures. The requirement for precision lenses to aim guns accurately meant that Saint-Étienne's engineers and designers became highly specialised in what is now known as optics, a field ranging from spectacles to cameras, from weapons to telescopes. The zoom camera lens, a revolution in photography, was invented in the city. To an outsider, the idea of creating an optics cluster, given the parlous state of Saint-Étienne's economy and its tradition of heavy industry, seemed a big leap and an almost random choice. Yet within a few years, the optics cluster based near the closed-down and restored Imperial Arms Factory is full with dozens of optics-related enterprises.

Saint-Étienne also has an environmental cluster, as does Lille, both acting to develop ideas and support small companies, often start-ups, pioneering ways of combining advanced manufacture with super-lightweight materials, low energy and minimal environmental damage. The work in Saint-Étienne on environmentally friendly methods of decontaminating land is extremely important in this.[35]

In the United States a similar model of cluster development has emerged under the title of innovation districts – a very close parallel with the Advanced Manufacturing Park in Sheffield, or the Science Park in Belfast. In both these cities, the local government, universities and private companies combine to provide space, support, infrastructure, start-up funds, access, advice, specialist skills, research – all made easier by the clustering on one site of different enterprises, interests, scales of operation and experience. Sheffield has become an international pacemaker for advanced manufacturing, thanks in large part to the success of the innovations in advanced manufacture. The University of Sheffield's decision to establish an Advanced Manufacturing Research Centre was far-sighted in laying the ground for the development and rapid take-off of the Advanced Manufacturing Park. Likewise there are high hopes that Belfast's Science Park in the old docks will become a world leader in both offshore wind and marine energy, both of which it is pioneering. Sheffield has recently decided to call its gathering strength in multiple forms of advanced manufacture, all clustered in the now quite crowded Advanced Manufacturing Park, an 'innovation district' – the first in Europe. In all but name, it was there already![36]

Small and medium enterprises

One of the biggest shifts in thinking following the financial crisis is the recognition that small and medium enterprises (SMEs) play a critical role, and always have done, in the economy of cities – they are the breakaway innovators, the start-ups, the inventors and discoverers that built the first industrial revolution, and just as surely they are building the third. They cannot be programmed or planned, as by their very nature, they grow out of experience, intuition, trial and error, learning by doing. The famous 1980s handbook for business, *In Search of Excellence*, showed how huge industrial giants like Honda, IBM and Procter & Gamble started in sheds and backyard experiments.[37] This is how many SMEs emerge.

Jane Jacobs, in *The Economy of Cities*, explains how success in cities, whether public or private, leads to over-growth and over-scaled structures, which in turn stifle innovation and stymie further growth. 'Breakaways' led by independent-minded entrepreneurs at this point literally break away from the larger structure, whether private or public, and form new, small, lithe enterprises. Many SMEs emerge as 'breakaways' but need 'fostering'. Incubators encourage bright ideas and give space for innovation to young entrepreneurs, often linked to university-led research, where enterprise incubators are often the offshoots of major research and training programmes. It also happens in much more marginal areas of cities, for example large social housing estates, where social enterprises can take off. Chapter Seven explores this. Strength in former industrial cities can come from any or all of these different routes.

SMEs are the backbone of private enterprise, but they are so numerous, so diverse in size and function, that they are hard for cities to 'get a handle on', or to sort into any kind of orderly structure. This seeming disorder does not fit with the bureaucratic methods or political cycles of local government – hence the belated and somewhat reluctant recognition of their critical contribution. However, as the 2008 crash and recession bit deeper into the economy of cities, it became clear that SMEs offered hope of more modest and in practice more manageable ways forward. They had many essential characteristics of the new order – small and hands-on; varied and adaptable, covering production, services and business. They ranged from shops to small factories; from social to private businesses; from high tech to modestly simple enterprises; from repair and restoration to making new; from micro start-ups to larger established firms.

A large majority of SMEs are extremely small with under ten employees. These micro-businesses, while often filling useful gaps, face many barriers to growth. They do not take big capital risks, and often lack the capacity or resources to take on young apprentices or graduate trainees. In the new climate of austerity and credit shortage, it is difficult for SMEs to borrow to invest. As a result they often have poor access to new markets; they are not necessarily up-to-date in information technology; they lack the capacity to reach out internationally; and they often do not have the resources for research, new machines and so on. Hampered by all these limitations, SMEs often punch below their weight. Some European countries impose additional charges, taxes and employer costs on SMEs when their workforces rise above 50 or another given limit. This can have a limiting effect on economic development and prevent job growth, which these cities desperately need. Spain, France and Italy impose financial burdens on SMEs as they expand that deter growth; a very high proportion of their enterprises have less than 50 employees. In Spain, the average number of employees is five.[38]

The German Mittelstand, medium-sized family firms, are a celebrated exception to the problems besetting SMEs. They are a vital part of Germany's manufacturing and major contributors to its success: specialist, skilled, experienced, productive; benefiting from stable management and ownership, recognition, access to investment, training and linkages. Family ownership is one of their hallmarks, giving a long-term investment interest. It is a model that is greatly envied in the UK as well as other countries.[39]

All the cities in our study have recognised the need for a strong, clear support framework for SMEs – to provide business advice; to facilitate audit; to provide key services such as IT support, marketing, international links; to offer training and apprenticeships; to inject graduate skills. Groupings of SMEs, as with clusters more generally, can help each other. There are significant networks developing. This mirrors the pattern of network development in US cities with their innovation districts.[40] Cities have set up enterprise hubs, converting large industrial buildings into digital hubs, such as Euratechnologies in Lille, based in a series of large former textile mills. An IT/digital cluster of high value with internationally recognised names offers single desk spaces and small cubicles to sole-operating entrepreneurs. The desks can be hired by the hour or occupied more regularly. These hubs are part incubator, part start-up space, part seedbeds for new ideas, part host to bigger names. Of course, the bigger names bring prestige and validity, but it is the SMEs that provide most of the new business and many of the new jobs.

Underpinning breakthroughs, as in the Advanced Manufacturing Park in Sheffield, is the provision of space for small enterprises, newer companies, receiving business support that they cannot afford one by one. Mondragon, near Bilbao, has around 140 mainly SMEs, all clustered around the headquarters of the Mondragon Cooperative Corporation, within walking distance of each other and the Caja Laboral, which offers business advice as part of its business loan scheme. The SMEs gain strength from the business support, training and exchange of skills that the umbrella cooperative group offers.

There are initiatives to build stronger skills and exchange networks, to encourage apprenticeship schemes and to part-fund graduate trainees to help expand the jobs and opportunities, bring in fresh blood and put more of the micro-SMEs on a growth path. By combining back-up to SMEs in several ways, it is possible to facilitate credit on borrowable terms to allow for expansion. It is a form of cooperation that offers real gains to individual members. This important sector is growing in the new post-crisis world, helped by its very diversity and extensive reach, and it is likely to keep growing. Since the cities are trialling new ideas constantly, the space for innovative start-ups is wide and populated by micro-enterprises that have the potential to become significant players in the new world of resource constraints. Their very modesty and leanness suggests the way of the future.

Outward focus

The umbrella structures help to foster international links. The seven cities long since became outwardly focused – as big national and international players in the industrial era. They also exported goods and imported materials on a vast scale. Leipzig, Lille and Torino grew and flourished because of their location on international routes and their trading advantage, still helping today. As major industries withdrew, so the outward-facing links weakened, although small, specialist suppliers often continued to trade externally. For example, an autoparts maker in a back alley in the old inner area of Saint-Étienne, a hands-on engineer, was producing specialist components for Peugeot engines in Northern France. Likewise specialist small engineering producers in Torino were linked to southern German car manufacturers. Lille, Sheffield and Leipzig have small specialist health-related manufacturers, producing plastic body parts for hospitals in different parts of Europe. Sheffield also produces ultra-fine blades for every kind of machinery including highly specialised medical uses.

One task the cluster support services have taken on is to foster international links. The cities of Bilbao and Torino even set up whole departments within the city councils to strengthen their international focus during the long period of austerity. Bilbao has a small team of dedicated staff within the council with the sole function of hosting groups of international visitors and promoting Bilbao's name and products. The Swedes come to learn about architectural design and urban planning; the Chinese to visit regenerated port areas and so on. These international visits allow Bilbao to put its stamp on everything made in the city and be sure it will be recognised internationally. Bilbao's constant stream of official foreign visitors come to learn about almost every aspect of city activity, from neighbourhood renewal, to port expansion, the Guggenheim to cooperatives. Sheffield likewise hosts international exchanges, connected to its Advanced Manufacturing Park.

Leipzig's history as an ancient centre for trade, interchange and university learning is turning it into an international gathering point for alternative green and progressive social movements and organisations. The design exhibition of Saint-Étienne attracts not only international visitors but promotes Saint-Étienne's specialisms in design engineering on an international stage. Torino's Slow Food movement attracts large international visitor numbers for its annual festival of food, and also for its newer international producer organisations network, Terra Madre (Mother Earth).[41]

The potential to internationalise more widely is built on by the cities to strengthen and grow their productive businesses, their revenue and therefore their jobs. Distances are small, compared with the US, and the many specialisms within cities are invaluable across the continent. Extensive international rail and waterway links make exchange easier than language and cultural differences suggest. International exchange encourages new ideas and approaches; it generates networks of trust and familiarity that facilitate further growth. This works both ways and major international companies, like Siemens, find investment in our cities both productive and valuable. Big international organisations, including industry, are important to manufacturing cities because they help foster international links, and internationalise the productive activities of cities.

Certain fields of activity and production are more internationally marketable – most forms of advanced manufacture and advanced materials, because of their novel and specialist nature; new technologies, which are changing and evolving fast, are likewise sought after everywhere and invite exchange of learning – particularly in university and research-related activity. In fact universities are often at the forefront of international links, hosting networks of many kinds – urban development, engineering, new technology, green innovation, even language study itself. The role of the European Union in building city networks, research exchanges, and cross-border investment in former industrial regions is one of the keys to rapid development of international exchange within Europe. Every city we visit forms part of some European programme. It is extraordinary that Europeans get by and progress on this confused medley of learning and exchange, but they thrive on it. Europeans are becoming more polyglot, and English is fast becoming the lingua franca of international meetings, specialist university courses and major companies.

Makers and Fab Labs

The Europe-wide focus is partly driven by the development of the European Union, the close historic and current ties between European countries, and the potential for new areas of growth in manufacturing. Many important new ideas are imported from the US and then spread like wildfire around Europe. Two related examples that match the growth mood of our cities are the Maker Movement and Fab Labs. Both are offshoots of university-led research in high tech engineering in US research universities, originating in the Massachusetts Institute of Technology (MIT).[42] The Maker Movement began with the idea of providing workshop space for people to put ideas of things they wanted to make into practise with ready, high tech equipment, learning how to use advanced digital design to make specialist designed objects.

The Maker Movement does not yet have a strongly commercial focus – it is more an experiment in design, production and application – giving people, mainly men, already in jobs, the chance to try out new ideas with new equipment using new materials hands-on. The Maker Movement attempts to reignite interest in making things. Fab Labs are a related experiment, often hosted by cities to encourage bright inventors to try things out, using a well-equipped and free space to do so. Fab Labs offer a mini factory environment with machines, advanced electronics, and a pool of walk-in inventors. Neither of these organisational forms was heard of in ex-industrial cities until the recession hit. Suddenly a Maker Movement developed in a regeneration area in the old port area of Bilbao in an abandoned warehouse.[43] Fab Labs have been formed in Torino, Lille and Saint-Étienne (linked to health) and in Belfast, part-funded by the Peace Fund. Sheffield is now developing a Fab Lab.

The core idea is to encourage engineering skills, galvanise the interest in making things, and demonstrate the powerful and ultra-modern link between computers, design, production, materials and machinery.[44] Technical skills are now the currency of these cities, and 'learning by doing' has become a kind of mantra. So they combine a new kind of education with a fun way of producing things, in the hope of matching consumer desires for more specialist products with real progress. There is a stronger than apparent link between the small scale activities of these seemingly 'declining' cities and the most avant-garde experiments in high-level, technical education and research in the most go-ahead centres of innovation in the US, such as MIT. The Maker Movement lies at the very hands-on end of advanced research and manufacture. According to the European coordinator of Fab Labs, neither Fab Labs nor the Maker Movement have yet become 'serious' about creating businesses and jobs.[45] Rather, they facilitate ideas and encourage experimentation in doing.

One recent development that has partly inspired them is the development of 3D printing. By this means, a computer can be programmed by the operator or Maker to design and 'print' an object. At the press of a button it will then print the designed object in three dimensions. A whole complex machine, such as a jet engine, can be built this way.[46] It means that it is becoming possible to custom design and produce usable, manufactured objects through the application of the highest technical skills and machinery.

Fab Labs will help transform the way things are made, so much so that the UK government has funded two bold experiments in Sheffield. The first is the Proving Factory, the prototype factory described above where innovative products, made by small producers, can be exhaustively tested to the point where they can be confidently taken up by mainstream producers. The other is the Fab Lab which Sheffield will open in a converted Cooperative store in the city centre to foster the kind of innovation and experiments we have described.

Fab Labs and Makers have a strong ethos of pooling and sharing ideas, in order to encourage faster growth in innovative making. In exchange for using the Labs, users must make their work available to the Lab. It seems likely that this new activity will lead to another round of innovations. Sooner or later links will be made between experiments, real needs, production and future jobs; between incubators and university-led research; SMEs and 3D manufacture; Fab Labs and green innovations. It is a whole new way of thinking about, fostering and supporting networks of creative companies.

Action dominates over strategies

Cities need to innovate across all sectors, private, public, social and civic. The focus on 'starting from where you are', getting on and doing things, hands-on making, rather than simply strategising and planning, now dominates city thinking. Activity that is entrepreneurial and skilled requires considerable confidence, motivation, knowhow and investment. So it is not for everyone. It does not do much for the large minority of urban workforces that are low skilled, lacking in confidence or up-to-date experience. However, the related back-up services that keep high tech enterprises going will offer many lower skill jobs – as used to happen within a large factory with its many sub-divisions or a city town hall.

Another hope is that low carbon industry, for example solar panels, requires many semi-skilled installers and maintainers, as do all energy saving technologies which will be crucial to the future of cities. The European Union estimates that 4 million jobs will be created from energy saving activity and a further 3 million in renewable energy.[47] There is no equivalent Maker Movement for low skilled but underemployed workers. On the other hand, in the last seven years, in France and the UK at least, there has been rapid growth in self-employment among exactly this group to carry out repair, small building works and other modest but essential activities, such as house cleaning, gardening and child care. If an equivalent movement for low tech and basic jobs was formed, then it could even help the Maker and Fab Lab movements flourish in unexpected ways.

In contrast, high unemployment and a desperate search for jobs has driven some negative developments. For example, the region around Leipzig is exploring new contracts for open-cast coal mining. Spain is encouraging oil exploration in environmentally sensitive coastal areas. The UK is anxious to start fracking in the industrial north of England, in spite of intense local opposition.[48] This conundrum – a tension between immediate needs, an unsustainable but still locked-in energy system, and longer-term ambitions – is yet to be resolved. We return to this challenge in the final chapter.

A new, low carbon growth model

There is an emerging new model, which Nicholas Stern refers to as a 'new industrial revolution'. It combines high tech invention with low carbon, alternative energy and materials, and considerable human endeavour to save energy and adopt more sustainable growth patterns. Cities have to escape their earlier locked-in model of high inputs, high waste, falling profitability and potentially irreversible environmental damage, for a new model that relies on:

- vastly lower inputs of materials and energy;
- as near zero waste as possible;
- minimal environmental damage that must afterwards be fully reinstated;
- high value added; and
- alternative infrastructure.

Box 6.8 gives some examples of the new low carbon growth model, related to the seven cities.

Box 6.8: Low carbon illustrations

TORINO benefits from strong government backing for domestic solar PV (photovoltaics) – eminently logical in a sunny climate – and Italy is rapidly expanding its renewable energy supply. It has one of the fastest growing solar electricity supplies in Europe. The city also heavily subsidises building retrofit. The city has one of the most extensive, energy efficient district heating systems in Europe. District energy systems coupled with energy efficiency have potential to reduce urban energy use by 58%.[49]

FRANCE encourages building retrofit and domestic energy saving alongside renewables. LILLE and SAINT-ÉTIENNE have strong, action-oriented environmental strategies. Wind turbines are highly visible in the countryside around Lille. The whole region, Nord-Pas de Calais, has adopted an ambitious strategy to become 100% renewable over the next two decades.[50]

The UK has passed a path-breaking Climate Change Act, obliging the country, on a multi-party basis, to stick to ambitious energy saving targets. The application of this commitment is hampered by spending cuts, and Conservative Government ambiguity. However, the UK is the world's leading producer of offshore wind, with a lot more in the pipeline. SHEFFIELD hosts a wind energy research centre and powers its city centre on a combined heat-and-power system. BELFAST has a dense network of electric vehicle chargers and a growing demand for electric cars. It is also expanding its production of sea-based renewable energy – both land and tidal.

Photo 6.1: Belfast's innovative electric car infrastructure makes the city a European pacesetter in the conversion to low energy vehicles

GERMANY, having been caught in the 1970s by the problem of acid rain and poisoned river systems due to its post-war boom in heavy industry, has legislated in steadily incremental steps for 40 years, to save energy, curb pollution and shift to renewables. For German cities like LEIPZIG, the incentives are strong, clear and stable. Leipzig became one of the largest solar panel producers in Europe. Leipzig is also a leader in Passiv Haus retrofit with almost zero energy requirements.

On several days in 2014–15, Germany has met all its electricity needs from renewable sources.[51] It is also an innovator in electric cars.

SPAIN adopted policies strongly favourable to renewable energy of which it has a rich supply, mainly solar and wind, but abruptly cut subsidies when the banking crisis hit, thereby provoking some loss of momentum. Iberdrola, Spain's largest energy company, is based in **BILBAO**. It is also the biggest renewable energy investor, and has major renewable energy investments in Glasgow.[52]

Source: City visits, 2006–15

This energy-light model will only work with major commitments, many experiments and upfront investment. The scale of change required helps explain why cities cannot make the conversion to sustainable growth work alone. The shift to a low carbon economy requires clear international frameworks and a steady regime of favourable financial incentives from governments, for example, to support renewable energy and energy saving in transport. Otherwise, the new alternative growth model could stay small and experimental – under-scale for the immensity of the task. Cities can do a lot at the experimental scale as we have shown; they can also produce at a large scale with proven technologies. City governments can be the prime movers in fostering this change of direction.

Box 6.9: Electric vehicles in Belfast

An exciting example to illustrate this shift comes from Belfast where energy supply problems, congestion, population dispersal due to the Troubles, and pollution combine. Northern Ireland is now near the top of the EU league for electric vehicle charge points and no one in the whole province is more than 8 miles from one. Electric vehicles increase by 40 every month from a zero base three years ago. With major subsidies, zero tax and a 75% fall in running costs, electric vehicles are increasingly popular in the public and private sectors. Belfast is now in line to become an international exemplar,[53] supported by the city, the Northern Irish and UK governments and the European Union.

There is little doubt that a bigger national and international framework is essential to the process.[54] This is at last emerging. The European Union has passed ever-stronger, cross-country and binding legislation on energy saving, renewables, waste, water, building, retrofit, among other things. It part-funds and facilitates many of the new approaches needed such as large scale battery storage, trans-European grids, new energy technologies, and more prosaically the urban renewal and retrofit projects that save energy at city level.[55] National governments are part of this Europe-wide commitment to 20:20:20 – a 20% energy reduction, a 20% increase in renewable energy, both to be achieved by 2020.

Conclusions: overcoming the risk of under-scale

Seven Phoenix cities, the cities that we tracked over the last decade, teach us that action on problems can reverse decline and bring new ideas and activities to the fore. They reuse existing urban capacity, both people and place, for new purposes. These experiments in post-crisis recovery take European industrial cities towards a new urban model that restores value to existing built environments, develops new skills on the back of old industries, experiments with new, more broken up, smaller scale enterprise, and creates new leadership and vision from the weakened threads of earlier models. There are lessons to be learnt from one city to another; and there are common developments across the cities. There are also big uncertainties over the future. The over 300 cities that made up the European Union's original Urban Audit provide a big picture within which lessons from seven 'Phoenix' cities can be set. The seven cities are pushing hard along the path towards more resource-constrained, more experimental futures, with new enterprises springing up, most still at micro-scale to date, to advance that process.[56]

It is not clear whether multiple small actions will be enough to get us out of the grid-lock of environmental damage and create the new industrial economy that Nicholas Stern argues is vital. Our post-industrial cities show a common resilience in the face of intense pressures. For they not only reinvented themselves during their post-war boom, then following their post-oil collapse, during their post-industrial recovery. Their bounce-back from the financial crisis of 2008 is full of new models, patterns, ideas and products. This chapter suggests how the new post-2008 challenges are helping to create a new industrial revolution.

Phoenix cities are not fading or dying, nor have their fortunes unravelled, tough as the great recession of the last six years has been. But they are poorer than they were at the end of their recovery period in 2007; less publicly funded; more precarious and uncertain. This means considerable hardship for the large parts of their populations that are not yet fully integrated into the new and still fragile economy. Chapter Seven takes up this theme. The story of Leipzig help us understand how cities actually survive and re-invent themselves.

Box 6.10: Tale of a city – Leipzig

Leipzig is a surprising story. It is one of central Europe's ancient cities, capital of the former German kingdom of Saxony, long before Germany became a unified country in 1879, a decade after Italy. In the middle ages, Leipzig developed a powerful international trading role and founded one of Europe's oldest universities in 1409, over 600 years ago. The city grew into an artistic and musical centre. Johann Sebastian Bach lived there from 1723 and was organist at the Thomaskirche where the Bach choir still performs and an annual Bach festival takes place.

Leipzig's medieval trade fair and the somewhat later book fair became Europe's biggest trade gatherings. They made the city into a dynamic hub of the industrial revolution just as railways were spreading across Europe. This made Leipzig's central station the biggest railway intersection in Europe. Leipzig was also a pioneer of many social reforms, often growing out of industrial hardship – the movement for women, the labour movement and the German allotment movement were all founded in the city in the 1860s. The allotment movement aimed to help poor families, crowded in tiny flats, to get some fresh air and grow

Photo 6.2: *Nikolaikirche: "open to all". The church where "Monday demonstrations" began as peace prayers which helped triggered the fall of the Berlin Wall*

healthy food. The combination of social movement, transport hub, high culture and trade have carried the city through to today when it is becoming one of Eastern Germany's most conspicuous success stories.

Both World Wars shook Leipzig, and the Second World War completely changed its sense of direction – though far less of the city was bombed than neighbouring Dresden, which was all but flattened. After the war and the occupation by Russia of Eastern Germany, Germany was divided in two, West and East, with Saxony, Leipzig and Dresden becoming part of a new and separate post-war Communist country, the German Democratic Republic.

Under Communism, Leipzig was turned into a centre for heavy industry with one third of its workforce employed directly in manufacture. Open-cast mining around the city caused environmental scars so deep that the city has not yet fully recovered, and the workforce became heavily dependent on industry and coal for jobs.

The East German government, determined to outpace its Western counterparts, built new housing on the edge of Leipzig on an industrial scale. The biggest estates, such as Grunau in West Leipzig, with 35,000 homes, became more famous for their scale than their beauty! Grunau was relatively popular with its 100,000 residents. Many such estates were built in Eastern Germany under Communism using a factory system, common also across Western Europe, called Plattenbau, using huge, manufactured concrete slabs, slotting and bolting them together with steel frames, to create identical high rise blocks swiftly and cheaply.[57] This industrial building allowed the authoritarian regime to move people out of the decayed, dense, turn-of-the-century inner city blocks of Leipzig's industrial heyday into brand new modern apartments on the outskirts. The old inner blocks were extremely dilapidated and outdated, often lacking modern plumbing and relying on coal fires for warmth. They gradually emptied and fell into disrepair, in spite of their historic style and solid built structure. Inner Leipzig became a shadow of its former self.

A turning point in Leipzig's history came with the unique role it played in bringing down the Berlin Wall that had been built to prevent East German citizens from fleeing to the West. An extraordinary combination of the Lutheran church, the Nikolaikirche in the centre of Leipzig, the people of Leipzig, both religious and non-religious, Communist and non-Communist, young and old, moved from the weekly Peace Prayer services in the church, to demonstrations in the public square outside the church. These became the famous Monday Demonstrations that over several years gathered hundreds, then thousands of supporters demanding freedom and justice. Finally, when 70,000 peaceful protesters marched through the streets of central Leipzig following a Monday Peace Prayer meeting in October 1989, the East German government allowed the Berlin Wall to be breached. The following year, East and West Germany were reunified.[58]

Leipzig entered a new period of radical change.
- Its industrial base collapsed. Within six years of reunification in 1990, 90,000 industrial jobs had disappeared, as one unviable industry after another closed. This was 90% of all manufacturing jobs.
- Many residents, boosted by the generous currency conversion into West German Deutschmarks, moved west and the city's population began to plummet: 90,000 left the city in the years following reunification.
- Unemployment shot up to 24% of the population, higher than East Germany's high average.
- There were thousands of property claims under the agreement forged in 1990, allowing former owners of expropriated property in East Germany to claim them back. This put a question mark over future investment in inner city blocks and led to even higher levels of abandonment within the old city. Meanwhile, vacancies also grew steeply in the post-war estates.

The new city government believed that the blight of empty homes, which tripled between 1990 and 2000 to over a quarter of the stock could only be solved by planned demolition – leaving many bare sites and a growing opposition to 'eliminating Leipzig's architectural heritage'. Many ways of retaining buildings were invented in Leipzig, including the 'guardian house' system, which encouraged young people to move into extremely run-down property and keep 'guard' over it by living in it until it could be upgraded. That idea is now being copied in the UK.[59]

In the early years post-reunification, government funding encouraged people to build and buy new homes outside the city boundaries, in order to produce relief from the monotony and uniformity of Communist blocks of flats. However, this policy encouraged wasteful sprawl building that further emptied the city. The city adopted a compelling strategy of countering sprawl and redensifying the inner city through renovation schemes to attract young residents; restoring the historic city centre; expanding the university; encouraging creative activity and citizen involvement. It focused heavily on developing new economic opportunities and skills to match. This approach worked and by the mid-2000s, Leipzig was growing again and gaining jobs alongside population.

Leipzig's economic strategy was to develop five enterprise clusters which were fostered with the help of Federal German and European funds.

- The **car industry**, a real success story, attracted Porsche and BMW to build new factories in the city, producing their most advanced models, including BMW's avant-garde 100% electric car.
- **Health and bio-tech industries** are now the city's biggest employer, including research, advanced medical care, advanced design and manufacture of artificial body parts.
- **Energy efficiency and the environment** has a target of upgrading the housing stock, including concrete estates and also public buildings like schools, to high energy standards. Many industrial sites have been reclaimed, including the former open-cast coal mines, a devastated zone which has been cleaned up and turned into lakes and wooded areas; a haven for wildlife and walkers, cyclists, boaters and picnickers.
- **Logistics** involves the conversion of the old Leipzig-Halle airport into a 24 hour cargo hub, attracting Amazon, DHL, Lufthansa and others to base their major European distribution centres in Leipzig, creating 1000s of jobs; the central station has also been upgraded and a high speed rail link to Berlin opened up.
- **Culture and media** has led to many festivals, musical, artistic, cultural and alternative events.

Photo 6.3: Spinnerei cotton mill: former industrial site, now an enterprise centre initiated and run by Leipzig artisans and community organisations

These clusters succeeded in attracting private and public investment. However, among all the features of the new Leipzig that have heralded its success, the appeal of the city to a youthful, creative and alternative population may be the most significant. Leipzig's population, having plummeted by 90,000 between 1989 and 2000, has been growing steadily since then, currently by 10,000 new residents a year. Whole sections of inner Leipzig are now popular, with a great cafe culture, old buildings reclaimed and reused, and new enterprises starting up. The city managed to encourage, tolerate and make easy the reoccupation of city spaces by informal groups, new enterprises, artists, architects and other start-ups.

The Spinnerai, a large group of former textile mills in West Leipzig, displays all these signs of regrowth from the bottom up. The large solid brick buildings were secured and structurally strengthened by the city. After that, active citizen groups simply colonised the buildings with new enterprises, ranging from architecture, cycle repair shops, to community cafes. In 2006, the Spinnerai was a glimmer of self-help hope among Leipzig's progressive planners.[60] By 2014, it had become a hub for creative, activist, alternative groups, alongside a more settled population of artisans, professionals and do-it-yourself residents. It hosts exhibitions, sales, city events and multiple new enterprises. It is lovingly restored and managed on site through a very basic structure.

Photo 6.4: Traditional Schrebergärten (small urban allotment) close to city centre. The Schrebergärten movement began in Leipzig in the 19th century

The growth in population is putting a huge strain on housing, schools and other infrastructure as the city had shrunk so significantly. So social tensions are growing, as older residents feel squeezed, while younger, newer residents face a shortage rather than a surplus of space, leading to rent rises. Meanwhile, poorer neighbourhoods in East Leipzig struggle with how to absorb immigrants and how to link residents themselves to new job opportunities, very far from

Photo 6.5: Derelict former factory ripe for conversion in low income area, East Leipzig

Photo 6.6: Cycle and pedestrain pathway along Leipzig canal

the buzz of the creative, arty activity of more popular areas. There are burning issues of inequality, as in all the cities. However, Leipzig has a far lower youth unemployment level than other European cities, in spite of its catastrophic levels in the 1990s. The city has managed to keep youth unemployment low during the economic crisis through special government support for traineeships, apprenticeships and short-term jobs.

Leipzig has a long history of citizen involvement, most conspicuous in the Monday Demonstrations that were instrumental in bringing down the Iron Curtain and the Berlin Wall. The city has built on that tradition with a whole new citizen-based approach to tackling the biggest challenges – housing, jobs, energy, the environment, transport, and so on. The city council organises participative assemblies – called 'Thinking Ahead' – with the aim of literally pooling ideas from as many quarters as it can reach. On this basis, it hopes to hold on to Leipzig's special qualities and build on its success, once the dedicated post-reunification funds run out.

Photo 6.7: New Leipzig University building –
Germany's second oldest university

Photo 6.8: *Historic restored shopping arcade, central Leipzig*

Photo 6.9: *Main square, Leipzig*

The story of this ancient city that lived through 40 years of Communism and was devastated by population and job losses in its aftermath, then recovered to the point where growth outstrips its empty spaces, has to offer hope for Phoenix cities. There are five main lessons to draw from Leipzig's experience.

First, the strong and determined adoption of the Compact City Model involved reinstating the city centre, reinvesting in pre-First World War inner city blocks that had often been abandoned and neglected for decades. This attracted young people and families to live in the inner city rather than on the periphery. It led to expanding public transport, densifying activities and population, creating a vibrant, mixed-use, culturally alive city centre that became a magnet for incomers.

Second, the urban environment had to be decontaminated and former industrial land reclaimed. The bare land left by demolition of derelict housing was turned into small parks, sometimes temporarily. Investing in energy saving by retrofitting homes, schools and public buildings helped to restore and make the existing stock sustainable. A special school dedicated to Passiv Haus training for builders has been set up. The city responded to protests and demand by reducing the scale of demolition. Cycle ways, footpaths and pedestrian routes were developed to encourage people out of cars. Solar panel production and the generation of renewable energy, mainly solar PV, added to the city's 'green' success.

Third, inward investment was attracted on a large scale matching the five strategic economic clusters – cars, health, energy and environment, logistics, media and creativity – drawing to the city big name, 'lighthouse' companies, such as BMW, Porsche, Amazon, DHL; and generating significant jobs and local back-up services. The city set up local employment and skills agencies and 'Job Shops' to support the local population in accessing the new jobs that were being created.

Fourth, the city revalued and exploited its historic assets, using the city's traditional economic and artistic base to enhance its progress. The art school, the medieval trade fair, the historic university, the Bach church and choir, the vast transport interchange at Central Station, all helped pave the way to Leipzig's recovery and conversion into an attractive tourist and artistic destination.

Fifth, the post-reunification, citizen-based approach to planning the 'reborn' city, involved difficult and controversial decisions around demolition particularly. Open participation led to the curtailment of much demolition and a renewed focus on restoration of the historic, compact city centre. Strong, civic, local leadership played a big part in this turnaround. Community-level projects, particularly in more disadvantaged areas, built bridges between poorer citizens and the new economy. A listening approach to pressing city challenges encouraged city leaders to look for new ways forward. In this, the historic Monday Demonstrations in Leipzig that led to the collapse of Communism offered a model from recent history of participative transformation which the city has followed in the 25 years since those eventful days.

SEVEN

The power of social innovation

Concentrated wealth can limit economic performance. Under the right rules, shared prosperity and strong economic performance reinforce each other. There is no trade off.

Joseph E. Stiglitz, *Rewriting the Rules of the American Economy*

Box 7.1: Torino – a story

Arrival in Torino by train is spectacular – you either head towards the Alps from Milan, or you descend into Torino from a majestic climb over the snow-capped passes of Europe's highest mountain range.

Torino is super-dense, so trains, trams, buses, metro and now yellow city bikes are everywhere. There is another, even more collective side to the city. Very few people know or remember Torino's 'social saints' who, in the 19th century, rescued the destitute, children, women, youth and men, from the gutters and shacks of a filthy, impoverished city. Even fewer people recognise the universal contribution of labour unions, resident-led housing protests, and mutually owned, non-profit businesses to the rapid social development of Italy, post-Second World War.

Social enterprise must have been born in Torino. New social movements of the 21st century seem to flourish in a city of engineers, tourist traders and civic activists. Non-profit cooperatives, alternative community organisations, religious charities, bank foundations warm to the city's appeal for help to meet a crisis of homelessness. The proactive, civic-minded city of Torino partners with these non-profit organisations in a battery of projects to help the destitute. Social enterprises organise community learning, social events, vegetable planting, libraries, music sessions. They invite people needing their help to become volunteers in providing the services – a true mutual aid.

Don Bosco, a famous social reformer of the 19th century, developed the now international movement to help combat homelessness through shelters and children's refuges in his home city of Torino; today, Torino's social inventions are carried across the world – just as they were 150 years ago.

Introduction

The major transformations in many of Europe's cities led to their social fabric wearing thin in many places. Europe has seen sharp increases in inequality, joblessness, particularly among young people, hardship of all kinds and simple poverty. These harsh realities are felt very unevenly. Struggling cities, which never fully caught up with the boom years of the 2000s either in incomes or in overall prosperity, have suffered harsher impacts than average. In particular, they have lost more public funding than average because they were more dependent on the public purse before the crisis – for decontamination, regeneration, infrastructure, renewal, economic and social development.

Yet, as Chapter Six argued, in many ways, cities also show more resilience and adaptability than expected, partly because they are used to coping with crises, partly because of an embedded culture of enterprise, partly because their traditional assets proved more valuable than expected in a time of resource shortage. Land, buildings, public transport, universities are four examples of resources that became underused while becoming scarce elsewhere. Their people are also an underused resource and, in spite of skill mismatches, their large populations offer untapped potential.[1]

This chapter looks at how cities, as social as well as economic engines, are faring in this long and troubled period of rebuilding; and what is being done to make conditions in communities match the progress in enterprises under a regime of ongoing austerity and resource constraints.

The growth of marginal communities

In the different phases of city growth, one problem is constant: the large marginal populations left behind in the race for growth and in the scramble out of decline:

- In the industrial era, manufacturing and labouring populations experienced extreme hardship, exploitation, ill health and shorter lives.[2]
- By the time major industries left, conditions had massively improved for the majority of workers, but a new layer of marginalisation had been added with large scale immigration from poorer regions of the globe and the marginalisation of lower-skilled and unskilled workers within existing populations. Their conditions deteriorated fast as better off workers moved out, from overcrowded, decayed and sometimes hostile environments.[3]
- During the recovery period from the mid-1990s to 2008, major efforts were made to close the gap – in neighbourhood conditions, services, skills and jobs. These publicly backed efforts made a measurable difference, particularly in conditions, but they did not close the gap between poorer areas and the rest of the city, and they did not remove the serious barriers to accessing work and education on an equal footing.[4]
- When the big recession of 2008–14 hit, poorer communities were particularly vulnerable and lost out heavily, in employment, housing and even cash for food.

Government sponsored mass housing to combat slums

Each phase of development produced its own community-level problems at such intensity that European national and local governments felt impelled to act. In the first phase of atrocious slum crowding and disease in the 19th century city governments emerged as powerful drivers of basic reform. Public health, sanitation, piped water, street lighting, paving and regulated minimal housing standards became accepted, though enforcement and implementation were uneven. Around the First World War, European governments unleashed ambitious subsidy programmes for rental housing to compensate for these gaps, help industrialists house their workers in healthier conditions and get rid of slums.[5]

After the First World War in Britain and Ireland, 'mass housing' was built by local councils and generously funded by government. A major 50-year slum clearance programme, beginning in 1930, led to around two thirds of council estates being built within inner cities. Both renting and owner occupation in new outer areas was often government subsidised as a way of relieving pressure on inner slums. But this private housing was out of reach for unskilled and casual workers.

Table 7.1: Government subsidised housing

Leipzig Outer estate	Grunau built on edge of city in west Leipzig, with 35,000 units and 100,000 population – socially mixed with many longstanding residents expressing strong attachment. Many shops, transport links, schools and other facilities – gradual demolition of least popular blocks – generated strong local oppositions. Major upgrading of remaining units to high energy efficiency standards.
Lille On Southern edge of city	Lille Sud is a large social housing area of around 3500 homes – very rundown and poor with high unemployment – feels cut off from main city centre. Spread out, unattractive. But new amenities being built. One large block to be demolished is now 100% occupied by West African families – some illegal. Most of estate will stay and be upgraded.
Saint-Étienne Outer estates	Two large outer estates, Quartier Sud Est and Monreynaud, both poor and difficult – experienced some disorders during the 2000 riots across France. Big reinvestment programmes with social, youth and enterprise provision. Extremely long 'wall' of flats (0.5km) – called Mur de Chine – was demolished and residents (mainly Algerians) dispersed around Quartier Sud Est, causing some racial tensions. Older parts of estate, built in late 1950s, are more settled, more attractive and mostly populated by indigenous French.
Torino Inner and outer social housing	Many publicly subsidised blocks of rented flats built in Fiat factory areas to house new workers in 1960s onwards. Serious decay as factories close. Many upgrading investments through neighbourhood programmes. Also old public (IACP) housing in inner city areas being retained.
Bilbao Outer housing developments relatively close to the centre	Lots of low cost, subsidised, owner-occupied, dense blocks all around edge of city. Tends to be quite socially mixed as low paid workers given incentives to buy at low interest – very little strictly social rented housing – about 4000 in whole city for emergencies. New housing developments in Miribilla and around coach station – using mixed income subsidy model. As a very dense city, even outer estates are not far out.
Sheffield Inner city large estate	Many large council estates built in post-war mass housing phase. Several now demolished and city is short of cheap social housing. Park Hill stands out as a brave experiment in high quality, imaginative upgrading, making virtue of concrete structure. New, renovated estate will house mixed 'social' and private residents.
Belfast Inner and outer estates	Belfast built lots of public housing with very big government subsidies in order to reduce community problems. Some estates such as Divis Flats in the city centre became so caught up in the Troubles they had to be demolished. The new social housing reinforces rather than reduces segregation. There are many interface communities within social housing areas, with diverse groups living in close proximity, where new housing is urgently needed but is disputed by communities.

Source: City visits, 2006–15

In other European countries a mix of private, charitable and government investment produced a similar outcome, though on a

Figure 7.1: Citizens of other countries (% of population), 2011

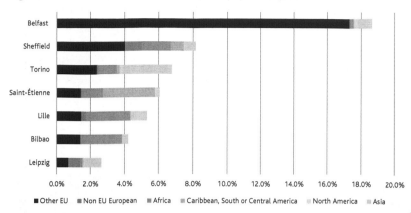

Source: Eurostat Population by citizenship and country of birth - cities and greater cities [urb_cpopcb]

smaller scale and not directly government owned. No other European country embarked on the mass–scale slum clearance that the UK did. Large subsidised estates often became marginal because they were generally built across Europe on the outskirts of cities. The building of mass estates set in train another kind of outward exodus. The huge building splurge which lasted up to the end of the 1970s eventually created a new phase of 'slum' problems of concentrated poverty and marginalisation in large estates.[6] Table 7.1 captures the conditions within mass housing estates.

Mass housing is now emblematic of social and management problems; but also a vital resource to the cities. That is why increasingly cities are restoring rather than demolishing estates. They are a lifeline for poor communities, but also a stark reminder of poverty, exclusion and minority concentration.

Migration and poor areas

One result of such strong dispersal of slum communities into new build estates was that post-Second World War immigrants increasingly filled the gaps left in inner cities. So as inner cities emptied of local working populations to fill the large, outer estates, so the old slums filled with newcomers, anxious to make a start somewhere. Slum areas deteriorated rapidly, due partly to increased overcrowding, partly to delinquent landlords, partly to the sheer neglect of conditions that results from their being classed as slums.

In Britain, where government demolition programmes were blighting most inner cities, slum properties were bought up cheaply by unscrupulous landlords and let out room by room to newcomers at exorbitant rents as 'furnished rooms', thereby escaping all rent controls. In France, Italy, Germany and Spain, the oldest, poorest, depopulating neighbourhoods, with no demolition in sight, became host to new arrivals, unmistakably foreign, living in unbelievably bad conditions. In 2008 in Torino, a city centre courtyard had improvised shelters (tarpaulin, plywood, tin) constructed on external balconies. These improvised 'rooms' literally hung off the balconies around the courtyards providing extra sleeping, washing, toilet and storage space. In Saint-Étienne, in a dense inner courtyard, intensively built into and closed off with primitive shed-like structures, without sanitation or running water, the going rent for a room in 2008 was 50 Euros a month. They were fully occupied. The immigrant population was heavily concentrated rather than large as a share of the city. Figure 7.1 shows the origins of immigrants in the seven cities in 2011.

Immigrants were initially attracted by booming industries. They were willing to take the undesirable jobs, increasingly shunned by native workers. They were paid less and often treated differently – for example, initially they were disqualified from union membership, from access to social housing and from many jobs relating to direct services with the public. Therefore they were pushed into accepting poor, overcrowded housing conditions in neighbourhoods that more established residents were leaving. So they became marginal in work and in communities, and they were invariably scapegoated and blamed for the very poor conditions they were forced to accept. When the concentration of problems became conspicuous, in the 1970s and 1980s, governments stepped in. Something would have to be done.[7]

Government energies and resources had been focused on mass housing estates and new private developments at the expense of existing homes. Particular inner city neighbourhoods with high concentrations of immigrants all over Europe eventually became such a running sore that governments felt obliged to tackle them head on. The older inner areas, with conspicuous ethnic minority communities, continued to house the more vulnerable and precarious members of the populations that were there previously – often now out of work, too low skilled and too poor to move, too fragile to find an alternative. These 'left behind' populations generally had poor levels of literacy and numeracy, were used to heavy industrial jobs, and were poorly adapted to the new, more mechanised and automated openings on offer or the new-style service jobs emerging. This made them not just poor and disengaged but often fairly hostile to the incomers who they saw as 'taking their jobs' and their homes. In addition there were language barriers, particularly among the incoming women who were often extremely isolated. These problems built up gradually over the late stages of industrial growth and then decline, compounded by poorly integrated, transient communities absorbing newcomers long after the industrial heyday was over. Sheffield, Belfast, Lille, Torino, Bilbao and Leipzig have all seen increases in minority populations over the last decade, in spite of the recession.

An uneasy peace prevailed in most of these marginal areas, and a modus vivendi emerged as people were living in such close proximity to each other. By the 1970s schools in such multi-ethnic areas had multiple mother-tongue languages and literally rainbow colours among children and parents. By rubbing shoulders with each other, social links often developed in spite of the cultural gaps, misunderstandings and occasional hostilities.[8] The problem of marginalisation continued and even grew however as poor literacy, poor work experience, language problems, crowding and poverty ground people down, removing them further from new opportunities and openings.[9] Schools became conspicuous separators of minorities within poor neighbourhoods.[10]

The threat of ghettos in European cities

The decay of inner neighbourhoods in Europe's industrial cities is different from the US in spite of many parallels. Urban racial ghettos divide American cities so sharply that the boundary of the ghetto is visible, a division only intensified with industrial decline as cities like Chicago, Milwaukee and Detroit show.[11] The concentration of African American and Hispanic populations reaches over 80% of the total population in large tracts of urban, 'rust belt' American cities.[12] On every measure, the gap between conditions in the most concentrated American urban ghettos and the average is extremely wide, far wider than in equivalent European cities.[13] The scale and depth of ghetto formation has been carefully documented by eminent scholars such as William Julius Wilson and Robert Sampson.[14] Interestingly, Barack Obama in his semi-autobiographical account of race in the US, *Dreams From My Father*, gives a vivid and detailed account of urban conditions in Chicago ghetto areas during the 1980s, based on his own experience.[15] His community-organising work with parents of school failures is a sharp reminder of how entrenched ghetto problems are in the city.[16]

One distinctive quality of ethnic minority incomers in Europe is their huge diversity, in skin colour, country of origin, language, cultural patterns, religious identity, affinity with the host country and many other aspects. This makes areas of ethnic minority settlement and concentration far more diverse, less uniform, less easy to categorise in Europe than the US. It is also unusual to encounter even small areas of cities where the share of minorities approaches 80%. And in those areas, there is usually considerable diversity. Even though white indigenous populations have dispersed and shrunk, many existing residents have stayed put, and still form a majority of households in almost all urban neighbourhoods where high concentrations of ethnic minorities have settled.

Ghettos are rare in today's Europe but are increasingly talked about and feared particularly with reference to disadvantaged neighbourhoods in declining cities. There is no room for complacency, given Europe's colonial history and the difficulties in absorbing foreign immigrants of a different colour in Europe; also given rising poverty and inequality.

Over the 1970s and 1980s, the older inner areas of the core cities we track experienced deteriorating schools, high unemployment and increasing poverty. The available jobs were often in the most precarious, lowest paid sectors with the least security or status. Quite often small ethnic minority businesses formed as family-run enterprises which eventually proved extremely valuable to recovering cities but grew on marginal profits. Housing was poor, whether it was in terraced streets like Sheffield's Burngreave, or dense blocks like East Leipzig, or central courtyards like Torino, or rundown streets in inner Saint-Étienne, Lille, or any other city in the study. Migrants inadvertently compounded and sped up the problem of decay and social polarisation.

Discrimination was a factor in both the concentration of problems and the disadvantages suffered by minorities. Civil disorders erupted in bigger cities in the 1980s – Lyon in France, Birmingham, Bristol and Liverpool in England, Berlin in Germany. Most heavy industrial cities managed to escape intense, racially provoked clashes with police until the 1990s and 2000s, when Bradford and the former cotton towns of Lancashire erupted. In 2000, riots also broke out in virtually every French city, including Saint-Étienne, mainly in outer estates, the former ZUPs. The riots were a clear sign that European cities were in real danger of following the American path. The troubles in poor inner and outer neighbourhoods served as a focus for city attempts to turn around what was in fact a much bigger problem – loss of jobs, loss of economic rationale, and as a result, loss of overall sense of direction and leadership.[17] All these losses hit hardest at the bottom.

Top-down meets bottom-up

Along with migrants, young student activists often moved into inner areas, close to central universities and nightlife, partly attracted by cheap accommodation and the lively mix, but partly drawn by political indignation at the exclusion of minorities from the mainstream and the marginalisation of poorer, more vulnerable traditional residents from more general prosperity.

Community-based protests in the different countries began to take shape – sometimes opposing demolition; sometimes fighting for the rights of squatters and insecure tenants; sometimes fighting 'gentrification', the upgrading of property for better off occupiers displacing existing residents.[18] These new protest movements exerted pressure on local governments to act, out of a combination of social concern, a continuing desire to eradicate slums, and a strong commitment to avoid the danger of ghettos emerging in Europe. The fear of ghetto formation in Europe had become a recurring theme in the wake of the US Civil Rights movement and the aftermath of decolonisation. There was also the stark reminder of the history of Jewish ghettos in Europe.

Allowing historic areas close to city centres to become such running sores was a potential threat to the social order that city governments in a crowded continent had to address.[19] An interesting shift in thinking took place, driven by governments' reluctance to offer new subsidised flats in new estates on the scale that was needed to relatively recent migrants ahead of longstanding, local slumdweller residents. So they embraced the idea that they had to improve the existing housing stock.[20]

A different approach to area renewal based on restoration and improvement emerged across Europe and quickly took root, drawing on two elements. First, local and central government could not simply impose solutions. As poor inner city areas were a large problem and a challenge that had to be tackled at the local level, governments realised that they needed the cooperation of existing residents in order to cope with such complex, diverse and volatile community dynamics. This represented a huge shift in city thinking towards smaller scale, more tailored solutions involving residents.

At the same time, community-based efforts to tackle such overwhelming pressures and problems created many micro-projects and innovative local initiatives that still relied on the wider community, official approval and external resources to get off the ground and succeed. Often predating public investment or large scale government action, local organisations developed play programmes, mothers' groups, youth clubs, tenants' action groups, legal advice centres, housing cooperatives and many other forms of local social action. Sometimes they were backed by local churches, charities, trade unions or other civic groups; sometimes by the local council; sometimes just by each other. These community initiatives strengthened the commitment to retaining and renewing existing areas.

In European cities, it is virtually impossible to escape planning constraints, public health laws, building controls, local political support, in establishing community-level projects. Small scale community projects are fragile without wider protection and backing; yet large scale projects are too clumsy without local voice. As a result a new form of 'top-down meets bottom-up' policy emerged in all our cities, taking different shapes in different European countries. Common patterns emerged nonetheless. The pressure on city governments, for example, to underpin cooperative and community enterprises matched the need for community representatives to help shape the delivery of programmes. These beginnings of a shift in the way cities worked with local communities reflected the economy of cities – the dominance of SMEs and the shift in city thinking towards smaller scale economic structures that occurred once large scale industries had gone. Local government and public programmes, backed at national and European levels, came to require community involvement and resident input into decisions.[21] The parallel trends in industrial and housing policy towards a more broken-up model are clearly visible at neighbourhood level.

Whole programmes of social innovation have been supported by the EU at neighbourhood level with a strong bias towards favouring ex-industrial cities. These projects range from raising skills to retrofit, resettling Roma communities, to upgrading legacy buildings. Most social reinvestment programmes target the most disadvantaged areas, and work by combining national and local government funding – as well as regional and European funding. This collective multi-level approach to renewal and recovery does buttress the poorest areas against the extremes experienced in US cities.[22] Even under austerity, there are more resources targeting the poorest areas in Europe than in the US. European programmes have been proactive in this agenda, but a lot now depends on how the next stage of the Eurozone crisis unfolds. So far the EU has clearly made a significant contribution in funds as well as focus – albeit with many limitations.[23] This is markedly different from the US experience.

Social action and neighbourhood management

One of the great values of neighbourhood projects in tackling marginalisation is that they helped poorer areas come through the shock of industrial decline and collapse in the late 1970s and 1980s. This is because community or area based initiatives spawned many levels of local activity and wider interventions which strengthened the viability and resilience of poorer neighbourhoods; took some steps towards integrating their distinct communities; and created local jobs and skills. In addition they generated commitment and confidence among both residents and the wider community by breaking down barriers. For example, neighbourhood renewal in inner neighbourhoods and outer estates was often linked to job creation projects, skill building and school programmes to improve literacy and numeracy.[24]

Councils and non-profit landlords upgraded local environments by enclosing open spaces to make them safer, creating play areas and gardens. They made entrances to blocks more secure and more attractive. They upgraded homes and neighbourhoods, working with private landlords and owners, as well as tenants.[25] These activities generated a demand for training and for jobs to go to local people, who wanted a bigger say in what happened. This chimed with local government ambitions to make disadvantaged areas and communities more resilient and more integrated.[26]

A major advantage of the 'local management' approach to poorer neighbourhoods is that it is job-intensive, it is not rocket science, and it involves a higher input of labour than either materials or machinery – compared with the construction of new housing, the production of cars or any other industrial process. Therefore some new opportunities opened up while industrial jobs closed.

Poor as social conditions were for the lowest income groups, residents had created a special kind of community solidarity, sharing and mutual support through local initiatives that was a response to shared needs and joint struggles to survive. The sense of solidarity and 'community identity' among very diverse groups, often newer residents, helped these neighbourhoods gain from the new public sector focus on the smaller scale.[27]

The focus of local government on area based renewal during a period of acute city decline helped in many ways. Some local shops and small enterprises survived or reopened in a wider context of major job losses, often run by minority entrepreneurs, sometimes taken over after the exodus of so many local residents.[28] The economic base of poor neighbourhoods shifted when immigrant communities became the leading entrepreneurs, often serving much wider groups. This trend was particularly conspicuous in Torino, where whole programmes, developed within a city-wide strategy targeting the poorest neighbourhoods and involving social development, including minorities.[29] Funding came from regional, national and EU sources. In German, Spanish and Italian cities, a focus on supporting minority enterprises encouraged skills and created more positive relations with minorities. It also recognised the contribution they can make in declining areas.

Box 7.2 shows how neighbourhood renewal developed in the poorest neighbourhoods. Table 7.2 shows the long-run social consequences of the phases of growth, decline, recovery, and crisis affecting the seven cities.

Box 7.2: Neighbourhood renewal

SHEFFIELD'S poorest, most migrant-populated inner area, Burngreave, was partially demolished and partially saved. It remains one of Sheffield's most deprived areas. Typically council estates were often built on slum-cleared inner city sites. In the late 1990s, the government selected Burngreave as a pilot for the New Deal for Communities programme with a £50 million investment in upgrading, better facilities and community development. Several earlier programmes had funded housing associations to upgrade street properties, and support this highly diverse community. The improvements to street properties increased the 'gentrification' of the area, in spite of its ongoing poverty and high proportion of minorities. There are now fewer dedicated neighbourhood programmes due to austerity.

Inner LEIPZIG began the process of renewal after reunification in 1989. Levels of vacancy unseen in any other city in the study, created a truly decimated and impoverished inner city zone. Nevertheless, following reunification, neighbourhood projects took off with similar patterns and purpose – to restore housing, remove surplus stock, and increase social provision and engagement. Leipzig faced the most extreme challenges, and one consequence of high abandonment was the startling levels of demolition in response to the scale of vacancies. This eventually became highly controversial and the policy of demolition in inner Leipzig was heavily curtailed, in favour of restoration and repopulation.

The French neighbourhood programme began in the late 1970s. Roubaix, the old industrial commune on the outer edge of **LILLE**, had lost coal mines and textile industries, devastating the local community. This early French experiment in neighbourhood renewal, provoking a new, far more locally tuned approach than the ZUPs, became widely copied in the European Union.

In Lille, comprehensive renewal programmes target most poorer areas of the city. In Lille Sud, there are ambitious renewal works going on through the 'Grands Projets de Ville', a major government investment programme in 'sensitive' urban areas. The challenge of integrating ethnic minority communities is huge. One plan is to demolish the biggest block of flats in Lille Sud, entirely occupied by African immigrant families, in order to 'weaken the control of criminal networks' in a highly vulnerable community and disperse the drug-dealing and other problems concentrated there.

SAINT-ÉTIENNE'S attractive but rundown inner areas, such as Tarentaize and Crêt de Roc, also became Grands Projets de Ville. The French government has so far kept in place the dedicated neighbourhood programmes with generous funding.

Extreme high density in cities like **BILBAO** and Barcelona and the integration of different incomes within inner city communities led to high levels of protection for the older stock. Bilbao targeted its two main central areas, the Casco Viejo and Bilbao la Vieja, the latter housing a dense concentration of minorities. Bilbao adopted a policy of partial demolition and rebuilding in this impoverished area, arguing that this was the only way in which the appallingly crowded and unhygienic conditions could be tackled. In spite of the financial crisis and Spain's difficulties, the city still has a major regeneration project in the large area around the bus terminal.

In Italy, chronic housing shortages in the 1960s and 1970s made inner cities unbearably overcrowded and worker housing provision was totally inadequate, during Italy's post-war industrial and urban growth spurt. **TORINO** began upgrading both old inner city areas and newer blocks in the late 1990s, building on a strong tradition of neighbourhood-based activity and community engagement, often supported by local church organisations, committed to helping migrants, providing for poor children and families, organising activities for young and old. Torino's publicly funded neighbourhood projects ended with the financial and debt crisis. Social enterprises, often taking cooperative form, arose from Torino's strong trade union movement and helped house people.

In **BELFAST**, neighbourhood renewal became embedded as a constructive and peacemaking approach to reconciling community divisions. It was an

Table 7.2: Long-run social consequences of growth, decline and recovery

Leipzig*	Leipzig is Germany's most unequal city Big contrast between West and East Leipzig, the centre and outer areas Strong neighbourhood focus – lots of upgrading Some job link efforts, and special neighbourhood focus More skilled jobs draw in outsiders Population regrowth Social enterprises flourish, such as Spinnerai
Lille	Big social impact of industrial job losses Strong socialist mayors combat worst poverty effects Investment in neighbourhoods Population re-attracted Some job growth Still generally poor by French city standards High concentrations of social housing in the south of the city
Saint-Étienne*	Poor city with extremely deprived inner and outer areas Strong minority concentrations Strong outer suburban growth because people flee poverty and decline Job retraining weak so big skills mismatch – still very working class city Serious attempts to attract people back to city Big restoration investments in poorest areas – Grands Projets de Ville
Torino	High illegal immigration and informal working Very over-crowded, dilapidated courtyard areas around train station Neighbourhood programmes cut Some innovative social initiatives backed by Compagnia San Paolo Strong cooperative development – social hotels
Bilbao	Very strong solidarity within Basque City Lan Ekintza – social enterprise and employment agency reabsorbed into council Neighbourhood renewal programmes still going But city budgets very hard hit so jobs shrinking and wages falling Older poorer areas visible Many cooperative initiatives
Sheffield	Big gap between richest and poorest areas Strong working class tradition, deprived areas and big social housing estates Major impact of public sector cuts Powerful community enterprise movement Neighbourhood renewal fund dries up Hard to access new jobs from low skill base Many initiatives to help access to jobs
Belfast	Social budgets protected to sustain Peace Agreement Uneasy peace between communities Community projects and renewal carefully brokered because of divisions Jobs are huge issue because of sectarian tensions Catholics are a rising share of population Population loss continues to suburbs, but some recovery Wider cuts on the way to match rest of UK Big local government reorganisation and reduction in staff More devolved decision making powers

Note: *Depopulation continued until very recently.

Source: City visits, 2006–15

alternative to belligerent, confrontational, defensive and often divided stands against authority by both sides. It has a more unifying effect than demolition and rebuilding. This approach to neighbourhood renewal had big advantages in creating some local jobs, supporting many local community organisations and enterprises. It forced the authorities to broker plans directly with community representatives. Almost all of Belfast's inner areas have been targeted with renewal programmes that are carefully overseen with inter-denominational representation. Since 2000, a new phenomenon of in-migration from abroad has created new conflicts and pressures within Belfast, which local initiatives were not ready for and so far have not been a match for.

Source: City visits 2008-2015

The general shift to a smaller, more local scale, and more project-based approach proved helpful in preventing the extreme polarisation, ghetto formation and abandonment that accelerated decline in American cities. European cities took steps to prevent a similar outcome.[30] Neighbourhood programmes have prevented the worst extremes of polarisation, but success in including ethnic minorities on an equal footing is at best partial, with many outstanding challenges.

Over the same period, similar problems undermined mass housing estates – lost revenue, high unemployment, reduced investment, a skills mismatch, poverty. This combination of factors caused falling demand for housing, particularly in outer estates as anyone with skill and ambition got out if they could. As a result, far more minority residents gained access to subsidised estates they had long been excluded from. Estates increasingly housed a high concentration of minorities as the estates lost popularity, so much so that French outer estates are increasingly referred to as 'ghettos'. They experienced a similar tension between 'left behind' traditional working class and newcomers as inner city areas. There were many eruptions of trouble in the estates during the decades of decline and recovery.[31]

The impact on large housing estates of industrial decline was especially acute as they had barely settled down as new communities, when they became truly marginal to the cities. Their very size and complex structures defies easy adaptation and there was much early talk of demolition. However, they house large, hard to integrate populations. They cost a lot to build, and although maintenance is expensive, renovation is clearly far cheaper than demolition and replacement.[32] On the other hand, their location, often outside the inner city, makes it harder to access jobs and harder to integrate into the city.

City recovery and neighbourhood renewal

When cities mounted wider recovery plans, it became clear that they would not work without attractive, restored inner city neighbourhoods and a clear rescue plan for mass housing estates. The restoration of inner neighbourhoods took root as cities began to recover in the 1990s. With government backing for the rescue attempts, local governments and non-profit landlords across European cities mounted community-level reinvestment programmes in 'difficult to let' estates. As with inner neighbourhoods, community involvement and backing were all important. It was impossible in high density estates to work around residents without involving them in the process. So upgrading programmes on large estates adopted a community-oriented approach.[33]

The estate rescue programmes, like the neighbourhood programmes they followed, focused on community provision of all kinds – youth centres, children's activity, local shops and markets, job training, environmental clean-ups involving families, play areas, tree planting, community centres, employer links. Governments felt particularly implicated in the fortunes of estates as they had driven their construction through subsidies and implanted them, often on the outskirts of cities with little thought for the ongoing costs of maintenance or the infrastructure needs of large new communities. The social consequences of the dislocation they caused lives with us still. Government reinvestment was crucial to their recovery, as no self-help or cooperative initiative was a match for the complexity of their problems.

In all seven cities, some demolition of subsidised post-war housing has taken place, but in most cases only a few blocks have been removed from each estate and the estates still stand as monuments to a Utopian dream. In fact, there is no real and affordable alternative. The aim of upgrading is to encourage established residents in work to stay and younger, more ambitious households needing a home to move in, thus creating that magic remedy of a 'mixed community'. This means repopulating empty property with working households which is different from the standard meaning of gentrification. It is not displacing poorer people; rather it is widening the income bands to ensure future viability by filling empty property. It mainly targets younger households in work who find it hard to afford a home in a better area – in other words, the kind of residents the estates were originally built for. This strategy is applied to outer and inner areas in Saint-Étienne, Torino, Leipzig and Sheffield. We call this 'low level gentrification'.[34]

Over the 2000s the outcome of these different efforts was vastly improved conditions in poorer inner and outer areas, rising popularity, particularly in inner areas, and new demand for low cost homes. The cumulative impact of community-level initiatives, government backed reinvestment, and city recovery plans showed that both outer estates and inner neighbourhoods with high poverty and unemployment were potentially accessible, attractive and cheap. Inner areas had the added value of being historic neighbourhoods which in European eyes is often highly appealing.

Job regrowth among low skilled populations

Inevitably low skilled industrial workers found it hardest to adapt to alternative jobs − mainly in services. 'Soft' skills and more flexible working, such as the service industry require, did not come easily to former industrial workers. Many were resistant to retraining, schooled to think that producing goods through your labour was what determined your social value and the value of what you produced. Minority communities in poor areas were even worse affected as they tended to lose their jobs first and have the least access to alternatives. The problem of skills is one of the biggest challenges. As industry declined inner city neighbourhoods became poorer and needier while city revenues fell in parallel, reducing local services.

Jobs became critical to a change in fortunes for poor neighbourhoods across many different skills and education levels. For young people, unemployment was and still is chronic − a majority of 16–21 year olds may be out of work in a single area; neither in training nor in college nor in a job. Unemployment is often at least double the local rate among minority groups − both in estates and inner cities.[35] Rates obviously vary between cities and countries but are invariably far higher in the poorest neighbourhoods.[36] Therefore finding ways of handholding people into new types of work became all important. Drawing on the lessons of neighbourhood renewal, local, small scale employment projects emerged in the 2000s in our cities.

The growth areas offering work opportunities include: housing and building renovation; retail; caring jobs; cleaning and maintenance services; catering and hospitality; transport, such as buses and taxis; urban tourism, including monuments, historic routes, conferences; maintenance of public spaces, parks, streets; security and caretaking; neighbourhood and housing management; infrastructure investment;

energy saving and renewable energy installation. A new phase of activity grew that needed a ready, available workforce at an affordable cost, which is exactly what poorer neighbourhoods could offer. For this reason, many employment projects emerged to complement the other neighbourhood activities, usually run by city councils or regional government, but occasionally set up or backed by employers, and sometimes operating as non-profit community-based enterprises.

Box 7.3 gives five examples of projects that help those most marginal in the job market through a combination of training, support and bridging between employer needs and job seeker capacity.

Box 7.3: Neighbourhood employment projects

GEMS NI Project, Belfast

GEMS NI began in 2000 as a charity working in inner Belfast to help marginal residents into jobs. It works intensively with individuals, over many months or more, handholding vulnerable people into jobs they otherwise could not hope to access. After placing over 2000 residents in work, GEMS NI has now spread all over the city and to other parts of Northern Ireland.

Arbeitsladen, East Leipzig

East Leipzig is the poorest and most rundown neighbourhood in Leipzig, with the biggest migrant population. The Arbeitsladen, or literally 'Job Shop', helps people find jobs, advises them on applications and interviews, steers them towards training and helps with officialdom. Its open door, informal, local focus helps win confidence and create bridges into work.

Kier Project, Sheffield

Kier is a large construction company that won the contract to manage most of Sheffield City Council's community facilities and open spaces. Over 600 such areas have been handed over for intensive management. The company, in its contract with Sheffield, agreed to invest in job opportunities for unemployed residents. One was to recruit and train young wardens to maintain and supervise open spaces throughout the city. Another was to create supported jobs for people with learning difficulties within special housing schemes. Both projects were popular, oversubscribed and transformed opportunities. Sheffield has now developed ambitious skills programs, apprenticeships and job training.[37]

Apollio Centre, Torino

Part of the neighbourhoods project in the central square of Porta Palazzo, the Apollio Centre helped illegal immigrant traders in the city centre gain official status and entitlements. One of its highly successful projects was to organise

Moroccan women into a bread-making cooperative. The locally-made, 'artisan' bread has become part of the Slow Food Movement and sells well across the city. The Apollio Centre itself has been subject to major cuts.

Lan Ekintza, Bilbao

An employment generating programme, funded by the city of Bilbao, Lan Ekintza was set up to encourage enterprise among young unemployed people. One project gave young people disposable cameras and sent them round the city to photograph any street activity they spotted that generated revenue from a single 'doer'. They uncovered literally hundreds of solo entrepreneurs, and made action plans from what they learnt. Lan Ekintza has now been reabsorbed into the city-wide umbrella body, Bilbao Ekintza, and employment related work has moved to provincial level, a move criticised by the city as it makes job support remote from local problem areas.

Source: City visits, 2006–15

A crucial lesson in accessing jobs lies in 'handholding'. This means investing time in face-to-face support and advice to overcome barriers of confidence, communication and presentation. The gap between the job market in services and the job-readiness of young people is frighteningly wide. Limited work experience, a poor schooling record and a family background in industrial, semi or low skilled work create special barriers. It seems that young women are more adept at crossing that boundary than young men.[38] Handholding can make a crucial difference. It needs to bring with it real knowledge of the job market and experience in bridging the gap. It involves a high upfront investment of time. Yet face-to-face support is one of the most direct areas in which cutbacks have happened. We found this to be the case in Sheffield, Torino and Bilbao.

The crash and its impact on jobs

The financial crisis provided a sudden, unexpected and severe blow to progress in job creation, affecting the poorest neighbourhoods most severely. In different cities different measures were adopted to minimise the losses and protect the gains. Jobs have begun to recover in most cities, but there is chronic youth unemployment everywhere except in Germany, where government supported jobs and apprenticeships have ensured that a large majority of vulnerable young people have stayed in work or training. Even so, Leipzig has higher unemployment

Table 7.3: Measures to increase jobs

Leipzig	City agency to recruit pool of local workers for new jobs Asbeitsladen – job shops in neighbourhoods to encourage and support people into work Alternative, new enterprises in empty buildings, such as the Spinnerai Government training and apprenticeship support to ensure young people have job opportunities
Lille	Strong encouragement of cluster growth to expand jobs Support for start-ups, self-employed, micro-enterprises Tight controls over employment standards which many believe discourages employers Close work with schools
Saint-Étienne	Maison de travail – government run local employment and advice centre Enterprise development and skills training in outer estates to encourage locals into work Investment in urban upgrading and environmental improvement creates jobs
Torino	Encouragement of SMEs, start-ups and incubators to create and hold jobs in the cities Work with charities to develop skills among marginal and homeless people so they can get jobs Training and job support among illegal immigrants Government funding to employers to sustain jobs in recession Development of retrofit as job intensive industry
Bilbao	City controlled job training and support until 2013, now a regional responsibility City encourages start-ups and solo enterprises Also offers many new jobs in hospitality and tourism Focus on 'learn by doing', encourages enterprise and cooperative development Reducing wages to protect jobs
Sheffield	Strong focus on skills training in technical subjects Job training programme for young people city-wide Special job-match agency to help employers find suitable local employees Training for low income residents to help them into jobs Encouragement of SMEs to expand and take on more workers Work with secondary schools to improve skills and employability
Belfast	Major training and retraining programmes to help people into work following the Peace Agreement Hospitality and call centre training, programmes by big employers to help local workforce secure jobs Work in further education to build skills among least qualified
Comments	In all cities there are major concerns about youth unemployment, and the low-skilled population. There are many small, self-run businesses in all cities. All the cities run training and job support programmes. Special government job subsidies to help employers keep people in work

Source: City visits, 2006–15

than Germany as a whole.[39] Overall, youth employment is double the adult rate in all the cities except Leipzig.[40]

In all countries, governments have taken some measures to keep existing jobs going (see Table 7.3). These job support measures have some impact, but it then becomes very difficult to discontinue the support as the economy recovers. In the UK, there are far looser controls over jobs and conditions, as a result of which many jobs have been created since 2013 when recovery got underway.[41] There is some evidence that the reforms to deregulate the labour market in Germany have resulted in expanded job opportunities for the unemployed. But the increase in temporary and short-term employment in Germany has expanded the number of part-time, insecure jobs. These poorer jobs obviously make struggling cities poorer, and may have an impact on productivity. [42]

Social innovation and green enterprise

Repeated crises in the cities from every stage of their development have pushed the boundaries of invention. Ex-industrial cities have such a deep legacy of poverty, social problems and low skill that they carry a great burden of need, which they are in practice unable to meet due to reduced economic viability, and lower public support. Central and local European governments have tried to compensate as part of their commitment to recovering cities, but the Eurozone crisis and austerity budgets have forced severe cutbacks in all kinds of support, hitting local and community budgets particularly hard.

In the United States, where the role of the federal government has never been strong and where state governments prioritise suburban and ex-urban populations over cities, the problems of neighbourhood and housing decline in cities are acute and highly visible due to racial segregation.[43] The gaps to close are truly daunting and few wider mechanisms are in place to do this. In spite of this, distressed cities in the US have displayed remarkable resourcefulness in innovating to tackle social needs while attempting to close budget deficits.

A remarkable study, *The Power of Social Innovation*,[44] explores how local governments, non-profit organisations and businesses can step in to plug the funding gaps left by cuts in public funding. The argument in this study is that the federal government will not and cannot do much to help depleted cities. Resources are too tight and priorities focused elsewhere, both at federal and state level. Cities are thus thrown back on their own initiative with extremely slender resources, given their heavy reliance on the local depleted tax base. They have no choice but to invent new ways. Yet without a wider scale of action, it is hard to generate a critical mass of projects that will foster real change. One example where this seems to be happening is the Harlem Children's Zone. Its goal is to help the most disadvantaged children in the very poorest areas progress through childhood from maternity and early post-natal stage, right through to college. Handholding families and young people is their key tool. So successful was this self-starting project that a national programme, the 'Promise neighbourhood', was launched by Obama to replicate the model, and it is now being tentatively copied in the UK.[45]

By far the most innovative social projects in European cities have been created at neighbourhood level. As city funds have shrunk, so non-profit community-based organisations have taken on bigger roles. Sometimes new organisations have emerged to fill gaps in provision. One example is the community enterprise, Zest, in Sheffield, which took over council-owned Victorian swimming baths in the early 2000s, and now runs it as a health centre with support from the area based NHS (National Health Service) trust. Attached to this, it runs a library, a community cafe, a youth programme, a sports programme, and more recently a job training programme for young people across the city. It has lost much of its public funding and has been forced to shrink some of its programmes, but in the words of the organiser, "We are constantly thinking of new ways of working and delivering".[46]

Torino may be the city that is richest in social innovation, partly because of a long and church-based tradition of social action to tackle the acute poverty of 19th and 20th century urban growth, partly due to the current budgetary problems of the city, partly because of a powerful civic and trade union tradition in the city, leading to strong working class social movements, partly through the independent role of the bank foundations, which are rich and powerful in Torino, and are required by law to support social projects in the city.[47] The current archbishop of Torino has helped progress social action in the city by calling on all churches, religious orders and other civic institutions to give over any spare rooms or space to help house and feed destitute people in the city as the city faces steeply rising rents and homelessness. The examples from Torino in Box 7.4 are most striking and offer other cities models that can inspire and offer lessons, even if the projects themselves cannot be replicated.

Box 7.4: Torino's social initiatives

Social caretaking: In old rundown blocks of social housing in inner and central Torino, many elderly low income, isolated tenants struggle to manage. The social landlord offers flats in the blocks at reduced rent – around 50 Euro per week – to young students in exchange for their offering around 10 hours a week to help elderly residents with shopping, medicines, company and community activity. One social caretaker arranges communal lunches on Saturdays to increase social interaction. The flats and the rooms are extremely small, so any activity is very cramped but residents in the block attend and the young renter-caretakers are animated by helping in this way. The payback in reduced hospital visits and general health problems is measurable.

Social hotels: Torino city council has too little cash to respond to the steep rise in homelessness in the city since 2008, partly driven by the steep rise in rents. The rate of evictions has accelerated greatly since 2010. One solution is for cooperative social enterprises, supported by Caritas, an international charity backed by the Catholic Church and bank foundations, to set up hotel-style accommodation in previously empty buildings, following full-blown renovation also carried out by cooperative organisations. These then function as part-hotel for paying visitors, part short-term flats for people needing immediate accommodation (for example, foreign students), part emergency rooms for homeless people. There are restaurants, leisure and training rooms in common ground floor areas that lead to spin-off activities in the neighbourhood. Social hotels are self-funding on a non-profit basis. There are five social hotels now functioning in the city, housing and feeding homeless people, alongside students and other visitors.

Neighbourhood centres (case del quartiere): Torino boasts several ambitious and multi-functional centres where an old abandoned building has been taken over by a locally organised community trust and run as a social enterprise. One centre in an old farmhouse on the outskirts of the city, Cascina Rocca Franca, combines a restaurant, cafe, crèche, meeting and training rooms, a large hall used for dancing, keep fit, games, events, an enclosed courtyard-cum-play area, IT suite, and many other facilities. It is run within the community with strong resident participation and real input into its programme. There are several other examples. For example, the San Salvario neighbourhood centre is run independently of the city council in some old, renovated swimming baths (echoing Zest in Sheffield!). A new neighbourhood centre is being developed in the inner Torino area, Barrio Milano, where many new immigrants are settling and where there is visible poverty and many community tensions.

Source: City visits, 2006–15

Most city councils were innovators in imaginative ways. Sheffield council recently launched a low cost and city-wide loan-and-save scheme linked to local credit unions, to help low income residents stay out of unpayable debt burdens and clear of loan sharks. The innovative social projects we uncovered during our site visits, and there were some in every city, reflected a kind of inspiration that brought immeasurable benefits in often quite significant, but hard-to-measure ways. The support and pride of the city councils in these projects was a big factor in this. The common thread we found everywhere was the commitment, enthusiasm and youthfulness of the organisers and the strong rapport they had with participants and beneficiaries. The projects themselves opened up job opportunities in the community, in the restaurants and cafes, in cleaning and maintenance, in reception and security, child care and support jobs. There was a conscious effort to prioritise local residents for these jobs and to offer training for them.

There were also much bigger movements of social innovation, such as the Slow Food Movement, born and based in Torino; the Mondragon cooperatives, based in the Basque country outside Bilbao; the Transition Town movement, based in the UK and found in Sheffield; the urban cycle movement, present in all our cities, but strongest in Lille, Leipzig and Torino; the allotments and community garden movement, strongest in Leipzig, but also important in Lille, Saint-Étienne, and growing in Belfast and Sheffield. All of these social innovations create some jobs, often not well paid, but offering real breakthroughs in confidence, new skills and engagement for those who get involved. They add real value and quality of life to cities struggling with large pockets of deprivation.

The Transition Town movement is particularly interesting because it combines a commitment to energy saving to combat climate change with a social commitment to community action without relying on government funding. Literally hundreds of informal groups have formed, beginning in Ireland, Wales and England, then spreading to many other communities in Europe and around the world.[48] Some of its social innovations are impressive.[49]

Neighbourhood and community resilience

Many projects supported by cities are specially designed to build community resilience – in other words, the ability to cope with shocks, get by and recover. One sign of community resilience is the response to social emergencies. We have already described alternatives to homeless hostels, the sharing hotels, and social caretakers in Torino. Food has become an unexpectedly critical problem in poor communities across Europe, mainly in cities, over the past eight years.[50]

Many of the neighbourhood innovations we discovered rely on traditional, tried and tested methods of survival such as food growing and sharing. They also reflect the much wider resource constraints on energy, land and the natural environment. There has been as a result a burst of community kitchens, free eating centres and food banks, where food is literally handed out in parcels. There are food centres of different kinds in most of the cities, and community cafes, while not free, are extremely cheap, basic and good quality. The aim is minimal profit and maximum social support. At the weekly dinner for destitute people, served in the Sister project in Torino, run by Caritas, people have to secure a ticket to come because the demand is so great.[51] In Bilbao there are also community kitchens, feeding centres and homeless refuges, supported and often run by Caritas or the Red Cross.

The whole Slow Food Movement, started in Piemonte and Torino, is based around local produce and the importance of local food growing to increase sustainability, reduce environmental impact and support low income producers and buyers. It creates local jobs in Torino by supporting many local cafes and restaurants, therefore reinforcing traditional food preparation. This protects small local farmers in the face of stiff competition. Torino has many small, local, 'Slow Food' restaurants.[52] It has also created a large market in Mirafiore for the sale of Slow Food produce.

The Slow Food Movement was in danger of becoming a transnational elite hobby, when the founder Carlo Petrini launched a sister organisation, Terra Madre, an international association of small scale food producers, invariably poor and producing on an artisan scale.[53] Collectively, the members of Terra Madre represent a significant mass.

The production of food within cities resonates with wider social movements for fair trade and the need for local food suppliers. Both Terra Madre and the Slow Food Movement hold large international gatherings in Torino generating more support and enterprise. Sheffield and Leipzig both have strong 'urban agriculture' projects involving residents in allotments, community gardens, and vegetable growing in pots and boxes. Belfast is now developing an 'urban agriculture' project in a deprived outer community in North West Belfast. There are many more examples.

The following box lists the most salient ideas we found of how to make social innovation work.

Box 7.5: What works to foster social progress

- Community and social enterprises – Job match / Job net – handholding young people into work – training opportunities
- Participatory budgets – where communities decide priorities
- Community brokering between different groups and interests – focus on social cohesion
- Constant social inclusion efforts to combat polarisation and segregation
- Low level upgrading – holding onto conditions
- Strong emphasis on retrofit – to save buildings and make them energy efficient
- Re-attracting working residents in renewed areas, particularly estates
- Neighbourhood management – holding onto neighbourhood conditions
- Community centres and community cafes, common areas/play spaces
- Summer youth programmes and after-school clubs
- Land reclamation/reuse, building restoration
- Conversion of industrial buildings for community uses
- Restoring historic facilities within neighbourhoods: parks, converted churches and shops
- Community festivals and celebrations
- Long-run social initiatives – keeping going since problems won't go away

Source: City visits, 2007-2015

Much remains to be done. Several cities, particularly Lille, Saint-Étienne and Belfast, have relatively low density in the city and damaging sprawl around the edges. All cities still struggle with the barriers to integration. They are far from achieving a strong and easy social mix. But the more cities attract life into their restored central areas, the more they generate casual encounters and informal social contact which in turn generates a sense of community. This evolution is particularly noticeable in central Belfast, where it was so conspicuously absent before. But it is also noticeable in central Lille, Torino, Bilbao and Sheffield.

Box 7.6 shows how the three phases of development of industrial cities interact with low income communities to build community resilience.

Box 7.6: Social impact on communities of three phases of city development

Phase One – industrial economy
- Unprecedented social dislocation in the 19th and early 20th century
- Rapid development of slum housing, crammed into inner cities near factories
- Concentrated poverty and brutally harsh work conditions
- Grotesque inequalities
- Gradual progress as factory owners need healthy workforce
- Emergence of city government
- Unionisation, democratic progress, wealth of cities gradually enhance worker's conditions
- Worker's housing movements are supported by local government
- Creation of mass housing estates with sanitary conditions, as factory system declines

The end of Phase One was marked by:
- Massive job losses; undermined workforce
- Manual job losses lead to economic inactivity
- Older inner areas and new estates fall into rapid decline
- Intense decay of housing stock
- Immigrant concentrations in inner areas suffer disproportionately
- New social dislocations – rise in lone parenthood; racial tensions; deskilling; crime
- Steep rise in inequality

Phase Two – recovering economy
- City centre recovery attracts newcomers, professionals, students and general population
- New flagship projects attract funds and people
- Reinvestment in estates and inner areas upgrades conditions for poorer communities
- Recovery in jobs and wealth often bypasses poorest areas but special employment projects help
- New skills are often in short supply – frequent job mismatches
- Some handholding into jobs

Phase Two lays the ground for Phase Three: resource-constrained economy:
- Public investment in physical infrastructure encourages private investment
- Improving public transport
- Reclaiming polluted and derelict land

- Recycling and remodelling former industrial building
- Revaluing and reusing vital infrastructure: canals, rivers, railways
- Creating public spaces and restoring public buildings
- Encouraging green innovation
- Strong emphasis on social integration, community enterprise and participation
- Social underpinning of neighbourhoods helps integration

Phase Three – resource-constrained economy
- Major public spending cuts – salary freezes or cuts
- Amalgamation/abolition of many special agencies
- Loss of major investment programmes (EU, national)
- Shrinkage in private sector investment
- Very high youth unemployment
- But recovery of inner city population

Phase Three begins to take shape:
- Growth in renewable energy and related engineering
- Innovative green technology companies
- Growth in advanced manufacture
- New interest and faith in SMEs and small scale community projects
- Enthusiasm for invention, hands-on making
- Stress on cycling and low energy transport
- Strong anti-sprawl measures
- Special focus on skills, training and apprenticeships

Source: City visits, 2006–15

Photo 7.1: Vista of Torino showing the Alps in the near distance

Photo 7.2: Porta Palatina, Torino

Conclusion

Poverty areas are much improved since reinvestment began in the 1980s, but they still persist, displaying the most worrying social trend of all, high youth unemployment, alongside a generally ageing population. These two pressures are in a way the strongest signs of how much remains to be done. European industrial cities have managed to hold onto and improve their poorest areas; re-attracting populations and increasing density. They have opened them up to more working residents without generally displacing the existing depleted populations. They expanded local social enterprises and therefore local job opportunities; reduced some of the harshest poverty enclaves, although poverty is constantly re-emerging in new forms; made areas greener and more attractive; improved links to the city centre. These improvements are more possible in cities that underwent such severe crises in the 1980s, and again in 2008–14, as these cities are still under far less development pressure than global capitals like London, Berlin and Paris, or regional capitals like Milano, Lyon, Barcelona, Leeds or Manchester. This makes their 'value added', estimated in cash terms, lower than richer cities. But their 'value added' in quality of life, scope for social enterprise and level of civic imagination is priceless.[54] This moves them closer to the model for the future, our third phase.

Photo 7.3: *Officine Grandi Riparazioni: Former railway repair sheds converted for the City of Torino's celebration of the 150th anniversary of the reunification of Italy*

Box 7.7: Tale of a city – Torino

Torino is the impressive capital of Piemonte, one of Italy's most prosperous and industrial Northern regions, a striking mixture of history, industry, innovation and decay. Arrival at the main station plunges you straight into the city's most avant-garde planning vision – a wide, sun-lit esplanade, lined with people, small businesses and restored buildings. This new thoroughfare forms a bridge over the now buried railway that cuts through the city. It forms the 'central spine' of the remade city, after more than a century of deep cleavage by multiple railway lines dividing the city in two. The 'Spina' is home to new and established sections of the famous Politecnico di Torino, which spawns the city's hugely successful technical incubators, research labs and advanced industrial design courses and start-ups. The 'Spina' also protects the old railway sheds, specially restored for the celebration in 2013 of Italy's 150th anniversary of unification, and its foundation as a single nation. Visitors poured into Torino, Italy's first capital, to celebrate the creation of the Italian state.

How did Torino become host to such a monumental event? A severely damaged and depressed, industrial city pulled off this feat by persuading the outside world that its two year stint as united Italy's first capital (1861–63) had earned it a unique place in Italian celebrations. Its industrial prowess as home to Fiat, Italy's most powerful and richest private company; and to Olivetti, the inventor of world-famous type writers, made it Italy's industrial champion. As host for the Winter Olympics in 2006, it restored its name as international tourist centre. So the historic celebrations of Italy's formation as a single, united, powerful European leader, in the preserved railway sheds, made every kind of sense.

Five major features make Torino a truly impressive model of recovery and reinvention today:

1 Its revaluing and repackaging of its history.
2 The reinvention and reuse of its industrial engineering prowess and legacy.
3 The revaluing and reinstatement of its buildings and infrastructure, both the historic centre, the dense, attractive inner neighbourhoods, and former industrial sites.
4 The revaluing of the city's natural environment, with its rivers and snow-capped Alps rising as a steep and majestic back-drop to the city, reminding it of the rich potential of tourism and the ready source of renewable energy on its doorstep.
5 Its social innovation, based on a long tradition of sharing and mutual aid.

Torino has a formidable reputation for cooperatives and social enterprises, citizen engagement and a historic commitment to helping the truly disadvantaged. But many strands of Torino's history are woven into this remarkable tapestry. The city came to life as a gateway to the rest of Europe for Julius Caesar in 29BC. Over the millennia, the boundary between Italy and France was blurred by this gateway status and Torino eventually became the capital seat of the Dukedom of Savoy, spanning Haute-Savoie across the Alps in France and the Piemonte region of which Torino is the natural capital. Internationalism, leadership and

Photo 7.4: Original Fordist conveyor belt in the model Lingotto FIAT factory

trade were thus woven into Torino's fabric, and help explain its ruling status as the first capital of Italy – albeit briefly. Italy's capital quickly moved to Florence in 1863, leaving Torino poorer, underemployed and somewhat stranded.

The bruising of the city's pride did not last. A group of rich, enterprising, innovative, young Torinese, determined to create a new future for the 'defrocked' capital, set up the Fabbrica Italiana Automobili Torino (Fiat) in 1899. With repeated and inspiring visits to Henry Ford's historic car factory in Detroit, Fiat quickly became the landmark industry in 'backward' Italy. By the First World War, Fiat was an established vehicle producer. Agnelli, its founding owner, became powerfully allied with Mussolini between the wars and expanded vehicle production to meet the dictator's military and industrial ambitions. Torino became a famous centre for automotive engineering, telecommunications and hydropower from the meltwaters of Alpine snow.

Agnelli drove the formation of an alternative, city-based welfare state, supported through the philanthropy and self-interest of Fiat, as hundreds of thousands of impoverished migrants from southern Italy poured into the expanding factories and already overcrowded housing of Torino. Fiat's role in tackling these social problems stood the city in good stead in the hideously hard times of the Second World War and its aftermath, but it also made the city over-dependent on the private giant, whose headquarters would eventually forsake the city – though not finally until late 2014.

FIAT-Torino-Direzione Generale (Lingotto).- FIAT-Turin-Direction Générale (Lingotto).- FIAT-Turin-General Direction (Lingotto).

Photo 7.5: Politecnico di Torino, a crucial hub of innovation and enterprise creation, based in former Fiat factory

The rapid and extreme growth of Torino's population, both before and after the Second World War to feed Fiat's need for workers caused huge social distress, vastly compounded by wartime bombing. Fiat was both the main magnet for rapid in-migration from southern Italy, the main provider of industrial welfare, including housing, and the main cause of social distress and social divisions – simply by virtue of its rapid expansion, its vast scale and industrial prowess.

Torino's fortunes began a major decline after a long boom, as the now huge industrial workforce became organised, militant and resistant to changes which would cut semi-skilled and low skilled jobs. Costs rose, along with industrial strife, and Fiat's production factories began the move to cheaper labour markets, including southern Italy where many of its migrants originated, devastating the employment base of the city.

The city's long period in the doldrums during Fiat's slow decline from the late 1970s showed signs of reversal when for the first time the city elected its own mayor with new powers to drive the city forward. The Politecnico di Torino, long the city's training ground for brilliant engineers, designers and communications specialists, moved to the fore, producing not only Torino's first mayor, Castellani, but some of the city's most important engineering and research breakthroughs in the new economy.

Three trends reshaped the declining fortunes of the once majestic capital:

1 Strong alliances between many partners, with the Politecnico and the city often in the lead, to encourage innovation, R&D, start-ups, design-oriented advanced engineering, SMEs. The rich bank foundations, set up by law in Italy to funnel a share of bank profits into significant local causes, funded many innovations. Torino has Italy's largest bank foundation, the Fondazione Compagnia di San Paolo, which backs many initiatives and enterprises in the city.
2 A strong international focus to encourage the export of Italy's design and engineering expertise, to expand international trade in the face of Fiat's decline and to foster the exchange of new ideas.
3 A new vision for the city, combining the restoration of the beautiful, historic, but decayed city centre and new investment in the 'Spina Centrale' with improved public transport, including the new metro system. The conversion by Renzo Pianno of industrial monuments such as the giant Lingotto factory in outer Torino to new uses, and the upgrading of Mirafiore, Fiat's now semi-defunct industrial and residential neighbourhood in the outer city, brought new life and new uses to the city. The new facilities to host the Olympic Winter Sports and subsequent tourist events made the city a magnet for visitors.

The city began to turn a corner and was set on a recovery path that seemed solid. Jobs were growing again and the city's population was no longer declining. Much of Torino's new found strength came from regional support from Piedmonte, one of Italy's most prosperous regions. Other innovations helped the city, such as the birth and rapid expansion of the 'Slow Food' movement, leading to further growth in tourism as visitors were drawn to the annual international Slow Food celebrations, the 'Salone di Gusto'. Expansion encouraged fast immigration, now often from Africa, north and south of the Sahara.

Yet the major international banking crisis was to hit the recovering city hard. The huge resources plunged into the restructuring of the city left Torino with an unfundable debt once the 2008 financial crisis hit, made vastly worse by the Eurozone crisis that followed, and Italy's chaotically shaky government under Berlusconi. In all this recent period of economic difficulty, immigrants have continued to pour into the city, helping fuel continuing population growth, but placing very heavy demands on the city's housing and other public resources.

It is therefore all the more remarkable that incubators, start-ups, design companies, advanced manufacturers, research-based innovation centres have continued to progress. International alliances, some harking back to Fiat's early links with Detroit, placed Torino's auto engineering skills at the forefront of developments in engine technology, electric cars, and hydrogen — a product of plentiful renewable hydroelectricity, potentially a major low carbon energy

Photo 7.6: Sharing project in converted Fiat worker flats: providing accommodation for visitors, students, short term residents and emergency homeless cases on a co-operative, non-profit basis

source. Torino has kept its focus on advanced technical and engineering skills; advanced transport innovation; the use and application of renewable energy, such as hydrogen; business support and services; information technology, linked to design and engineering; international outward facing alliances and enterprise developments; major events and the continuing expansion of tourism; social innovation and investment.

Torino has experienced many ups and downs and its low income population has suffered many setbacks. It has shown many times over that it can respond to the problems that beset it and has learnt to invent new responses to seemingly insuperable challenges. This is especially true of the new housing initiatives that the city is banking on in response to rising rents, a steep rise in evictions and an acute lack of affordable housing. Out of funds and almost bankrupt, the city is working with charities, churches, cooperatives, bank foundations and property owners to develop 'sharing social hotels'. These innovative models house a wide mix of people looking for accommodation, so the social hotels can be self-financing. 'Social hotels' use renovated and remodelled property that had become obsolete, and function as cooperative enterprises. They help some of the most destitute people, alongside international engineering students and business visitors in a deeply impressive and workable mixture of charity and business. The cooperative organisations that run them work to improve neighbourhood conditions as well as integrate marginal people within the city. They train locals

Photo 7.7: *Community event at the San Salvario neighbourhood centre adjacent to Torino's main station – a multi-racial low income area*

in the jobs they need, including the building work to repair and maintain the buildings, the cafe and restaurant work within the centres. The social hotels welcome newcomers, offer meals to people running short of food, restore disused buildings, provide training and many other functions. They also encourage residents and neighbours to join in social and learning activities in the hotel.

Torino has developed some impressive neighbourhood centres in the poorest areas, run by and through community groups that provide multiple social services such as child care, elderly support, integration of foreigners, training and jobs. They also generate revenue by hiring out space to local groups and for community events. Their simple, basic 'Slow Food' cafes and restaurants generate revenue to help cover costs and also create a dynamic social environment in deprived areas. These different social initiatives contribute to Torino's progress in spite of pain; bank foundations invariably help with funding and wider expertise.

The strong and continuing development of advanced engineering, much of it specialising in the auto skills that are embedded in Torino's history, has made Torino a leader in electric cars, the development of hydrogen as a non-polluting renewable energy source for transport, advanced train technology. SMEs in Torino make specialist parts for Germany's powerful and highly successful vehicle industry. Torino is becoming the inventor of environmentally friendly transport, using old hydro-energy skills based on water sources from the Alpine foothills nearby with auto engineering skills from its car-making heyday, to develop hydrogen and electricity based transport – many times less environmentally damaging than petrol. Torino is home to the invention of the first all-electric, city-wide car share scheme, now operating successfully in many cities, including Paris.

Now the environmental challenge is coming to the fore. There is an explosion of solar PV installations and retrofitting old buildings to save energy. There is a highly ambitious scheme to provide a unified combined heat and power energy system across the city, operating at vastly greater efficiency, providing all domestic energy needs from recycled waste and renewable sources. It already covers over half the city.

The constant attempt to attract tourists has placed Torino fourth in Italy's enviable record-breaking tourist magnetism – behind only Rome, Venice and Florence. Torino has built on the success of Olympics, the celebration of Italian unification, the exhibition of the Holy Shroud, a revered relic attracting many devout and curious visitors, the 150th anniversary of the founding of the Carabinieri (Italy's National Guard), the original 'Slow Food' movement and its renowned Salone del Gusto.

Torino is set to become a city of tomorrow through its national and international role, its strong enterprise creation, its high level design and engineering skills, its density and social commitment, its plethora of SMEs, incubators, experiments and participative practices. It faces huge challenges in the sluggish Italian economy, the heavy debt – the highest in debt laden Italy – which it still has to pay down. The integration of the fast growing immigrant population is a huge challenge. The loss of European and state support has cramped, but not crushed, the city's style. But Torino works as a model for social, economic and environmental survival in troubled times.

Photo 7.8: *Politecnico di Torino: a crucial hub of innovation and enterprise creation based in former Fiat factory*

Photo 7.9: *Politecnico di Torino: a crucial hub of innovation and enterprise creation based in former Fiat factory*

EIGHT

Shoots of growth in older industrial cities in the US

Bruce Katz and Alex Jones

The boarded up homes, the decaying storefronts, the aging
church rolls, kids from unknown families who swaggered
down the streets – loud congregations of teenage boys,
teenage girls feeding potato chips to crying toddlers, the
discarded wrappers tumbling down the block – all of it
whispered painful truths, told them the progress they'd
found was ephemeral, rooted in thin soil, that it might not
even last their lifetimes.

Barack Obama, *Dreams from my Father*

Box 8.1: Detroit – a story

High up in the Austrian Tyroll, a young journalist, just returned from six weeks
in Detroit, read to a small group of artists and academics some of the personal
stories she had picked up as she wandered around the half empty, somewhat
scary neighbourhoods of Detroit, which declared bankruptcy in 2013. One story
struck home.[1]

A young, white jazz music lover and record collector, Brad, opened a shop,
'People's Records', in 2003 selling old vinyl records, mainly 45s. His shop was
in an insecure shopfront in a half-abandoned neighbourhood. Brad searched
boarded up, abandoned houses, their attics, garages and basements, for old
records. "Old records are the last thing people want to take with them when
they move – they're heavy." These discarded records were often of famous but
long forgotten Motown greats. Now that vinyl records have become the pure
fashion sound in music, particularly jazz, they are worth something. Brad gets
specialist collectors from Europe and even Japan coming in search of his vinyls.
Occasionally, they sell for $100s – often for $35. He has about 11,000 records
in his store, many in crammed, barely sorted boxes.

Brad has built lots of friendships with local teenagers who help by searching abandoned properties and bringing old 45s into Brad's shop for a couple of dollars. He enjoys their company, knows there are far too few opportunities, and teaches them about their 'damn cool' grandparents and their music. He encourages them to find music they like for themselves.

One young lad, who is lame and with a bad eye, finds two old gospel records among the thousands Brad holds. He is hoping to invent a new kind of Motown music, 'Gospel hip hop', with help from his brother's computer. Brad is enthusiastic. He believes every idea has promise. All Detroit's best creations came from the "something in the air". "Someone tries something, a new idea, even when others think he's mad. That's how it's always worked in Detroit."

Brad talks about the poverty and worries how the new creative economy links with the mass of young people he is friendly with. "For lots of people, it's going really badly." Brad is part of the creative economy – "I try to show them what a great culture is buried in these labels". He goes to the local hip hop clubs – "that way, everyone's together. I make no distinction". For Brad the connection between his young business and his young helpers, including the gospel hip hop creator, is vital. Otherwise the new recovering Detroit will not succeed. Brad says he makes enough to get buy and help a few others with a 'couple of dollars' he has even though now moved his store to a more secure and upcoming neighbourhood near the university. He makes sure the local Detroiters still come and feel at home. He says that does not make him creative – it makes him part of the local scene.

Introduction

The future of American cities has not looked brighter in decades. After an era of suburbanisation, changing demographic preferences and the restructuring of the broader economy have begun to favour the city, reversing years of declining population and employment even in some of the nation's hardest hit regions.

As Brookings demographer Bill Frey has observed, 2010 was the first year that core city population growth outpaced that of the suburbs since the Second World War.[2] Despite a slowdown in growth in the most recent data, rates remain above those of the late 20th century. A January 2015 report from the City Observatory noted that employment is following those new residents: since the beginning of the recession in 2007 through to 2011, job growth saw a 0.5% increase in the city core, while employment in the periphery dropped by 0.1%.[3]

These trends reflect changing dynamics in the United States and across the world. People in older and younger age bands, retiring Baby Boomers and millennials, are changing household patterns and revaluing the urban amenities that cities have to offer. At the same time, globalisation and technological change are disrupting business models, ushering in a period of 'open innovation,' where collaboration (and the proximity and density that foster it) is an economic imperative.

The result is a new found appreciation of what makes cities unique – walkability, density, diversity. This, in turn, is fuelling a rebirth in the downtowns – and the band surrounding the downtown – of American cities, where these attributes are most common.

Still, the urban revival of the past decade has been uneven. By the end of 2014, five years after the end of the Great Recession, only 52 of the United States' 100 largest metropolitan areas had fully recovered the jobs lost.[4] Downtown revitalisation, however substantial, has generally not been strong enough to induce widespread neighbourhood regeneration. Just as was the case through the 1990s, the challenge for US policymakers and urban advocates is to ensure that the revaluing of 'city-ness' – and the related economic benefits – extends through to our most distressed cities and most distressed neighbourhoods within them.

To take full advantage of the moment, we need to understand the way the world – and our cities – work. These cities are fundamentally co-governed, by their mayors and elected leaders, but also by networks of businesses, philanthropies, non-profit groups, universities and the individuals who lead these institutions. The most successful economic development strategies are developed and carried out through partnerships and between networks. These strategies are also firmly rooted to their place – building off of existing assets and advantages rather than trying to imitate other places.

Such strategies apply to the continuum of cities. They apply to economic winners such as Boston, San Francisco and New York that are now struggling to face the challenges of prosperity like traffic congestion, the lack of affordable housing, and the growing gap between the rich and poor. These strategies apply even in cities that have struggled for decades. This chapter will highlight emblematic examples in Pittsburgh, Philadelphia, Cleveland and Detroit – where shoots of growth are emerging that can be leveraged into a broader economic renewal. Each is at a different stage in the development of their cores, but understanding their progress is critical, not just to spread benefits throughout the city and region, but also to spread the lessons across the country, and to struggling cities through the world.

Older industrial cities in the US

The 'state of the city' in the United States was not always so healthy. Decades of suburbanisation, globalisation and economic restructuring decimated both the population and employment base of many of the country's core cities.

Even ten years ago, while strong market cities such as San Francisco and New York and those in the growing South and Southwest were thriving again, many cities in the United States remained mired in post-industrial decline. A 2007 Brookings report focused on those cities in the direst straits – the older industrial US cities. The 65 cities identified, including the four we explore in this chapter, lagged behind the rest of the nation in both economic conditions – employment and business growth – as well as residential wellbeing – income and poverty, unemployment, and labour force participation rates.

Restoring Prosperity found that the economies in these cities were unable to retool and renew through the latter half of the 20th century in the face of the challenges posed by rapid globalisation and deindustrialisation. They were specialised in manufacturing at nearly double the rate of other cities – accounting for 27% of their workforce in 1970 versus 17% in the rest of the country – and they struggled to shift from an industrial economy to a knowledge-based economy. Between 1970 and 1990, manufacturing employment in these older industrial cities fell by 33%.[5]

As jobs left, so too did residents – average population in these cities during the same period dropped 2%, but that obscures the severity in some cities. Philadelphia shed 19% of its residents; Pittsburgh Pennsylvania, Cleveland, and Detroit lost nearly one third of their residents. At the same time, those left behind were often those who could not afford to leave. Poverty rates in this group of cities climbed steadily to 22% by 1990. These economic conditions exacerbated the effects of 'white flight' to the suburbs that began in the 1950s, leaving behind segregated cities with many intensely disadvantaged communities.

While examples of acutely distressed cities are dotted across the United States, the Rust Belt region – previously renowned for its manufacturing prowess – contained the greatest concentration of struggling urban cores such as Cleveland, Ohio, Detroit, Michigan, Philadelphia and Pittsburgh. Table 8.1 shows the economic distress of these cities, relative to other US cities, in 2000, using the measure detailed in *Restoring Prosperity*.[6]

Table 8.1: Older industrial cities evidence

Older Industrial Cities[7]					
	Pittsburgh	Philadelphia	Cleveland	Detroit	Average of other 237 cities
City Economic Condition Index (1990–2000)					
Change in employment	-7.80%	-12.7%	-12.00%	-12.80%	18%
Change in annual payroll (County)	20.80%	11.40%	17.70%	13.20%	45.10%
Change in establishments (County)	0.80%	-9.10%	3.20%	1.90%	18%
Residential Economic Wellbeing Index (2000)					
Median household income	$28,588	$30,746	$25,928	$29,526	$38,510
Per capita income	$18,816	$16,509	$14,291	$14,717	$20,424
Unemployment rate	10.10%	10.90%	11.20%	13.80%	6.50%
Labour force participation rate	58.50%	55.90%	57.40%	56.30%	65.50%
Poverty rate	20.40%	22.90%	26.30%	26.10%	15.20%

Source: Vey, 2007

While employment grew in cities across the country, these older industrial cities continued to lose jobs. Household and per capita incomes remained stubbornly below the national average. And between higher unemployment rates and lower labour force participation, significantly less of the residential population was gainfully employed. These were economies – and workers – that continued to be rocked by the economic transformation of the late 20th century.

With its economy singularly focused on steel manufacturing, Pittsburgh suffered greatly through the deindustrialisation of the 1980s. The economy bottomed out in 1983, when peak unemployment in the region rose to over 17%. Over that decade, it is estimated that 100,000 manufacturing jobs alone were lost in the region, with severe impact on secondary supply chains and the service and retail sectors.

The city of Philadelphia was more a victim of decentralisation and suburbanisation, as the surrounding region retained a diverse economy and growth through the second half of the 20th century. Still, manufacturing in the city collapsed, from over 350,000 employed in the sector in the 1950s to 35,000, barely one-tenth of that, by 2000. In the decade between 1990 and 2000, the core city population declined 4.5% while total metropolitan population increased 3.2%.

Cleveland, like Pittsburgh, was a city battered by both urban decline and regional economic collapse. The whole metro lost 13% of its employment base in the latter half of the 20th century – manufacturing jobs fell by 40%.[8] The city sat smack in the middle of a Rust Belt economy that offered no hope of a comeback: neighbouring cities such as Akron and Youngstown suffered jobs losses as bad, if not worse.

In Detroit, the auto industry expansion that by 1930 made the city the fourth largest in the United States also contributed to its demise. A steady decline began in the 1960s that would eventually hollow out over 60% of the city's peak population. Both the suburbanisation and globalisation of the auto industry, combined with decades of political mismanagement and corruption, left Detroit as the poster child of urban decline and dysfunction, culminating in its 2013 bankruptcy.

The impact of this deindustrialisation continued through the 2000s: A 2012 Brookings report on manufacturing jobs found that between these four cities, manufacturing job losses continued over the decade 2000–10, exacerbated by the impact of the Great Recession. Losses ranged from 32% in Pittsburgh to 52% in Detroit.[9]

Cities rebound

Yet, in the years since the *Restoring Prosperity* report, and through the economic restructuring post-Great Recession, things have begun to turn around for some of the US' older industrial cities. Driven by growth in their downtown and surrounding cores, some cities are adding population and jobs for the first time in decades.

Table 8.2 shows the steep population decline in the four cities between 1970 and 2010. From 2010–13, population began to grow again in Philadelphia and Pittsburgh while the rate of population loss slowed significantly in the other two cities, Detroit and Cleveland. The overall citywide pattern is encouraging.

The revival of major downtowns across the United States has been underway for some time. According to Philadelphia's Center City District, from 2000 to 2010, the country's ten largest downtowns, generally the stronger coastal or Sunbelt cities, grew 77% faster than the country as a whole.[10]

But a broader shift in population patterns began after the Great Recession. 2010 marked the first time in decades that population growth in the 50 largest US cities exceeded growth in their suburbs. As recently as 2000–10, suburban population growth was triple that of primary cities (1.38% annually in suburbs versus 0.42% in cities). That changed in 2010 as core city growth reached 1.03% and suburban growth 0.96%. This trend has continued in the years since 2010.[11]

Table 8.2: Population development in selected cities, 1950–2013

	1950	1970	2000	2013	Cumulative change 1970–2010	Cumulative change 2010–13
Cleveland	914,808	751,046	478,403	390,113	-1.583%	-0.556%
Detroit	1,849,568	1,511,336	951,270	688,701	-1.858%	-1.189%
Philadelphia	2,071,605	1,948,609	1,517,550	1,553,165	-0.609%	0.590%
Pittsburgh	676,806	520,167	334,563	305,841	-1.320%	0.015%

Source: US Census (http://www.census.gov/prod/www/decennial.html)

Much of this population growth is the result of the changing preferences of young, highly-educated new residents. A recent analysis found that since 2000, the education profile of young adults in cities has jumped, from a college-attainment rate of 43% in 2000 to 55% in 2014. These educated young workers are more than twice as likely as other residents to live close in to the core of cities and, in most cities, they make up a majority of new residents.

The young and talented move in where businesses are starting up, and vice versa, setting in train a virtuous circle of population and job growth. An analysis by City Observatory of 41 large metropolitan areas found a reversal of the 'job sprawl' that dominated economic development up until the recession. Between 2002 and 2007, job growth in the periphery of metros was 12% annually, while city centre employment was stagnant at 0.1%. This trend reversed post-recession, as city centres – defined as a 3 mile radius from the urban core central business district – added jobs at a rate of 0.5% annually and peripheral jobs declined 0.1% annually. In Pittsburgh and Philadelphia, the trend was even starker, with core city growth rates of 1% and 2% while peripheral jobs stagnated.

What's happening and what's next

The shoots of growth in struggling cities are not akin to the old model of urban regeneration – both in terms of leadership and focus.

Rather than being financed by the federal government or driven by large locally subsidised projects like stadia or convention centres, much of the growth has been the product of local public, private and civic actors taking advantage of broad demographic and market dynamics that revalue the cores of cities as live, work and play communities. This reflects a shift in the United States, away from centralised leadership and towards a networked approach.

This is at the heart of what we call 'the metropolitan revolution' that is sweeping across the United States. In the aftermath of the Great Recession, the federal government has become mired in partisan gridlock and succumbed to structural budget challenges that all but assure its declining relevance in the next decade of urban growth. In its place, collaborative local efforts have taken on the challenge of renewing and stewarding metropolitan economies.

The focus of these efforts is also more economic in nature, rather than just oriented towards real estate development. The brightest spots in these cities are places that are restoring and reviving their urban amenities – dense, walkable neighbourhoods with plentiful retail, restaurants and recreation – while also leveraging their economic assets – universities, medical campuses, research facilities – to advance an economic transformation at the same time as a physical transformation.

Progress remains uneven. Those cities with legacy assets and strong institutions have thrived, while those in the direst straits are struggling to convert the economic potential into sustained renewal.

Among the four cities highlighted in this chapter, each is at a different point in its economic restructuring. For some, the work will take decades – to replace the jobs and residents lost in the downturn. But in all the cities, the downtown and inner cores contain a spark of economic potential that offers a path towards a vibrant and prosperous 21st century economy. Table 8.3 highlights the job growth in the central business districts before 2011, except in Detroit which is now changing.

Pittsburgh is perhaps the furthest along in its economic evolution. Its industrial past left behind shuttered factories and thousands of unemployed; yet it also left significant assets – institutions like Carnegie Mellon University, which owes its existence to the founders of

Table 8.3: Employment change in central business districts, 2002–11

	Philadelphia	Pittsburgh	Cleveland	Detroit
2002	250,359	145,991	128,399	143,555
2011	275,248	155,169	137,855	128,203
2002 to 2011	+24,889	+9,178	+9,456	-15,352

Source: US Census, 2011 (http://www.census.gov/population/metro/data/)

Carnegie Steel and Mellon Bank. Carnegie Mellon along with fellow advanced research institutions such as the University of Pittsburgh and the Pitt Medical Center have been critical to the economic evolution in Pittsburgh and are central to the resurgence of the city centre and the city as a whole.

Together, the institutions in the greater downtown area and the nearby Oakland neighbourhood house nearly 70,000 students and steward over $1 billion in annual research and development funding in Pittsburgh's core. This research base has been an engine for both new business – such as Aquion Energy, a start-up battery manufacturer that grew out of Carnegie Mellon University – and for attracting existing firms into the city – both Google and Uber were drawn to establish operations there to take advantage of the innovation ecosystem in Pittsburgh's core. This dynamic has enabled the city to attract and retain an educated workforce: 36% of adults are college graduates, well above the national average of 29%.

Spurred by the institutional research platform and entrepreneurial job creation, Pittsburgh's economy has come back to life. From a peak of 9% in the immediate aftermath of the recession, the unemployment rate across the city dropped to 4% by the end of 2014, a full point below the national average.

Philadelphia, too, has experienced growth after years of decline. Its core is adding both employment and population: the Center City neighbourhood grew by 16% between 2000 and 2010, while employment in the adjacent University City district grew by nearly 30%.

Together, these two pockets alone concentrate roughly 43% of all jobs in Philadelphia into just 6% of the city area and demand is growing. Office vacancy rates are declining and average asking rent is increasing. Retail and tourism are expanding. But the main economic driver continues to be 'eds and meds' – the universities and medical centres – which account for 21% of all jobs in the centre and inner core of the city and 79% of all jobs in University City.

The seeds of Philadelphia's evolution were planted early. In 1963 a consortium of research institutions both in the city and throughout the region founded the University City Science Center, the nation's first urban research park. Today, the centre has 30 teaching staff and its campus is home to hundreds of start-ups and spin-offs from nearby research labs. It anchors a constellation of research institutions that together oversee $1 billion of research and development money into the University City district.

The revival of **Cleveland**'s core, as in Pittsburgh and Philadelphia, owes itself to the concentration of globally significant institutional actors. Its University Circle district, to the east of the downtown expanded from the home of Case Western Reserve University to a thriving neighbourhood containing dozens of research and medical facilities such as the Cleveland Clinic; cultural amenities, such as the Cleveland Museum of Art; and public spaces.

Those established institutions enabled the district to survive the economic downturn that plagued the broader region, and their recent expansion and new investments have brought new energy to the city. The latest analysis has found that the square mile area of University Circle generates $14.3 billion in direct and indirect annual economic output for the city and 80,000 direct and indirect jobs. This growth has been overseen by University Circle Inc., a non-profit civic organisation that promotes everything from economic development to place making to local services within the district.

Similar, though less rapid, growth is occurring in the downtown of Cleveland. Traditionally housing very few residents, the downtown population is at an all-time high, with residential occupancy rates of over 98%. It can thank its share of anchor institutions such as the Cleveland State University but the downtown is also seeing the fruits of 30 years of large investments in amenities such as sports stadia, museums, theatre, and new public transport catalyse growth in residential and retail projects.

Among the four cities, **Detroit** clearly remains furthest from economic recovery. The city has long symbolised the extremes of urban decline in the United States. Its bankruptcy declaration in the summer of 2013 was the largest municipal bankruptcy filing in US history. This was preceded by years of deindustrialisation, population loss, and political mismanagement.

Unsurprisingly, the birthplace of the automobile was also home to endless urban sprawl; at 139 miles squared, the city itself is larger than Manhattan, San Francisco and Boston combined. After its mass population exodus from the 1960s onwards, the city, in many ways, became one of empty places and ungoverned spaces. A 2013 report commissioned by a coalition of public, private, and philanthropic organisations, *Detroit Future City*[12], chronicled the state of the city: nearly 80,000 vacant housing units, over 50,000 non-functioning street lights, a water system that was only 40% functional. Just like its physical infrastructure, the economic infrastructure was also crumbling in the city: the Detroit metropolitan area has some of the worst job sprawl in the country, with 77% of jobs located more than 10 miles from downtown, and the city itself, now a little more than one third of its former size.

But even in Detroit, there is a turnaround occurring; one that had been underway quietly for years prior to the city's bankruptcy, but that has grown stronger since. Germinated in the absence of a well-functioning city government, the evolution has been led by a loose network of private business, active philanthropic organisations, and engaged citizens. This network is reviving Detroit from its core – in the greater downtown area that sits along the Detroit River – with Canada located on the far bank. Remarkable things are happening in a 7.2 square mile area, fuelled by private and civic energy and investment. The downtown itself is being transformed by an evangelical urban billionaire, Dan Gilbert. In 2007, Gilbert moved the headquarters of Quicken Loans – his online mortgage company – from the suburbs of the city into downtown Detroit. Since then, he has attracted more than 12,000 employees into the downtown and purchased over 60 buildings in the downtown area.

Gilbert's confidence has sparked decisions by other firms, large and small, to expand their downtown presence – health care companies such as Blue Cross Blue Shield, which brought 3,400 jobs into the downtown, energy companies like DTE Energy, architecture and creative firms. A lively community of tech start-ups is also emerging – galvanised by the alluring notion of building a company while rebuilding a city. And people are moving back into the downtown at such a pace that developers cannot build housing fast enough to meet

Photo 8.1: Basketball pitch within Downtown Detroit attracting young people from surrounding neighbourhoods

the demand – occupancy levels in the downtown neighbourhood are at all-time highs of 98% and the greater downtown population has grown to over 35,000. The people and firms moving in crave the physical 'bones' and amenities of old Detroit – walkable streets, historic buildings, cultural and sports venues, access to waterfronts, formal and informal gathering places.

A few miles away another revival is underway, fuelled by the expansion of anchor institutions in the Midtown neighbourhood. Henry Ford Hospital System – the largest in the city – has embarked on a $1 billion expansion that would include not only new and enhanced health care and medical distribution facilities but a community health park with commercial, retail, and housing. Wayne State University – the largest public research university in the city of Detroit – is building a $90 million biomedical research facility. The College for Creative Studies, one of the top design colleges in the world, has turned the historic General Motors' research facility – the famed Argonaut building – into a college campus, a special high school and the production home of Shinola, a watch and bicycle manufacturer that employs former automotive production workers. Shinola bikes are prominent in shop window displays in the centre of London, the ultimate accolade.

All this activity – corporate relocation, anchor expansion, entrepreneurial growth, housing and retail – is now fuelling the next infusion of energy and capital, the building of M1 Rail, a light rail line from Downtown to Wayne State University in the Midtown, the area around the city centre. A consortium of public, private, and philanthropic institutions, including Dan Gilbert, the Kresge Foundation and the Big 3 auto companies – Ford, Chrysler and General Motors – have committed over $100 million to construction of the light rail project, 3.3 miles long, which will link downtown Detroit with the university area.

These are a few examples illustrating more than $9 billion that has been invested in the city core since 2006, according to a 2015 report by the Hudson-Weber Foundation. The momentum behind these investments is only increasing: of that $9 billion, $5.2 billion was invested since only 2013.[13]

These cities are not alone. There are nascent signs of renewal throughout older industrial cities. In Buffalo, NY, the downtown has been remade with the 2001 founding of the Buffalo-Niagara Medical Center, which currently employs 12,000 and has spurred billions of dollars in new investment. And in St. Louis, Missouri, a coalition of universities, medical centres, and philanthropies formed the CORTEX innovation district in the heart of the city, a $2 billion project expected to create over 10,000 jobs upon completion.

Photo 8.2: Detroit: The Auburn – a new residential development with cyclists reclaiming the streets

Innovation districts

These regeneration efforts are frequently grounded in the heart of cities – in areas of concentrated economic activity in urban downtowns and midtowns, which we and others have termed 'innovation districts.' These districts offer languishing cities the ability to reach a critical mass of innovation, financial resources, and talent that can lead to the creation of globally competitive firms and job creation – which in turn can generate ancillary services and job recovery.

This trend reflects a fundamental shift in the spatial geography of innovation and innovative industries. For the past 50 years, the landscape of motivation has been characterised by places like California's Silicon Valley – isolated corporate campuses surrounded by sprawling suburban developments.

Today, innovation districts are emerging as a complimentary model.[14] These districts are dense, urban environments that concentrate economic, physical and networking assets – research universities, medical campuses, incubators and entrepreneurs; public transport, broadband and quality public space; a culture that promotes collaboration through formal and informal programming, face-to-face meetings and networking events.

Innovation Districts are emerging throughout the United States and abroad, taking multiple different forms. In cities with traditionally strong anchor institutions – universities or medical facilities – *anchor-plus districts* are growing, leveraging the platform of institutional research and development activity offered by the anchors. In former industrial cities, 'reimagined urban areas' are developing, spurred by strong public transport access, historic building stock, and lower real estate prices relative to the rest of the city. A further model is offered by 'urbanised science parks,' where auto centric suburban campuses that were developed in the mid-20th century, such as North Carolina's Research Triangle Park, are evolving to compete in response to new demographic and industry preferences by adding residential and retail elements to their footprint. They are essentially attempting to bring 'city-ness' into a formally suburban landscape.

The creation and success of innovation districts relies upon networks of individuals and institutions working in concert – from mayors and local governments, to real estate professionals, to university and philanthropic leaders, and ultimately private industry and entrepreneurs. If done right, the development of innovation districts offers a unique opportunity to restore broader prosperity to our cities, and even into the distressed neighbourhoods within them. Many innovation districts – whether developed on former industrial sites or near longstanding anchor institutions – tend to be proximate to lower income neighbourhoods. As they develop, they offer not just the opportunity for new secondary and service jobs, but also the potential for access to unique educational and professional experience within the innovation cluster itself.

In Philadelphia, Drexel University is planning a specialised high school that will integrate local students into research labs, offering experience that could translate to a job even right out of high school. The fact is, as recent Brookings research has pointed out[15], that many of the jobs even in the advanced economy do not require a baccalaureate degree.

Innovation districts can also promote *sustainable* growth by enhancing employment and residential density in urban cores, by inventing sustainable products and services for the market and by using the area as a living laboratory to test new sustainable solutions.

While the cores of these cities offer hope for economic revival, there is still much work to be done. Across all four cities, poverty remains well above the national average; home values remain well below. Lagging per capita income and labour force participation rates are evidence that the broader economy has yet to spread the growth in the city's core into broadly shared prosperity and more jobs. The challenge is to transmit the dynamism of these cores throughout the rest of the city.

Spreading prosperity

Ten years after identifying the struggles of older industrial cities in the United States, there are clear signs of improvement. Still, the employment and residential growth remains, in many cases, inaccessible to the broader population. Decades of racial segregation and the concentration of inner city poverty have made these challenges more intractable. It remains to be seen whether Detroit – and other reviving cities – can translate the growth in their downtowns and midtowns into broader urban prosperity and economic rejuvenation. Still, several strategies stand out to link economic growth with the rest of the city.

First, the jobs created in these cities must be physically accessible to residents throughout the city region. This requires improvements in urban and metropolitan transportation systems to ensure there are connections between neighbourhoods that are growing and those that are stagnant. It also demands smart housing solutions that pair the increasing development of market rate housing with incentives to build and expand affordable housing.

Second, jobs must also be accessible in terms of education and skills. The economic restructuring in cities is shifting employment away from traditional manufacturing industries into more knowledge intensive and service based industries, such as health care and information services. While many of these jobs require advanced education, many do not. A 2015 Brookings report[16] found that over half of the jobs in advanced industries are available to workers with sub-baccalaureate degrees that have specialised training and skills. The colocation of firms and educational institutions in small geographical areas like innovation districts offers a unique opportunity for collaborative education programmes that focus on career skills relevant to the local cluster.

Finally, the employment and population growth in these cities offer some promise of improving the fiscal balance sheets of central cities. A healthy tax base is critical to enable cities to make smart investments in infrastructure, public services and social programmes, particularly during a period when the federal government and many state governments are likely to scale back these kinds of investments. These developments broadly match the changes under way in struggling European cities too.

Implications

The resurgence within the US' older industrial cities, grounded in a needed economic transformation and fuelled by a downtown revival, offers lessons for cities in Europe and around the world that have been left behind by globalisation and deindustrialisation.

First, the successes in these cities have been driven by networks of public, private and civic institutions and leaders rather than government alone. Sometimes institutions and leaders work on joint, collaborative initiatives for example, the M1 Rail project in Detroit. Often they make investments on their own, for example, the relocation of a company or the expansion of a hospital or university. Sometimes, special institutions such as a business improvement district or an economic development corporation facilitate the process. Sometimes, the local government leads the way; often they support the development of new markets and place making through land use, flexible planning, and other policies. The key insight is that cities are co-governed and market revival is co-produced in ways that make them more nimble, affirmative and pragmatic than federal and state governments.

Second, and related to the first, the revival of cities has been driven by a combination of public, private and civic capital rather than government subsidies exclusively. As seen in Detroit and elsewhere, capital from local institutions – philanthropies, universities, corporations – is being smartly deployed to improve the public realm and spark business growth and job creation. The public sector is present but not omnipresent. In essence, a new field of metropolitan finance is being created, which aggregates not only the public balance sheet of the city and traditional municipal finance tools but also, critically, the private balance sheets of anchor institutions, corporations and philanthropies. Once local markets achieve a certain momentum and critical mass, outside capital from large national and global institutions is attracted, starting a virtuous cycle of investment, revenue generation, job growth and increasing prosperity.

Finally, the revival of cities can be accelerated, deepened and shared with all citizens if higher levels of government act with greater purpose and reliability. The growth of anchor-led innovation districts is a product, in part, of routine federal and state investments in, for example, health care, higher education, and research and development. These districts are essentially commercialising for the market ideas generated through federal and state investments. Maintaining if not expanding these investments would be a sign of true leadership.

At the same time, enabling and empowering local institutions and leaders to align federal and state resources, for example around housing or skills with the distinctive needs of their local areas rather than the arbitrary 'one size fits all' prescriptions of federal programmes, would fuel inclusive growth and promote the efficient use of valuable resources.

By the end of the 20th century, older industrial cities in the United States found themselves in a deep economic hole. At the start of the 21st century, there is a roadmap out: these cities have the physical bones to take advantage of a renewed appreciation of 'city-ness'; many have the legacy institutions and assets to drive the transition towards an advanced economy; and all these cities are composed of networks of leaders who, given a shared vision, can collaborate to make their city better.

Box 8.2: Tale of a city – Detroit

Detroit may hit international headlines more often than any other 'rust belt' city. It is famous in Europe for its bankruptcy in 2013, its ugly race riot in 1967, its Cadillacs and its Fords, both created in the city. It has experienced the highest murder rate of any large US city, the highest poverty rate, and some of the country's most notorious drug gangs, with devastating heroin and crack cocaine epidemics in the 1970s and 1980s. Its city government became notorious for mismanagement and corruption. In sharp contrast, Wayne State University and the Detroit Institute of Arts flourish in a city that is only one third of its former size and where one third of the city's land is disused.

The population has gone from 70% white in 1970 to 83% black in 2014. The city's powerful music tradition – Motown Jazz – and the city's world-famous boxer – Jo Lewis – lend glamour to a city that seems 'on a fast track to economic desolation'. Yet this chapter has shown that an economic revival is underway, based on renewed confidence and new investment, fast growing jobs and enterprises. It is important to tie the two Detroits together – on the one hand, a sense of hopelessness; on the other, signs of hope.

Detroit began in the 17th century as a small trading settlement on the borders with Canada. By the 19th century, it was a thriving industrial city and by 1900 had a population of 250,000.

Henry Ford, the genius inventor of modern cars, founded his great enterprise in the city, changing forever the face of modern transport and the world economy. Ford inspired young entrepreneurs from Torino to found Fiat, borrowing many ideas from his path-breaking factory system, and establishing links that were to continue to the present.

Henry Ford was so successful he established a 'city within a city', Highland Park, with its revolutionary assembly lines and unheard of high wages. Chrysler and General Motors also established themselves in and around Detroit, and the big three became renowned for their super-fast, oversized, gas-guzzling cars. Workers flocked to Detroit and the population boomed, reaching nearly 2 million by 1950.

At this time, the flow of impoverished former share croppers from the Deep South, descendants of African slaves, poured northwards, just at the point when the city's population peaked and began to decline as suburbs grew under federal land and mortgage subsidies. The rapid growth of Detroit's suburbs made 'white flight' a byword for growing segregation in the city. Racial troubles quickly mounted and Martin Luther King made a key speech in Detroit at the height of his civil rights campaign in 1964, shortly before his famous 'I have a dream' speech in Washington.

Civil rights legislation, passed by President Lyndon Johnson in 1965, paved the way for the 'Great Society' programme, possibly the most ambitious and generous investment in poor minority communities across the States. Leading cities like Detroit with deeply divided communities and intense poverty were major beneficiaries, encouraging the emergence of many young black community leaders. Detroit became a model city in the federal anti-poverty programme, and its first black mayor was a leading player in attracting federal support to the city.

However, conflicts arose over where large investments should focus, the downtown business district or the impoverished inner city neighbourhoods, intensely segregated and harshly policed by a predominantly white police force. Clashes between black youth and white police eventually spilled over into a devastating riot with a death toll of nearly 50, 450 injured, and 2000 buildings razed to the ground. At that point, businesses began to flee the city and investment almost dried up. The city seemed convulsed with irreversible losses. Empty buildings were set on fire, guns could be heard, and schools were deeply segregated. As the population declined — which it did steeply and continually from 1950 up to the present — so the share of white people fell until the city became today an almost all black city.

Detroit and the State of Michigan were accused of creating de facto segregation in the city's schools by virtue of the restrictive housing covenants in the city and suburbs, the concentration of public housing in segregated ghetto neighbourhoods, the red lining of ghetto areas, and the exemption of growing suburbs from housing or schooling obligations to help the city. In 1970, after a long legal battle, the Supreme Court judge in the case against the State of Michigan ruled that de facto segregation was as culpable as de jure segregation, as in Detroit's case, and asserted that Michigan State 'washes its hands of its own creations', by implication becoming responsible for the de facto segregation that state policies caused and supported. Public (state) schools are still struggling with this problem today and poor literacy and school drop-out are both major problems. So bad is the city's school record that fully one half of Detroit's children do not attend the city's public schools. Parents opt for religious schools, charter schools or schools outside the city boundary (which is now allowed by the State of Michigan). The spaces created by a falling population facilitate this rejection of the public system.

Empty buildings and empty land, deserted offices and factories, boarded up mansions of the motor barons all tell the same story as efforts in the 1970s failed to revive the city's fortunes, shaken by the riots. While Chicago, Washington DC, Philadelphia, Los Angeles and other US cities suffered similar riots in 1968 and after, Detroit was extremely hard hit by the added disaster of the international oil crisis of 1974, undermining its still strong car industry. Not only was the city over-reliant on the three car giants; their product was suddenly oversized, over-energy consuming, over-embedded in the throwaway mass-production pattern of the post-war boom era. As large, rusting derelict cars piled up on huge waste sites around the country, Detroit was forced to scale back on everything – the size of its cars, its factories, its workforce, its housing stock, its schools. The city was left with an infrastructure vastly too big for the shrinking city. The main railway station closed in 1988, a major transport severance that cut off Detroit's rail links for the future.

The scale of the problems defied the powers of the city government with its sharply declining tax base and levels of bureaucratic incompetence. The historic liabilities of oversized buildings, roads and public services such as street lights, water, power and sewage systems were simply beyond the capabilities or capacity of the city government. The generous pension commitments made to city employees and private industrial workers in the city's heyday now looked unfundable, while basic services such as water and street lighting failed. Thus the threat of city bankruptcy gradually loomed. Federal and state aid did not come near to bridging the gap, although several federal programmes and grants helped the city in smaller ways. A new mayor made efforts to reform the city, and citizen groups made heroic efforts to close the gaping holes in provision. But Detroit seemed beyond rescue.

The international financial crisis of 2008 hit Detroit particularly hard because its cheap housing stock and its low income population had offered fertile ground for subprime mortgages – specially subsidised loans that allow people, with incomes too low to justify a conventional mortgage, to borrow on the value of the home to be purchased. Cheap homes in Detroit plummeted in value as this system took hold, with mortgaged homes sometimes reaching almost no value at all by 2010. Average house prices in Detroit fell from $98,000 in 2003 to only $15,000 in 2007, and then on down. There were 60,000 empty properties in 2009; rising to 80,000 by 2014 in spite of ambitious city clearances. In 2013, the city declared the largest municipal bankruptcy in the country's history.

So desperate was the funding crisis that, by 2014, thousands of homes were cut off (for non-payment) from water and sewage services. Tenants holding Section 8 housing vouchers have been evicted from 'unsafe' downtown blocks and city pension holders voted for a cut in their pensions. On the other hand, over 50,000 broken street lights have been reinstated with LED lights, and violent crime, still extremely high, has continued to fall.

Detroit did not lose its enterprising spirit, its committed citizens, its richly endowed heritage and infrastructure, its powerful and wealthy philanthropic institutions. Bright entrepreneurs set up the first electric car company in the US in Detroit, in 1908, 'Detroit Electric'. Electric cars were made and sold between 1911 and 1939 when they were considered more reliable, more sedate and more 'Ladylike' than the new petrol version which required cranking. The company went bankrupt in 1939 but the revival of Detroit Electric in 2008, albeit by a British based firm, provoked massive efforts by the 'old school' big three to undermine it. This rearguard move eventually backfired and by the time Chrysler and General Motors were bankrupted themselves in 2011, with Ford also on the brink, electric cars offered a new future – as did electric trains – to be embraced and fostered in an alliance with the Politecnico di Torino and Fiat. Chrysler amalgamated with Fiat in 2012. Electric cars are now produced for Detroit Electric in Holland and England.

Many citizens' organisations fought hard for the communities they represented. No task seemed too daunting, from doing up houses, to creating public works of art; developing market gardens and urban farms, to running special schools for school-age mothers. At the same time, the economic impact of the financial crisis made suburbs less attractive and less affordable, helping cities like Detroit begin a comeback. Nonetheless, the poverty, joblessness and deep racial divisions in the city remained overwhelming. The city continued to lose population.

Native Detroiter and billionaire Dan Gilbert decided in 2009 to move his Quicken Loans, a highly lucrative business, back into the city centre from the suburbs. He argues with passion that "we can do well by doing good". He has moved a total of 7000 employees back into the city; created residential units in disused buildings, now virtually fully occupied; developed start-up spaces in old buildings; and is backing the new 3 mile light rail linking the downtown with the university area. The plan is to extend this to the edge of the city. Other initiatives have followed. Detroit's 'New Economy' initiative has set up an enterprise zone called Tech Town with 250 new businesses, from the most mundane and practical dry cleaners, to the most avant-garde and speculative tech start-ups. A total of 10,000 new jobs were created in the downtown area between 2011 and 2013.

One exciting young manufacturing company, Shinola Detroit, is breaking new ground in two surprisingly related fields – specialist watches and bicycles. They link to Detroit's past because they comprise wheels, metals, mechanics and advanced manufacturing. Shinola watches are now acclaimed in Switzerland, the watch capital of the world. And Shinola bikes, made in Detroit, are conspicuously on sale in Oxford Street, London, the new biking city. Maybe Detroit itself will become a cycle city, at least within the compact, mixed-use, desegregated inner neighbourhoods it is trying to rebuild.

Such is Detroit's growing reputation for a new buzz, space and freedom of operation that both Baltimore and the Bronx report young artistic, musical and digital entrepreneurs are opting for Motown Midwest rather than the better connected, but more crowded and costly Eastern seaboard. There is more freedom to create and more space to colonise. But there remains a big question over how welcoming and inclusive the new buzz is in a city of nearly 700,000 with a reputation for community activism, protest and poverty.

The city faces immense problems of joblessness, violence, discrimination and intense concentrations of minorities. One half of all black males are jobless and one third of males in their 30s have been in jail. Nearly 40% of Detroiters live below the poverty line. Public transport is so bad that, on average, city residents can only reach one third of all city jobs in under 90 minutes; 61% of working Detroiters work outside the city. These embedded problems cannot be solved by community initiatives or business development alone. They are exactly the kind of deep social divisions and threats to order that led to the emergence of local government in Europe in the 19th century, strongly backed by national legislation, powers and funding mechanisms for public action.

The earnings gap between white and black in the US is still huge – almost double; and the wealth gap is vastly more extreme – an average of $11,000 for African

Americans, compared with almost 13 times as much for whites, $142,000. Seventy-one percent of African American babies are born outside marriage, compared with 30% for white babies.[17] The rate has tripled since the 1960s. In Detroit, these figures are more extreme still. In order to close these gaps, a massive commitment is required rather than the hope that a 'trickle down' recovery will remedy such deep-set ills. The public sector will need to adopt and promote the strategies that are working.[18]

Major city-based foundations are backing some of the positive initiatives that are pulling Detroit back from bankruptcy and from social unravelling – investing in better schools, enterprise and start-up areas, the new light rail, and many neighbourhood initiatives. There is a new proposal to support a technical high school to equip young local students with the STEM skills (science, technology, engineering, maths) for the many technical jobs that require less than a degree but more than high school drop outs. At the moment, only 11% of 24–35 year olds have a degree. Such initiatives need to multiply fast to close the gap that is widening as the city's business district starts to grow again. Detroit's future hinges on its ability to spread its new found success out from the centre and downwards to poorer, more African American neighbourhoods.

It is hard to imagine a bankrupt city starved of population not seeking to attract and welcome bright young entrepreneurs and investors. But the biggest risk is a failure to reverse the still intense segregation of the city by failing to invest in the very communities that are currently classed as too hard to save. Tensions over gentrification will grow as the city pursues a policy of abandoning the worst in favour of better areas and pushing poor people out of potentially desirable areas to allow upgrading. European experience highlights this danger. Therefore urgent public action is needed to attract investment and urban pioneers to the poorest areas as well as the most promising ones.

One unsung, but compelling, social initiative by young locals that demonstrates the enterprising culture in the heart of the city is the Detroit Soup. Once a month, young people of the city meet to share bright ideas to help the city recover, tackle its community problems, create new jobs, change conditions. The group meets in a community venue to share soup, each paying a small contribution into a fund. Everyone proposes a new idea to help Detroit communities and the participants vote for their favourite. The winner gets the collection money to help launch the idea.

From such small beginnings come big ideas. The internal combustion engine, electric cars, new light rail, Tech Town, the art collections and theatre, new bars and residences were all once just dreams. Detroit is a comeback city. It is not hard to find signs of hope. But the scale of the task can seem to swamp the progress that is in evidence. Detroit's 700,000 citizens must be part of this comeback, thereby overcoming a bitter history. **Doing well** needs to be closely bound with **doing good** if racial and social harmony are to be achieved, alongside the downtown recovery. It is surely a burden that the country as a whole should carry, just as Lyndon Johnson foresaw in his Great Society and Barack Obama talked of in his inaugural speech in 2008. There is little time to lose.

Photo 8.3: Campus Martius Park: a new square in a restored part of Downtown

Photo 8.4: Eastern Market in the heart of Detroit with fresh food, restaurants, businesses, art and culture and over 150 years of rich history

About the authors

Bruce Katz is a vice president of the Brookings Institution and founding co-director of the Metropolitan Policy Program. He is the author, along with Jennifer Bradley, of *The Metropolitan Revolution* (2013).

Alex Jones is a senior policy and research assistant at the Brookings Metropolitan Policy Program.

NINE

Finding new ways out of the woods

Given the irreversibility, the relatively modest overall levels of investment required ... and the potentially very large co-benefits of action, we can surely be confident in saying the costs of inaction are much higher than the costs of action ... much of what is likely to be necessary will have a strong community focus.

Nicholas Stern, *Why Are We Waiting?*

Box 9.1: Green cities – four short stories

Detroit's imposing Art Nouveau railway station, closed since 1988, may become a 16 storey, stacked market garden, growing vegetables and salad for the local farmers' market. In an urban food desert, food growing makes sense. All the hype about Detroit's decline overlooks the promise and potential of a green and liveable city. Around 300 green, open spaces replace what were once well laid-out, built-up streets. Many have become urban farms. Urban agriculture and tree planting are one of Detroit's new enterprises. So is land reclamation for environmental and ecological reasons.[1]

Industrial cities remind us not of woodland, but of smoke stacks and 'satanic mills'. Yet **Sheffield**, the archetypal industrial city in England's northern manufacturing heartland, a pioneer in the industrial revolution, sometimes called England's ugliest city, has 2 million urban trees, more per citizen than any other city in Europe. Sheffield borders the Peak District National Park, where, before its creation in the 1930s, workers from Sheffield, Manchester and other industrial cities invaded the protected moorland in a mass trespass to open up the grouse shooter's private land to city dwellers, and changing for posterity the way a shrinking natural environment is shared.

The city has 170 woodlands within its borders, 80 of them ancient, dating from long before Sheffield's urban-industrial explosion. Its early 19th century botanical gardens and its 21st century, glass-covered Winter Garden, with 2500 trees, shrubs and flowers from around the world, show the value of green, shared spaces within cities. They make cities cleaner, quieter, cooler and they absorb CO_2, helping to combat climate change. Seven public parks are packed within this dense city, built on seven hills. Today, Sheffield's residents are fighting in the terraced and semi-detached city streets to stop private contractors chopping down mature trees, which lock up thousands of tonnes of carbon, on the basis that mature trees are more expensive to maintain.

Saint-Étienne also has a national park on its door step at the source of the great river Loire at Mont Pilat. Saint-Étienne, a crowded, dense, working class city like Sheffield, learnt from Barcelona's citizen-based experiment in pocket parks and squares throughout the city. All over Saint-Étienne are micro-open spaces and green verges, planted with decorative, multi-coloured cabbages. In the very central square, trees are trained overhead to form a green canopy shading outdoor cafes and restaurants. Saint-Étienne now promotes green design internationally through its Design Centre.

In the Ruhr, city authorities, like **Dortmund**, encourage green verges to grow wild instead of being mown. Within a year they are full of wild flowers – and bees. Playgrounds have climbing frames sculpted from old tree trunks and heavy branches to create an urban play forest that children swarm over.

Greenery helps make 'clapped out' cities take on new life – countering environmental damage, combatting climate change and making them liveable.[2]

Introduction: European cities grow, decline and recover

Below the radar, European cities have been changing out of all recognition, above all former industrial cities. Most people know about the dramatic turnaround of Barcelona and Manchester, two large, heavily industrial, damaged and declining cities in the 1980s. But we are less familiar with the comeback of hundreds of Europe's former industrial cities, and how this growth–decline–recovery pattern reflects the broader trajectory of cities worldwide. Cities pass through many periods of decline, conflict, revolution that change their workings and lead to 'shrinkage', 'managed decline', 'abandonment', 'collapse'. Yet it is rare in Europe for that decline to go far before city governments take action. Western Europe spent the 70 years after the Second World War rebuilding its cities and economies, passing through phases of intense industrial growth, deep decline, concerted recovery efforts and recent troubles with the ongoing Euro crisis. Eastern Europe is still struggling with post-Communist population flight, the abrupt closure of uneconomic industries, the unravelling of state control. Many of its industrial cities are still in acute decline.[3] Europe cannot afford to abandon its cities when they hit trouble. Besides, we are part of the global economy, and people from all over the world are drawn by Europe's immense wealth in comparison with the chronic poverty of fast developing cities. Immigrants from the Middle East, Asia, Africa and South America pour into Europe through its many borders. So Europe's 'shrinkage' is not materialising and regrowth, albeit slow and uneven, is happening.[4] Even smaller, more beleaguered cities, such as Saint-Étienne, are recovering population.[5]

Several hundred European cities, housing around 80% of Europe's 500 million citizens, have been on a rollercoaster ride since the 1970s. How they ended up in such trouble, how they recovered, only to hit trouble again and create a new model of regrowth is the storyline of this handbook, woven around the tale of seven cities. It is an exciting and encouraging story – still leaving many questions unanswered. This handbook uses the experience of seven cities across Europe, north and south, east and west – Leipzig, Torino, Bilbao, Lille, Saint-Étienne, Sheffield, Belfast – to argue that most cities go through a process of intense growth with ever multiplying productive activities. They end up burning themselves out through environmental degradation, sprawl building, rising economic costs and competition.[6] The collapse that follows generates a strong public response and attempts to reverse the decline. In Europe, that response has been particularly intense and widespread since the 1990s.

The story of *Cities for a Small Continent*

We chose the seven cities in 2006, at the outset of our study, because they had lost so many jobs and people. They were struggling to recover, and were not chosen because they were already proven success stories. Our ten years of visiting European industrial cities have shown how common the pattern of over-rapid growth, steep decline and recovery is.[7]

Chapter One set out the core challenges facing urban Europe, finding ways of restoring, sustaining and improving the urban industrial legacy of the former wealth-creating giants of the last two centuries.

Chapter Two explored how European history has shaped its cities, with centuries of conflict and rivalry culminating in two world wars that all but devastated the continent. These cataclysmic events forged the beginnings of a united Europe, which now helps to shape the way European economies and cities function. The Second World War also divided Europe, with an 'iron curtain', forging a new 'social' model of city development, neither 'free market', anti-Communist American; nor planned, Soviet-style Communist development. European governments built strong welfare states and the European Union to unify their people and avert the risk of communism. This 'social' model shaped Europe's post-war cities.

Chapter Three explained how all seven cities in this handbook were central to Europe's explosive industrial revolution. They became internationally renowned centres of invention and wealth creation based on intense exploitation of human and environmental capacity. The post-war boom in industrial and population growth fuelled extreme development, only to crash when the 1974 oil crisis hit. This represents Phase One of our Recovery Framework – industrial economy.

Chapter Four detailed the public response to intense industrial decline, which led to job and population losses in the seven cities. City governments, backed at regional, national and European levels, invested in recovery and persuaded their citizens that a new order was vital, based on reclaiming and restoring existing assets. Cities are rich in assets – civic buildings, public spaces, anchor institutions, particularly universities. They also have wasted, obsolete and severely damaged assets, caused by industrial pollution, and extreme environmental damage of all kinds. Recovery based on reuse, reinvention and reinvestment made European cities attractive again. City-led partnerships gradually drew back private sector investment. Jobs and population stabilised and began to regrow. This represents Phase Two of our Recovery Framework – post-industrial economy. During this phase the Iron Curtain collapsed and Eastern Europe became integrated. Leipzig helps us tell this distinctive part of the story.

Phase Two did not last – the international banking crisis of 2008 which shook the world economy and its entire financial system, sent huge shock waves through our cities. **Chapter Five** showed the job losses, cuts in public investment, stalled projects, withdrawal of private investment, raising serious worries about the future of these vulnerable cities. However, the reinvestments of Phase Two, the 'steady hand at the tiller' of city governments, the overarching role of the European Union, push cities towards Phase Three of our Recovery Framework – resource-constrained economy. Cities embrace a more diverse, more producer and service-oriented economy that promises to be more environmentally friendly. This marks the beginning of Phase 3. Both populations and jobs continue to grow in the face of severe resource constraints.

Chapter Six explored in more detail how cities have reshaped their economies, building on their 'producer' traditions. They have worked with their technically oriented universities and their strong engineering traditions to create new specialisms in advanced manufacturing, materials and digital communication, building new jobs through incubators, skills training, support for small and medium enterprises, and technical back-up. Small and medium enterprises (SMEs), which survived two major crises, have proved resilient and adaptable.

City leaders and investors, supported by European Regional Development funds and national programmes, are backing new ways of running things, more broken up, more dispersed, more private–public. Increasingly public and private feed off each other – particularly because SMEs, start-ups and innovation grow together with the help of public bodies and the enterprise of private investors. Cities cannot thrive unless their private enterprises do. Private and public must reinforce each other. Chapter Six illustrated the potential of Phase Three, to become more environmentally friendly in spite of the high carbon patterns we are still locked into. The threat of climate change fuels the potential for green innovation.

Recovering cities cannot ignore poorer neighbourhoods that house the low skilled workers, immigrants, minorities and unemployed youth. **Chapter Seven** examined both the problems and responses of European governments and cities. Cities target efforts at poor areas and public services stay in place albeit with severe cutbacks, to help bind cities and communities together. The very density and proximity of Europe's cities require this. Europe's public infrastructure underpins many social enterprises, while cutbacks in public funding generate community initiatives – another form of SME. Overall, European cities retain significant levels of service infrastructure and commitment to integration, in spite of resource shortages and renewed pressures.

American Rust Belt cities are also recovering, in spite of far weaker federal and state support and in markedly similar and yet distinct ways. **Chapter Eight** showed how American city governments have lost the capacity to play a strong public interventionist role, so familiar in Europe. Depopulation, suburban sprawl and racial segregation are so entrenched that public services have been seriously weakened.[8] In spite of this, 'innovation districts', strong economic growth corridors, are emerging in the centres of some of the US' most distressed core cities, like Detroit, Cleveland, Philadelphia and Pittsburgh. These 'innovation districts' are driven by the private sector, but also by universities, foundations and citizens. They are backed by city governments. The regrowth signs within American cities are newer and weaker, but unmistakeable.[9] This experience reinforces our Phase Three resource-constrained economy, driving proximity, density and low carbon, a new economy that revalues city assets.

The framework we outline for city regrowth promotes the idea of the compact city,[10] making the core city the heart of and magnet for the wider city region. This chapter provides an overview of developments in the light of this evidence.

Compact cities: a European model of density

The historic pattern of closely packed, narrow, pedestrianised streets clustered around a multi-functional centre is now being revalued. European cities fight to retain their vitality, helped by their mixed use, diverse patterns based on close proximity. Many physical and cultural assets support this: the conversion of ugly industrial buildings into historic landmarks and workshops; the upgrading of dense public transport systems to limit car use and favour walking and cycling; the orchestras, theatres, choirs, museums, theatres, art galleries and other cultural attractions; the renewal of outdated housing stock, particularly large estates and dense inner neighbourhoods. More fundamentally, the high level of engineering and research skills of the universities and technical schools in the cities strongly underpin their regrowth from the centre outwards. These institutions provide a constant source of stimulus, creativity, innovation and invention, feeding new enterprises, sustaining existing ones, and providing well-qualified young graduates.

As the seven cities have battled to find new uses for almost everything – space, buildings, land, people, skills – so they have revalued their core and fought against further suburban expansion. The trend away from more out of town and peripheral shopping and business parks, towards growing networks of city-based businesses and small enterprises reflects this ambition. Euratechnologie in Lille, the Spinnerai in Leipzig and the Maker Centres in Bilbao and Sheffield demonstrate this trend. Torino's alliance between the city, the Politecnico, business and residents has reclaimed many city spaces and buildings for enterprise development. Lille, Bilbao and Belfast are planning urban business development parks to strengthen and intensify the core city, rather than the more spacious periphery. Although European cities are dense by American or suburban European standards, they have not recovered all their lost population, particularly working families but also entrepreneurs and businesses.

The stronger the core city, the more the density increases, the greater the energy saving becomes, the greater also the chances of recovery for the wider city and even surrounding towns. Core cities are regional anchors, driving metropolitan viability, even though relations with their surrounding metropolitan areas can be more competitive than collaborative. Generally smaller industrial towns around industrial cities struggle more and take longer to recover than core cities, but eventually gain as the core city improves.

One technique European cities have used to strengthen their core is to devise special projects that create a 'wow' effect – places and spaces that stand out as making the city more attractive. Special city projects reinforce the compact city idea, that people and activity are drawn in by other people and activities. So Sheffield's Winter Garden and Peace Square, Belfast's Titanic Quarter, Bilbao's Guggenheim and adjacent conference venue, Torino's historic centre and palaces, Lille's Citadelle, Leipzig's Nikolaikirche and main square, Saint-Étienne's enclosed green city squares, all in different ways create city appeal, and make cities come alive as compact, concentrated cores. The more this happens, the more public transport becomes viable, and the more energy is conserved through concentrated heating grids like Torino's and Sheffield's. As a result, cities become more environmentally sustainable through density.[11]

Rebuilding core cities

Strengthening the role and the fabric of core cities to combat industrial decline requires direct, hands-on city leadership and shared, participative governance. This public leadership role builds on strong European civic traditions. During the post-war growth era, public bodies played a huge role in rebuilding the economy of cities through mass housing provision, regional economic development, zoning to favour industry, motorway road building, public infrastructure such as new schools, hospitals and universities, a massive expansion in development of all kinds, energy use, land appropriation and many other forms of heavy impact activity. There was also considerable intervention in industries themselves, sometimes through direct ownership, sometimes through subsidies, controls or related investments. Whole new settlements were created around industry, more often as dormitories for nearby cities.[12] All this led to powerful local governments with many functions and competencies, albeit subject to central government rules, funding and ultimate control.

When the first big post-war crash came in 1974, neither central nor local governments were ready for a diminished role – if anything the opposite was true. The crisis provoked strong responses from cities and governments alike. Over a 20-year period, they moved from defence and protection of failing industries and systems, to proactive search for new solutions. This gave a powerful but different role to both local and central governments.

There were five main elements to the public focus on the recovery of 'shrinking' cities in the 1990. First, *investment in restoring city centres, upgrading public transport, renewing neighbourhoods* generally made cities more attractive. The physical infrastructure of cities had to be made to work in new ways in order to attract new investors, enterprises and residents.

Second, *environmental reclamation from industrial damage* restored large, ex-industrial wastelands, large, disused industrial buildings, contaminated land and canal systems, toxic waste dumps, and so on. In many cases, the restored environments were enhanced by green growth of all kinds – trees, gardens and parks.

Third, the *economy, jobs and skills* took far longer to move forward, partly because the new knowledge economy gravitated to cleaner, less harsh environments. Gradually, however, the pain of industrial losses was softened by the rapid growth in services and the continuing, now dominant role of smaller enterprises. Skills are still a major barrier, with many of the high level technical skills imported from elsewhere, but local technical universities and colleges, supported by cities, are playing a growing role in reskilling the population, setting up incubators, research labs and graduate retention programmes.

Fourth, a growing emphasis on *increasing density* and *fighting against sprawl* requires ever stronger partnerships with outer suburban authorities. The cities are winning. All seven cities now show overall population regrowth, in spite of the hard hit they took in the big recession of 2008 onwards. Urban planning took on a difficult, new role, revaluing and renewing the public realm, public buildings and the characteristically dense structure of European cities.

Fifth, *finding new uses for old* has become a main function of *public and private institutions* together. This applies not only to buildings, spaces and infrastructure, but also to skills, production, specialist knowledge, jobs, cultural activities, heritage of all kinds.

The overarching, core role of government facilitates change with many different partners, private, community, civic and public, from the European Union (EU) down to neighbourhood level. Today the brokering role of city governments becomes more important in a context of scarce resources, a massive recycling of everything cities once were into what they must now become, viable economic engines in an environmentally sustainable economy, making cities socially more integrated. One constant challenge for recovering cities is to involve existing populations into the new, 'creative' economy.

It is hard to imagine European cities surviving and prospering without a clear public role, public investment and public underpinning, so embedded is it in city workings of both public and private sectors. However, none of it would work or be fundable without a much stronger private sector. The main source of strength for the future of the public sector lies in the strength of the private sector, which explains why cities passed through a 20-year period of acute decline when big industries began to fail. However, it was public intervention that pulled cities out of the doldrums and set them on a new path, with a new vision, new strategies and new vitality in the 1990s. 'Public entrepreneurs', 'social entrepreneurs' and private entrepreneurs gradually found they could learn from each other. The private sector never actually left these cities, but it faded from prominence, as it shrank and relied on the central function of European governments to push forward reforms,[13] only to regain prominence, alongside universities, local councils and other agencies. SMEs are in the lead in all cities by sheer volume of activity and numbers of jobs.[14]

The European city story shows how central the linkage between public and private, large and small, central and local is.

Heavy impact cities drive climate change

All seven cities had a pre-industrial story: they existed as settlements of 15,000 to 50,000 people in 1800, and grew into great cities of 200,000 to over 1 million by 1950. The sheer pace and scale of growth had significant impact. Over the post-war years of rebuilding and boom expansion, interventions were ambitious in scale and disproportionate in impact; traffic, pollution, concrete dominated city landscapes, hit limits, sometimes before new buildings were finished. Plans outran resources and demand.[15] This left city governments with a huge challenge. Some like Leipzig and Sheffield were forced to 'rationalise' their infrastructure, under protest, by the sheer scale of oversupply. Today, Leipzig struggles with a shortage of school places and rising rents as the city has become more popular in its strong millennial recovery period.[16] Similarly Sheffield and Belfast are short of housing after large scale demolition, particularly in the now fast growing Catholic areas of inner Belfast.

Virtually all development has a high environmental impact, due to high embodied energy in materials and infrastructure, whereas reuse of existing buildings, materials and infrastructure may have as little as one tenth the impact.[17] Holding onto, protecting and reusing valuable infrastructure has become a central tenet of progress. It is more environmentally sustainable, and invariably lowers the cost when all factors are taken into account. New development risks locking us in to unsustainable infrastructure unless we adopt and enforce the highest energy saving and low carbon standards.[18] Recovering, former industrial cities can limit the inescapable costs of building our way out of reliance on fossil fuels, high energy consumption, high wastage and high environmental damage by focusing on reuse and retrofit.

The EU plays a key role in securing agreement and enforcing the adoption of high energy saving standards in all activities from housing to transport to offices and industry itself, to reducing waste, and prioritising renewable energy. It also invests heavily through its regional development and research funds in environmental protection, climate change prevention and international leadership in the fight for planetary survival.[19] However, the environmental odds are heavily stacked against Europe's cities because of their high energy consumption, high impact activities, over-reliance on oil, gas and sometimes coal, over-depletion of forests and wood, overuse of land and so on.

Low impact, low carbon plans

The EU adopted ambitious environmental goals, captured in a plan for a 20% reduction in energy use and at least 20% rise in renewable energy use by 2020. There are more ambitious plans being promoted for a trans-European grid, a grid connector to North Africa, across the North Sea and even to Iceland to facilitate renewable energy transfers; a massive solar plant in the Sahara desert with enough sunshine to power much of Europe; wide-scale development of marine energy and offshore wind. Many of these ideas are far off, but they underline the value of Europe's overarching ambition to unite and pioneer critical ways forward.

Other overarching plans include a fast rail network, connecting all European countries and main cities. These are proving more divisive in the implementation than the idea with the high speed train proposals linking Torino to Lyon, and Bilbao to Madrid. Overall, trains are more environmentally benign compared with cars and air, but this equation is challenged with high speed.[20]

In the industrial sector, cutting edge technology and advanced materials attract experimentation and investment. So the application of graphene in Manchester, hydrogen in Torino, electric vehicles in Leipzig, Torino and Bilbao, renewable marine technology in Belfast and

Glasgow stand more chance of breaking through into a wide market with European support because they involve a high level of research collaboration across European specialisms. Europe is bigger than the sum of its parts. These advanced industrial, research based activities have the potential to reduce environmental impact by significantly reducing the material and energy inputs, the waste and pollution. They also generate many back-up jobs. The underlying idea behind Phase Three of our framework is to convert industrial cities to low impact, low resource use, low waste economies. The tension lies between not being able to afford to do this, while also not affording not to.[21]

In spite of progress towards a more sustainable future, more so in Europe than most continents, there is a long way to go. Europe falters in environmental protection because it wants short-term economic growth, even if this requires energy intensity and high impact development. So it lags behind its own ambitious targets for both energy saving and low carbon growth.[22] Economic growth brings jobs, prosperity, and revenue to support services to vast populations, so the Union risks prioritising short-term over longer-term growth, sidelining climate change, long-term sustainability and environmental protection in favour of jobs.[23] According to Nicholas Stern, one of the world's leading experts on the economics of climate change, this is short-sighted and wrong.[24] The economic benefits of investing in climate change mitigation for the long term include intense job creation.

We know from the history of industrial collapse and the exodus of jobs from our cities that the consequence of intense energy use and environmental overuse is economic and environmental exhaustion and near-collapse. As materials and energy became scarcer and more costly, so too did labour. Competition arose in newer economies where the environment was yet to be exhausted. Today many cities in fast developing economies, such as China, India, Brazil, Mexico, are swamped by pollution and other environmental and resource pressures, which pose a similar threat today. There are many examples of a return in Europe to short-term, environmentally blinkered thinking, including Leipzig contemplating a return to open-cast coal mining in its surrounds to create jobs.[25]

However, progress is being made towards renewable energy targets and many other environmentally friendly, energy-light measures. For example, the UK is now a world leader in offshore wind generation, and there is huge potential around Britain's windy and wave-hit shores, receiving 40% of Europe's total wind resource.[26] Belfast will soon host the largest and most ambitious offshore wind development so far. It is also expanding the world's first commercial sea turbines, based in Strangford Lough.[27] Italy has the most rapidly growing solar electricity generation, helped by generous subsidies. Germany, for one day in the summer of 2015, met all its energy needs from renewable sources. Leipzig is a leading solar PV manufacturer. Iberdrola, a Spanish energy giant, based in Bilbao, is one of Europe's largest, multinational renewable energy producer. France has pioneered the most successful tidal barrier to generate electricity.

One of the biggest barriers to progress with renewable energy is the need to store it. Batteries are a key and currently they are bulky, expensive and often of themselves environmentally damaging. A small, relatively new engineering company, Faradion, based in Sheffield, has recently discovered a breakthrough that would reduce the cost, increase the efficiency and greatly extend the storage and use of renewable energy. With rapid acceleration of development and falling costs, the members of the EU could yet reach their 20:20 target by 2020.

Greener cities protect the wider environment

Environmental protection has become a major imperative in the seven cities, as a way to reduce their 'heavy impact'. As European cities become greener, they enhance local environments, combat pollution, reabsorb greenhouse gases and soften harsh urban environments. Dense European cities rely on small gardens, courtyards, balconies, small, paved backyards. This makes the protection, care and expansion of urban parks and other shared spaces crucially important, even in straightened times. As important is the creation of small local neighbourhood parks, tree planting, allotments, community gardens, green roofs. These reduce air pollution, flooding and temperature rises caused by climate change.

Bilbao has nearly doubled its open, green space in 30 years; Sheffield has created community-owned woodland, an urban city farm and impressive botanical gardens; Leipzig has dotted the city with pocket parks, community gardens, allotments, play spaces, green cycleways. Urban food growing has become popular, not only in Leipzig but other cities too. Lille has built whole eco-neighbourhoods with water recycled through reed beds and homes insulated to Passivhaus standards, a now internationally recognised measure of energy efficiency.[28] City squares are commonly traffic-free, cycle-adapted, environmentally friendly civic spaces. There is all but universal adoption of publicly sponsored cycle routes, running alongside far more pedestrian streets and highly developed bus and tram systems.

Public transport in European cities has gained ground as density has increased, car use has fallen, bus and tram ridership has risen.[29] Low carbon electric and hydrogen powered vehicles are becoming more common, supported by leading edge research in the transport field in Leipzig and Torino. Belfast meanwhile is a European leader in electric vehicle-charging infrastructure and the electric vehicle adoption rate is accelerating fast.[30]

These steps to 'green' cities help rescue cities from the environmental doldrums and open the door to a more green way of thinking, seeing cities as within, not against, nature. Green cities are vital to Europe's urban survival, given the level of congestion, brown and grey development that dominate.

Meanwhile, green innovation is percolating into almost every form of activity, in spite of heavy over-reliance still on fossil fuels. The EU expects not only energy intensity to reduce, that is the amount of energy needed for a unit of output, but for overall energy consumption to fall as energy efficiency accelerates, and total energy needs decline particularly in buildings and transport. It is possible, even now, to reduce energy use in buildings by 50% at minimal additional cost.[31] Because cities are built environments and buildings comprise nearly 50% of all energy use, a 50% reduction would make a major contribution to cutting energy demand in spite of growth, thereby making much higher renewable energy targets achievable more quickly. Energy saving measures, particularly in buildings, are highly labour intensive – so this investment is good for jobs and skills too. The skills required to retrofit building are tried and tested, and quick to learn. The shift to electric and hydrogen powered vehicles is gathering pace too, with research happening in Leipzig and Torino and electric vehicle infrastructure expanding in Belfast.

Creating a circular economy

The real urgency of these tasks lies in the risk of runaway climate change. Not only are the risks real but the impact on European cities is likely to be particularly harsh, because of their heavily built-up, overused environment. By December 2015, there was a decision to put in place global climate change action which will shape the future. Europe has no choice. The European Union strongly backed the ambition agreed by all country participants, to keep global temperature rises below 2 degrees centigrade.[32]

Cities and national governments know they have to accelerate the change, but there is no easy shortcut. Yet many of the conditions are ripe for a shift towards a circular economy, where any short-term environmental impact of economic activity is offset through reuse, recycling, restoring the damage – creating a zero waste, self-replenishing economy.[33] Eleanor Ostrom, the Nobel prize-winning economist, has studied societies where resource protection, sharing and renewal are so critical to survival, that some basic rules about access to resources, distribution, fairness, legal controls and sanctions have evolved over generations. She makes a crucial point that what she calls 'common pool resources' must be conserved and only used as fast as they can be replenished to avoid eventual exhaustion. The application of her theory and methods to our cities shows just how pivotal the circular economy is to city survival.[34]

We call the recycling in old cities the Re-economy because around 30 words are commonly used in English and other European languages (French, Italian, Spanish) to describe the restorative actions that make good what is damaged and make what is already there new again. Our environments, our economies, our interlocking infrastructure and dense network of already built-up cities make restorative, renewable action both economically sound and environmentally imperative.[35]

There are three main transformations we need to take on board if we are to keep climate change and greenhouse gas emissions within safe limits: changes in cities, land use and energy.[36] Everything that relates to city recovery involves all three.

The economy of cities is changing

There is evidence that restorative action in cities is job intensive and therefore helpful to industrial cities. Former industrial cities have large workforces with a work history that no longer matches job needs of the 21st century. This poses a huge challenge for cities and often leads to city governments attempting to support and even create jobs – certainly to protect jobs wherever they can. However, cities that rely heavily on the public sector for job creation tend to struggle to regrow private jobs. Saint-Étienne and Sheffield have faced this problem, because of the extreme dominance and then disappearance of heavy industry. Belfast and Bilbao face it, because of their history of civil disorder and violent independence movements in the 1980s and 1990s. Leipzig was maybe the worst affected because of Communist control of virtually the entire labour market until 1989. Now that public sector investment is shrinking virtually everywhere, job creation and economic growth have become city obsessions.

Only a generation ago these cities were dominated by heavy industry, but manufacturing jobs have plummeted, as technology has replaced people. In contrast to the overall decline in manufacturing, the growth in *advanced manufacture* in all the cities is impressively strong. Sheffield, Torino, Bilbao, Leipzig and Lille are all leading edge research and application centres, high up the European league table in technical, engineering and materials research. In optics and design, Saint-Étienne leads; in marine and offshore wind renewables, Belfast leads. In fact, advanced manufacture is a crowded European and global field, with universities competing and collaborating to discover usable breakthroughs in super-lightweight, low energy, light impact products, which are essential if we are to save the planet and continue to grow. However, advanced manufacture is extremely high tech by definition and therefore job-light, although it does generate between five and seven ancillary jobs for every one in the cutting edge industries of the new economy.[37]

There are some fields where jobs grow rapidly such as renewable energy, as it involves not only production but also installation and maintenance. This applies even more to energy saving and retrofitting buildings. Growth is particularly strong in services, many of which directly relate to and support the much smaller manufacturing base. Other socially valued parts of the fabric of cities survive and grow – shops, cafes, domestic and child care, elderly support, public transport and so on. Rapidly expanding activity in the health and social care fields results from an ageing population, household fragmentation and migration which are putting pressure on core services which Europeans pride themselves on providing.[38] The social economy has become central to survival.

New growth new enterprise

There are many fields where the new economy of cities flourishes. Several stand out.

The digital revolution generates new start-ups at a phenomenal rate. This relates closely to advanced manufacture, new services and new methods of production, trade and information sharing. Digital technology now underpins future development in myriad ways, from design and engineering, to production, marketing and applications, services and even mundane functions like shopping, ordering food or finding your way through city streets. Lille has created a whole advanced technology centre in remodelled textile mills.[39] Sheffield universities support a 'digital quarter'. Moving SMEs into the new digital economy is a major goal.

Design has become a major growth area, partly because of the complex demands of advanced manufacture and the use of new materials, partly because the digital revolution makes design more accessible, but mainly because careful, clever design lies at the heart of making cities work – at every level, from the most banal paving stones to the most elevated building, from the shape of batteries and charge points to electric vehicles.[40] There are so many small design and design-related firms in Saint-Étienne that a whole design, advice and mentoring centre has been created. Torino's Politecnico runs several specialist design engineering courses feeding into its incubators. To a greater or lesser extent all cities use design as a tool for innovation and enterprise creation.

Advanced manufacturing is clearly linked to advanced design and digital invention. It also draws on advanced materials and expanding vital areas of the new economy. Advanced manufacture, while job-light, adds high value to local economies and attracts many ancillary design, digital and supply chain activities. It is so leading edge in the Sheffield region that manufacturing jobs are actually growing.[41]

Green innovation based on the engineering, design and research strengths of the seven cities uses advanced materials, manufacture and technology to develop green inventions at every level – from relatively low skill energy saving into high skill products. Superlight materials, nanotechnology, energy and waste reductions and precision design all create breakthroughs in green technologies.

Hands-on microenterprises and Maker activities create a rapidly expanding field of self-employment. The spread of the Maker Movement and Fab Labs from the US across Europe reaches all our cities in one form or another, demonstrating the ambition to try out new ideas, to make things for ourselves.[42] It illustrates the idea that we have to reinvent ourselves and allow ourselves to apply our urge to 'do something' to the daily challenges we face.[43] This activity is potentially extremely creative, if as yet not very visible – for example, the embryo Maker Movement we discovered, by chance, on a neglected island in the decayed port of Bilbao; or the Maker Centre in Sheffield, to be set up in a boarded-up department store. The idea of 'learning by doing' has strong purchase and validity in cities that are used to and grew through hands-on work. Bilbao and the University of Mondragon have taken this idea to new heights with their full university degree that involves developing a viable new cooperative business over four years of learning as part of the Learn by Doing degree programme.[44] Cities thrive on production – of ideas, enterprises and goods.

New and old skills

City remaking and rebuilding is another striking field of economic activity. Although this task took off in the 1980s, heavily backed and driven by public support, it is still far from complete today due to the sheer scale of land use loss and contamination, the volume of empty buildings and sites, the industrial–urban infrastructure and machinery. Empty, underused space is recreated in a continuous flow as activities change and evolve.[45] Much of it, such as railways and canals, offers opportunities today. Many of the starkest eye-sores and immediate opportunities have been taken up, but myriad smaller and some bigger spaces, buildings, facilities remain to be fully exploited. Former industrial cities in the US have a similar pattern of regrowth taking place in their very centres, as yet to spread out to embrace the whole core city.[46]

New uses for old, recycling and reinventing are a fundamental part of the new job opportunities as land is so short and so precious. This is particularly true in housing and neighbourhood renewal. Upgrading activity is also a tool for redensifying the city and drawing people and enterprises back in. The notion of urban pioneers is crucial here – adventurous, imaginative, ambitious young people are attracted into damaged underused city spaces, both for living and working, and make them come good. In spite of lower wages and poorer working conditions, many measures of quality of life are both better and cheaper in less competitive older cities, and young 'pioneers' thrive on challenge.[47] A very new strand of economic activity based on sharing and exchange, recycling and cooperation, is emerging among this new generation of city lovers, as several studies show.[48] Tool shops in Leipzig, where people borrow what they need and repay with labour; clothes swap sessions; Freecycle websites for redistributing goods; furniture restoration workshops; community energy generation; and many other sharing ideas proliferate in cities.

An outstanding challenge for ex-industrial cities is the low skill, low wage economy in which many city dwellers are caught. These areas of activity attract foreign immigrants, as low-paid jobs require few qualifications, offer generally poor conditions and few opportunities for progress. There are not enough local workers willing to take them so immigrants often do – in retail, social care, cleaning and maintenance, odd jobs of all kinds. Competition is fierce, with a real race to the bottom of falling wages, particularly since the recession, deteriorating job security and a shrinkage of low skilled jobs.[49] An important focus, particularly in Torino, has been to legalise informal jobs in order to ensure that migrants and casual labourers have at least minimal entitlements.

Overall jobs have grown, unemployment has fallen, breakthrough new technologies and products, linked to historic specialisms, have expanded, and weak market cities are regrowing their now very different economies. The biggest economic and social challenge remains youth unemployment.

Social divisions and social cohesion

Huge social challenges press on European cities, particularly in older industrial cities. The three most pressing challenges are: youth unemployment, immigration, and falling wages for low skilled populations. Unemployment, particularly youth unemployment, is far more serious and challenging in the cities in this study than in capitals. There are new jobs, but matching these jobs, some requiring high, some low skill, to the aspirations and experience of city populations is notoriously difficult. Ambitious young people, often recent graduates of local universities, want to move away, leaving behind less qualified, less adaptable young people who are less connected to new job markets, less experienced and less confident.

Several cities have developed highly enterprising programmes to hold onto and encourage graduates — often the most technically skilled and entrepreneurial. Sheffield has launched a highly successful graduate apprentice scheme, feeding into its growth-oriented SMEs, and helping Sheffield's graduates find exciting, challenging work in the city. New or expanding employers need reliable workers they can train, but they often cannot bridge the knowledge and experience gap. City governments in partnership with colleges, universities and businesses, are developing special training and job access schemes. Nonetheless, youth unemployment remains around double the country average, with long-lasting and blighting impacts on young peoples' lives. European cities will suffer far into the future as a result of workless youth.

Immigration and incipient segregation divide European cities. The concentration of minority populations in certain neighbourhoods reflects deeper divisions. Previously run down areas, following years of upgrading and social investment, often remain minority concentrations. East Leipzig, Sheffield's Burngreave, South East Saint-Étienne and the Bario Milano in Torino all show this. In South Lille, whole blocks have become occupied entirely by African migrant families. The starkest example may be Bradford, where relatively small but growing areas within the city have shifted from majority white, to mixed, to almost entirely minority.[50] White flight is a European, as well as American, phenomenon.[51]

Immigration raises strong fears about undercutting the local population in jobs and wages. Although there are grounds for this fear, it is exaggerated as migrants usually fill the gaps in the economy which locals are not ready or able to fill. De-industrialisation, economic inactivity and unemployment have destroyed traditional job structures and expectations, often leaving local populations devalued, demoralised and hard to employ. Belfast in the 2000s experienced rapid job growth and high immigration, running alongside extreme low skill and high economic inactivity among existing, former industrial workers. This problem is compounded by low wages at the bottom of the scale and far more precarious working conditions. The protection of worker conditions won in the 1960s is long since gone.[52]

European city leaders are acutely aware of these gaps in urban society due to the physical proximity of diverse social groups. They therefore organise and support job access programmes, building in handholding and brokering. This and other forms of social underpinning help to dilute the extreme impacts of exclusion.[53] However, city governments on their own cannot resolve the current problems of mass migration, with the cost, social pressures and potential for conflict it brings. They need national back-up and international cooperation to cope. Cities, like Torino, Sheffield and Bilbao, have been at the receiving end of national refugee dispersal. In all cases, a combination of civic, faith-based and public responses ease the transition. However, it is an issue where the EU itself is floundering and leadership seems lacking for want of a reasonable and manageable way forward.[54] Nonetheless these acute problems are Europe-wide as well as local, calling for Europe-wide collaboration on policy and action.[55]

In spite of such major social challenges, cities have held together, partly explained by the strong social infrastructure that was built up over the post-war era and is largely intact in spite of austerity. This method of managing social problems has helped. As Bilbao's city manager explained, they built slack into the system to allow for 'wastage' when cuts came.[56] The city then shed jobs without unravelling the core social infrastructure that keeps Europe's dense cities functioning and together. This applies even where austerity has hit hardest: Sheffield, Torino, Bilbao.[57] It does not mean that there are no losses and no pain.

Strong public sector-led reinvestment, particularly in neighbourhood renewal, has also helped avert deeper social problems. It not only brought conditions up to a reasonable standard in the most decayed neighbourhoods – with ongoing work in some of them – but it also encouraged many forms of social enterprise, community infrastructure and concerted efforts at integration. These neighbourhoods, while still generally poor have been made more viable and sustainable. Today they are repopulating.

The role of public brokering

There is no magic bullet for the complex, interlocking social problems of unemployment or underemployment, immigration and community relations, low wages and poverty. But continuing public social underpinning, albeit at a reduced level, has helped avoid severe social dislocation in cities. Voluntary organisations, community enterprises, cooperatives and church groups plug many important gaps. This steady stream of social investment and support rely on the good offices of leading city officials, able to broker deals between citizens, business, civic institutions and services, such as universities, health, and environmental agencies, charities, regional, central and European governments. There is no question that brokering the combined action needed, from community level to international level, is vital to resolving such deep and internationally driven problems. The quiet measured chief officers in city councils as far apart as Torino, Bilbao, Lille, Sheffield, Belfast, Saint-Étienne and Leipzig have shown these qualities in extraordinary degree.[58] There are many unsung heroes and heroines within cities who play exactly this brokering role.

There remains the core problem that inequality has been rising in Europe, as conditions in the low wage economy have deteriorated; these cities are particularly harshly affected at the bottom. As support has been cut back in the public sector, so voluntary effort has increased, but some of it is an emergency infill – for food, housing, debt advice, job links, family support. Cash resources have been shrinking, along with people's incomes, therefore poverty was bound to rise. But people support has increased dramatically, invariably operating within a public framework. Torino's cooperative homelessness projects are an example; so are Bilbao's food and homeless centres. They do not fill the gap, as reports of growing poverty across Europe show.[59] So there is a question mark over whether austerity can go much further before things go seriously wrong. There is now also a serious risk of deep divisions re-emerging within Europe between the weaker European economies worst hit by the Euro crisis and stronger European economies that have more resources to cope.[60]

Austerity, resource shrinkage and community sharing

Within dense cities, the problem of poverty and resource shortages is always 'in your face', inescapable. Therefore, any 'sharing' initiative is welcome, from street celebrations to growing food, community suppers, to food, clothes and tool banks. Torino, as we stressed in Chapter Seven, is highly socially enterprising, cooperative, 'sharing', even calling its most pioneering projects the Sharing Hotel, and the Sister Project. Bilbao is also strongly cooperative in its organisations and focus. Other cities, like Sheffield, Belfast and Leipzig, are bursting with social and community enterprises. The French cities, Lille and Saint-Étienne, stand out as having so far retained a large part of their public funding for regeneration and social support, but they also have their community action centres and social movements.

Thus, in the seven cities, there is little sense of social unravelling, rather of intense social pressure that is being met with serious countervailing initiatives in the public, charitable and community spheres. European enterprises, private, social and public, will rely increasingly on people's resourcefulness in a very unpredictable environment. But community endeavours will not be strong enough to withstand the turmoil of resource constraints, climate change and the instability of the Eurozone. Some communities themselves cannot manage the turmoil of Eurozone crisis without more help. Hence the ongoing battle within the EU between anti-austerity social movements and pro-austerity governments.

Meanwhile, unforeseen and acute social needs arise from the regrowth in city populations, putting pressure on the public purse – schools, health, housing. Overall, regrowth gives hope and is positive. It means more younger people; more new families; more workers and local taxes; more income to circulate in the local economy; and more urban pioneers. Young urban pioneers tend to get involved in social enterprise, community relations and fight for greater equality and integration. Since our cities are laboratories of change, the social field offers fertile soil for new ideas and new social enterprises. New experiments at the grass roots appear faithful to the social ideals on which Europe's post-war vision was formed – pro-equality, pro-integration, pro-community control.[61] Extreme counter movements that evoke memories of fascism and Nazism are still greatly feared.

European government and citizen groups tend to respond to counter such trends.

City and regional level inequalities provoke European-wide responses, with additional funds flowing to poorer cities, regions and countries in an effort to stimulate growth and equalise conditions for progress. This applies particularly to Eastern Europe, but also to Mediterranean countries and more peripheral regions of the Union, like Ireland. Leipzig, Bilbao, Torino and Belfast have particularly benefitted this way. European regional funds help, but do not solve structural problems in European economies, such as: under-recognition of SMEs; the need to transition much faster to energy saving and renewable energy; high unemployment, particularly among youth; high immigration pressures; the Eurozone crisis affecting many cities; and austerity programmes affecting them all.

These overarching challenges underline, at European and national levels, the bigger problems facing core cities and their surroundings, making Europe, as a continent of cities, seem weighed down. Yet its ponderous, compromising, halting but constant attempts to respond to unfathomable challenges in cities has held up better than feared.[62] Austerity is extremely harsh. Yet resource constraints are forcing cities to think afresh and search for new solutions.

Europe's overarching structures

The seven former industrial cities are in five different countries, with five different languages and cultures. They are highly distinctive with unique histories and all are several centuries, even thousands of years old. Europe's Union, troubled as it appears, has been forged by shared borders, a common urban heritage, a history of trade, conquest and union, two world wars. This history creates an intense need to cooperate to ensure survival in a small, densely built-up continent. Cities are at the heart of these developments.

The industrial revolution, which began in Britain over 250 years ago, and quickly spread across Northern Europe, made European countries and cities both competitive and collaborative. The railways that linked cities by trade in the 19th century still link them today right across Europe – many of them now high speed. The porous borders that led to rapid immigration into cities from regional and national hinterlands soon became porous to international incomers. The vast majority of migrants seek their fortune in cities which fill and refill their gaps with newcomers. Manchester attributes much of its recovery to rapid immigration in the 2000s.[63] It also happened in Belfast following the Peace Agreement in 1998.[64]

Cities dominate Europe's landscape, particularly industrial cities, as they are the wealth creators and ideas generators throughout history.[65] Action within cities often starts small and, if successful, grows. It filters up through local, regional, national and European governments, to build the collaborative structures and exchanges that support progress. Yet this often criticised centralising trend also generates powerful movements of decentralisation. So the regions and cities we study have gained powers and responsibilities that allow them to initiate and innovate. The European ideal of collaboration is matched by the urban ideal of autonomy, fostering innovation and enterprise. The secret of city recovery lies in combined city, national and European supports.[66] Governments can become too big, just as leading industries can. So the move to break up oversized structures in response to the big economic downturn of the 1970s, which felt like defeat at the time, in fact became a precursor of innovation and recovery efforts.[67] Renewed efforts operate at a more local scale so even European-level development programmes target the most struggling cities and the poorest regions, almost without exception the ones with declining industries. The powerful idea of a 'social Europe', integrated, tolerant, harmonious, cohesive, played out albeit in uneven ways in the seven cities.

The framework of external, higher level support, running in parallel with local leadership, city initiatives and bold local recovery strategies, helps explain why European cities neither fell into the intense decay and levels of abandonment that afflicted the US' industrial core cities, nor did European cities take so long to recover.[68] Europe's core cities cannot be replaced by or simply subsumed into their metropolitan areas. They are not designed or built to be suburbanised metropoles. Their density, proximity, internal and external links give them a vitality all of their own that positively drives regrowth and recovery which spill over into their metropolitan areas.

The dominating role of core cities led to the EU, supporting networks of core cities, meeting to exchange and develop ideas, lessons and strategies – from the ground up.[69] This network approach, fostered at the highest governance level, feeds up from the bottom, strengthening the connection between overarching interlinking Union approaches, and of ground-level activity. A combination of top-down and bottom-up seems to fit European cities. But cities are more like jigsaws than iron grids, fitting together, but sometimes breaking up, part of a bigger whole but made up of distinct pieces.[70]

European governments invest heavily in core cities, through universal programmes such as education, health and transport; through dedicated, if declining, city funds for social support; through public amenities, such as parks, libraries, swimming pools; and through 'rescue' programmes, whether for housing and neighbourhoods, environments and reclamation, skills training and enterprise development. National programmes underline the way national governments intervene to support local development. These programmes wax and wane but rarely disappear. The City Deals in England focus heavily on economic development.[71] The Grand Projet de Ville in France focuses on neighbourhood upgrading and amenities.[72] The Sozialstadt in Germany focuses on community and social development.[73] These national programmes are brokered regionally and delivered locally.

More universal programmes, such as education, aim to sustain a baseline of provision that includes all communities and at least in theory prevents any person, group or area from falling far behind.[74] The commitment to provide equal services everywhere for all its limitations has helped Europe's ex-industrial cities, ensuring a commitment at European, national and regional levels, to greater equalisation and integration than has been possible in the United States. Although divisions and inequalities in Europe's cities are still acute, there is a recurring focus on addressing them through policy.[75]

Patchwork cities: a working model of city recovery

This handbook outlines multiple forms of help, micro and macro projects, public and private initiatives, social, environmental and economic imperatives. Combined they form a patchwork quilt of solutions. Every piece in every city is different, the patterns are distinct, the combinations special to that place. The myriad strands of action summarised in this concluding chapter do not offer a pattern book for survival and recovery. But they offer many compelling ideas which underline the urgency of action:

- a still powerful and dominant public role, showing the importance of partnerships with the private sector;
- technical and engineering prowess to advance new solutions;
- the capacity and value of community-based and neighbourhood initiatives;
- action under threat of energy shortages and climate change;
- responding to the glaring inequalities and social challenges of poverty, youth unemployment and immigration;
- fomenting city restorations and regrowth;

- greening their environments – literally planting trees, creating parks, reclaiming canals, creating allotments; and
- constant searching for ways to avoid energy shortages and environmental disaster through climate change action and a shift to renewable energy.

This dense patchwork of ideas is driving city regrowth and attracts support both within countries and across Europe. Meanwhile Europe as a whole still struggles with its history of divisions and reconciliation as it faces external pressures such as refugee inflows from the upheavals in the Middle East.[76]

The recovery in European cities diverges from the American experience. But the pattern of city recovery and regrowth is beginning to show in US Rust Belt cities in spite of many adverse countertrends, such as strong outer sprawl, growing poverty concentrations and stark inequalities.[77] Their incipient recovery underlines the intrinsic value of 'played out', still declining cities, like Detroit and Cleveland, and their potential to recreate themselves like Pittsburgh and Philadelphia. While Europe becomes more open to public–private partnerships, the US rediscovers the value of overarching city and state governments in brokering environmentally and socially sustainable models of city recovery.[78] This convergence underpins our core argument that the finite resources of a finite planet drive rediscovery and reinvention of urban assets.

Former industrial cities are diversifying their economies. They now work with their highly varied SMEs to develop new ideas, encourage apprenticeships, foster international links, adopt new technologies, and respond to new demands. Cities are attracting support and investment from major enterprises, governments and also start-ups, for cities offer space and opportunity for new growth. Many of the new projects are small; many are university linked and research based; many are hands-on, labour intensive, reworking the city's assets. All over Europe, underused capacity is being rediscovered.

Conclusion

We need to ask whether our handbook on city decline and recovery does offer the promise of a more sustainable future; whether our framework for understanding city recovery in the European context in three distinct phases matches the new reality. Phase One, the first industrial revolution, postulates that extreme, exploitative industrial growth, discounting environmental and social costs, inevitably collapses, leaving industrial cities in a parlous state, just as the public resources that underpin city growth also shrink. Therefore, a long period of decline forces painful recognition of a failed model as jobs and populations shrink, and environmental resources are destroyed.

Phase Two, the post-industrial economy, is very different. A determined effort to create a new vision, to rebuild played out infrastructure, to turn cities into attractive, dense hubs for regrowth, pays off in job and population regrowth. Enterprises start to move back in and startling innovations are born of traditional industrial and engineering skills. Cities become a cross between old and new. Their anchor institutions thrive and become life-savers; new city leadership emerges; and community programmes tie highly unequal neighbourhoods into a shared frame. Cities show strong signs of recovery.

Phase Three, the resource-constrained economy, underlines the resource limits confronting all European cities and the urgency of tackling climate change, reinforced by the international financial crisis of 2008, the Eurozone banking crisis, continent-wide austerity programmes and the path-breaking climate change agreement in Paris, December 2015. Former industrial cities are hardest hit, but have least far to fall and are most practised at finding new ways out of problems. Resource problems, starting with the war, then the oil crisis of 1974, have forced Europe's cities to think differently about their assets, to revalue them, reuse them and recreate them. Phase Three shapes a custodial approach to city rebuilding which fits with Europe's tight environmental limits and soaring environmental ambitions – dense, highly urbanised, highly populated, highly developed, energy constrained, yet rich in urban, social, economic and environmental assets.[79]

Ways forward can be found through the acute environmental and climate change threats we face. But European cities, governments and enterprises have to work harder under more severe resource constraints in order to achieve the rapid progress in energy saving and conversion to renewable energy required by Phase Three – an energy-light, labour intensive, socially equalising phase of regrowth; a new, circular economy that constantly self-replenishes, that bases growth on replaceable, not irreplaceable, resources, that endorses 100% reliance on renewable energy as a must, that values people with place. It is hard to imagine our common future with depleted resources in a small continent, full of crowded cities, without transforming cities into renewable resources. That future is within reach.

Endnotes

Chapter 1: Lessons from cities in a crowded continent

[1] A large city is defined as having a population of 150,000 or more; vom Hove (2014).

[2] Power and Zulauf (2011)

[3] Glaeser (2011)

[4] Geim (2009); Novoselov et al (2012); Kumar (2015)

[5] Power et al (2010)

[6] Stern (2015)

[7] Hald (2009)

[8] Nivola (1999)

[9] Winkler (2007b)

[10] Urban Task Force (1999)

[11] Massey and Denton (1993); Jargowsky (1997); Wilson (2009)

[12] Sampson (2012)

[13] Vey (2007): McGahey and Vey (2008)

[14] Burdett et al (2011)

[15] Vey (2007)

[16] Katz and Bradley (2013)

[17] Stern (2015)

[18] Power (1993)

[19] Marsh (2012)

[20] Holy Father Francis (2015)

[21] Author's visits to the Ruhr, 2006, 2012

[22] Tsoukalis (2014)

Chapter 2: Divided and united Europe

[1] This quotation comes from the information board in the Kings Cross Regeneration site, adjacent to the temporary swimming pool, built in the middle of a vast building site June 2015. The source was quoted as The European Commission in Joint Research Centre Institute for Environment and Sustainability.

[2] Academy of Achievement (2009)

[3] Diamond (2006)

[4] Reader (2005)

[5] Fiat (Fabbrica Italiana Automobile Torino) was a major force. Olivetti was founded in Piedmont near Torino.

[6] Large cities like Manchester were even more extreme, doubling in size in ten years in the early 1800s, then doubling again between 1820 and 1830.

[7] European Union display in the Millennium Dome, London, of the International Rail Network of Europe, 2000

[8] Eurostat (2014b)

[9] Fields of Battle – Lands of Peace 14–18

[10] Gies and Gold (2009)

[11] 'Hand me downs' refers to second-hand clothes and other items passed between siblings, generations, extended families and friends. 'Any old iron' was the government controlled effort to collect and recycle iron and other metals as part of the war effort.

[12] Power (1993)

[13] Inman et al (2015)

[14] Balabkins (1964)

[15] Wollmann (1985)

[16] Marshall Plan (US Congress, 1948); George C. Marshall Foundation (nd)

[17] Treaty of Rome 1957, founding of European Economic Community (European Community, 1957)

[18] Barraclough and Stone (1989)

[19] Lutz et al (2002)

[20] Tosi and Vitale (2009)

[21] Tosi and Vitale (2009)

[22] Fuhrer (2009)

[23] British customs and economy were considered incompatible with the system of the European Economic Community by Charles de Gaulle who exercised the French veto.

[24] Tsoukalis (2014)

[25] Sundquist (2010)

[26] Forster (1989)

[27] McKittrick and McVea (2002)

Chapter 3: Grit and vision

[1] Pope Francis, *Laudato Si*, full reference listed under Holy Father, Francis

[2] Atkinson (2003)

[3] *The Economist* (2014a)

[4] *The Economist* (2015l); de Kok et al (2011); Bakhshi et al (2011); *The Economist* (2014c)

[5] Osborne and Gaebler (1993); Titmuss (1958)

[6] Brown (2014)

[7] Wilkinson and Pickett (2010); Hills et al (2015)

[8] Gies and Gold (1987)

[9] IPCC (2015)

[10] Donnison and Ungerson (1982)

[11] Steffen et al (2015): Green Alliance (2015)

[12] Power (1993)

[13] La Fabrique de la Cité (2014)

[14] Personal communication with Northern Ireland housing officials during official visit to Belfast, 2009

[15] UK National Ecosystem Assessment (2011)

[16] Eurostat (2014a)

[17] Whyte (1956)

[18] Volti (2011): Bibby (2012)

[19] Jackson (2009)

[20] Lacey (1972)

[21] *The Economist* (2015d)

[22] ZUP stands for *Zone à urbanisation prioritaire* or urban priority zones.

[23] Schumacher (1993)

[24] Porritt (2005)

[25] Ehrlich et al (2012)

[26] IPCC (2014); UN Environment Program (2014)

[27] Bernt (2009); Haase et al (2013)

[28] Lee et al (2014)

[29] Dodds et al (2013)

[30] The Global Commission on the Economy and Climate (2014)

[31] UN Habitat (2013)

[32] *The Economist* (2015g)

Chapter 4: Struggle and Strive

[1] Reader (2005)

[2] Hunt (2005)

[3] Quilliot and Guerrand (1989)

[4] Briggs (1968); Power (1993)

[5] Mallach and Brachman (2013)

[6] Mallach (2012)

[7] Winkler (2007a); Elcock (2006); Booth (2005)

[8] Power and Zulauf (2011)

[9] EU Objective 1 and Objective 2 funding, EUR-Lex (nd)

[10] European Commission (2005)

[11] Dodd et al (2013)

[12] Gobierno Vasco (2012)

[13] Neumann and Seidel-Schulze (2010); ONS (2012)

[14] Herden and Power (2016)

[15] Parkinson et al (2006); Liverpool John Moores University (2012); European Commission (2007)

[16] Eastern Germany as a whole received large transition subsidies from West Germany and some European funds. Special funds will gradually phase out by 2019.

[17] European Commission (2003); European Union Agency for Fundamental Rights (2014); European Commission (2014b)

[18] In 2006, Sheffield City Council hosted a visit from experts representing the cities in this study, including an American delegation headed by Bruce Katz, of the Brookings Institution, who made this statement.

[19] Urban Task Force (1999)

[20] Department of Energy and Climate Change (nd) 2050 Calculator

[21] Sheffield City Council (2014)

[22] Author's city visits, 2009–11.

[23] Jargowski (2013)

[24] IPCC (2014)

[25] Keep (2015)

[26] Power et al (2010)

[27] Power et al (2010)

[28] Power et al (2016)

[29] Provan and Power (2016a)

[30] Rifkin (2011)

Chapter 5: Threats and Opportunities

[1] These quotations from City Staff during site visit, 2007.

[2] Leunig and Swaffield (2007)

[3] Within-country financial and currency adjustment was not possible if things went wrong within the Spanish, Irish, Portuguese or Greek economies. They simply had to follow the Euro line. This loss of sovereignty over the single currency with very divergent regional conditions and without the accompanying central banking controls, rendered weaker economies within the Euro, including Greece, Portugal, Ireland, Spain, and to a lesser extent Italy, virtually powerless in the face of the Euro crisis.

[4] Youth unemployment is relatively low in German cities as special support is introduced nationally to support jobs.

[5] The German federal model is distinctive as it was devised with the opposite motivation from the European Union to keep Germany's many parts from combining to become too strong again.

[6] IMF 2015

[7] Eurostat (2015a)

[8] Krugman (2012)

[9] *Guardian* (2015b)

[10] Krebs and Scheffel (2013); Power (2016a, 2016b); Herden and Power (2016); Provan and Power (2016a, 2016b); Lane and Power (2016a, 2016b)

[11] OECD (2015)

[12] Kovats et al (2014)

[13] Jackson (2009)

[14] Stern (2015)

[15] IPCC (2012); IPCC (2014)

[16] National Energy Foundation (2015) – Simple Carbon Calculator

[17] City visits, 2007-2015

[18] Briggs (1968)

[19] Stern (2014)

[20] World Economic Forum (2015); European Council (2015c)

[21] Scottish National Party (2015); *Guardian* (2015a)

[22] Klein (2014)

[23] Saint Étienne's Schema de Coherence Territoriale, the SCOT plan, has a strong environmental focus, stresses the compact city model and favours protection of the surrounding green areas of city regrowth

Chapter 6: Over-scale and under-scale

[1] Jacobs (1970)

[2] IPCC (2014)

[3] Pearce (2010)

[4] Briggs (1968)

[5] Le Grand (2009)

[6] Osborne and Gaebler (1993)

[7] Ente Vasco de la Energia (2012)

[8] Bernt (2009); Haase et al (2013)

[9] Hatton (1988)

[10] Author's meeting with private sector leaders, following visit to Liverpool with Michael Heseltine, 1982

[11] Liverpool City Representative in City Reformers Workshop, LSE 2006

[12] Demographia (2006); ONS (2014a)

[13] Demographia (2006); ONS (2014a)

[14] Katz and Wagner (2014)

[15] Jackson (2009)

[16] Author's visit to Cedemi, Barakaldo, 2012

[17] Author's visit to Bochum, 2012

[18] Marsh (2012)

[19] IPCC (2014); UN Environment Program (2014); Stern (2015)

[20] *The Economist* (2015f)

[21] *Guardian* (2013)

[22] Invest in Bradford (2015)

[23] Lane et al (2014)

[24] MacKay (2009)

[25] Belfast City Council (2012)

[26] Environment Agency (2008)

[27] *The Economist* (2015b)

[28] *Guardian* (2015c)

[29] Geim (2009); Novoselov et al (2012); Kumar (2015)

[30] World Energy Council (2009)

[31] European Commission (2010)

[32] European Commission (2010)

[33] Mondragon Team Academy (2015)

[34] Anderson, R (2015)

[35] Provan and Power (2016b)

[36] Katz and Wagner (2014)

[37] Peters and Waterman (1983)

[38] *The Economist* (2015c)

[39] *The Economist* (2013)

[40] Katz and Wagner (2014)

[41] Petrini (2010)

[42] Troxler (2014)

[43] Maker Faire Bilbao (2014)

[44] Troxler (2014)

[45] Troxler (2014)

[46] *The Economist* (2015a)

[47] European Commission (2010)

[48] Klein (2014)

[49] UNEP (2015)

[50] Rifkin (2011); Region Nord-Pas De Calais (2013)

[51] Power and Zulauf (2011)

[52] Scottish Power Renewables (2015)

[53] European Commission (2010)

[54] Stern (2015)

[55] European Commission (2010)

[56] Mason (2015); Rifkin (2014)

[57] Ward (1976)

[58] Fuhrer (2009)

[59] Acorn Guardians (2015)

[60] Stadt Leipzig / Dept. of Urban Development (2006)

Chapter 7: The power of social innovation

[1] Reich (1992)

[2] Thompson (1990)

[3] Pétonnet (1973)

[4] Hills et al (2009)

[5] Power (1993)

[6] Power (1997, 1999)

[7] Dubedout (1983)

[8] Parenting Partnership Programme, funded through the Single Regeneration Budget, Birmingham, 1997.

[9] Jacquier (1991)

[10] Burgess (2014); Ratcliffe et al (2001)

[11] Sampson (2012)

[12] Jargowski (1997; 2013)

[13] Sampson (2012)

[14] Wilson (1987); Wilson and Taub (2006); Sampson (2012)

[15] Obama (2004)

[16] Emanual (2015)

[17] Wacquant and Wilson (1989)

[18] CDP Inter-project Editorial Team (1977)

[19] Francois Mitterand, in Dubedout (1983)

[20] Milner Holland Report (1965)

[21] Dodd et al (2013)

[22] *The Economist* (2015m)

[23] Dodd et al (2013)

[24] Power (1993); Power (1997)

[25] Power (1987); Power (1997)

[26] Délégation interministérielle à la ville (DIV) (1989)

[27] Power (2007); Power and Tunstall (1995)

[28] Power and Tunstall (1997)

[29] Power (2016a); Winkler (2007b)

[30] Power and Mumford (2003)

[31] Power (1997)

[32] Power (2008)

[33] Van Kempen et al (2005)

[34] Rogers and Power (2000)

[35] ONS (2014b); ILO (2014); MacInnes et al (2014)

[36] Power et al (2010)

[37] Lane and Power (2016a)

[38] South East England Councils (SEEC) (2009); Power et al (2004)

[39] East Germany overall has significantly higher unemployment compared to the West.

[40] Herden and Power (2016)

[41] BBC News (2015)

[42] Kelly and D'Arcy (2015); *The Economist* (2013)

[43] Sampson (2012)

[44] Goldsmith (2010)

[45] Dyson et al (2013)

[46] Contribution by Zest manager at Lille City Workshop, organised by Fabrique de la Cité, September 2014 in Gare Saint Sauveur, Lille.

[47] Compagnia di San Paolo (2014)

[48] Hopkins (2008)

[49] Transition Town Brixton (2015)

[50] Harvey (2006)

[51] Power (2016); Winkler (2007b)

[52] Kingsolver (2007)

[53] Petrini (2010)

[54] Power (2007)

Chapter 8: Shoots of growth in older industrial cities in the US

[1] Kullman (2012)

[2] Frey (2013)

[3] Cortright (2015)

[4] Friedhoff and Kulkarni (2015)

[5] Vey (2007)

[6] Vey (2007)

[7] Vey (2007)

[8] Warf and Holly (1997)

[9] Helper et al (2012)

[10] Levy and Gilchrist (2014)

[11] Frey (2013)

[12] Detroit Strategic Framework Plan (2012)

[13] 7.2 SQ MI (2015)

[14] Katz and Wagner (2014)

[15] Katz, B (2013)

[16] Muro, M et al (2015)

[17] *The Economist* (2015e)

[18] De Souza Briggs et al (2015)

Chapter 9: Finding new ways out of the woods

[1] Thomas Sugrue, expert on Detroit's history, set out Detroit's environmental potential in *Detroit Rising?: Crisis, Bankruptcy, and Reinvention*, a public lecture hosted by LSE Cities on Tuesday 12 January 2016 at the London School of Economics

[2] Rogers and Power (2000); Power and Houghton (2007)

[3] Dodd et al (2013)

[4] Power et al (2010)

[5] INSEE (2008; nd)

[6] UN Habitat (2007, 2009, 2011); Reader (2005); Girardet (2004)

[7] Power et al (2010); Katz et al (2013)

[8] Wilson and Taub (2006); Desmond (2013)

[9] Power et al (2010)

[10] Urban Task Force (1999)

[11] Stern (2015)

[12] Power (1993)

[13] Heseltine (1983)

[14] *The Economist* (2015l); de Kok et al (2011); Bakhshi et al (2011); *The Economist* (2014c)

[15] Power (1987)

[16] Herden and Power (2016)

[17] UK-GBC and The Crown Estate (2015)

[18] LSE Cities (2013)

[19] European Commission (2010)

[20] Velasco (2015); Aona (2015)

[21] Klein (2014)

[22] European Commission (2014a)

[23] Hutton (2015)

[24] Stern (2015)

[25] Plöger and Power (2012)

[26] Stern (2015)

[27] Lane et al (2016)

[28] International Passive House Association (nd)

[29] Eurostat (2014b)

[30] Personal communication, City of Belfast, June 2015.

[31] LSE Cities (2013)

[32] UN (2011); United Nations Framework Convention on Climate Change (2015)

[33] Girardet (1999); Rees (1999)

[34] Ostrom (2009)

[35] Rogers and Power (2000)

[36] Stern (2015)

[37] Katz and Wagner (2014)

[38] Glennerster (2013)

[39] Provan and Power (2016a)

[40] Burdett et al (2011)

[41] Lane and Power (2016a)

[42] Sheffield Culture Consortium (2016)

[43] Troxler (2014)

[44] Author's visit to Mondragon, 2015

[45] Katz and Wagner (2014)

[46] Katz and Bradley (2013)

[47] Power and Houghton (2007)

[48] Mason (2015); Rifkin (2014)

[49] *The Economist* (2014b)

[50] City of Bradford MDC (2013)

[51] Power (1997)

[52] MacInnes et al (2014); Belfield et al (2015)

[53] Winkler (2007a); Plöger (2007a); Lane and Power (2016a, 2016b)

[54] European Commission (2015d)

[55] Atkinson (2015)

[56] Meeting with Bilbao City Manager, June 2014

[57] Lane and Power (2016a and 2016b); Provan and Power (2016a and 2016b); Herden and Power (2016); Power (2016a and 2016b); Hills et al (2015)

[58] Personal interviews with city leaders, 2008–14.

[59] International Federation of the Red Cross (2013)

[60] European Council (2015a, 2015b)

[61] Revolting Europe (2015); Green Party (2015)

[62] *The Economist* (2015h; 2015i)

[63] City of Manchester – meeting with senior officials in 2006.

[64] Northern Ireland Statistics and Research Agency (NISRA) (2015)

[65] Jacobs (1970)

[66] European Commission (2010); European Commission (2014a); European Commission (2015a; 2015d)

[67] Power (1993)

[68] McGahey and Vey (2008); Mallach (2012)

[69] UrbAct (2015)

[70] Power and Houghton (2007)

[71] HM Government (2012)

[72] Grand Projet de Ville (2013)

[73] BMVBS (2008)

[74] OECD (2014)

[75] Atkinson (2015); Piketty (2015)

[76] European Commission (2015d)

[77] Jargowski (2013)

[78] EDA (2011)

[79] Power et al (2010)

References

7.2 SQ MI (2015) *A report on greater downtown Detroit*, 2nd ed., http://detroitsevenpointtwo.com/resources/7.2SQ_MI_Book_FINAL_LoRes.pdf

Academy of Achievement (2009) 'John Hume Biography – Academy of Achievement', www.achievement.org/autodoc/page/hum0bio-1

Acorn Guardians (2015) 'What we do', https://carlitamcknight.wordpress.com/what-we-do-3/

Anderson, R. (2015) 'Heat pumps extract warmth from ice cold water', BBC News, 10 March, www.bbc.co.uk/news/business-31506073

Aona, A. (2015) 'TAV: spesi finora 32 miliardi. Manca il nodo di Firenze', *Il Sole 24 Ore*, 17 March, www.ilsole24ore.com/art/notizie/2015-03-17/tav-spesi-finora-32-miliardi-manca-nodo-firenze-063705.shtml?uuid=ABZDKOAD

Atkinson, A.B. (2003) 'Social Europe and Social Science', *Social Policy and Society*, 2, 261–72.

Atkinson, A.B. (2015) *Inequality: What can be done?*, Cambridge, MA: Harvard University Press.

Bakhshi, H., Edwards, J., Roper, S., Scully, J. and Shaw, D. (2011) *Creating Innovation in Small and Medium-sized Enterprises: Evaluating the Short-term Effects of the Creative Credits Pilot*, Working Paper, CESME/70, London: NESTA.

Balabkins, N. (1964) *Germany under direct controls: economic aspects of industrial disarmament 1945–1948*, New Brunswick, NJ: Rutgers University Press.

Barraclough, G. and Stone, N. (eds) (1989) *The Times Atlas of World History,* 3rd ed., London: Times Books.

BBC News (2015) 'Election 2015: David Cameron speech in full', www.bbc.co.uk/news/uk-politics-32661073

Belfast City Council (2012) 'Back to the Future: Future Cities and urban empowerment for resilient, low carbon communities', Submission to Technology Strategy Board, Future Cities Competition, November.

Belfield, C., Cribb, J., Hood, A., and Joyce, R. (2015) *Living standards, poverty and inequality in the UK: 2015*, Institute for Fiscal Studies, www.ifs.org.uk/uploads/publications/comms/R107.pdf

Bernt, M. (2009) 'Partnerships for Demolition: The Governance of urban renewal in East Germany's shrinking cities, *International Journal of Urban and Regional Research*, *33*(3), 754–69.

Bibby, A. (2012) 'Co-operatives in Spain – Mandragon leads the way', *Guardian,* 12 March, www.theguardian.com/social-enterprise-network/2012/mar/12/cooperatives-spain-mondragon

Booth, P. (2005) 'Partnerships and networks: the governance of urban regeneration in Britain', *Journal of Housing and the Built Environment,* 20(3), 257–69.

Briggs, A. (1968) *Victorian Cities,* Harmondsworth: Penguin Books

Brown, G. (2014) *My Scotland, our Britain: A future worth sharing,* London: Simon and Schuster.

Bundesministerium für Verkehr, Bau und Stadtentwicklung (BMVBS) (2008) *Statusbericht zum Programm Soziale Stadt: Kurzfassung,* Berlin, http://www.difu.de/publikationen/2008/statusbericht-2008-zum-programm-soziale-stadt.html-0

Burdett, R., Sudjic, D. and Cavusoglu, O. (2011) *Living in the Endless City,* London: Phaidon Press.

Burgess, S. (2014) *Understanding the Success of London's Schools,* The Center for Market and Public Organization, University of Bristol, Available at: www.bristol.ac.uk/media-library/sites/cmpo/migrated/documents/wp333.pdf

CDP Inter-project Editorial Team (1977) *Gilding the Ghetto: The state and the poverty experiments,* London: Community Development Project.

City of Bradford MDC (2013) *Bradford City Centre Area Action Plan 2013–2028 Summary Document,* www.bradford.gov.uk/NR/rdonlyres/1C4A1304–85FC-4960-AB2E-95F2FF36D1A1/0/2BradfordCityCentreAreaActionPlanFurtherIssuesandOptions2013SummaryDocument.pdf

Compagnia di San Paolo (2014) *Rapporto 2014,* Torino: Compagnia di San Paolo.

Cortright, J. (2015) 'Surging City Center Job Growth', *City Reports,* http://cityobservatory.org/city-center-jobs/

De Souza Briggs, X., Pendall, R. and Rubin, V. (2015) *Inclusive economic growth in America's cities: What's the playbook and the score?* World Bank Policy Research Working Paper No. 7322, http://papers.ssrn.com/sol3/papers.cfm?abstract_id=2621876

Department of Energy and Climate Change (DECC) (nd) 2050 Calculator, http://2050-calculator-tool.decc.gov.uk/#/home

Délégation Interministérielle a la Ville (DIV) (1989) Justice et Quartiers, Paris: DIV

Demographia (2006) 'International: Selected cities with declining population ranked by annual loss rate', http://demographia.com/db-intlcitylossr.htm

Department for Transport (2014) *Road - DfT Statistics, 2016: Table TSGB0101 Passenger transport: by mode, annual from 1952*

Desmond, M. (2016) *Evicted: Poverty and profit in an American City*, London: Allan Lane

De Kok, J et al (2011) *Is Small Still Beautiful?* Literature Review of Recent Empirical Evidence on the Contribution of SMEs to Employment Creation. International Labour Organisation/Deutsche Gesellschaft für Internationale Zusammenarbeit (GIZ) GmbH.

Diamond, J. (2006) *Collapse: How societies choose to fail or survive,* London: Penguin.

Detroit Strategic Framework Plan (2012) *Detroit Future City*, Detroit: Inland Press.

Dodd, J., Fox, T., Güntner S., Provan, B. and Tosics, I. (2013) *Housing investments supported by the European Regional Development Fund 2007–2013* European Commission, Brussels, http://ec.europa.eu/regional_policy/sources/docgener/studies/pdf/housing/2013_housing_study.pdf

Donnison, D. V. and Ungerson, C. (1982) *Housing Policy*, Harmondsworth: Penguin Books.

Dubedout, H. (1983) *Ensemble, refaire la ville: Rapport au premier ministre du président de la Commission nationale pour le développement social des quartiers*, http://aquitaine-pqa.fr/mini-sites/politique-ville-aqui/wp-content/uploads/sites/17/2014/12/Rapport-Dubedout-Ensemble-refaire-la-ville-1983.pdf

Dyson, A., Kerr, K. and Wellings, C. (2013) *Developing Children's Zones for England, What's the evidence?* London: Save the Children.

The Economist (2013) 'Dissecting the miracle', 13 June, www.economist.com/news/special-report/21579145-ingredients-german-economic-success-are-more-complex-they-seem-dissecting

The Economist (2014a) 'European labour mobility: On the move', 13 January, www.economist.com/blogs/freeexchange/2014/01/european-labour-mobility

The Economist (2014b) 'The onrushing wave', 18 January, www.economist.com/news/briefing/21594264-previous-technological-innovation-has-always-delivered-more-long-run-employment-not-less

The Economist (2014c) 'Don't bank on the banks', 16 August, pp. 57–59.

The Economist (2015a) '3D printing under the knife', 15 April, http://gelookahead.economist.com/3d-printing-under-the-knife/

The Economist (2015b) 'How renewable energy can become competitive', 3 June, www.economist.com/blogs/economist-explains/2015/06/economist-explains-1?zid=313&ah=fe2aac0b11 adef572d67aed9273b6e55

The Economist (2015c) 'Supersize me', 21 February, www.economist. com/news/business/21644172-lack-larger-firms-means-fewer-jobs-and-less-resilient-economy-supersize-me

The Economist (2015d) 'The end of industry', 27 June, www.economist. com/news/britain/21656198-impending-closure-britains-last-deep-coal-mines-moment-reflection-and-awe-end

The Economist (2015e) 'The fire and the fuel', 9 May, www.economist. com/news/united-states/21650533-what-dead-white-man-can-teach-america-about-inner-city-decay-fire-and-fuel

The Economist (2015f) 'The great incubator', 31 January, www. economist.com/news/britain/21641266-makers-are-thriving-capitalbut-perhaps-not-long-great-incubator

The Economist (2015g) 'Under the Bonnet', 30 May, www.economist. com/news/britain/21652310-britains-stall-productivity-more-serious-any-rich-world-peer-closer-look

The Economist (2015h) 'Europe's future in Greece's hands', 4 July, www. economist.com/news/leaders/21656662-whatever-its-outcome-greek-crisis-will-change-eu-ever-europes-future-greeces

The Economist (2015i) 'The euro-zone recovery is losing momentum', 14 August, www.economist.com/blogs/freeexchange/2015/08/economic-growth-europe

The Economist (2015l) 'To have and to hold', Special report: Family companies, 18 April, pp. 3–16.

The Economist (2015m) 'Why rioting makes things worse', 2 May, www.economist.com/news/united-states/21650158-angry-youths-burn-their-own-neighbourhood-why-rioting-makes-things-worse

EDA: US Economic Development Administration (2011) *Strong Cities, Strong Communities*, www.eda.gov/challenges/sc2challenge/

Ehrlich, P.R., Kareiva, P.M. and Daily, G.C. (2012) 'Securing natural capital and expanding equity to rescale civilization', *Nature*, 486(7401), 68–73.

Elcock, H. (2006) 'Local political leadership in Britain: Rake's progress or search for the Holy Grail?', *Public Policy and Administration*, 21(2).

Emanual, R. (2015) 'Inaugural Address of Mayor Rahm Emanual', City of Chicago, www.cityofchicago.org/city/en/depts/mayor/press_room/press_releases/2015/may/inaugural-address-of-mayor-rahm-emanuel.html

Ente Vasco de la Energia (EVE) (2012) *Report from ENNERREG Pioneer Region, Basque Country, Spain*, Bilbao: EVE, www.regions202020.eu/cms/assets/Uploads/Resources/13Jan29-Basque-Inspiration.pdf

Environment Agency (2008) *Greenhouse gas emissions of water supply and demand management options*, Science Report SC070010, www.gov.uk/government/uploads/system/uploads/attachment_data/file/291728/scho0708bofv-e-e.pdf

EUR-Lex (nd) 'Objective 1', http://eur-lex.europa.eu/legal-content/EN/TXT/?uri=uriserv:g24203EUR-Lex (nd) 'Objective 2', http://eur-lex.europa.eu/legal-content/EN/TXT/?uri=uriserv:g24206

European Commission (2003) *Support for Roma Communities in Central and Eastern Europe*, Brussels: Enlargement Information Unit, http://ec.europa.eu/enlargement/pdf/brochure_roma_oct2003_en.pdf

European Commission (2005) 'Urban Audit Perception Survey: Local perceptions of quality of life in 31 European cities', Eurostat.

European Commission (2007) *State of European Cities: Executive Report*, May.

European Commission (2010) *Europe 2020: A strategy for smart, sustainable and inclusive growth,* COM(2010) 2020 final, http://eur-lex.europa.eu/LexUriServ/LexUriServ.do?uri=COM:2010:2020:FIN:EN:PD

European Commission (2014a) *Annexes to the Communication from the Commission to the European Parliament, the Council, the European Economic and Social Committee and the Committee of the Regions: Taking stock of the Europe 2020 strategy for smart, sustainable and inclusive growth*, COM(2014) 130 final/2, http://ec.europa.eu/europe2020/pdf/europe2020stocktaking_annex_en.pdf

European Commission (2014b) *Roma Health Report: Health Status of the Roma Population – Data Collection in the Member States of the European Union*, http://ec.europa.eu/health/social_determinants/docs/2014_roma_health_report_en.pdf

European Commission (2015a) 'European regional development fund', http://ec.europa.eu/regional_policy/en/funding/erdf/

European Commission (2015b) 'European social fund', http://ec.europa.eu/esf/main.jsp?catId=35&langId=en

European Commission (2015c) 'Remarks of Commissioner Avramapoulos after the Justice and Home Affairs Council on 20 July 2015', Press Release Database, http://europa.eu/rapid/press-release_SPEECH-15-5421_en.htm

European Commission (2015d) 'Managing migration and financing a safer and more secure Europe: €2.4 billion to support Member States', Press Release Database, Brussels, 10 August, at: http://europa.eu/rapid/press-release_IP-15-5483_en.htm

European Community (1957) Treaty of Rome, European Union, Treaty Establishing the European Community (Consolidated Version), 25 March, www.refworld.org/docid/3ae6b39c0.html

European Council (2015a) 'Ministerial statement on 27 June 2015', Press releases and statements, www.consilium.europa.eu/en/press/press-releases/2015/06/27-ministerial-statement/

European Council (2015b) 'Remarks by President Donald Tusk after the Euro Summit of 7 July 2015 on Greece', Press releases and statements, www.consilium.europa.eu/en/press/press-releases/2015/07/07-tusk-remarks-euro-summit/

European Council (2015c) *Leaders' Declaration G7 Summit, 7–8 June 2015*, Schloss Elmau, Germany, https://sustainabledevelopment.un.org/content/documents/7320LEADERS%20STATEMENT_FINAL_CLEAN.pdf

European Union Agency for Fundamental Rights (FRA) (2014) *Education: The Situation of Roma in 11 Member States, Luxembourg: Publications Office of the European Union*, Roma survey – Data in focus, http://fra.europa.eu/sites/default/files/fra-2014_roma-survey_education_tk0113748enc.pdf

Eurostat (2014a) *Modal split and road freight transport performance in the EU*, news release 147/2014, http://ec.europa.eu/eurostat/documents/2995521/5181618/7–01102014-AP-EN.PDF/27ff9bda-5a54–4321–94c6–9f8a446ee431?version=1.0

Eurostat (2014b) 'Passenger transport statistics', Statistics Explained, http://ec.europa.eu/eurostat/statistics-explained/index.php/Passenger_transport_statistics#Rail_passengers

Eurostat (2015a) 'Euro area unemployment rate at 11.1%', news release 98/2015, http://ec.europa.eu/eurostat/documents/2995521/6862104/3–03062015-BP-EN.pdf/efc97561-fad1–4e10-b6c1-e1c80e2bb582

Eurostat (2015b) 'Unemployment statistics', Statistics Explained, http://ec.europa.eu/eurostat/statistics-explained/index.php/Unemployment_statistics

Fab Labs, http://fablabsuk.co.uk/ accessed 15th March 2016

Fields of Battle – Lands of Peace 14–18 (2014) A major photographic exhibition by Micheal St Maur Sheil, www.fieldsofbattle1418.org

Forster, R.F. (1989) *Modern Ireland 1600–1972*, London: Paladin.

Frey, W.H. (2013) *A Big City Growth Revival?*, Brookings Institution, www.brookings.edu/research/opinions/2013/05/28-city-growth-frey

Friedhoff, A. and Kulkarni, S. (2015) 'Metro Monitor – July 2015', Brookings Metropolitan Policy Program and LSE Cities, www.brookings.edu/research/interactives/metromonitor#/M10420

Fuhrer, C. (2009) *Und wir sind dabei gewesen: Die Revolution, die aus der Kirche kam*. Berlin: Ullstein.

Geim, A.K. (2009) 'Graphene: Status and Prospects', *Science, 324*, 1530–4.

George C. Marshall Foundation (nd) 'The Marshall Plan', http://marshallfoundation.org/marshall/the-marshall-plan/

Gies, M. and Gold, A.L. (1987) *Meine Zeit mit Anne Frank*, Frankfurt am Main: S. Fischer Verlag, GmbH.

Gies, M. and Gold, A.L. (2009) *Anne Frank Remembered: The Story of the Woman Who Helped to Hide the Frank Family*, New York: Simon & Schuster

Girardet, H. (1999) *Creating Sustainable Cities* (No. 2), Totnes: Green Books Ltd for the Schumacher Society

Giradet, H. (2004) *Cities people planet: Liveable cities for a sustainable world*, New York, NY: John Wiley & Sons

Glaeser, E. (2011) *Triumph of the city: How our greatest invention makes us richer, smarter, greener, healthier and happier*, New York: Penguin Press.

Glennerster, H. (2013) *Paying for Welfare*, 3rd ed., New York: Routledge.

Gobierno Vasco (2012) *25 años de Euskadi en Europa: La ayuda a Euskadi de los fondos estructurales europeos 1986–2011*, Departamento de Economia y Hacienda, www.ogasun.ejgv.euskadi.eus/contenidos/informacion/politica_regional/es_2340/adjuntos/25-anos-de-Euskadi-en-Europa.pdf

Goldsmith, S. (2010) *The Power of Social Innovation: How civic entrepreneurs ignite community networks for good*. San Francisco, CA: John Wiley & Sons.

Grand Projet de Ville (2013) ANRU 2008–2017, https://www.data.gouv.fr/fr/datasets/grand-projet-de-ville-gpv-ods/

Green Alliance (2015) *Inside Track 35: The great acceleration – what should the UK do to protect natural systems?* www.green-alliance.org.uk/inside_track_35.php

Green Party (2015) 'General election manifesto', www.greenparty.org.uk/we-stand-for/2015-manifesto.html

Guardian (2013) 'Stoke on Trent travel tips: Wedgewood and the industrial revolution', 4 February, www.theguardian.com/travel/2013/feb/04/stoke-on-trent-travel-tips-industrial-revolution

Guardian (2014) 'Electric 'Boris cars' are coming to London – how do they work in Paris?' 9 July, www.theguardian.com/cities/2014/jul/09/electric-boris-car-source-london-how-work-paris-autolib

Guardian (2015a) 'Election 2015: Sturgeon says Tories bullied Miliband into rejecting SNP support, 27 April, www.theguardian.com/politics/live/2015/apr/27/election-2015-labour-stamp-duty-first-time-buyers-5000-small-businesses-cameron

Guardian (2015b) 'Greek debt crisis: EU agrees €7bn loan as Germany backs new bailout talks – as it happened', 17 July, www.theguardian.com/business/live/2015/jul/17/greek-debt-crisis-germany-bailout-package-lagarde-debt-relief-live

Guardian (2015c) 'The innovators: cheaper batteries could help electric cars hit the mainstream', 9 August, www.theguardian.com/business/2015/aug/09/the-innovators-cheaper-batteries-could-help-electric-cars-hit-the-mainstream

Guardian (2015d) 'Three sisters, nine children, one dangerous journey to the heart of Isis. What is the lure of the caliphate?', 21 June, www.theguardian.com/world/2015/jun/21/three-sisters-nine-children-what-is-the-lure-of-the-isis-caliphate

Guardian (2015e) 'UK and Norway to build world's longest undersea energy interconnector' 26 March, www.theguardian.com/business/2015/mar/26/uk-and-norway-to-build-worlds-longest-undersea-energy-interconnector

Haase, A., Bernt, M., Großmann, K., Mykhnenko, V. and Rink, D. (2013) 'Varieties of shrinkage in European cities, *European Urban and Regional Studies, 0*(0), 1–17.

Hald, M. (2009) *Sustainable Urban Development and Chinese Eco-City: Concepts, Strategies, Policies and Assessments,* FNI Report 5/2009, Fridtjof Nansen Institute, www.fni.no/pdf/FNI-R0509.pdf

Harvey, G. (2006) *We want real food: Why our food is deficient in minerals and nutrients-and what we can do about it,* London: Constable.

Hatton, D. (1988) *Inside left: The story so far,* London: Bloomsbury Publishing.

Helper, S., Krueger, T. and Wial, H. (2012) *Locating American manufacturing: Trends in the geography of production,* Washington DC: Brookings Institute

Herden, E. and Power, A. (2016) *Leipzig City Report,* LSE: CASE.

Heseltine, M. (1983) *Reviving the Inner Cities,* London: Conservative Political Centre.

Hills, J., Cuncliffe, J., Obolenskaya, P. and Karagiannaki, E. (2015) *Falling behind, getting ahead: the changing structure of inequality in the UK, 2007–2013, Social Policy in Cold Climate, Research Report 5*, London: The London School of Economics and Political Science.

Hills, J., Sefton, T. and Stewart, K. (2009) *Towards a More Equal Society? Poverty, inequality and policy since 1997,* Bristol: Policy Press.

HM Government (2012) *Unlocking Growth in Cities: City deals wave 1,* www.gov.uk/government/uploads/system/uploads/attachment_data/file/221009/Guide-to-City-Deals-wave-1.pdf

Holy Father Francis (2015) Encyclical Letter *Laudato Si: On care for our common home* (24 May), Libreria Editrice Vaticana, http://w2.vatican.va/content/francesco/en/encyclicals/documents/papa-francesco_20150524_enciclica-laudato-si.html

Hopkins, R. (2008) *The transition handbook: From oil dependency to local resilience,* White River Junction, Vermont: Chelsea River Publishing.

Hunt, T. (2005) *Building Jerusalem: the rise and fall of the Victorian city.* London: Phoenix.

Hutton, W. (2015) *How Good We Can Be: Ending the Mercenary Society and Building a Great Country*, London: Little, Brown Book Group.

International Labour Organization (ILO) (2014) *Global employment trends 2014: Risk of a jobless recovery?* www.ilo.org/wcmsp5/groups/public/---dgreports/---dcomm/---publ/documents/publication/wcms_233953.pdf

IMF (2015) Statement by IMF Managing Director Christine Lagarde on Greece. Press Release No. 15/381. August 14. https://www.imf.org/external/np/sec/pr/2015/pr15381.htm

Inman, P., Elliott L. and Nardelli, A. (2015) 'IMF says Greece needs extra €60bn in funds and debt relief', *Guardian*, 2 July, pp. 10–11.

INSEE (nd) *Municipal Population at the Census - Saint-Étienne*, Macro-economic database, http://www.bdm.insee.fr/bdm2/index?request_locale=enINSEE (nd) 'Population', www.insee.fr/fr/themes/theme.asp?theme=2&sous_theme=0&type=1&nivgeo=0&produit=OK

INSEE (2008) 'Loire: un léger regain démographique', *La Lettre-Analyses*, No. 93, July, www.insee.fr/fr/insee_regions/rhone-alpes/themes/syntheses/lettre_analyses/02093/02093_loire_projection_population_2020.pdf

International Federation of the Red Cross (2013) *Think Differently: Humanitarian impacts of the economic crisis in Europe*, www.ifrc.org/PageFiles/134339/1260300-Economic%20crisis%20Report_EN_LR.pdf

International Passive House Association (nd) 'Passive House certification criteria', www.passivehouse-international.org/index. php?page_id=150

Invest in Bradford (2015) 'Bradford economy', www.investinbradford. com/bradford-economy.html

Intergovernmental Panel on Climate Change (IPCC) (2012) *Managing the Risks of Extreme Events and Disasters to Advance Climate Change Adaptation. A Special Report of Working Groups I and II of the Intergovernmental Panel on Climate Change* [Field, C.B., V. Barros, T.F. Stocker, D. Qin, D.J. Dokken, K.L. Ebi, M.D. Mastrandrea, K.J. Mach, G.-K. Plattner, S.K. Allen, M. Tignor, and P.M. Midgley (eds)]. Cambridge, UK and New York: Cambridge University Press.

IPCC (2014) *Climate Change 2014: Impacts, Adaptation, and Vulnerability. Part A: Global and Sectoral Aspects. Contribution of Working Group II to the Fifth Assessment Report of the Intergovernmental Panel on Climate Change* [Barros, V.R., C.B.Field, D.J. Dokken, ,Cambridge, UK and New York: Cambridge University Press.

IPCC (2015) *Fifth assessment report*, www.ipcc.ch/report/ar5/

Jackson, T. (2009) *Prosperity without growth: The transition to a sustainable economy*, London: Sustainable Development Commission.

Jacobs, J. (1970) *The economy of cities*, New York, NY: Random House

Jacquier, C. (1991) *Voyage dans dix quartiers européens en crise*, Collection Objectif Ville, L'Harmattan.

Jargowski, P. (1997) *Poverty and Place: Ghettos, barrios, and the American city*, New York, NY: Russel Sage Foundation.

Jargowski, P.A. (2013) *Concentration of Poverty in the New Millennium: Changes in prevalence, composition, and location of high poverty neighbourhoods*, The Century Foundation, www.tcf.org/bookstore/ detail/concentration-of-poverty-in-the-new-millennium

Katz, B. and Bradley, J. (2013) *The Metropolitan Revolution: How cities and metros are fixing our broken politics and fragile economy*, Washington DC: Brookings Institution Press.

Katz, B. and Wagner, J. (2014) *The Rise of Innovation Districts: A new geography of innovation in America*, Brookings Institute, www. brookings.edu/~/media/Programs/metro/Images/Innovation/ InnovationDistricts1.pdf

Keep, M (2015) Public expenditure by country and region. BRIEFING PAPER Number 04033, 8 March 2015. London: House of Commons Library. [www.parliament.uk/briefing-papers/sn04033.pdf]

Kelly, G. and D'Arcy, C. (eds) (2015) *Securing a Pay Rise: The path back to shared growth*, The Resolution Foundation, www.resolutionfoundation.org/wp-content/uploads/2015/03/Securing-a-pay-rise-the-path-back-to-shared-wage-growth-web-version.pdf

Kingsolver, B. (2007) *Animal, vegetable, miracle,* London: Faber and Faber.

Klein, N. (2014) *This Changes Everything: Capitalism vs. The Climate*, New York: Simon and Schuster.

Kovats, R.S., Valentini, R., Bower, L.M., Georgopoulou, E., Jacob, D., Martin, E., Rounsevell, M., Sousanna, J-F., Corobov, R., Kajfež-Bogotaj, L. and Vallejo, V.R. (2014) 'Europe', in IPCC, *Climate Change 2014: Impacts, Adaptation, and Vulnerability*, Cambridge, UK: Cambridge University Press, pp. 1267–326.

Krebs, T., and Scheffel, M. (2013) 'Macroeconomic evaluation of labour market reform in Germany', *IMF Economic Review*, *61*(4), 664–701.

Krugman, P.R. (2012) *End This Depression Now!* New York, NY and London: W.W. Norton.

Kullmann, K. (2012) *Rasende Ruinen: wie Detroit sich neu erfindet*, Berlin: Suhrkamp Verlag.

Kumar, A. (2015) 'The fuss about graphene', *Economist*, 9 June, www.economist.com/blogs/economist-explains/2015/06/economist-explains-7

La Fabrique de la Cité (2014) *Recovering Cities: How to create value for cities - Experience of seven "Phoenix Cities"*, www.lafabriquedelacite.com/fabrique-de-la-cite/data.nsf/B1D62B37F6E0A5CBC1257BFA004A21DF/$file/lse_study_eng_def.pdf

Lacey, G.N. (1972) 'Observations on Aberfan', *Journal of Psychosomatic Research*, *16*(4), 257–60.

Lane, L. and Power, A. (2016a) *Sheffield City Report*, LSE: CASE.

Lane, L. Grubb, B. and Power, A. (2016b) *Belfast City Report*, LSE: CASE.

Lane, L., Power, A. and Provan, B. (2014) *High Rise Hope Revisited: The social implications of upgrading large estates*, CASEreport 85, London: London School of Economics.

Le Grand, J. (2009) *The Other Invisible Hand: Delivering public services through choice and competition*, Princeton: Princeton University Press.

Lee, N., Sissons, P., Hughes, C., Green, A., Atfield, G., Adam, D. and Rodrigue-Pose, A. (2014) *Cities, Growth, and Poverty: A review of the evidence,* York: Joseph Rowntree Foundation.

Leunig, T. and Swaffield, J. (2007) *Cities Unlimited: Making Urban Regeneration Work*, Policy Exchange, www.policyexchange.org.uk/images/publications/cities%20unlimited%20-%20aug%2008.pdf

Levy, P.R. and Gilchrist, L.M. (2014) *Downtown rebirth: Documenting the live-work dynamic in 21st century U.S. cities*, Prepared for the International Downtown Association by the Philadelphia Center City District, http://definingdowntown.org/wp-content/uploads/docs/Defining_DowntownReport.pdf

Liverpool John Moores University (LJMU) (2012) *Second tier cities in Europe: In an age of austerity why invest beyond the capitals?* European Institute of Urban Affairs (LJMU), Metropolitan Research Institute (Budapest), Sente (University of Tempere), Institut Français d'Urbanisme (Université Paris-Est), University College London, www.liv.ac.uk/media/livacuk/publicpolicypractice/euconference/Second,Tier,Cities,in,Europe,-,Final,Version.pdf

Louv, R. (2008) *Last child in the woods: Saving our children from nature-deficit disorder*, Chapel Hill, NC: Algonquin Books.

LSE Cities (2010) *Global Metro Monitor: the Path to Economic Recovery*, Metropolitan Policy Program at Brookings and LSE Cities, London School of Economics and Political Science, www.brookings.edu/~/media/research/files/reports/2010/11/30-global-metro-monitor/1130_global_metro_monitor.pdf

LSE Cities (2013) *Going Green: How cities are leading the next economy,* https://files.lsecities.net/files/2013/06/Going-Green-Final-Edition-web-version.pdf

Lutz. W., Scherbov, S. and Volkov, A. (eds) (2002) *Demographic trends and patterns in the Soviet Union before 1991,* London: Routledge.

MacInnes, T., Aldridge, H., Bushe, S., Tinson, A. and Barry Born, T. (2014) *Monitoring poverty and social exclusion 2014*, York: Joseph Rowntree Foundation, www.jrf.org.uk/report/monitoring-poverty-and-social-exclusion-2014

MacKay, D.J.C. (2009) *Sustainable energy without the hot air*, Cambridge: UIT Cambridge.

Maker Faire Bilbao (2014) 'Crazy maker faire!', http://bilbaomakerfaire.com/2015/03/18/crazy-maker-faire/

Mallach, A. (ed) (2012) *Rebuilding America's Legacy Cities: New Directions for the Industrial Heartland*, New York: American Assembly Columbia University.

Mallach, A. and Brachman, L. (2013) *Regenerating America's legacy cities*, Cambridge, MA: Lincoln Institute of Land Policy, www.lincolninst.edu/pubs/2215_Regenerating-America-s-Legacy-Cities

Marsh, P. (2012) *The new industrial revolution: consumers, globalization and the end of mass production*, London: Yale University Press.

Mason, P. (2015) *PostCapitalism: A guide to our future*, London: Allen Lane.

Massey, D. and Denton, N. (1993) *American apartheid: Segregation and the making of the underclass,* Cambridge. MA: Harvard University Press.

Mayor of London (2012) *London ERDF Programme 2007–2013: Annual Implementation Report*, European Regional Development Fund 2007–13.

McGahey, R. and Vey, J.S. (eds) (2008) *Retooling for growth: Building a 21st century economy in America's older industrial areas*, Washington DC: Brookings Institution Press.

McKittrick, D. and McVea, D. (2002) *Making sense of the troubles: The story of the conflict in Northern Ireland*, Lanham, MD: New Amsterdam Books.

Milner Holland Report (1965) *Report of the committee on housing in Greater London*, Cmnd. 2605, HMSO.

Mondragon Team Academy (2015) 'About us', http://mondragonteamacademy.com/1/about-us

Muro, M., Rothwell, J., Andes, S., Fikri, K and Kulkarni, S. (2015) *America's Advanced Industries: What They Are, Where They Are, and Why They Matter*, Washington DC: Brookings Institution Press

National Energy Foundation (NEF) (2015) 'Simple Carbon Calculator', www.carbon-calculator.org.uk

Neumann, U. and Seidel-Schulze, A. (2010) *Urban Audit Analysis II: Research Project for the European Commission, General Directory Regional Policy*, www.staedtestatistik.de/fileadmin/vdst/Muenchen2010/Vortraege/M0403_Scorus_Neumann_Seidel-Schulze_.pdf

Nivola, P.S. (1999) *Laws of the landscape: How policies shape cities in Europe and America*, Washington DC: Brookings Institution Press.

Northern Ireland Statistics & Research Agency (NISRA) (2015) *Long-Term International Migration Statistics for Northern Ireland*, NISRA Statistical Bulletin, www.nisra.gov.uk/archive/demography/population/migration/Mig1314-Bulletin.pdf

Novoselov, K.S., Fal'ki, V.I., Colombo, L., Gellert, P.R., Schwab, M.G. and Kim, K. (2012) A Roadmap for Graphene, *Nature, 490,* 192–200.

Obama, B. (2004) *Dreams from my father: A story of race and inheritance*, New York, NY: Three Rivers Press.

Organization for Economic Co-operation and Development (OECD) (2014) *PISA 2012 results in focus*, Programme for International Student Assessment, www.oecd.org/pisa/keyfindings/pisa-2012-results-overview.pdf

OECD (2015) *OECD Employment Outlook 2015*, Paris: OECD Publishing, Paris, http://dx.doi.org/10.1787/empl_outlook-2015-en

Office of National Statistics (ONS) (2012) *Urban Audit IV: United Kingdom Cities Compared with European Cities, 2008*, www.ons.gov.uk/ons/dcp171766_259161.pdf

ONS (2014a) 'Neighbourhood statistics: Liverpool (Local Authority)' http://tinyurl.com/gtcrlmm

ONS (2014b) *Young people not in education, employment or training (NEET), November 2014*, Statistical Bulletin, www.ons.gov.uk/ons/dcp171778_383815.pdf

Osborne, D.E. and Gaebler, T. (1993) *Reinventing government: how the entrepreneurial spirit is transforming the public sector*, New York, NY: Plume.

Ostrom, E. (2009) *Beyond markets and states: Polycentric governance of complex economic systems*, Prize Lecture, The Sveriges Riksbank Prize in Economic Sciences in Memory of Alfred Nobel 2009, 8 December, Aula Magna, Stockholm University, www.nobelprize.org/nobel_prizes/economic-sciences/laureates/2009/ostrom-lecture.html

Ostrom, E (2015) *Governing the Commons: The Evolution of Institutions for Collective Action* (Canto Classics), Cambridge: Cambridge University Press

Parkinson, M., Champion, T., Simmie, J. Turok, I., Crookston, M., Katz, B. and Park, A.(2006) *State of the English Cities: A Research Study*, London: Office of the Deputy Prime Minister.

Pearce, F. (2010) 'The overpopulation myth', *Prospect*, 8 March, www.prospectmagazine.co.uk/magazine/the-overpopulation-myth

Peters, T.J. and Waterman, R.H. (1983) *In search of excellence: Lessons from America's best-run companies*, New York, NY: Warner Books.

Pétonnet, C. (1973) *Those people: the subculture of a housing project (Ces gens-là) (No. 10)*, Westport, CT: Greenwood Press.

Petrini, C. (2010) *Terra madre: Forging a new global network of sustainable food communities*, White River Junction, VT: Chelsea Green Publishing Company.

Piketty, T. (2015) *Capital in the 21st century*, Cambridge, MA: Harvard University Press.

Plöger, J. (2007a) *Belfast City report*, CASEreport 44, London: London School of Economics.

Plöger, J. (2007b) *Leipzig city report*, CASEreport 42, London: London School of Economics.

Plöger, J. and Power, A. (2012) *Staying on track? Recovery of European Cities,* City Reformers Group Workshop: ILS – Research Institute for Regional and Urban Development, 10 October, www.ils-forschung.de/files_projekt/pdfs/Recovery%20of%20European%20Cities_Ploeger_Power.pdf

Porritt, J. (2005) *Capitalism as if the world matters,* London: Sterling.

Power, A. (1987) *Property before people: the management of twentieth-century council housing,* London: Allen & Unwin.

Power, A. (1993) *Hovels to high rise: State housing in Europe since 1850,* London: Routledge.

Power, A. (1997) *Estates on the edge: The social consequences of mass housing in Northern Europe,* New York: St. Martin's Press.

Power, A. (1999) 'High-rise estates in Europe: is rescue possible?' *Journal of European Social Policy, 9*(2), 139–63.

Power, A. (2007) *City survivors: Bringing up children in disadvantaged neighbourhoods,* Bristol: Policy Press.

Power, A. (2008) 'Does demolition or refurbishment of old and inefficient homes help to increase our environmental, social and economic viability?' *Energy Policy, 36*(12), 4487–501.

Power, A. (2013) *Recovering Cities: How to create value for cities. Experience of seven "Phoenix Cities",* Paris: La Fabrique de la Cité Available from: http://www.thecityfactory.com/fabrique-de-la-cite/site/en/index.htm

Power, A. (2016a) *Torino City Report,* London: LSE.

Power, A. (2016b) *Bilbao City Report,* London: LSE.

Power, A. (2016b) *Torino City Report,* London: LSE.

Power, A. and Houghton, J. (2007) *Jigsaw cities: Big places, small spaces,* Bristol: Policy Press

Power, A. and Mumford, K. (2003) *Boom or abandonment: Resolving housing conflicts in cities,* Coventry, UK: Chartered Institute of Housing.

Power, A. and Tunstall, R. (1995) 'Swimming against the Tide: Polarisation or Progress on 20 Unpopular Council Estates, 1980–1995' York: York Publishing for the Joseph Rowntree Foundation

Power, A. E and Tunstall, R.H (1997) *Dangerous disorder,* York: Joseph Rowntree Foundation

Power, A. and Rogers, R. (2000) *Cities for a small country,* Faber and Faber, London.

Power, A. and Zulauf, M. (2011) *Cutting carbon costs: learning from Germany's energy saving program,* Washington DC: Brookings Institution Press.

Power, A., Plöger, J. and Winkler, A. (2010) *Phoenix cities: The fall and rise of great industrial cities,* Bristol: Policy Press.

Power, A., Richardson, L., Seshimo, K., Firth, K. and others (2004) *London Thames Gateway: a framework for housing in the London Thames Gateway*, London: LSE Housing.

Provan, B. and Power A. (2016a) *Lille City Report*, London: LSE.

Provan, B. and Power, A. (2016b) *Saint Étienne City Report*, London: LSE.

Quilliot, R. and Guerrand, G.H. (1989) *Cent Ans d'Habitat: une utopie realiste*, Paris: Albin Michel.

Ratcliffe, P., Harrison, M., Hogg, R., Line, B., Phillips, D. and Tomlins, R. (2001) *Breaking down the barriers: Improving Asian access to social rented housing* (Action plan by Anne Power), published by the Chartered Institute of Houseing on behalf of Bradford City Council, Bradford Housing Forum, the Housing Corporation and Federation of Black Housing Organizations, www.bradford.gov.uk/NR/rdonlyres/F638DC26–72A2–42F0-B182-DF473125EC6A/0/6BreakingBarriers.pdf

Reader, J. (2005) *Cities,* London: Vintage.

Rees, W.E. (1999). "Achieving sustainability: reform or transformation?" In D. Satterthwaite (ed.) *The Earthscan Reader in Sustainable Cities*, Earthscan, London, pp. 22–52.

Region Nord-Pas De Calais (2013) *Nord-Pas De Calais: La troisieme revolution industrielle est en marche*, http://fr.calameo.com/read/00282096041bbcee430b3

Reich, R.B. (1992) *The work of nations: Preparing ourselves for 21st century capitalism*, New York: First Vintage Books.

Revolting Europe (2015) 'Spain's Podemos – neither left nor right?', Radical manifestos, http://revolting-europe.com/radical-manifestos

Rifkin, J. (2011) *The third industrial revolution: How lateral power is transforming energy, the economy, and the world*, London: Palgrave Macmillan.

Rifkin, J. (2014) *The zero marginal cost society*, New York: Palgrave Macmillan.

Rogers, R. and Power, A. (2000) *Cities for a small country*, London: Faber & Faber.

Sampson, R. (2012) *Great American City: Chicago and the Enduring Neighbourhood Effect*, Chicago: University of Chicago Press

Satterthwaite, D. (ed) (1999) Earthscan reader in sustainable cities, London: Earthscan Publications.

Schumacher, E.F. (1993) *Small is beautiful: A study of economics as if people mattered*, London: Vintage.

Scottish National Party (SNP) (2015) *Stronger for Scotland: SNP Manifesto 2015*, http://votesnp.com/docs/manifesto.pdf

Scottish Power Renewables (2015) 'Whitelee Windfarm Visitor's Centre', www.whiteleewindfarm.com

Sheffield City Council (2014) 'Cycling Inquiry', Economic and Environmental Wellbeing Scrutiny and Policy Development Committee, www.sheffield.gov.uk/your-city-council/council-meetings/scrutiny-committees/cycling-inquiry.html

Sheffield Culture Consortium (2016) 'A Year of Making 2016', www.sheffieldculture.co.uk/what-we-do/a-year-of-making-2016

South East England Councils (SEEC) (2009) *A perspective on the impact of the downturn on the Thames Gateway*, www.secouncils.gov.uk/wp-content/uploads/pdfs/_publications/467-Recession_in_Thames_Gateway___July_2009.pdf

Stadt Leipzig / Dept. of Urban Development (2006) *Monitoringbericht 2006 – kleinräumiges Monitoring des Stadtumbaus.*

Steffen, W., Broadgate, W., Deutsch, L., Gaffney, O. and Ludwig, C. (2015) 'The trajectory of the Anthropocene: The great acceleration', *The Anthropocene Review*, 2(1), 81–98.

Stern, N. (2014) 'The state of the climate — and what we might do about it', Talk at TED@Unilever, September, www.ted.com/talks/lord_nicholas_stern_the_state_of_the_climate_and_what_we_might_do_about_it/transcript?language=en

Stern, N. (2015) *Why are we waiting? The logic, urgency, and promise of tackling climate change*, Cambridge, MA: MIT Press.

Stiglitz, J.E. (2015a) *Rewriting the Rules of the American Economy – an Agenda for Growth and Shared Prosperity*, New York: Roosevelt Institute.

Stiglitz, J.E. (2015b) *The great divide: Unequal societies and what we can do about them*, New York: W.W. Norton & Company.

Sundquist, V. (2010) 'Political terrorism: A historical case study of the Italian red brigades', *Henley-Putnam University Journal of Strategic Security*, 3(3), 53–68.

Sugrue, T. (1996) *The Origins of the Urban Crisis*, Princeton: Princeton University Press.

The Global Commission on the Economy and Climate (2014) *Better growth, better climate: The new climate economy report*, Washington DC: New Climate Economy, https://files.lsecities.net/files/2014/11/NCE-2014-Better-Growth-Better-Climate-Synthesis-Report.pdf

Thompson, F.M.L. (1990) *Cambridge social history of Britain, 1750–1950, Vol 2: People and their environment*, Cambridge, UK: Cambridge University Press.

Titmuss, R.M. (1958) *Essays on 'The Welfare State'*, London: George Allen & Unwin

Tosi, S. and Vitale, T. (2009) 'Explaining how political culture changes: Catholic activism and the secular left in Italian peace movements', *Social Movement Studies*, 8(2), 131–47.

Transition Town Brixton (2015) 'Transition worldwide', www.transitiontownbrixton.org/about-ttb/transition-worldwide/

Troxler, P. (2014) 'Everyone is a designer', 30 May, http://petertroxler.net/fab-labs-3d-printing-the-3rd-industrial-revolution-and-their-impact-possibly/

Tsoukalis, L. (2014) *The Unhappy State of The Union: Europe Needs A New Grand Bargain*, London: Policy Network, www.policy-network.net/publications/4602/The-Unhappy-State-of-the-Union

UK-GBC (Green Building Council) and The Crown Estate (2015) *Tackling embodied carbons in buildings*, www.ukgbc.org/sites/default/files/Tackling%20embodied%20carbon%20in%20buildings.pdf

UK National Ecosystem Assessment (2011) *The UK National Ecosystem Assessment: Synthesis of the Key Findings*, UNEP-WCMC, Cambridge.

UN (2011) 'Ad Hoc Working Group on the Durban Platform for Enhanced Action (ADP)', Framework Convention on Climate Change, http://unfccc.int/bodies/body/6645.php

UN Environment Program (UNEP) (2014) 'Annual report 2013', www.unep.org/annualreport/2013/home_climatechange.asp

UNEP (2015) *District energy in cities: Unlocking the potential of energy efficiency and renewable energy*, www.unep.org/energy/portals/50177/DES_District_Energy_Report_full_02_d.pd

United Nations Framework Convention on Climate Change (2015) Paris Agreement, http://unfccc.int/files/meetings/paris_nov_2015/application/pdf/paris_agreement_english_.pdf

UN Habitat (2007) *State of the world's cities 2006/2007*, http://unhabitat.org/books/state-of-the-worlds-cities-20062007/

UN Habitat (2009) *State of the world's cities 2008/2009 – Harmonious cities*, http://unhabitat.org/books/state-of-the-worlds-cities-20082009-harmonious-cities-2/

UN Habitat (2011) *State of the world's cities 2010/2011 – Cities for all: Bridging the urban divide*, http://unhabitat.org/books/state-of-the-worlds-cities-20102011-cities-for-all-bridging-the-urban-divide/

UN Habitat (2013) *State of the world's cities 2012/2013: Prosperous cities*, http://mirror.unhabitat.org/pmss/listItemDetails.aspx?publicationID=3387

UrbAct (2015) 'UrbAct at a glance', http://urbact.eu/urbact-glance

Urban Task Force (1999) *Towards an urban renaissance*, Urban task force, Department of the Environment, Transport and the Regions, Wetherby.

US Congress (1948) Marshall Plan: Act of April 3, 1948, European Recovery Act [Marshall Plan]; Enrolled Acts and Resolutions of Congress, 1789–1996; General Records of the United States Government; Record Group 11; National Archives, http://legisworks.org/congress/80/publaw-472.pdf

Van Kempen, R., Dekker, K., Hall, S. and Tosics, I. (2005) *Restructuring large housing estates in Europe*, Bristol: Policy Press.

Velasco, J. (2015) 'Euskadi-Madrid, cuarenta minutos mas cerca un tren a finales de 2015', *Sociedad*, 28 January, www.elcorreo.com/bizkaia/sociedad/201501/28/euskadi-madrid-cuarenta-minutos-20150128130158.html

Vey, J. (2007) *Restoring prosperity: The state role in revitalizing America's older industrial cities*, Washington DC: Brookings Institution Press.

Volti, R. (2011) *An introduction to the sociology of work and occupations*, London: Sage Publications.

vom Hove, T. (2014) 'Some 212 million people live in Europe's 500 largest cities', City Mayors Statistics, www.citymayors.com/features/euro_cities.html

Wacquant, L.J. and Wilson, W.J. (1989) 'The cost of racial and class exclusion in the inner city', *The Annals of the American Academy of Political and Social Science*, *501*(1), 8–25.

Ward, B. (1976) *The Home of Man*, London: Penguin.

Warf, B. and Holly, B. (1997) 'The rise and fall and rise of Cleveland', *The Annals of the American Academy of Political and Social Science*, *551*(1), 208–21.

Whyte, W.H. (1956) *The Organization Man*, New York, NY: Simon & Schuster.

Wilkinson, R. and Pickett, K. (2010) *The spirit level: why equality is better for everyone*, London: Penguin UK.

Wilson, W.J. (1987) *The truly disadvantaged: he inner city, the underclass, and public policy*, Chicago, IL: University of Chicago Press.

Wilson, W.J. (2009) *More Than Just Race*, London: W.W. Norton & Co.

Wilson, W.J. and Taub, R.P. (2006) *There goes the neighbourhood: Racial, ethnic, and class tensions in four Chicago neighbourhoods and their meaning for America*, New York: Knopf.

Winkler, A. (2007a) *Sheffield City Report*, CASEreport 45, London: London School of Economics.

Winkler, A. (2007b) *Torino City Report*, CASEreport 41, London: London School of Economics.

Wollmann, H. (1985) 'Housing policy: Between state intervention and the market' in K. von Beyme and M. Schmidt, *Policy and Politics in the Federal Republic of Germany*, Aldershot: Gower.

World Economic Forum (2015) 'Global Risks 2015', http://reports. weforum.org/global-risks-2015/?_ga=1.31889278.1118043875.14 48878676

World Energy Council (WEC) (2009) *Survey of Energy Resources: Interim Update 2009*, www.worldenergy.org/publications/2009/ world-energy-resources-2009-interim-update/

Afterword

The financial crisis of 2008 and its repercussions on the real economy have shown that Europe's former industrial cities must reinvent themselves to continue to prosper.

Ex-industrial cities today face two major challenges: less public investment and a more restrained use of natural resources. Therefore infrastructures, buildings, public spaces must be reused to retain existing residents and attract new populations that can promote positive territorial development.

Cities for a Small Continent is the result of ten years of intensive research focused on struggling former industrial cities in Europe. Anne Power provides a concrete and in-depth look at life in these cities that managed to recover in the 1990s but had to deal with the economic crisis of 2008 and its aftermath. She decodes the political decisions and economic strategies that have allowed these cities to rise from their ashes like the mythological phoenix. She analyses the beneficial effect of public-private collaboration and highlights the impact of cluster strategies. She stresses the importance of these cities' industrial legacy and their history of invention and engineering prowess, now driving technological innovation to gain a foothold in the global economy.

What does the future hold for these cities at the beginning of this new industrial revolution? The book provides some clues. Their strength depends on their leadership, their shared vision, their flagship infrastructure, and their leading-edge innovations in green technology, renewable energy and social enterprise.

Anne Power offers thought-provoking insights into the role of cities in the world to come. This book is timely. Cities are the main users of fossil fuels and the main emitters of greenhouse gases, but they must become the new solution in the fight against climate change. They will play a leading role in the transition to a low-carbon society. The value of this book lies in providing concrete and convincing arguments in favour of this exacting transition.

Cécile Maisonneuve,
Chairperson – La Fabrique de la Cité

La Fabrique de la Cité

Created by VINCI, La Fabrique de la Cité is a Paris-based think tank promoting discussion and leadership on urban transitions. Its interdisciplinary approach brings together thought leaders and international players to uncover good urban development practices and put forward new ways of building and rebuilding cities. La Fabrique de la Cité has been an endowment fund since December 2010.

A grant from La Fabrique de la Cité supported the research into the seven cities, documented in Cities for a Small Continent, and supported the production of seven City Reports, published in May 2016.

Index

References to figures, tables and boxes are in *italics*. References to photos are in **bold**